Surrealism

Emerging from the disruption of the First World War, surrealism confronted the resulting 'crisis of consciousness' in a way that was arguably more profound than any other cultural movement of the time. The past few decades have seen an expansion of interest in surrealist writers, whose contribution to the history of ideas in the twentieth century is only now being recognized. *Surrealism: Key Concepts* is the first book in English to present an overview of surrealism through the central ideas motivating the popular movement. An international team of contributors provide an accessible examination of the key concepts, emphasizing their relevance to current debates in social and cultural theory.

This book will be an invaluable guide for students studying a range of disciplines, including Philosophy, Anthropology, Sociology and Cultural Studies, and anyone who wishes to engage critically with surrealism for the first time.

Contributors: Dawn Ades, Joyce Suechun Cheng, Jonathan P. Eburne, Guy Girard, Raihan Kadri, Michael Löwy, Jean-Michel Rabaté, Donna Roberts, Bertrand Schmitt, Georges Sebbag, Raymond Spiteri, Michael Stone-Richards

Krzysztof Fijalkowski is Professor of Visual Culture and Senior Lecturer in Fine Art at Norwich University of the Arts, UK. He is the author of a number of articles and book chapters on the subject of international surrealism, including contributions to the exhibition catalogues *Surreal Things: Surrealism and Design* (2007), *Surreal House* (2010) and *Magritte A–Z* (2011).

Michael Richardson is Visiting Fellow at the Centre for Cultural Studies, Goldsmiths–University of London, UK. He is author of *Otherness in Hollywood Cinema* (2010), *Surrealism and Cinema* (2006), *The Experience of Culture* (2001) and *Georges Bataille* (1994). He has worked with Krzysztof Fijalkowski on a number of publications, including the books *Refusal of the Shadow: Surrealism and the Caribbean* (1996) and *Surrealism against the Current* (2001).

Key Concepts

The Key Concepts series brings the work of the most influential philosophers and social theorists to a new generation of readers. Each volume is structured by the central ideas or concepts in a thinker's work, with each chapter in a volume explaining an individual concept and exploring its application.

Theodor Adorno: Key Concepts
Edited by Deborah Cook

Hannah Arendt: Key Concepts
Edited by Patrick Hayden

Alain Badiou: Key Concepts
Edited by A. J. Bartlett and Justin Clemens

Pierre Bourdieu: Key Concepts
Edited by Michael Grenfel

Gilles Deleuze: Key Concepts
Edited by Charles J. Stivale

Derrida: Key Concepts
Edited by Claire Colebrook

Michel Foucault: Key Concepts
Edited by Dianna Taylor

G.W.F. Hegel: Key Concepts
Edited by Michael Baur

Martin Heidegger: Key Concepts
Edited by Bret W. Davis

Immanuel Kant: Key Concepts
Edited by Will Dudley and Kristina Engelhard

Merleau-Ponty: Key Concepts
Edited by Rosalyn Diprose and Jack Reynolds

Jacques Rancière: Key Concepts
Edited by Jean-Philippe Deranty

Jean-Paul Sartre: Key Concepts
Edited by Steven Churchill and Jack Reynolds

Wittgenstein: Key Concepts
Edited by Kelly Dean Jolley

Jürgen Habermas: Key Concepts
Edited by Barbara Fultner

Georges Bataille: Key Concepts
Edited by Mark Hewson and Marcus Coelen

Surrealism
Key Concepts

Edited by
Krzysztof Fijalkowski and Michael Richardson

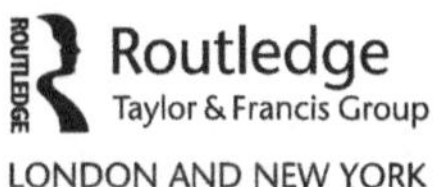
LONDON AND NEW YORK

First published 2016
by Routledge
2 Park Square, Milton Park, Abingdon, Oxon OX14 4RN

and by Routledge
711 Third Avenue, New York, NY 10017

Routledge is an imprint of the Taylor & Francis Group, an informa business

British Library Cataloguing in Publication Data
A catalogue record for this book is available from the British Library

Library of Congress Cataloging in Publication Data
Names: Fijalkowski, Krzysztof, editor.
Title: Surrealism : key concepts / edited by Krzysztof Fijalkowski and Michael Richardson.
Description: 1 [edition]. | New York : Routledge, 2016. | Series: Key concepts | Includes bibliographical references and index.
Identifiers: LCCN 2015045938| ISBN 9781138652071 (hardback : alk. paper) | ISBN 9781138652118 (pbk. : alk. paper) | ISBN 9781315622071 (e-book)
Subjects: LCSH: Surrealism.
Classification: LCC N6494.S8 S876 2016 | DDC 700/.41163--dc23
LC record available at http://lccn.loc.gov/2015045938

ISBN: 978-1-138-65207-1 (hbk)
ISBN: 978-1-138-65211-8 (pbk)
ISBN: 978-1-315-62207-1 (ebk)

Typeset in Times New Roman
by Taylor & Francis Books
Printed in Great Britain by Ashford Colour Press Ltd

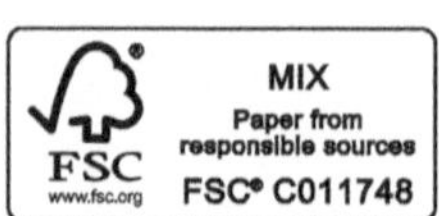

Contents

Figures

Contributors

Dawn Ades is Professor Emerita at the University of Essex. Her publications include *Dada and Surrealism* (1974), *Photomontage* (1976), *Salvador Dalí* (1982), *André Masson* (1994), *Marcel Duchamp* (with Neil Cox and David Hopkins, 1999), *Surrealism in Latin America: Vivisimo muerto* (with Rita Eder and Gabriela Speranza) (2012). Among the exhibitions she has curated or co-curated are: *Dada and Surrealism Reviewed* (1978), *Art in Latin America: The Modern Era 1820–1980* (1989), *Art and Power: Europe under the Dictators* (1995), *Dalí's Optical Illusions* (2000), *Undercover Surrealism: Georges Bataille and Documents* (2006), *Close-Up: Proximity and Dematerialisation in Art, Film and Photography* (2008) and *The Colour of My Dreams: The Surrealist Revolution in Art* (2011).

Joyce Suechun Cheng received her PhD from the University of Chicago in 2009, where she studied European art of the nineteenth and twentieth centuries. She has published articles and book chapters on Symbolism, Dada, surrealism and the art theories of Carl Einstein. She recently completed a book on the avant-garde art theories in the interwar period, entitled *The Mask and the Subject: The Avant-Garde Art Criticism of Carl Einstein, Walter Benjamin and Surrealism*. She is now working on a new project on late nineteenth-century painting and music in France and Belgium.

Jonathan P. Eburne is Associate Professor at the Pennsylvania State University. He is founding co-editor of *ASAP/Journal*, published by Johns Hopkins University Press (2016) and author of *Surrealism and the Art of Crime* (2008) and co-editor of *Paris, Modern Fiction, and the Black Atlantic* (with Jeremy Braddock, 2013) and *This Year's Work in the Oddball Archive* (with Judith Roof, forthcoming). He has edited or co-edited special issues of *Modern Fiction Studies*

(2005), *New Literary History* (2011), *African American Review* (2009), *Comparative Literature Studies* (2014) and *Criticism* (2015).

Krzysztof Fijalkowski is Professor of Visual Culture and Senior Lecturer in Fine Art at Norwich University of the Arts, UK. He is the author of a number of articles and book chapters on the subject of international surrealism, including contributions to the exhibition catalogues *Surreal Things: Surrealism and Design* (2007), *Surreal House* (2010) and *Magritte A–Z* (2011).

Guy Girard is a painter and poet born in Normandy who has participated since 1990 in the activities of the surrealist group of Paris. His paintings have been widely exhibited and he has published several volumes of poetry, among them *L'Oreiller du souffleur* (2008), *Maillot d'hécatombes pour Jeanne D'Arcula* (2013) and a collection of essays, *L'Ombre et la demande, projections surréalistes* (2005). He has also edited *Insoumission poétique, tracts, affiches et déclarations du groupe de Paris du mouvement surréaliste, 1970–2010* (2011).

Raihan Kadri was a writer, lecturer and theoretician specializing in modern intellectual history and surrealism, author of *Reimagining Life: Philosophical Pessimism and the Revolution of Surrealism* (2011). At the time of his death in 2014, he was researching a second book: *Deserters: Avant-gardism, Anti-nationalism, and the Modern World.*

Michael Löwy was born in Brazil and has lived in Paris since 1969. Presently emeritus Research Director at the CNRS (National Center for Scientific Research), his books and articles have been translated into twenty-nine languages. Among his main publications are *Georg Lukács: From Romanticism to Bolshevism* (1981), *Romanticism against the Tide of Modernity* (with Roster Sayre, 2001), *Fire Alarm: Reading Walter Benjamin's 'On the Concept of History'* (2005) and *Morning Star: Surrealism, Marxism, Anarchism, Situationism, Utopia* (2009).

Jean-Michel Rabaté has been Professor of English and Comparative Literature at the University of Pennsylvania since 1992, is a curator of the Slought Foundation, an editor of the *Journal of Modern Literature* and a Fellow of the American Academy of Arts and Sciences. He has authored or edited more than thirty books on modernism, psychoanalysis and philosophy. Recent books include *Crimes of the Future* (2014), *An Introduction to Literature and Psychoanalysis* (2014) and the edited collection *1922: Literature, Culture, Politics* (2015). Forthcoming in 2016 are *Pathos of the Future* and *Think Pig! Beckett's Animal Philosophies.*

Michael Richardson is Visiting Fellow at the Centre for Cultural Studies, Goldsmiths–University of London, UK. He is author of *Otherness in Hollywood Cinema* (2010), *Surrealism and Cinema* (2006), *The Experience of Culture* (2001) and *Georges Bataille* (1994). He has worked with Krzysztof Fijalkowski on a number of publications, including the books *Refusal of the Shadow: Surrealism and the Caribbean* (1996) and *Surrealism against the Current* (2001). With Ian Walker, they also published *Surrealism and Photography in Czechoslovakia: On the Needles of Days* (2013), and with Dawn Ades *The Surrealism Reader: An Anthology of Ideas* (2015). Together with Dawn Ades, Steven Harris and Georges Sebbag they are currently working on an *Encyclopaedia of Surrealism*.

Donna Roberts holds a PhD in Art History and Theory from the University of Essex, and has taught on surrealism in the UK, Mexico, and Finland. She has written widely on surrealism, including Czech surrealism, the photographer Emila Medková, and the relations between the Grand Jeu and the Czech painter, Josef Síma. On the theme of nature, she has written on Edward James' rural Mexican 'folly', *Las Pozas*, on the relation between Freud's evolutionary psychobiology and Salvador Dalí's *The Tragic Myth of Millet's Angelus*, and on surrealism and the discourse of natural history, with particular focus on the writings of Roger Caillois. At the time of publication, she is completing a book on this theme, titled *A Feeling for Nature: Surrealism, from Natural History to Ecology.*

Bertrand Schmitt is a poet, film director and essayist. In 1990 he became a member of the Paris group of the surrealist movement, contributing regularly to its journal *S.U.RR* (*Surréalisme, Utopie, Rêve, Révolte*). Since 1997 he has divided his time between Paris and Prague, participating in the activities of the Czech and Slovak surrealist group and contributing as a member of the editorial committee of the journal *Analogon* and has published the following collections of his work: *J'ai du bon tabac* (1992), *Le Gré des rues* (1995) and *Dynamika Křiku* (2006). He has also worked extensively with Jan Švankmajer and Eva Švankmajerová, about whom he has frequently written and also made the 1999 film *Les chimères des Švankmajer*. Many of his articles have appeared in catalogues and monographs.

Georges Sebbag is a writer with a doctorate in philosophy, and participated in the activities of the surrealist group in Paris from 1964 to 1969. He has written texts on time and many books about surrealism. His most recent are *Potence avec paratonnerre, Surréalisme et philosophie* (2012) and *Foucault Deleuze, Nouvelles Impressions du Surréalisme* (2015).

Raymond Spiteri teaches art history at Victoria University of Wellington, New Zealand. In his research and publications he focuses on the culture and politics of surrealism. He is the co-editor (with Don LaCoss) of *Surrealism, Politics and Culture* (2003), and is currently working on a study of surrealism circa 1930.

Michael Stone-Richards is professor in the department of Liberal Arts, College for Creative Studies, Detroit, where he teaches Critical Theory and Comparative Literary and Visual Studies. He has published widely in English and French on the history and critical theory of the avant-garde. His book *Logics of Separation* (readings of Fanon, Cha, Celan, Ellison and Du Bois) appeared in 2011. He is completing two books: *Care of the City: Participation, Community, and Post-studio Practice in Detroit and Beyond* and *Surrealism and Critical Theory.* He is the founding editor of *Detroit Research* a journal devoted to post-studio practices and critical theory. He is also a founding member of the Program Committee, MOCAD (Museum of Contemporary Art Detroit), and a member of the Board of the Friends of Modern and Contemporary Art, Detroit Institute of Arts.

Introduction

Krzysztof Fijalkowski and Michael Richardson

In the English-speaking world surrealism has historically been understood principally as a project of creative expression – foremost in the visual arts – rather than a movement committed to challenging received modes of thought to connect intellectual and practical experience. Founded by poets in France in the early 1920s, gathering around it not only writers, artists, photographers and film-makers but also scholars, ethnographers, psychoanalysts, doctors, architects and many others and spreading to all corners of the globe, surrealism cannot easily be reduced to the model of avant-garde modernism that is too often imposed on it. First and foremost a meeting of *sensibilities* – occurring on the plane of passions and elective friendship (even if these did not preclude bitter quarrels) – surrealism must be recognized as addressing a coherent, if perpetually renegotiated and sometimes paradoxical, philosophical engagement. As such it has also established itself as a centre of gravity for a reorientation of life away from the stagnant existence the structures of contemporary society give it, towards the promises of desire, freedom and the overcoming of debilitating forces. Its central *raison d'être* has always been to transform the world and to change life.

If a generalized idea of the 'surreal' can be found almost everywhere in Western popular discourse, it is hard to know where to begin in tracing the impact of surrealist thought and practice on the intellectual history of the twentieth century. One might venture, for argument's sake, that without it much contemporary critical thinking would be unimaginable. In France, thinkers like Sartre and Camus defined themselves against surrealism, while others like Lacan, Blanchot, Lefebvre or Debord drew crucial aspects of their own thinking from it even in departing from it. The Frankfurt School theorists, especially Benjamin, Adorno and Marcuse, also owe it much and engaged critically with it. Even those fashionable doyens of post-war French theory like Barthes, Sollers, Kristeva, Baudrillard, Deleuze or Foucault are deeply marked by it, although largely without direct critical engagement. Indeed, several of these thinkers set themselves explicitly *against* surrealist thought, in the process often gravely misunderstanding or misrepresenting it.

The latter is especially the case with the Tel Quel circle of critics (notably Sollers and Kristeva) who celebrated marginal surrealists like Georges Bataille and Antonin Artaud (while separating them from surrealism) as a strategy to diminish surrealist thought in general. This was expressly directed against André Breton, the most prominent surrealist theorist, and appears to have been so successful that Breton's name is today largely absent in global accounts of modern and contemporary critical thought. This is all the harder to understand given that in recent decades academic scholarship on surrealism and its environs has proliferated on an unprecedented scale. But it is notable that even when much of this scholarship explores surrealist ideas, at least in an abstract way, it rarely engages with its significance to broader intellectual debates.

Yet from the outset, surrealism presented itself first and foremost as an engagement of the mind. As Gérard Legrand points out (1992: 13), the classic definition of surrealism in the first manifesto is precisely set in terms of a revolution of the understanding of thought, in a format that could not be more explicitly philosophical:

> SURREALISM, *n.* Pure psychic automatism in its pure state, by which one proposes to express – verbally, by means of the written word, or in any other manner – the actual functioning of thought. Dictated by thought, in the absence of any control exercised by reason, exempt from any aesthetic or moral concern.
>
> ENCYCLOPEDIA. *Philosophy.* Surrealism is based on the belief in the superior reality of certain forms of previously neglected associations, in the omnipotence of dream, in the disinterested play of thought. It tends to ruin once and for all all other psychic mechanisms completely, and so substitute itself for them in solving all the principal problems of life.
>
> (Breton 1972: 26)

How then should we begin to understand and situate surrealism's philosophically grounded claim to solve life's key problems? During 1920 and 1921, Breton and Aragon engaged in two 'classifications' of thinkers who interested them. The only ones to receive consistently positive appreciations were Freud (average 17), Hegel (14), Pascal (13), Sade and Einstein (both 12¾), Rousseau (12½), Kant (10), Nietzsche

(9) and Vauvenagues (5). Those most disliked were Voltaire (−14), Marcus Aurelius (−11¾), Bergson (−9¾) and Schopenhauer (−4) with Comte alone on an absolute −20 (see Sebbag 2012: 16). These sorts of defining activities served a double purpose of establishing elective affinities as a basis for collective binding on the one hand, and on the other serving to situate the surrealists' own position within intellectual history. In 1923 they published the typographic diagram 'Erutaréttil' in which major influences were set out as intellectual constellations. Most were poets, but we also find several thinkers. Shining with the greatest magnitude is Hegel, with Fichte, Diderot, Agrippa, Lulle, Flamel, Rousseau, Leibniz and Pascal following in order of importance.[1] Later, the verso of José Corti's 1931 catalogue of surrealist publications carried a list of recommended and disapproved authors. 'Lisez … Ne lisez pas' gives us a challenging snapshot of surrealism's preferences for critical models, even if this is only one of a number of its ever-changing intellectual audits. While many on the list are literary (or anti-literary) figures, nearly half of them are in fact thinkers, from which one might extract the following names to give a flavour of the mental constellation they map out:

> READ: Heraclitus, Lulle, Agrippa, Berkeley, La Mettrie, Rousseau, Diderot, d'Holbach, Kant, Sade, Fichte, Hegel, Feuerbach, Marx, Engels, Lenin
>
> DON'T READ: Plato, Aquinas, Montaigne, Voltaire, Schiller, Schopenhauer, Renan, Comte, Bergson, Durkheim, Lévy-Bruhl, Gandhi, Benda.
>
> (Pierre 1980: I 202)[2]

Of course, these lists are playfully presented and represent no doubt hotly debated *collective* interests rather than coherent statements of surrealist engagement. Nevertheless, what is notable is how consistent they have remained with surrealism's historical development. Even if a preference for unorthodox, marginalized or *maudits* authors may be noted, one can imagine the same distinctions being more or less drawn at any point in surrealist history, with only minor variations (one might expect Schelling, Nietzsche and Fourier to be given greater prominence, while Lenin might not find such favour). What should be noted, however, is that such preferences reflect the fact that surrealist thinking is not eclectic. The surrealists did not dip into everything to see what might turn up, even if they might allow an impassioned intuition to prevail over careful intellectual examination. As such the above lists do not constitute stipulations of prescriptions and proscriptions, but rather function as kinds of manifesto laying down a statement of intent.[3] Another list of intellectual endorsements from a decade and a half later, in circumstances altogether more challenging, was issued by the Bucharest surrealists Gherasim Luca and Trost:

> We agree with dream, madness, love and revolution.
>
> We reject in all their aspects art, nature, utility, the class division of society, the law of gravitation, idealism, the therapeutic, painting, the separation between dream and life, psychology, white magic, poverty, memory, diurnal remnants in oneiric functions, Euclidean geometry, unfavourable numbers and death.
>
> We agree with delirious inventions, tears, somnambulism, the real functioning of thought, the elixir of long life, the transformation of quantity into quality, the concrete, the absurd, the negation of negation, desire, hysteria, furs, black magic, the delirium of interpretation, the dialectics of the dialectic, the fourth dimension, simulacra, flames, vice, objective chance, manias, mystery, black humour, cryptaesthesia, scientific materialism and bloodstains.
>
> (Luca and Trost 1945: n.p.)

We can note the deliberate provocation and hyperbole; the drift towards para-scientific or occult knowledge; and the incorporation of by now well-established surrealist concepts into this pronouncement. But this is also, nonetheless, a coherent, rigorous and above all philosophical set of positions.

These successive lists of preferences and rejections give a sense of surrealism's thought as a galaxy in which attraction and repulsion are constantly in play, and in which an idea might be scrutinized, challenged and assigned a place with a spirit that is at the same time critical and ludic. It helps if we recall that the first generation of surrealists shared the sense of disillusion with received ideas born out of the direct experience of the First World War, in which the majority of them had served, and that would make the revolt of Dada such an attractive strategy. But this alone is not enough to explain the critique of positivism, rationalism and reason that would characterize the group as it gathered impetus far beyond this founding generation. For the Parisian surrealists, it might equally be rooted in the poetry and thought of Romanticism (and to a lesser extent of Symbolism), of Gothic literature, and of marginal but spectacular anti-literary figures such as Jarry, Lautréamont and Vaché. But one would also note that all surrealists of French origin would have possessed a basic grasp of philosophy and its concepts, since philosophy was part of the French school curriculum (in a far more programmatic way than in other European secondary-education systems). Breton's teacher, for example, was André Cresson, a well-known writer on philosophy with a dozen or so monographs to his credit (the last of which, on Hume, was written in collaboration with Gilles Deleuze). These included one on Hegel, although if we are to believe what Breton tells us in *Entretiens,* Cresson only treated Hegel with positivist sarcasm.[4]

Naturally this example, given the future surrealists' general antipathy to state-sponsored intellectual structures and the education system in general, would be just as likely to have turned the young poets and artists away from the models and ideals they had been offered and set them in search of something more satisfactory. The extent and significance of Breton's understanding of Hegel (read in sometimes poor translations) have been debated: Alquié, for example, questions the congruence of Hegel's system with Breton's thought (Alquié 1965: 41ff.). But here is the perfectly clear passage from *Entretiens*:

> It was undeniably Hegel – and no one else – who put me in the condition necessary to perceive [the supreme point], to strain toward it with all my might, and to make this very tension my life's goal. No doubt there are others whose knowledge of Hegel's works far surpasses mine: any specialist could teach me a thing or two when it comes to interpreting his Writings ... To my mind his method has bankrupted all others. Where the Hegelian dialectic does not operate, for me there is no thought, no hope of truth.
>
> (Breton 1993: 118, translation slightly modified)

Notwithstanding some dissenters like Wolfgang Paalen, who saw Hegel's thought as providing the basis for totalitarianism, Hegel permeates surrealism in complex ways. For instance, René Magritte frequently invokes him in his painting in a way that reveals some of its intricacies. Let's consider *Hegel's Holiday,* a painting from 1957 in which a half-full glass of water is balanced on top of an open umbrella.

At first glance we may think Magritte was simply making a joke inspired by nothing more than the mystery of an image which brings together objects with contrary uses in an impossible encounter. From this perspective, the invocation of Hegel may be considered simply to play upon vulgar understandings of the Hegelian dialectic and the title may be nothing but a poetic evocation. As soon as we start to think about the painting in relation to its title, however, we recognize some complexity.

First of all, it is not Hegel the philosopher who is in fact being invoked, since he is on holiday. Moreover, if we take account of the associations of the French title, *Les Vacances de Hegel*, it is also his *vacancies*, his *abdication* that may be being referred to. We can thus say that Hegel, made present in the painting by Magritte's invocation, is at the same time absent from it or, more precisely, that Hegel is simultaneously present and absent in a way that resembles Marcel Duchamp's famous door that is both open and closed at the same time.

The level of paradox in this painting is typical of Magritte's work in general, and in common with much surrealist work it tends towards tearing thought from its hinges. In so far as the glass of water and the umbrella are suspended in time and space, it emphasizes the bringing together of opposites in a complementary way to form an image rather than a strictly Hegelian negation that gives rise to the formation of a third element. At the same time this is not a simple balancing that denies negation but rather suggests that progression and advance are not inevitable, or necessary, results of the dialectic. Surrealism as a whole has always been suspicious of any idea of progress and Magritte's image implies that movement may be held in check by the very dynamic of the dialectic itself, which can just as easily turn back on itself, to fall into stasis, as it can result in progress.

In this respect, Magritte's image is consistent with how surrealists in general have understood the workings of dialectic, which is viewed not simply as the dynamic of progress but as an explanatory model for thinking about the process of communication and the ways in which phenomena act upon each other. The painting is thus also a reflection on imaginative process. Magritte explained in an illustrated letter to Suzi Gablik how he came to this work:

> [It] began with the question: how to show a glass of water in a painting in such a way that it would not be indifferent? Or whimsical, or arbitrary, or weak – but, allow us to use the word, with genius? (Without false modesty.) I began by drawing many glasses of water, always with a linear mark on the glass.
>
> This line, after the 100th or 150th drawing, widened out and finally took the form of an umbrella. The umbrella was then put into the glass, and to conclude, underneath the glass. Which is the exact solution to the initial question: how to paint a glass of water with genius. I then thought that Hegel (another genius) would have been very sensitive to this object which has two opposing functions: at the same time not to admit any water (repelling it) and to admit it (containing it). He would have been delighted, I think, or amused (as on vacation), and I call the painting 'Hegel's Holiday'.
>
> (Quoted in Gablik 1970: 121–2)

As the letter and its accompanying drawings make clear, Magritte did not have in mind an image of Hegel on holiday and try to realize it visually, but rather played with images until a painting emerged; through this process, in a sense, Hegel can be said to have made an intervention into it.

We also have here a clear reference to the Sunday of Life, by which Hegel meant a reconciliation (of philosophy and religion) that lies beyond either negation or progress. In addition, Magritte makes it clear that this desire to imbue a glass of water with 'genius', far from denying negation, is dependent upon it: the glass needs to be interrogated until it gives rise to the umbrella, so that water can be simultaneously repelled and collected. At the same time, Magritte is playing upon the relationship between image and idea in the pact he makes with the viewer. This image of a glass partly filled with water and resting on an umbrella suspended in the air calls for the viewer to make several leaps of the imagination. We are presented with two material objects with contrary uses, as Magritte himself says, the purpose of one being to collect water; the other to repel it. We also have two elements: the water in the glass and the air in which the umbrella is suspended. It is an image that could not be realized other than in an artwork, since a glass cannot be balanced on an umbrella and in turn an umbrella cannot be suspended in empty space. The impossible nature of the image inscribes into it the very negativity that may at first appear to be missing from it, which emerges not within the image itself but in the viewer's relationship with it. This appears to correspond with a purely Hegelian understanding that identity is formed through the process of reflection on the object of perception taken, admittedly, in a purely 'poetic' direction: the identity of the glass is questioned through reflection, via Magritte's action as a painter, on its dialectical affinity with an umbrella.

We can further illustrate this by considering another famous artwork, Giacometti's *Suspended Ball*, which offers a similarly dazzling reflection on the dialectical process as a moment when elements come together at a moment of danger and are transformed, but *not necessarily* surpassed. What we see in both of these works – and to some extent throughout surrealism – is that a surpassing (even a sublation in the Hegelian sense) is possible and is always glimpsed, but whether or not it occurs doesn't detract from the significance to the encounter itself. What matters here – and perhaps this is a fundamental difference from Hegel – is not the development that results, but the moment of dispersion itself and the communicative action it initiates. The negation is present, therefore, but as a quickening point rather than a motive point; in other words, it excites without necessarily implying transcendence. The surrealist

Absolute, then, can perhaps be described as a 'temptation' rather than an aim, founded in a dialectical thinking which surrealists adopted as a means to emerge from what they considered to be the abyss of rationalism and Enlightenment logic. It tantalizes, entices and gives meaning to the condition of being alive, but it does not offer a solution to that condition. It may perhaps be described as the *frisson* that results from coming into contact with what is a dialectical *other* to oneself (most often a lover, but in fact anything with which a communicative relation is possible) through which the sublation of life and death may be glimpsed and even momentarily experienced but not consecrated.

Surrealists in general appear to be constitutionally antithetical to any closure or finality of thought and, if sublation is not an essential element of either its conception of the Absolute or its use of the dialectical process, surrealism can hardly be described as 'Hegelian' in any orthodox sense; but nor is its approach abusive or arbitrary. It responds to essential elements within surrealism itself, and the dialectic as the surrealists understood it is applied fairly consistently throughout the range of surrealist activity. It does not reject negativity (if stasis may be an important aspect of the surrealist understanding of dialectic, this does not at all imply a balancing of opposites) but refines it: the elements of the dialectical relation can never return to their condition prior to the encounter; they can never escape unscathed, let alone retain their previous identities. But the result of the encounter is not predictable: it does not *necessarily* lead to the creation of a third term.

Surrealism as a whole thus can be seen as a dynamic, passionate but above all collective encounter with ideas. Lists such as 'Lisez … Ne lisez pas' show such a range of positions and points of contact, many of them representing tangential rather than orthodox readings, that it makes little sense to try and draw up a family tree of the ancestry of surrealist thought. Surrealism's thinking has its revered guiding figures, its beacons of clarity, but few of them are beyond reproach and many are viewed in a mode of contestation or against the grain: they represent not a lineage but, in a Benjaminian sense, a constellation of ethical reference points or markers gathered by all involved into a fulgurant expansion of ideas that move outwards in all dimensions. Individual surrealists' engagements with philosophy, meanwhile, were experienced as an encounter like any other, driven by an elective affinity. Their interest in bodies of philosophers' work tended not to be systematic or wholesale but intuitive and partial, and made in response to a wider ethical spirit, and Legrand (himself a philosopher) may be right when he suggests that Breton, for example, is ultimately more interested in philosophers than philosophy (Legrand 1992: 18).

This does not mean that the engagement could not be sustained and detailed: along with other surrealists, Breton attended Alexandre Kojève's influential lectures on Hegel during the 1930s, in the company of Bataille and Raymond Queneau among others. The case of Max Ernst is also notable: an artist who never enrolled at an art academy but studied philosophy, among other subjects, at the University of Bonn. His level of familiarity with philosophical thought is clear (see Bataille 1994: 134–5). But these encounters could also be partial, impetuous and made wilfully against the grain. Here is Dalí (whose surrealist writings are crammed with direct but often highly unorthodox references to philosophers) describing his intellectual formation as a student:

> As for myself, I had already made up my mind. I turned to silence, and began to read with real frenzy and without order of any kind. … The work which had the greatest effect on me was Voltaire's *Philosophical Dictionary*. Nietzsche's *Thus Spake Zarathustra*, on the other hand, gave me at all times the feeling that I could do better in this vein myself. But my favourite reading was Kant. I understood almost nothing of what I read, and this in itself filled me with pride and satisfaction. I adored to lose myself in the labyrinth of reasonings which resounded in the forming crystals of my young intelligence like authentic celestial music. I felt that a man like Kant, who wrote such important and useless books, must be a real angel! … But one day I did [understand] it. In a short time I actually made unbelievable progress in understanding the great philosophical problems.
>
> (Dalí 1993: 140–2)

Kant, however 'important and useless' he may have been, remained a specific reference point for Dalí in a number of writings and artworks, notably an assemblage entitled *Monument to Kant* (1936) combining a marble base with found objects including inkwells and pens that from photographic evidence seems also to have been imposing and excessive but to defy utility.[5]

For all its references to figures such as Kant or Hegel, surrealism at the same time maintained an ingrained suspicion of the systematizing principles they wished to build, and beneath this, of the logical or rationalizing methodologies drawn from the classical philosophy upon which they relied. The experience of Dada, of course, injected a strong inoculation of derision against any stable system of thought, and while Dada's impact on the emergent surrealist group in Paris diminished rapidly, in Spain, for instance, the surrealist-oriented Logicophobista group of artists in Barcelona of the 1930s could still advertise its dismissal of traditional modes of reason through its very name. The tone of early French surrealism, particularly in Artaud's writings and tracts, tended to present Western philosophy and its attendant normative structures as the province of elderly, irrelevant fogeys.

Paul Éluard's text 'Les Philosophes' attacks philosophy's intent to turn the unknown into the known in a pointless quest for truth:

> They have built magnificent staircases that lead to the truth. They followed them down and when they got to the bottom, they whispered to each other: 'it's too high.' The knowledge that came from their intelligence never convinced them that they were right. On every landing, their stillborn image had no need of them. They are the ones who've understood, they've conquered surprise, they've vulgarized the unknown. …
>
> They have willingly been enslaved by what was most basely human within them, their reason showed them the inanity of all things and they wallowed in their ideas. But now comes the time of pure men, of unexpected acts, of walls suspended in mid-air, of illusions and ecstasies, of blasphemies and the love that dreams, now that fire and blood regain their primal splendour, now that suffering and delight haunt body and soul at will, that thought has no more doors to open, has no more need to come and go, and that random bullets pierce those 'Great Pudding Brains', those Wonderful Calculating Machines, as they sit in their boutiques.
>
> (Éluard 1924: 32)

In contrast to classical models of thought, surrealism often used the tools of philosophy against their intended function, generating intellectual theories from poets (such as Rimbaud's 'JE est un autre') and poetic ideas from philosophers (for instance, the use made of the notions of 'objective humour' and 'objective chance' derived from Hegel). One of the most distinctive and influential aspects of surrealism's methodology was its desire to reorient the power of thought towards apparently trivial or inadmissible subjects, focusing serious reflection on something as incidental as a rolled-up bus ticket or a mass-market film. This informs the emphasis surrealism placed from the outset on seeing its activity in terms of *research*, for example in setting up a study centre, the Bureau de recherches surréalistes, in parallel to founding the journal *La Révolution surréaliste* on a model that referred not to literary publications but a popular science magazine, *La Nature*.

Finally, surrealism's interest in philosophical thought sees it as just one means among many of generating insight or establishing truth. Participants in Czechoslovak surrealism, for example, have frequently referred to the idea of 'complementary knowledge', drawing in particular upon Hermetic and alchemical traditions of thought to balance and 'correct' the currents of scientific or poetic understanding that, once brought together rather than being considered as mutually exclusive, can develop coherent, dynamic and holistic models. Roger Caillois's development of the notion of 'diagonal science' during the 1950s could be seen as another example of surrealist thought practices in which an attempt is made to fuse poetic and scientific approaches through the motor forces of interdisciplinarity and analogy. This is emphasized by the subtitles of journals associated with surrealism. For instance, the subheading of *Documents* was 'Doctrines, Archaeology, Fine Arts, Ethnography', with 'Varieties' replacing 'Doctrines' in the second year. This was followed in more directly surrealist journals like *Mandragore*, in Chile, with its rubric 'Poetry, Philosophy, Painting, Science, Documents', or the journal of the Czechoslovak surrealists, *Analogon*, subtitled 'Surrealism, Psychoanalysis, Anthropology, Diagonal Science'.

Contrary to the strictures of a science based on inductive or deductive logic, however, it would be the principle of analogy combined with a dialectical engagement with the discordance of opposites that would be the guiding motor for a thought that returns to a system of insight rooted in much deeper patterns of knowledge. This convergence of analogy and dialectic is crucial to an understanding of surrealist modes of thinking. Gérard Legrand has spoken of analogy as the '"clasp" of the dialectical necklace', noting how '[t]he supreme relation of reconciled being does not cease to be dialectical, but it proves to be (or becomes) equally analogical' (1971: 154). Thus Breton could explain that

> Only on the level of analogy have I ever experienced intellectual pleasure. For me the only *manifest truth* in the world is governed by the spontaneous, clairvoyant, insolent connection established under certain conditions between two things whose conjunction would not be permitted by common sense. As much as I abhor, more than any other, the word *therefore*, replete with vanity and sullen delectation, so do I love passionately anything that flares up suddenly out of nowhere and thus breaks the thread of discursive thinking. What comes to light at that moment is an infinitely richer network of relations whose secret, as everything suggests, was known to early mankind.
>
> (1995: 104)

The essential nature of surrealist thought, then, balances on the tensions between the spark of revelation and the reanimation of hidden but profoundly rooted certainties: between quicksilver and fossil. Rather than propose global or systematic models, surrealist knowledge adopts the characteristic of a permanently reviewed construction made from encounters between ideas and between levels of thought. It is this character that not only permits but encourages the introduction of the incongruous, the heterogeneous, the anomalous and the irrational, into this building process, and that generates the kind of intellectual heat that could also lead to dissent. Contrary to many of the attempts of critics and scholars to divide and distinguish its intellectual patterns (for example, spuriously to differentiate between a 'Bretonian' surrealism and a 'Batailleian' one) taken as a whole surrealism is thus fully equipped to cope with varying, even competing models and approaches, and to privilege variety rather than coherence in its research.

Distinctive intellectual interests could characterize local differences, and were a focus for debate: in the context of early Parisian surrealism, one could cite the importance of Nietzsche for the surrealists such as André Masson associated with rue Blomet,[6] or the Grand Jeu group's focus on Eastern philosophy. Meanwhile, surrealism's temporary or more enduring external alliances were almost always made for philosophical rather than purely circumstantial or political reasons: in France the collaborations with the dissident Marxist Philosophies group in the 1920s, or with Contre-attaque in the 1930s; in Czechoslovakia one might point to the links between surrealists and the Prague Linguistic Circle during the same period. These practical/intellectual links are another indication that it makes less sense to look for a 'philosophy of surrealism' as Alquié (1965: 2) does – something Legrand (1992: 14) strongly rejects – than to see surrealist thought as emerging from a series of dialogues and tensions between groups, texts and ideas that constitute, more accurately, a philosophical anthropology or a 'philosophy of living'.

The contents of this book indicate the tremendous range of surrealism's interests and intellectual engagements, and its willingness to encounter existing ideas, not only absorbing some of their aspects but also challenging some and diverting others towards its own purposes while generating distinctive concepts for its own use. The first part thus deals with the most significant contexts within which surrealism was oriented, dealing with themes such as revolution, imagination and utopia. Some of these ideas had emerged only as surrealism was taking shape, while others were older – in some cases considerably older – offering a diverse set of founding principles that complicates the prevailing view of surrealism as a typically modern or avant-garde critical current. Emblematic of this tendency is Jonathan P. Eburne's opening chapter (Chapter 1) on surrealism and the dialectic, in which Hegelian strains of the dialectical thinking that is crucial to surrealism's intellectual strategies are problematized and traced back to more distant sources in Heraclitus. Guy Girard's chapter (Chapter 2) on Hermeticism and the magical tradition traces surrealism's interests in currents of thought more usually considered fanciful or irrational, notwithstanding the complex origins of many more recent intellectual systems (notably science) in some of these traditional bodies of knowledge. Among the intellectual origins of surrealism, the significance of Freud's discoveries for the first development of the movement is well known (though not all surrealist groups followed Parisian surrealism's lead in advocating them). Here, Jean-Michel Rabaté's chapter (Chapter 3) traces some of the key moments of a complex and sometimes fraught engagement between surrealism and Freudian psychoanalysis in interwar France.

The notion of utopia is a central tenet of surrealism's relationship with the world, negotiated between a fervent engagement with the everyday realm and an evocation of states ruled by dream, desire and imagination. Georges Sebbag's chapter (Chapter 4) on utopian thought examines surrealism's espousal of philosophical currents marrying revolutionary exigency with a vivid poetic attitude. That this intense combination – the famous meeting of Marx's call to 'transform the world' and Rimbaud's desire to 'change life' – may be easier to accept at the level of a poem or a painting than in the arena of lived experience is demonstrated by the explosive case of the life and ideas of the Marquis de Sade (Chapter 5, by Michael Richardson), in whose exaltation of violent desire the surrealists discerned an exemplary attitude that raises fundamental issues about the human condition. For surrealism Romanticism, as examined here by Michael Löwy (Chapter 6), represented a revolutionary current (sometimes betrayed by the Romantics themselves), of which they were content to consider themselves the 'prehensile tail'. The significance for the Parisian surrealist group of its immediate precursor, Dada, is considered in the final chapter of this section (Chapter 7, by Krzysztof Fijalkowski), showing that if the tendency to see the two as a complementary pair is an oversimplification, Dada's rebellion would continue to stamp surrealism in its commitment to humour, confrontation and collective action.

Part II of the book presents – without any intention of imposing a hierarchy in its order – the key concepts developed by surrealism itself. While here again the sheer range of themes suggests that the movement's ambitions give it an entirely different status in relation to almost any comparable contemporary intellectual movement, this list of topics may also be seen to anticipate a great sweep of late twentieth- and early twenty-first-century critical currents whose intellectual turns surrealism would appear repeatedly to have anticipated, albeit in very different terms. Raymond Spiteri (Chapter 8) begins this section with an examination of a crucial aspect of surrealism's philosophical and ethical attitude, the idea of community and collective action, without which no individual surrealist activity can be said to hold sway. Yet at the same time, as the following chapter (Chapter 9, by Michael Richardson) on otherness and identity argues, surrealism was also profoundly concerned with the interrogation and opening up of the notions of selfhood and alterity, challenging received models of identity with more complex – and more inclusive – ones that explicitly strove to undermine the authority of Western and colonial positions. The next chapter (Chapter 10, by Michael Richardson), on surrealism's poetics, looks to the ways in which the movement cherishes poetry as a sovereign value in its intellectual engagements – specifically, as argued here, in the ways in which poetry provided a contested ground within which its 'practical truth' could be recovered and set to work as an ethical tool. Breton's key articulation of objective chance is considered by Raihan Kadri (Chapter 11, with Michael Richardson and Krzysztof Fijalkowski), who traces it not only within the thought of Hegel and Engels, but also in its links to themes in Nietzsche's thought. As a reconciliation between internal and external forces – between one necessity generated by the hidden aspects of individual unconscious impulses and another manifested in the workings of the external world's apparently random events, rendered meaningful through encounter and interpretation – objective chance exemplifies surrealism's claim to resolve contradiction and reveal once again the individual's place in the 'forest of symbols'.

Two themes given a newly charged significance by surrealism are examined in the next two chapters: madness and dream. Often recognized as central to the movement, both were actually seen by the surrealists not as exemplary states but as *critical* concepts in need of investigation. While Michael Stone-Richards (Chapter 12) examines the former in the context of surrealism's use of language – above all, the core value of automatism for the foundation of the movement – Georges Sebbag (Chapter 13) traces surrealism's interest in dream back to philosophical currents long predating Freud's focus on the subject, and which allowed it to develop a concept of dream far more radical than those of psychoanalysis, which remain wedded to a dichotomy between waking and dreaming life. To these two primary colours of surrealism's palette might be added another, that of love, explored by Dawn Ades and Michael Richardson (Chapter 14) in a speculative dialogue that locates Breton's notion of 'amour fou' within the revealing discussions around love and sexuality in the Parisian surrealist group, as well as against the background of the surrealists' lived experiences and relationships. The complex mechanisms of desire drive another of Breton's major conceptual formulations, that of convulsive beauty, presented in the following chapter (Chapter 15, by Krzysztof Fijalkowski), and in which conventional and static models based on ideas of taste and form are rejected for a concept of beauty privileging motion, erotic desire, anxiety and indeterminacy. A parallel set of disruptive co-ordinates characterizes surrealism's attitude to the object, as considered in the following chapter (Chapter 16, by Krzysztof Fijalkowski), highlighting some of the mechanisms through which the surrealists invested physical objects with latent and revelatory meanings, above all through a strategy of suspending utility that gave their use-value a poetic charge.

Surrealism's positing of the notion of black humour (Chapter 17, by Michael Richardson) – an often violent, pessimistic attitude born from the experiences of war and from Dada and pre-Dada attitudes – attests to the movement's spirit of recalcitrant refusal mixed with an assertion of sovereign freedom. This confirmation of fundamental truths has echoes in the subject of the following chapter by Donna Roberts (Chapter 18), which discusses the relevance of ecological themes in surrealism, arising from its attempt to reorient knowledge away from anthropocentric models towards a more profound and respectful attitude to the world. Bertrand Schmitt's examination of Breton's concept of magic art (Chapter 19) also emphasizes this desire to realign received understandings of human agency, in this case by formulating creative practice as a form of inspirational but research-based knowledge. The profound but most frequently ignored connections between the self and the external realm also figure in yet another of surrealism's central concepts, examined here by Joyce Suechun Cheng and Michael Richardson (Chapter 20): the idea of the marvellous, those rare moments of exhilarating revelation in which the possibility of a reconciliation of opposing forces springs to life as a form of transformative encounter. This leads into the concluding chapter (Chapter 21, by Michael Richardson and Krzysztof Fijalkowski) and consideration of the idea of a 'supreme point', a notion that offers a key to surrealism's aims as a whole, and yet at the same time as a concept striving to actualize what is fundamentally fleeting, ambivalent and beyond expression.

Throughout this volume, authors have focused in particular on primary texts; all translations, except where otherwise noted, are by the authors.

This volume is itself the culmination of an extended encounter over a period of many years with both the concepts of surrealism, and with many of its current or former participants, and while the list of individuals whose willingness to debate and elucidate surrealism's ideas would be too long to draw up here, the editors wish to thank in particular those members of contemporary and historical surrealist groups in Paris, Prague, Leeds, Madrid and Stockholm who have helped us eventually to shape and direct this project. Special thanks are also due to Tristan Palmer, who originally commissioned this volume and whose commitment to it was decisive in bringing it to fruition. A Research Fellowship from Norwich University of the Arts offered invaluable time and support for the completion of Krzysztof Fijalkowski's chapters. At the same time, we also gratefully acknowledge the precious help of all of the contributors, especially that of Georges Sebbag, all of whose enthusiasm and erudition have been indispensable. Finally, this book is dedicated to the memory of Raihan Kadri, whose writing was to have been substantially more present in this volume but whose thought helped encourage and construct its planning, and epitomizes surrealism's ability, nearly a century after its inception, to continue to engage the minds of successive generations.

Notes

1 Published in *Littérature*, nos. 11–12 (October 1923).

2 We would take this opportunity to correct a printer's error that crept into this list as reproduced in our 2001 book *Surrealism against the Current*, in which Durkheim surreptitiously slipped over into the 'Read' side.

3 These collective games around surrealism's intellectual points of reference particularly characterize the movement's early years, but they continued to be relevant as groups refreshed their membership and their positions: see for example the enquiry 'Ouvrez-vous?' (published in the first issue of *Médium* in 1953), in which participants cited a crisp, usually personal, reason for agreeing or refusing to 'Open the Door' to given thinkers, writers and artists; the results, a treasury of the constellations of surrealist thought, are often surprisingly varied.

4 Breton nevertheless must have had some respect for Cresson in 1925, since his book *La Position actuelle des problèmes philosophiques* was included in the small library assembled for the Bureau de recherches surréalistes (see Sebbag 2012: 71).

5 Thanks to William Jeffett for details of this no longer extant assemblage.

6 References to Nietzsche in the letters of Simone Breton – whose importance to the development of early surrealism is only now being recognized and who could read German, English and Spanish – suggest that his work was also a matter for discussion in Breton's circle (S. Breton 2005: 52).

Part I
Contexts

1 Heraclitus, Hegel, and dialectical understanding

Jonathan P. Eburne

The surrealist movement was – and remains – resolutely dialectical. In the classical sense of the term, denoting the pursuit of truth through disagreement, surrealist dialectics encompass the argumentative basis of the group's activities from the early 1920s onward: it points to the meetings, inquiries, investigations, debates, ruptures, and exclusions that characterize surrealism's aesthetic and political pursuits alike. Such contentiousness extends throughout the movement's history, from the group's inaugural rupture with Parisian Dada through its restless engagement with leftist politics; its polemical interactions with Maurice Barrès, Georges Bataille, Jean-Paul Sartre, and other intellectual contemporaries; its militant anti-nationalism and anti-colonialism, and of course, its numerous exclusions. Though contentious, such relations are constitutive of surrealism's collective project, generating some of its most profound contributions to the intellectual and political life of the twentieth century. Rather than considering such disquiet as extraneous to surrealist activity, it is worth considering the degree to which surrealism's history is grounded in a dialectal movement of its own, inviting the very disagreements that might even tear it apart. Far from denoting the rhetorical excesses of a fractious band of poets and artists – or the consequences of André Breton's authoritarian grip – surrealist dialectics characterize the movement's procedural, as well as ethical, imperatives.

The surrealist movement famously refused to limit its activities to the sphere of art. The question of whether or not surrealism designated a philosophy – the subject of a 1956 'debate' published in *Le Surréalisme, même* (Legrand and Patri 1956: 140–4) – only begins to address the extent to which the surrealist group left its impression on twentieth-century philosophy. From the movement's inception, the surrealists thought seriously about the dialectical procedures characterizing their collective work and, increasingly, made this a central philosophical and methodological concern. In the aftermath of the First World War, these young Parisian poets turned defiantly to German Romanticism as a double-edged rejoinder to a post-war French intellectual climate dominated by nationalism and positivism wherein, broadly speaking, scholars delimited and codified the rational basis for knowledge as deriving from sensory experience – and, implicitly, from experience on French soil.[1] Breton derides this empirical restriction in a famous passage from the 1924 surrealist *Manifesto*:

> The absolute rationalism that is still in vogue allows us to consider only facts relating directly to our experience. Logical ends, on the contrary, escape us. It is pointless to add that experience itself has found itself increasingly circumscribed. It paces back and forth in a cage from which it is more and more difficult to make it emerge. It too leans for support on what is most immediately expedient, and it is protected by the sentinels of common sense. Under the pretense of civilization and progress, we have managed to banish from the mind everything that may rightly or wrongly be termed superstition, or fancy; forbidden is any kind of search for truth which is not in conformance with accepted practices.
>
> (Breton 1969: 10)

From Dada onward, the surrealists' recourse to German Romantic poetry and idealist philosophy – including Novalis, Achim von Arnim, and Hegel, as well as, more belatedly, Marx and Engels – could be considered first as a provocation, a counter-nationalist appeal to the literary inheritance of the vanquished enemy. The real appeal of Romanticism had more to do, however, with the generative powers of the imagination it celebrated, as well as with its insistence that truth could emerge from evidence beyond immediate sensory experience. Surrealism could, in this sense, be considered the tail end of Romanticism – but it was, as Breton put it in 1938, a *prehensile* tail (Breton 1969: 153).

The full methodological significance of the surrealist recourse to German idealism emerged during the mid-1920s, when the group, with other leftist intellectuals in Paris, sought to formalize their growing political convictions and launched a series of systematic discussions about Marxian dialectical materialism and Communist Party affiliation. The surrealist movement would not only exercise its own characteristic dialecticism – the 1925–29 period was one of the most turbulent, as well as the most intellectually animated, phases in its history – but would also contribute substantively to the resurgence of dialectical thinking in France, as well as to its transformation as a conceptual framework. As intellectual historians have begun to examine, surrealism was at the forefront of the French philosophical 'return to Hegel' of the 1920s and 1930s. The influential public lectures of Alexandre Kojève on the master–slave dialectic presented at the École Pratique des Hautes Études during 1933–39, have often been cited as the formative event in the French philosophical reception of Hegel and dialectical reasoning, influencing an entire generation of intellectuals that included attendees Georges Bataille, Raymond Queneau, Jacques Lacan, Jean-Paul Sartre, Simone de Beauvoir, and André Breton.[2] The modern French reception of Hegel begins earlier, however. Even as Kojève and his colleagues at the École Pratique des Hautes Études were beginning to reconsider Hegelian philosophy, and particularly the *Phenomenology of Spirit*, in light of contemporary pragmatism (James, Whitehead) and phenomenology (Husserl, Heidegger), the surrealists were also approaching the Hegelian dialectic as a key philosophical concern within their own thinking about knowledge, consciousness, materialism, and the determining forces in world history. The surrealist group's recourse to Hegel – especially in the work of Breton, Louis Aragon, and René Crevel in the early decades of the movement – did as much to transform the contemporary understanding of dialectical thinking as that of Kojève and his colleagues, including Jean Wahl, Alexandre Koyré, and the philosopher of science Gaston Bachelard – the work of the latter would be especially contiguous with surrealism in the 1930s. This doesn't mean that the surrealist attention to Hegel was grounded in systematic study, however. Though Breton certainly studied Hegel's *Aesthetics* in 1931 and 1932, and though others in the movement would address surrealism's Hegelianism directly in the 1950s, the movement's general contribution to 'the French Hegel' and dialectical thought in the twentieth century had as much to do with the group's oblique – indeed, dialectical – approach to German philosophy.

Earlier French philosophers had evaluated Hegel on account of his idealism, a philosophical system that subsumed the violent tribulations of historical change within the panlogism of a transcendental consciousness or *Geist*. By contrast, the surrealists and their philosophical contemporaries radically recast Hegel's system, privileging the dynamism (and incompleteness) of dialectical movement rather than the abstract totality of Spirit. This meant that dialectical negation operated as something other than a logical formula or a world-historical pattern; rather, it described the dynamic functioning of consciousness in its relationship to the world. Consistent, in many ways, with Jean Wahl's influential 1929 study *Le malheur de la conscience dans la philosophie de Hegel* (The unhappy consciousness in Hegel's philosophy), the surrealists understood the work of consciousness as intrinsically restless, incomplete, and self-contradicting. This restlessness was exacerbated, moreover, by the work of the unconscious: because the mind is not fully present to itself, the work of thought was itself dialectical, to the extent that the mind, as René Crevel insisted in 1927, could work *against* reason (Crevel 1986). This restlessness was productive, of course: both poetic creation and historical change comprised dynamic processes that came about through negation. The unfolding of the human world over time, like the unfolding of thought, takes place according to a process through which closed, knowable entities (an object, the self, a nation) become divided and oppose themselves, negating their former, limited, totality. In traditional dialectics, this divided, antithetical condition could be surmounted in turn by various forms of *Aufhebung* or synthesis, a provisional 'negation of the negation' that yields a new arrangement in turn. For the surrealists, however, the poetic or worldly 'productiveness' of dialectical negation consisted in this very restlessness itself: art and revolution were not the utopian fruit of dialectical synthesis, but the concrete forms of persistent negation, at once the result and the medium for what Breton called a necessary *crise de conscience* (crisis in understanding) (Breton 1988: 781).[3]

In his 1929 *Second Manifesto*, Breton outlines a naturalistic version of the surrealist dialectic in terms that explicitly register its distance from Hegel. Citing Friedrich Engels' critique of Hegelian panlogism in *Anti-Dühring* (1877), Breton portrays surrealism – along with Marxian dialectical materialism – as extending from the 'avortement colossal' (colossal abortion) of the Hegelian system. As Breton writes, 'Surrealism, although a special part of its function is to examine with a critical eye the notions of reality and unreality, reason and irrationality, reflection and impulse, knowledge and "fatal" ignorance, usefulness and uselessness, is analogous at least in one respect with historical materialism in that it too tends to take as its point of departure the "colossal abortion" of the Hegelian system. It seems impossible to me to assign any limitations – economic limitations, for instance – to the exercise of a thought finally made tractable to negation, and to the negation of negation' (Breton 1988: 140).[4] While agreeing with Engels' rejection of Hegelian panlogism, Breton doesn't simply present Hegelianism as a failure, but instead casts surrealism and dialectical materialism as the twin offspring of this failure: the *avortement* is itself a negation of Hegelian systematics. As a result, Breton argues that surrealist dialectic was bound neither by the totalizing framework of Hegel's system nor by the socio-economic rhetoric of party communism. 'How', Breton asks, 'can one accept the fact that the dialectical method can only be validly applied to the solution of social problems?' (Breton 1969: 140). The aim of surrealism was instead to engage dialecticism in a movement 'toward the concrete', as Wahl would later put it: to furnish dialecticism 'with practical possibilities in no way competitive in the most immediate realm of consciousness' (see Wahl 1932; Breton 1969: 140). Breton substantiates his position by continuing to paraphrase Engels. In the *Second Manifesto*, he goes so far as to abandon the 'dialectical method, in its Hegelian form', in favour of Engels' defence of the dialectic as an organic (rather than metaphysical) principle of change requiring no external, transcendental, force of causation. For Breton, as for Engels, dialectic is far more than an epistemological function or interpretation of the 'rifts and disorders' of Western (and capitalist) nations; rather, the dialectic describes a principle of change that extends to concrete, worldly action as an extension of its knowledge and praxis.

Even beyond its rejection of Hegelian systematics, Breton's understanding of the dialectic is peculiar, progressing less through contradiction and synthesis than through a proliferation of *rencontres*, that is, of meetings or encounters that staged negation as a constitutive event in its own right. For Breton, that is, the so-called 'negation' in dialectics signified a transformation that was already an affirmation (if not an *Aufhebung*) in itself: there is no self/other, master/slave hierarchy; there is only the process itself though which 'life and death, the real and the imagined, past and future, the communicable and incommunicable, high and low, cease to be perceived as contradictions' (Breton 1969: 123). Bruce Baugh has described this 'unlimited negation' as an animating concern of the surrealist movement, a creative project that levied the work of negation toward 'destroying the antinomies and contradictions which the Surrealists say was the source of human unhappiness'. As Baugh puts it, the surrealists wanted Hegel's method, but not his metaphysics (Baugh 2003: 58 and 55).

To a large extent, the surrealist group's early understanding of the dialectic as an operative worldly and cognitive function could elide the particularities of the Hegelian system because the group's approach to dialecticism was not, in fact, drawn from Hegel; nor was it entirely deducible from Engels or Marx. Rather, the group's thinking about negation, mediation, and dialectical notions of change and causality drew upon a far less contemporary source. Beginning in the mid-1920s, the surrealists looked to one of Hegel's own avowed precursors as an object lesson in an unrecuperable dialectics, drawing upon the fragmentary work of the pre-Socratic philosopher Heraclitus of Ephesus (535–*c*.475BCE). 'Heraclitus', as Breton would put it in 1934, 'is surrealist in dialectic', an insistence that would persevere within surrealist thinking well into the post-Second World War period.[5] The significance of

Heraclitus is twofold: first, the pre-Socratic thinker introduced a dialectic anterior to Hegelian panlogism, which characterized negation in terms of an elementary volatility to which knowledge (*logos*) and the world (*physis*) were mutually subject. Second, as a body of ancient work available only through textual fragments, the very condition of Heraclitus's work allegorized this twofold volatility, demonstrating the extent to which its concept of negation would be mediated by its own concrete conditions, its status as a material text. Heraclitus's work thus doubly articulated the 'practical possibilities' to which Breton dedicated surrealist activity: the medium for dialectical movement would no longer be the Hegelian systematics of panlogism and 'Spirit', but the vicissitudes of consciousness, and of textual and material media alike.

The October 1927 issue of *La Révolution surréaliste* published a pair of articles introducing Heraclitus into the group's intellectual genealogy. The first of the two articles is a brief biographical sketch of the pre-Socratic philosopher reprinted from François Fénelon's 1726 *Abrégé des vies des anciens philosophes.* The second, a book review by Aragon, is more polemical, representing as much an incursion against 'the sentinels of common sense', as Breton had written of the state of contemporary philosophy, as a panegyric to ancient philosophy. Entitled 'Philosophie des paratonnerres' (Philosophy of lightning-conductors), Aragon's review addresses the contemporary scholarly interest in the ancient philosopher, which approached Heraclitus as a knowable and ideologically consistent precursor to Hegel and Marx, an ancient source of dialectical thought.[6] The recourse to Fénelon stressed, however, that any such approach could hardly be straightforward, since Heraclitus has always been considered 'obscure, because he only spoke through enigmas', as Fénelon (1927: 43) put it. Aragon notes that Hegel famously regarded Heraclitus as his precursor in developing a theory of dialectical change. Yet unlike Hegel, Heraclitus left behind no complete system, no coherent body of philosophical work. The conceptual and material difficulty of any approach to Heraclitus's philosophy – which was not only notoriously enigmatic, but extant only in fragmentary form – resisted such totalizing systems. To this end, Heraclitus offers a corrective not only to the instrumentalism of contemporary philosophy, but also to the panlogicism of Hegelian idealism; the fragments enabled the surrealists to approach the dialectic as a worldly, material dynamic rather than as the movement of a transcendental Mind.

Aragon's approach to Heraclitus is framed in explicitly post-Hegelian terms. Asking 'what is living and what is dead in the philosophy of Heraclitus', Aragon reprises the title of Benedetto Croce's 1907 commentary on Hegel, which likewise questioned the Romantic philosopher's panlogicism (which Croce (1915: 192) called a 'morbid excrescence', if not the 'colossal abortion' cited by Engels). Aragon is deeply critical of contemporary scholarship's reduction of Heraclitian philosophy to stable, doctrinaire political values – as if seeking to retrench the pre-Socratic philosophy within a panlogistic 'excrescence' never fully his own. His essay indicates by contrast how a 'return' to Heraclitus offers a new basis for thinking about the nature of empirical, historical, and ultimately political change. In both its fragmentary form and its philosophical content, Heraclitus's work reflects on the difficulty of knowledge and the commonality of flux and revolution in the empirical world, a theory whose very language insists upon confusion, contradiction, and wordplay. Heraclitus sketches a complex epistemology in which the 'real' of the natural world is as difficult to grasp as the articulation used to grasp it. This acknowledgment of a 'missed encounter' inherent within understanding indicates an implosion of panlogism from within: rather than appealing to grand idealist abstractions, Heraclitus testifies to the notion that the empirical is never immediately graspable in itself, a problem exemplified by the very medium of the textual fragments.[7] As bewildering as they are influential, the cryptic and often dubious fragments of Heraclitus's lost work *On Nature* maintain, Aragon writes, 'a prestige that ends up serving the most irreconcilable ends' (Aragon 1927: 47). Yet, precisely for this reason, the pre-Socratic philosopher became a useful figure for surrealism's efforts to recast the dialectic as a concrete basis for their creative and political activity. In this respect, the surrealist interest in Heraclitus indicates the group's proximity to the philosophers in the École Pratique des Hautes Études such as Jean Wahl and Alexandre Koyré, in that both, by *approaching*, rather than presuming, the concreteness of the empirical world treated dialecticism as a phenomenology that resists both positivism and idealism. At the same time, however, Aragon's remark about irreconcilable ends bears the surrealist movement very much in mind; for in the years immediately following his review, the ancient philosopher would become a kind of 'lightning-conductor' (*paratonnerre*) for the group's own most irreconcilable ends, its fiercest debates, and its efforts to think through its dialectical functioning as an avant-garde collective.

Just as a lightning conductor's usefulness only fully emerges during a storm, at a time of crisis, allusions to Heraclitus begin to appear in surrealist writings at the very moment when the group entered its turbulent period of adhesion to the French Communist Party and to revolutionary Marxism. Rather than grounding this exigency within a restricted version of Marxism – by which dialectical materialism would come to resemble the very panlogism against which Marx and Engels fought – Heraclitus's fragments offer no easily instrumentalizable political doctrine. Not only do the fragments suggest a cosmology based on contradiction, fire, and constant transformation, but their fragmentary form is itself also rife with inconsistency and internal conflict. Thus exacerbating rather than neutralizing the surrealists' polemical energies, the instability expressed in and by Heraclitus's work almost uncannily reflects the movement's own volatility, even fragmentation, at this moment of internal conflict. Indeed, in the years following their initiation into leftist politics in 1925 and 1926, the surrealists would dramatically restructure themselves as a group based on a commitment to collective political action, either expelling or alienating members who refused to adhere to such a programme.[8] It would be a mistake, though, to equate this turn to militancy with a lapse into orthodoxy; instead, Heraclitian instability might be said to 'ground' surrealist political discourse during this period, in the sense that it redirected the group's polemical energies toward its own epistemological foundations. As Breton's struggle to redefine the Hegelian system suggests, the surrealist group's ideas about revolutionary action were mediated by its approach to dialectical thought, as much as by its artistic prerogatives.

Breton, too, draws upon Heraclitus in his continued effort to rethink the dialectic; in his 1932 text *Communicating Vessels* he cites Heraclitus as a way to conceptualize what he refers to as the 'harmony' between seemingly opposed ideological systems – in this case, the relationship between Marxist and Freudian methodology, as well as between the two 'realms' of experience they each describe as well, the material sphere of political economy and the cognitive sphere of the unconscious. Breton writes that the challenge for most modern ideologies (but especially for surrealism) is 'to maintain that what opposes them is in accord with them'. Heraclitus, he continues, 'expressed it precisely: "Harmony of opposed tensions, like [that] of the bow and [that] of the lyre"' (Breton 1990: 134). The Greek term *harmonie* here – which derives from the verb *harmozein*, 'fitting together' – connotes both 'connection' and 'attunement'. Heraclitus's bow and lyre thus suggest that these two 'communicating vessels' are not only bound up in communicative tension with each other, but both are also vessels of communication in themselves, each operating by means of the 'harmony' created by the tension in their strings.[9] Breton cites this passage to articulate a functional substitute for the notion of dialectical synthesis, an updated version of his recourse to Engels in 1929. In place of either a logical totality or an unfolding 'negation of the negation', Heraclitus articulates the opposing 'tension' both between and within seemingly incompatible modes of negation.

What emerges is, in short, a theory of mediation that allows Breton to champion surrealism's ability to engage simultaneously in both political and artistic commitments; citing a harmony between the bow of political action and the lyre of poetic activity, Breton explains that any revolutionary potential is the product of their *tension,* their non-synthesis. Instead, the bow and the lyre each become the mediating form that concretizes the negative potential of the other. The bow and the lyre illustrate not only the analogy between political and pastoral instruments (which each use tension and disruption as means of attaining a greater harmony), but also the similarity of their power to obtain 'great animation ... though this alteration of attraction and repulsion', as Breton puts it (Breton 1990: 135). Mediation, in this heterodox sense, thus comes to describe the concrete formations – whether material, linguistic, cultural, or corporeal – that structure the very possibility of intellectual and political labour, whether this labour consists in the leftist interrogation of historical causality or in the phenomenological description of cognitive experience.

In exploring what was living and what was dead in the philosophy of Heraclitus, Breton and Aragon implicitly identify the very question the surrealism movement consistently asked of itself: what is living and what is dead in the work of surrealism? Aragon's 1927 essay on Heraclitus anticipates how such questions about the movement's relevance would be motivated by the same criticisms to which the group subjected Hegel: how to function as a political as well as artistic movement without succumbing to reductive 'explicative ideologies', without foundering on the shoals of its panlogism. Just as Aragon was critical of contemporary scholars' reduction of Heraclitian philosophy to stable, doctrinaire political values, by 1929 the surrealist group was submitting itself to a profound critique of its own interpretations of the nature of historical, political, and empirical change. Under renegotiation was surrealism's very *raison d'être,* its value as an intellectual phenomenon rather than as a mere art movement.

Georges Bataille's more sceptical reaction to Breton's new positioning of surrealism – 'too many idealistic twits'[10] – demanded a similar renegotiation of whether an art movement could in fact position itself not within 'the paltry sequence of literary history, but in history itself, seen in its widest application, something that correctly considers the development of our sensibility from the most distant time'.[11] Although it may be tempting to consider such disagreements as evidence of the movement's descent into rhetoric – or panlogicistic formalizations of its own invented dialectics – it is crucial to remember how extensively these disagreements were inherent to the concepts surrealism embraced. The reverse is also true: as I have suggested, surrealism restructured itself around the very disagreements that might tear it apart. For as we have already seen, it wasn't only Bataille who sought to purge surrealism of its tendency toward 'idealism' and logical abstraction; so did Aragon and Breton. This restlessness continued into the 1930s, with heightened intensity. As the culmination of the group's political engagements, Aragon's poem 'Front rouge' (Red front) was notable for its rejection of surrealist discourse in a precipitous turn to agitprop. The 1931 poem, published after Aragon's return from the Second Soviet Writers' Conference in Kharkov, sought to abolish the forms of mediation upon which other politically committed surrealists insisted. Whereas Breton, along with René Crevel and Paul Éluard, could espouse dialecticism in a 'harmonious tension' that mitigated the apparent ideological separation between experimental poetry and politics, Aragon's poem assumed the orthodox position that dialectical materialism was a force of historical causation in itself, a force incarnated in the concrete reality of revolution and the triumph of the Red Army. Aragon's recourse to Stalinism was, in short, another 'avortement colossal' of a reified system, representing – for many in the surrealist group – a lapse into the reductive ideological formulae Aragon criticized in his essay on Heraclitus. The ensuing 'Aragon affair' provoked a concerted effort among the surrealists to redress the conceptual shortcomings and ideological inadequacies of the Stalinist presumption of 'direct action' and direct speech. To disavow the work of mediation, they maintained, was to fall prey to dangerous ideological mythmaking. A few years later, Jean Paulhan published his influential study of language, *Les Fleurs de Tarbes* (1938), in which he likewise tempers the 'terrorist' project of seeking 'direct meaning' free from the flowery excesses of rhetoric; as Paulhan (2006) argues, any such claim to immediacy, however admirable in theory, was itself a rhetorical effect of language. The surrealists recognized instead the 'profound meaning', as Breton put it, of experimental poetic language, precisely insofar as it *resisted* its ready instrumentalization for political ends: like the fragments of Heraclitus's work, poetic language demonstrated the *tension,* as well as the distance, between mind and world, as well as between an idea and its material or textual form, rather than the collapse of all such negations into an instrumental synthesis (see especially Breton 1992: 5–45; partly translated in 1978: 76–82).

One of the more substantive theoretical contributions to this discourse was the brief polemical tract published in 1934 by writer and photographer Claude Cahun, entitled *Les Paris sont ouverts* (All bets are off). Written in response to the Aragon affair, Cahun's tract emerged from her participation in the AEAR, the Association des Écrivains et

Artistes Révolutionnaires, in 1932 and 1933, an association that galvanized her collaboration with Breton, Crevel, Éluard, and other surrealists. *Les Paris sont ouverts* was dedicated to Leon Trotsky, countering the Stalinist mythmaking of Aragon's poem.[12] It stressed instead the political significance of understanding poetic language as a medium that negates, misdirects, and disrupts the very relations of communicability or action it purports to enable. Formalizing and redoubling the surrealist attention to mediated political expression, Cahun argues that the strength of poetic language lies in its resistance to the cognitive certainty presumed by propaganda and protest writing alike: poetry 'keeps its secret' even as it paradoxically 'hands over its secret [*livre son secret*]' (Cahun 2002b: 500–34; 519). This latter idea is expressed through a pun on 'livre' (book) that both demonstrates and parodies the openness of meaning Cahun ascribes to language.

Distinguishing a poem's manifest content from its 'latent' content, Cahun argues that language is an agent of conflict as well as of connection and communicability. As she writes in a conceptual postscript to the volume,

> Given that language is an *agent of conflict* – that is, of *contact* – in the relation of a man to himself, of men with each other, and, as a consequence, of men with nature; and given that science is oriented toward a direct understanding of the universe, and philosophy an indirect understanding of the universe; poetry intervenes here, there, and everywhere, provoking short circuits within this human coming-into-awareness – those 'magic' short cuts to which sexual love and extreme suffering also hold the 'secret'.
>
> (Cahun 2002b: 532)

Cahun's term 'magic short cuts' (*raccourcis magiques*) is a pun on 'raccourci', denoting at once a short cut and a pithy turn of phrase. The term thus demonstrates as well as formalizes linguistic play as a technology of communicative condensation and displacement; such short cuts and short circuits become the medium, in turn, for the latent elements of thought, imagination, and desire that keep 'all bets off' (or open, to translate Cahun's title literally) resisting the foreclosure implicit in any claim to direct action. In distinguishing poetry from propaganda, she articulates the function of poetry doubly – first in naturalizing it as a *drive,* a basic human instinct, which she likens to a sexual drive, and thus impossible and foolish to purge from any revolutionary future; and second in conceptualizing it as a *medium.* Poetry, in this double sense, functions according to a relational dialectic that mediates any other social or political system. In contrast to Georges Bataille's revision of the Hegelian dialectic in the form of a critical materialism, which stresses the documentary value of media such as painting, photography, film, literature, and criticism as means for assessing the power of raw phenomena, Cahun articulates the vital (dys)function of the 'raccourcis magiques' of poetic media. Mediation, in this sense, delineates not only the harmonious tension of 'communicating vessels', but also the volatile malfunctions of a short circuit.

In her subsequent participation in surrealist activities – including a short-lived collaboration with Bataille in the anti-fascist Contre-attaque group in 1935, as well as an exhibition of surrealist objects in May 1936 – Cahun pursued her investigation into the political resonances of poetic short circuits in her photographic work, which came increasingly to dominate her artistic output. A polymath and multimedia artist in her own right, Cahun locates the dialectic of 'medium' on two distinct fronts: in the photographic and textual media in which she worked, and in the fascinating household objects her work depicted, including her own face and body. In both cases, her work stresses the simultaneous plasticity and resistance of such media; as she writes in her 1936 essay for the exhibition of surrealist objects, the participatory exercise of discovering and making strange new material objects was a process that could help us 'make ourselves ductile – good conductors of liberating forces' (Cahun 1998: 59–61; 60). The point, it seems, was to heed the noisy call of medium.

Cahun's insistence upon the mediating function of artistic media in the dialectic of political communicability finds its continuation in two other major developments in surrealist thinking of the interwar and wartime period. The first is the work of the self-taught philosopher of science Gaston Bachelard, whose writings from the early 1930s, particularly *The New Scientific Spirit* (1934) were especially influential to the group. Drawing from an intellectual genealogy that dovetailed with that of the surrealists – invoking Novalis and Lautréamont, as well as psychoanalysis and alchemy – Bachelard taught philosophy at the École Pratique des Hautes Études and collaborated with Wahl, Koyré, Kojève, and others on the journal *Recherches Philosophiques* throughout the 1930s. Espousing what the philosopher Jean Hyppolite dubbed a 'romanticism of the intelligence', Bachelard proposed that the history of science opened itself up to new discovery on the basis of its irrational, imaginative, or even failed works (Hyppolite 1957: 13–27). Rather than a triumphal narrative of forward scientific progress, Bachelard's history of science proceeds dialectically. Most profound for the surrealists, though, was Bachelard's claim in *The New Scientific Spirit* that such progress-through-negation demanded a new understanding of rationalism altogether: 'rationalism', he writes, 'need not be a closed system; *a priori* assumptions are subject to change' (Bachelard 1984: 3). Such changes, moreover, were necessary to scientific creativity; a closed rationalism, bound by habit, became an 'epistemological obstacle' that foreclosed its capacity to think rationally. The encounter with unfamiliar ideas, by contrast, could induce the kinds of 'epistemological ruptures' that could inaugurate an open rationalism (Bachelard 1984: 38; see also 2004: esp. 15–28). Most importantly for the surrealists, Bachelard attributed such encounters not to empirical experiment alone, but to imagination, reverie, and even the history of unscientific ideas. What Bachelard named 'surrationalism' thus operated as an open system similar in character to the surrealist movement's Heraclitian dialectics.

Bachelard's thinking was instrumental to surrealism's own dialectical interests of the 1930s, particularly in abolishing the categorical distinction between scientific (or political) reason and the imagination, while maintaining the mediated integrity of either function. Proposing a theory of epistemological ruptures – if not a 'harmony of opposing tensions' – Bachelard stimulated the surrealist group's turn to sciences other than psychoanalysis, and especially drew their attention to material objects, as epitomized by the contemporary exhibition of surrealist objects at the Charles Ratton Gallery in 1936.[13] Indeed, Claude Cahun's notion that poetic mediation could 'make ourselves ductile – good conductors of liberating forces' finds its complement in Breton's introductory essay to the exhibition, which frames this conductive possibility in Bachelard's terms as a 'continuous assimilation of the irrational, a process during which the rational is required to remould its own image constantly, both in order to reassert itself, and to develop' (Cahun 2002b: 539; 1998, 60; Breton 1972: 276).

A second major development in surrealist dialectics took place at a remove from the Parisian group, in the philosophical and artistic work of the surrealist group in Bucharest. Self-consciously responding to the Bretonian group at a geographical and historical remove, the Bucharest surrealists conducted their post-war activities in dialogue with the pre-war and wartime activity of the Parisian group; they at once recognized the surrealists' attention to medium and 'epistemological rupture' and yet also noted the extent to which such practices tended to become reified in spite of themselves. In their own aesthetic experiments and critical writings, they took up anew the critical dialecticism of Aragon, Bataille, Cahun, and others, in both interrogating and refusing the tendency of some surrealists to consider their art, speech, or political intentionality to be somehow 'revolutionary' in themselves, once again succumbing to the idealisms and panlogisms that surrealism sought to dismantle.

In a polemical 1945 tract addressed to the Parisian group, Gherasim Luca and Dolfi Trost seek to formalize their own dialectical language of epistemological rupture in the reflexively titled *Dialectic of the Dialectic.* They explain their project 'despairingly to give an objective character to the desire to encounter the image of the universe' (Luca and Trost 2001: 41). This giving of 'objective character' to otherwise inchoate – or flatly metaphysical – phenomena may seem at odds with the more explicitly Marxian concerns of the interwar surrealist group. Yet insofar as 'le vol de la consistence' itself represents a concrete expression of the group's political intentionality – its desire – such ontological inconsistency is significant for its categorical opposition to the kind of instrumentalization Aragon once resisted (in 1927) before succumbing to it (in 1931). The Bucharest group's goal here is not to 'realize' its desire – that is, in a manner consistent with political and artistic spectacle – but to find the means for rendering this desire concrete, even if this concreteness consisted, as in the case of Heraclitus, in fragments or obscurity. The Parisian surrealists of the early 1930s first defended – and then decried – Aragon's poem on behalf of the non-instrumentality of poetry; yet they nevertheless insisted on the dialectical continuity between poetic activity and political action. Luca and Trost, on the other hand, indicate the Bucharest group's negation of this very idea, in positing what they called 'l'idée noire de la révolution' in place of any positive 'revolutionary' politics: their position *presumes* disappearance and suspension as the negative conditions of its possibility, whether this obscurity signified the retreat into poetic abstraction or the hypostatic production of artistic techniques and methods.

The surrealist inquiry into dialecticism and the active work of mediation continued, with increasing precision, after the Second World War. Turning its sights from Freudo-Marxism to the social forms that mediated the forces of historical determination, surrealism's post-war work is considerably more ethnographic and anthropological in focus, dwelling on an expansive – even exploded – set of cultural tendencies, from anti-colonial insurgence to cinema, humour, myth, science, and the history of occultism. Indeed, this project represents a shift away from the movement's interwar dialecticism insofar as it understands 'mediation' in methodological rather than in purely instrumental terms. The surrealist journal *Médium*, produced in two series between 1952 and 1955, presents an extensive inquiry into the possibilities of such an historical impression; the journal's driving concern, I propose, is the study of the social forms through which avant-garde practices are impressed upon by historical conditions, and through which they might, in turn, also leave their impression. Indeed, as we will see, the surrealist group of the early 1950s explored forms of intellectual agency beyond the revolutionary instrumentality implicit in pre-war Marxisms; they turned instead to experiential modes of thinking wherein cultural and material forms of mediation – the human sciences, artistic practices, language, bodily experience, and even consciousness itself – could predicate something resembling a new political subjectivity.

Without losing their commitment to political insurgence, the surrealists who contributed to *Médium* explicitly cast aside a *surrealist* project of revolutionary militancy in order to concentrate on the social forms – whether myths, disciplinary conventions, or historical models – through which historical change takes shape. In the decade after the Second World War, surrealism's task of 'poetic illumination' sought new ways to heed, rather than apply mechanically, Marx's appeal to a futurity discontinuous with the existing course of history. This meant reinventing the nature of discontinuity itself. In a manner that resonates with the work of Cahun, Bachelard, Luca, and Trost, post-war surrealists sought alternative conceptual models, aiming to break with the continuities presumed even in Marxian and Hegelian dialectics, while maintaining their investment in entertaining the possibility of transhistorical patterns in general. Rather than aspiring to a politics of pure immanence, for example, the surrealists compiled alternatives to existing models of historical continuity and discontinuity, whether the capitalist myth of progress or the 'phases of development' of dialectical materialism. The group's approach to this project was to study such historical abstractions as social forms in themselves: that is, as cultural products whose transhistorical scope was itself historically determined, and, at the same time, as conceptual apparatuses that shaped the very phenomenon of historical and social experience itself.

'Surrealism is not a philosophy', writes Gérard Legrand in 1956. 'It is the crossroads, the meeting place of several philosophies that have significance only in mutually completing themselves before the flaming hearth of poetry. But if it has been able to coincide, under precise conditions, with contemporary humanisms for the defence of interests and values belonging to "the mind", this is not because man was the bearer of these values; in my opinion it's for these values, and for the mind itself' (Legrand and Patri 1956: 144).

As Legrand suggests, surrealism posited its own form of mediation. Indeed, the group's very reason for existence, especially throughout the 1950s, might be described as its desire to organize the relationship between political revolution and art in a way that would short-circuit not only the totalizing panlogism of the Hegelian system and other humanisms, but also the orthodoxies to which the surrealist movement was itself prone. Such an organization demanded a redefinition not only of the relationship between political thought and aesthetics – a relationship the surrealists configured as a dialectic – but also of the nature of poetry and art themselves as something other than a means for human expression. In place of a traditional understanding of art as representation, the surrealists posited the role of art in political thought as constituted within and by the dialectic of interpretation that takes place between and among objects, concepts, forms, and spectators. Surrealism is dialectical insofar as it strove, from Heraclitus to anti-humanism, to position its thought at this crossroads: that is, at the point of encounter where the work of negation could take effect apart from the 'avortement colossal' of Hegelian systematics.

Notes

1 On surrealism's ties to the nineteenth century, see Drost and Reliquet 2014.
2 On the influence of Kojève, see, for instance, Hollier 1996: 69–3; Stewart 1996: 1–16.
3 In Breton (1969) this term is translated as 'an attack of conscience'.
4 The notion of the Hegelian system as an 'avortement colossal' derives from Engels' parody of Hegel's rhetoric of childbirth in the preface to the *Phenomenology of Spirit*; the English version of Engels' text translates it as 'The Hegelian system, in itself, was a colossal miscarriage.' See Friedrich Engels, *Anti-Dühring* (1987a: 25).
5 For a genealogy of the surrealist recourse to Heraclitus, see Hussey and Stubbs 1997: 151–66; Eburne 2000: 180–204. References to Heraclitus can be found, for instance, in the work of André Masson, who not only cites him in several early letters, but also publishes an illustration to Michel Leiris's entry on the philosopher in the 1937 edition of Leiris's *Glossaire: J'y serre mes gloses* (also in *Minotaure*, illustrating the text by Calas). The Belgian surrealist Louis Scutenaire prints a 'portrait' of Heraclitus in his *Pêle-mêle* (1934). Breton, in his later work, from the *Dictionnaire abregé du surréalisme* (1938) to his interviews after the Second World War, repeatedly adopts Heraclitus as a figure of unpopular but objective speculation.
6 The three books Aragon reviewed are Pierre Bise's *La politique d'Héraclite d'Ephèse* (Paris: Félix Alcan, 1924); André Fauconnet's *Oswald Spengler, le prophète du 'Déclin de l'Occident'* (Paris: Félix Alcan, 1926); and Salomon Reinach's *Lettres à Zoé* (Paris: Hachette, 1926). Aragon writes that Pierre Bise's book is 'the only French-language work entirely consecrated to Heraclitus currently in stores'. Fauconnet's book is concerned less with Heraclitus than with Spengler, who nonetheless 'finds his philosophical point of departure in the thought of the Ephesian'. Likewise, Reinach's book, insofar as it 'presents the history of philosophy to a young girl, gives Heraclitus intercurrently his place in the universe, as it suits a young girl to imagine it in order not to fail her baccalaureate' (Aragon 1927: 45).

7 As Andrew Benjamin has written of Heraclitus, 'it is possible to draw an analogy between interpreting the fragments and the problems involved in understanding the empirical. Neither a particular fragment nor the empirical can be understood literally, that is as an end-in-itself, rather both demand the recognition that understanding is never immediate but is the result of the process of interpretation' (A. Benjamin 1988: 124).

8 The archival documents concerning the movement's turn 'toward political action' have recently been published as part of the Archives du surréalisme collection: cf. Bonnet 1988b and 1992b. For English-language accounts of this period, see Lewis 1990.

9 On the translation of *harmonie*, see T.M. Robinson's useful commentary, Heraclitus (1987: 115–6).

10 'Beaucoup trop d'emmerdeurs idéalistes' is Bataille's response to Breton's and Aragon's inquiry, 'A suivre: petite contribution au dossier de certains intellectuels à tendances révolutionnaires (1929)' (Pierre 1980).

11 Bataille later revised his position on surrealism, intending this statement positively, in an article published in *Combat* in 1945. See Bataille, 'The Surrealist Revolution' (in 1994: 53).

12 On Cahun's Trotskyism and her ties to the Brunet group of Trotskyite writers, see especially Löwy 2009: 65–82. See also Leperlier 1992: 167–87.

13 On surrealism's ties to Bachelard, see Parkinson 2008a; also Caws 1966.

2 Hermeticism and the magical tradition

Guy Girard

Are there several esotericisms or just one? Let's consider the possibility that each civilization, without necessarily contradicting its most widespread conceptions about relationships between mankind and the universe, has developed other conceptions, other understandings of them, as well as other ways of being and acting, which are taught by recourse to an initiatory framework responding to a specific symbolic ensemble. The aim of this initiation is to approach, experience and understand the harmony between being and the world, a condition available to humanity in a far off time, and to make this understanding the agent of a transformation in the individual who can master it and interpret its signs. It then falls to him to transmit them, once he knows that he is a link in a chain whose origins are laid out in the story of a primordial Tradition, a mythical story that interconnects, interferes with, or sometimes contradicts those that are conveyed by religions. In this way, if we need to locate the esoteric quest in relation to religious faith, one might suggest that this quest cannot be satisfied just by contemplation of divinity, but must aspire to decipher what the latter veils, and by so doing find the effect or the ferment that an action has upon the phenomenal world.

In this way all esotericism remains dependent upon magic thought, even if it is diversified through practices such as astrology, alchemy, geomancy, theurgy or Kabbalah (to list only those from the West). This form of thought privileges analogy, in so far as it allows the establishment of signifying correspondences between microcosm and macrocosm, between mankind and nature, between mortals and supernatural beings. It begins with the principle that everything in the universe is encrypted, that everything acts as a sign and is linked to other signs whose interpretation is accessible to the initiate, for whom human language itself participates in this infinite play of signification that drives universal harmony. Very close to this extremely ancient principle, if not indeed founded upon it without having clearly formulated its origin, is the one adopted at the dawn of modernity by Romantic and Symbolist poets like Novalis, Hugo, Nerval, Baudelaire, Rimbaud or even Saint-Pol-Roux, and that claims that the poet is able to read in the clouds or in any other natural spectacle the forms taken by the turmoil of his own mind, and that in themselves allow him to recognize that 'Nature is a temple whose living pillars/Sometimes issue obscure messages' (Baudelaire, 'Correspondences', in 1975: 11). Those 'obscure messages' that Victor Hugo heard uttered by the 'Bouche d'ombre' (Hugo 1947: §26; 801) are the ones whose origins and meaning surrealism sought when it interrogated the indications linking the unconscious to the objective world in its most disconcerting as well as its least known forms, through its appeal to automatism and objective chance, even to the point of proposing that they demonstrate that poetic thought – far better and more evidently than rational thought – leads to a 'certain point of the mind' (Breton 1969: 123) at which the contradictions between being and the world are erased. Poetic thought, as tested by surrealism following the example of Rimbaud, is effectively activated by *illuminations* that have the value of truths for the one who is dazzled by them. But André Breton and his friends did not regard them as accidental, and they felt free to speculate as much on the causes as on the scope of this new enlightenment within which is played out a fundamental calling into question of the relations between language and a reality it henceforth no longer describes but on the contrary seems potentially able to control. In this way, from the earliest years of surrealism, and contemporaneous with the research on Freud and the theoretical scope of psychoanalysis, the promises of automatic writing and mediumistic experiments, in the attention given to dreams, and of the quest for the marvellous in the workings of chance, all bespeak a correlation with what is communicated by traditional sciences. This is because surrealist research, if its principal aim is the will to liberate the unconscious, proposes as much in its conception of language (as Breton writes, 'Language has been given to man so that he may make surrealist use of it'; 1972: 32) as in the very conditions of thought, to restore mankind's lost powers, for instance those that once (or still can), allow it to understand the 'language of the birds' and so rediscover the paths of a fundamental harmony between being and the world, an achievement that was also the aim of initiates in the esoteric tradition.

This proximity of the surrealist adventure to the traditional legacy can be discerned from the outset of surrealism. Indeed, numbers 11–12 of the journal *Littérature* (October 1923) offered under the title 'Erutaréttil' an extremely varied list of authors, ranging from antiquity to the beginnings of the 1920s, that included names familiar to any disciple of

Hermeticism: Hermes Trismegistus himself, but also Lulle, Flamel, Corneille Agrippa and Louis-Claude de Saint-Martin (Pierre 1980: 12–13). Among the other writers selected, it is known that Nerval, Hugo, Baudelaire, Rimbaud, Jarry, Péladan and even Raymond Roussel were all to different degrees aware of the traditional sciences. Later, a collective declaration dating from 1931, in other words during the period when the surrealist group declared its support for Marx's dialectical materialism, proposed a renewed list of authors recommended for reading as well as others that are advised against ('Lisez – Ne lisez pas' in Pierre 1980: 202). This, much longer, list still contains the names of Lulle, Flamel and Agrippa. Hermes Trismegistus and Saint-Martin have admittedly been omitted, but the essential difference in relation to the list of 1923 lies in the contribution of Marxist theorists: Marx himself, as well as Engels, Lafargue and Lenin. In the intervening period surrealism had defined its political position in support of communism (at that time mistakenly identified with the regime installed in the Soviet Union). This shift was not without its debates, notably with Antonin Artaud, that set out (and continues to do so) the essential question of surrealism: if the human condition is one of revolt, is this essentially its ontological nature, or is it relative to the given historical conditions? Is the surrealist revolution, approximating the play on words, the object of its own revelation or is it inscribed, within a play of causalities needing better definition, in a social revolution? In the face of the prevailing decision in favour of the need for a political dimension for this movement with its revolutionary ambitions, Artaud on the contrary defended the viewpoint of the absolute, according to which it would be vain to change the frame of this 'breaking up of appearances, this transfiguration of the possible that surrealism was to help bring about' (Artaud 1976: 142) and these concepts of the absolute and of transfiguration, remind us of the essential themes of esoteric thought, which distinguishes several levels of reality that the initiate has to experience in turn. It is indeed thus desirable to relate these qualitative differences in the grasp of reality within the notion of surreality adopted by the surrealists in order to distinguish between the banal perception of things and a poetic experience opening onto a superior dimension of reality, one that might equally be described by the notion of the marvellous.

Around 1925 the surrealists wanted to contact René Guénon. Apparently the author of *The Multiple States of Being* (*Les États multiples de l'être*) did not respond to their overtures, and moreover would come to consider surrealism as a counter-initiation typical of the confusion of the dark ages in which we live. But during this period in which the surrealists were enthused by the myth of the Orient, when they wrote to the Dalai Lama or to the schools of Buddhism, but at the same time they were also soon to subscribe to the tenets of historical materialism, the notion of surreality really might have acted as a here and now made from a sudden encounter between a millenarian or progressive conception of history, one that was Hegelian-Marxist in inspiration, and another stemming from the primordial Tradition according to which the golden age lay in the past rather than before us. Before Breton and his friends, during the 1940s, discovered the work of Fourier that contained the dialectic of this relationship, this notion of Tradition, in other words the interrogation of the legacy and the transmission of a founding myth subject to the test of 'the reign of quantity and the signs of the times' (to use the title of Guénon's book of 1945), would not have been investigated without misgivings. This was because surrealism saw itself as a radically new poetic experience, beginning with the automatic writing of *The Magnetic Fields* by Breton and Philippe Soupault (1919), and as the dynamic actualization of the quests for liberty and knowledge launched by a long line of ancestors whose list, as we have just seen, is never complete or definitive. In this way surrealism should never be considered as an avant-garde: it does not claim to wipe the slate of the past clean, but rather to rediscover and, if necessary, retranscribe the teachings of the Emerald Tablet by the legendary Hermes Trismegistus to serve the modern poetic movement. But does this mean that surrealism, following the example of all traditional teachings, aims to establish a wisdom that a master might teach to avid disciples? In due consideration of the relationship between revolt and desire that surrealism has always considered its essential driving force, this presumptuous wisdom would be as disconcerting as the *Poésies* of Isidore Ducasse, Comte de Lautréamont, in comparison to his *Chants de Maldoror*.

But the surrealists would never consider the miseries and riches of this world mere appearances, and for them there is no beyond, neither in this life, nor in some hypothetical survival of the soul after death. Their atheism is irreducible, they have no belief in a divine transcendence, and the analogies they discern as much in the spheres of language and human behaviour as in the natural realm are facts of nature – incomprehensible, admittedly, but which can still be grasped. The study of esotericism can in this way offer them a method of thought rather than a fixed conception of the world; in this regard it is a different logic that can better respond to their enquiries into mythic thought and poetic facts that they research in their play with the unconscious and with chance. It is a logic that can thus sometimes be compared to those of dream and madness which likewise deploy a symbolism to challenge the signifying opacity of the real. But alchemical symbolism, for example, if it often draws upon classical mythology, doesn't aim to respond to psychic conflicts, and many surrealists, fascinated or inspired by these, would turn this Hermetic language to a 'surrealist use' that, with a few notable exceptions, did not lead them to work in alchemical laboratories. Does the 'gold of time' (*l'or du temps*) Breton sought – as well as the suggestion, made with malice but perhaps something more, that it is shadowed by something outside of time (*hors du temps*) – fuse its light on the peaks of surrealism's utopia with that of the philosopher's gold of Nicolas Flamel or Fulcanelli? Breton noted in the *Second Manifesto* that surrealism shared a 'remarkable analogy in its goal' with alchemy (Breton 1972: 174, translation modified), and there is no doubt that in this domain subsequent efforts by surrealists were able to focus and expand upon the significance of this analogy.

The same manifesto affirms the existence of 'a certain point of the mind at which life and death, the real and the imagined, past and future, the communicable and the incommunicable, high and low, cease to be perceived as contradictions' (Breton 1972: 123), the mental place that would subsequently be named the supreme, or sublime, point and in search of which Breton would call for the occultation of surrealism. In truth surrealism has never been inclined to become a school or a party (or a group like the Grand Jeu, whose poetic proximity to the surrealist movement rests on its substantial interest in esotericism), nor to open itself up to all comers. In this it is comparable to the various more or less secret groups or societies practising esoteric knowledge, and if no surrealist was ever asked to create a poetic or artistic work, the mutual recognition between surrealists was to be found in the purlieu of this mental location. Henceforth the contradictions inherent in surrealism's development in the face of the vagaries of history would no longer be called upon to resolve themselves more or less effectively in a dialectic inherited from Hegel, but to pass onto the other side of the 'mirror of the marvellous', to borrow the title of Pierre Mabille's great book.

Through its demand for an overcoming of all profane misery, this is a passage that can be compared to that which crosses an initiatory threshold leading to an experience of the sacred. This moment is indeed found at the heart of all esoteric research but for the majority of Hermes' disciples, unlike surrealist research, it is attained or revealed on the basis of the transcendence offered by religious faith, even when – as, for example, for Raymond Abellio, who was well aware of surrealism – this basis could nevertheless be described using Husserl's phenomenology. In contrast, the surrealists do not accept that they should just be limited to the resources of the human psyche, but combine them in particular with those of the liminal states between conscious thought and the outbreaks of the unconscious, and the possibilities offered by intuition or mediumistic trances, in order to grasp a qualitatively different relationship to the real, in such a way that the distinction between subjectivity and objectivity might cease to be conceived or even experienced. In this way the facts and consequences of objective chance would be sought out or even provoked, in parallel with the investigations into the contribution of psychic automatism to the fields of poetic expression and their confrontation with the paranoia-critical method proposed by Salvador Dalí. But do these all constitute the stages of an initiation, or – to borrow Walter Benjamin's phrase – a 'profane illumination'? It is worth remembering how Victor Brauner, after the accidental loss of one of his eyes, discovered that for many years he had been concerned unconsciously with the expectation of this event, to the extent that this tragic occurrence oriented the painter towards making work that was entirely impregnated with esotericism, even towards the creation of a magic art that, from the end of the 1930s, symbolized the extent to which the links between surrealism and the traditional sciences were growing closer and more fertile. It was during the years of the Second World War that Breton discovered simultaneously the work of Charles Fourier, and those in the esoteric domain of Eliphas Lévi and of Saint-Yves d'Alveydre, subsequently redefining surrealism's task as the creation of a new myth. Thus in his *Prolegomena to a Third Surrealist Manifesto or Not*, published in 1942, Breton proposed that the mythological imagination of his contemporaries should be crystallized around the image of the Great Transparents, the modern enchantment of the era of relativity that demands leaving behind the deplorable dead end of anthropocentrism (Breton 1969: 293–4). This put at stake a different relationship between microcosm and macrocosm, a relationship based on analogy rather than opposition, following the wisdom of what Lévi-Strauss called the 'wild' or 'untamed' thinking of the indigenous peoples of the Americas and elsewhere as much as that of esoteric thought. But this was also the period in which Breton wrote *Arcanum 17*, a work in which a love song to his wife Elisa is inextricably intermingled with the claim not only for a libertarian feminism but also for the feminine principle itself, as an essential basis of the psyche whose given task will be both to 'reshape human understanding' (Breton 1996: 97; 1999b: 759 'Surrealist Comet') and to renew contact with the objective world, both of these becoming the object and subject of the mythical thought of which surrealism sees itself as the bearer. But where and how should this mythical thought, as proclaimed by the sixth International

Surrealist Exhibition of 1947, be grasped, and how can it be given life? The solution lies in desire; it's at hand: the cover of this exhibition's catalogue was conceived by the group's long-time friend, Marcel Duchamp, and consisted of the presentation of a female breast, accompanied by the caption 'Please Touch' ('Prière de toucher'). Was this an invitation for esotericism and eroticism to join together in order between them to push back the frontiers of knowledge?

For the surrealists, when the human sciences study myth they do so from a perspective that is too external to their object of study. This indicated to them that the deepening of the relationship between surrealism and the esoteric tradition, as they engaged with it, should not only extend intellectual knowledge, but also put their poetic sensibility, and thus the deepest layers of both their psyche and their sensitivity towards the signs and symbols with which the real is marked out, to the test. Unlike the then currently fashionable ideologies (the Marxism manhandled by Stalinism or the existentialism whose poetic contribution was negligible) surrealism and esotericism were placed together under the 'ascendant sign' that, according to Breton, is the true domain of analogical thought that 'tends to hint at and bring to account truly "absent" life' (Breton 1978: 281). This ascendant sign was open to misunderstanding, and some considered that this notion, borrowed from astrology, would lead the surrealist imagination astray into an aestheticization of the marvellous. But in fact it was a matter of activating, in the domain of the exploration of the resources of the imagination, what the alchemists effected upon matter in their crucibles and their athanors before it became transmuted in the course of the various decoctions to which it was subjected. And, in the dispiriting context of the Cold War, for the surrealists it was now a question of demanding more than ever that poetic thought should be requalified, that language and human passions should be re-enchanted. For Breton and his friends, these were, on the basis of analogy, as perfectible as the lead that the alchemist persists in transmuting into gold. A surrealist greeting card of 1925 had moreover already announced this fact with admirable insolence: 'You who have lead in your head/ melt it so it turns into surrealist gold' (Pierre 1980: 33).

By resembling the entrance into a Masonic temple, the 1947 exhibition was thus conceived as a veritable initiatory journey. Divided into a number of rooms as so many stages and tests to which the visitor's (or the applicant's) sensibilities were subjected, it notably included a staircase with twenty-one steps – the same number as the Major Arcana of the Tarot, not including the Fool. These steps were painted to resemble the spines of books, those of the surrealists' ideal library: in it of course were found the permanent reference points like Ducasse,

Jarry and Apollinaire, but also authors of the Hermetic tradition like Valentin Andreae, Swedenborg and even John, author of the Apocalypse. Taking this staircase, the visitor entered the Hall of Superstitions in which twelve altars had been erected, devoted to a being or an object 'susceptible to being endowed with mythic life' (Breton 1999b: 1367). Taken from the works of the surrealists or their immediate precursors, naturally they included one of the Great Transparents created by Jacques Hérold. This imposing sculpture with its anthropomorphic bearing brought together various elements borrowed from the natural kingdom, in this way accomplishing the fusion of microcosm and macrocosm, and its belly resembled an athanor. These altars were not inspired by concern with ridiculing Christian religion (against which the surrealists nevertheless remained implacable enemies) but by the memory of the voodoo ceremonies witnessed by Breton, Mabille and Wifredo Lam in Haiti. If they were twelve in number it was because there are twelve signs of the zodiac. Each altar corresponded to one of these: thus the altar to the Great Transparents/Invisibles was aligned with the sign of Aquarius, logical to the extent that the '*inversion of the sign*' claimed by Breton at the time (in 'The Lamp in the Clock', a text to which we shall return; Breton 1995: 111) corresponded by analogy to the passage from the age of Pisces to that of Aquarius that, according to astrology, characterizes the end of the twentieth century and the beginning of our own.

Moreover Breton and many of his friends did not underestimate astrology. As we have seen, the *Second Manifesto* demanded the 'occultation' of surrealism, a word borrowed from astrological vocabulary (and not from that of occultism, a term admittedly popularized by Eliphas Lévi but that subsequently designated a composite mixture made up of borrowings from the traditional sciences, spiritualism and various oriental mythologies and linked by an attitude that was positivist in spirit). But in a long footnote, he proposed that surrealists should pursue the task of 'probing seriously into those sciences of astrology and parapsychology which for various reasons are today seriously discredited' (Breton 1969: 178, translation modified). It continues, after formulating, by analogy with the surrealist project, the idea that love might be 'the site of ideal occultation of all thought' (181), by inviting the reader to reflect on the influence of the planet Uranus upon surrealism itself. In the late 1920s Breton had learned to draw up and interpret astrological charts, and subsequent surrealist journals published the birth charts of several of the movement's precursors.

Nineteen forty-seven was also the year that the surrealists became aware of the work of Malcolm de Chazal. Made up of notes and fragments combining a profound sense of the observation of humanity and nature with a specific science of analogy, this attracted Breton's attention as much because this poetic thought was entirely oriented towards a grasp of the sensual pleasure and the harmony at work in all the manifestations of life as because its author was a descendant of one of Swedenborg's disciples. Thus in a text celebrating de Chazal, 'The Lamp in the Clock', Breton demands a refounding not so much of literary history as of the history of ideas, those that currently fail to acknowledge the itinerary and legacy of esotericism. Attacking 'your wretched Sorbonne' (Breton 1995: 121), he proposes among other things that we should prefer Martinez de Pasqually and Saint-Yves d'Alveydre to Chénier or Renan. And so during the 1950s and beyond the surrealists were very keen to extend their knowledge of various esoteric sciences, in a period when they considered both psychoanalytic research and political criticism derived from Marxism to have stalled. During this time they encountered figures such as René Alleau, Eugène Canseliet and Robert Amadou. In this period Breton also sent his enquiry into magic art (to accompany the book of the same name) as a matter of urgency to a number of scholars of Hermeticism. The visual creations of the surrealists, just as much as their poetry, were from that moment increasingly influenced by a range of symbols from the traditional sciences: this is discernible not only in the work of Brauner but also, to cite just a few others, that of Maurice Baskine, Leonora Carrington, Remedios Varo and Jorge Camacho (who would actually practise alchemy). Certainly surrealism, from its origins to the present day, has never sought to confine itself to the banks of the Seine; in parallel to the evolution of the Parisian group, a certain number of the members of groups in other countries directed their research towards one or other aspect of esotericism, including (to give just a few examples) Toni Del Renzio and Ithell Colquhoun in Great Britain, Antonio Maria Lisboa in Portugal, Philip Lamantia in the United States, or today, in the Czech Republic, Jan Švankmajer and Martin Stejskal. This study led some of them to conduct genuine works of exegesis in order to reveal what some specific precursor owed to the traditional sciences. Breton set an example for this approach with his text 'Fronton-virage' which introduced a study by Jean Ferry devoted to Raymond Roussel (Breton 1995: 175–95). According to Breton, the latter's work might be seen as entirely suffused with alchemical symbolism. In a similar vein Marcel Jean and Arpad Mezei investigated the messages of Lautréamont, Rimbaud and Jarry.

But unlike academic scholarship, the aim of these researches was not to enclose a given subversive work within the nets of a discursive rationality, but to stimulate the rebellious power of poetic thought, in the face of all that would pitifully wish to convince it of its inanity, through the revelation of the correlations between the 'alchemy of the word' – which, ever since Rimbaud, should be the practice of all poetry worthy of the name – and spagyric procedures. It is in this that surrealism constructs both its myth and its own culture which conducts it. Through this its task is also to learn about those mythologies and traditions that have been ridiculed or ignored by the civilization against which it struggles. Non-Western esoteric thought would be included in this, and for example Benjamin Péret translated (into French based on a Spanish version) the *Book of Chilám Balám of Chumayel* (Péret 1955). In Japan the surrealist Fukuzawa Ichirô became interested in Zen, which would also attract Breton's attention on several occasions. But Breton would also be led to a passionate engagement with Celtic poetry and art, whose esoteric significance would be outlined to the surrealists (who had long marvelled at the Arthurian cycle) thanks to the work of first Lancelot Lengyel and then Jean Markale. Even more than with ancient Egyptian art, in which they were struck by the figure of Isis, the surrealists found in the art of the Celts, rich in esotericism, a confirmation that in order to orient the project of civilization along the lines of an 'absolute divergence' (Fourier) from the civilization that currently dominates the globe, it is necessary to exalt the power of the feminine in order to interpret the dynamic of the forms of the world and of thought. It is a power whose revelatory aspect is, in the surrealists' eyes, the love that is for them the initiatory test itself, but one which, like poetry and freedom, is within the grasp of all who are prepared to devote their hearts and minds together to it. In this surrealism, in so far as it simultaneously offers and demands at the same time both complexity and evident facts, has the status of a gnosis: it is even the unresolved gnosis of modernity. At the conjoined heart of absolute revolt and a no less absolute thirst for the knowledge that Tradition promises in a golden age, a mythic reminiscence that it insists, in the wake of revolutionary Romanticism, on transmuting into a concrete utopia, surrealism thus sets itself the task, in the words of Michel Zimbacca, of embracing a 'collective initiation' (Zimbacca, personal communication). And this is truly what it obtains, what it transforms, following the perspective of a surrealist revolution, from the most ancient *Science of Symbols* (Alleau 1976) laid out on the Emerald Tablet, not far from the Fountain of Youth.

3 Freudian origins

Jean-Michel Rabaté

If surrealism can be seen as a continuation of psychoanalysis by poetic means, this was due almost exclusively to Breton's initial fascination for Freud's main concepts and discoveries. Breton appealed to Freud's ideas when he pioneered psychic automatism, the unconscious dictation of the Unconscious, and saw hysteria as a revolutionary form of artistic activity. However, this transfer was not without high doses of ambivalence. These had remained private until *Le Surréalisme au service de la Révolution* published polemical letters between Breton and Freud to document a tense rapport caught up in paranoid accusations. This loaded ambivalence was partly due to Breton's formation. He began his career as a medical student specializing in psychiatry and it was in this function that he served during the First World War. He read Freud closely then, at a time when French schools of psychiatry ignored him. Breton was sent to the neuropsychiatric ward of Saint-Dizier in August 1916, which was supervised by a former assistant of Charcot. There Breton devoured all the psychoanalytic literature available. Breton strenuously defended Freud's ideas against his friend Théodore Fraenkel's scepticism (Bonnet 1992a: 121). He copied entire pages for him and provided him with accurate synthetic notes on Freudian concepts such as resistance, repression and sublimation (Bonnet 1992a: 125–7). At the same time, Breton took notes on what psychotic patients would tell him, which provided a first-hand acquaintance with war-induced trauma. And then he was transferred to Doctor Babinski's service in 1917. This shift led him to address the issue of hysteria more directly.

Babinski had just then refuted Charcot's elaborations on hysteria and at first Breton had accepted his theories. However, Breton did not like his mentor's harsh treatment of shell-shocked soldiers who had come back from the front during the First World War; they were treated as male hysterics, which led to accusations of medical abuse, since treatments often included electroshock therapy. A strange coincidence:

after the war, in 1921 when the actor and playwright Pierre Palau was writing a disturbing play, *Les Détraquées* (literally, The deranged women), for Les Deux Masques, a theatre specializing in gory melodramas, Babinski was advising him. The theatre was just a few doors from Breton's apartment in rue Fontaine and he gives an account of it in *Nadja*. He'd been impressed by Blanche Derval, the stunning actress playing the main role: she is Solange, an upper-class sex and opium addict who, in complicity with the 'perverse' school headmistress, murders a shy little girl after torturing her with steel pen nibs! Breton sums up the rather trite and blood-curdling plot at some length in the first part of *Nadja* (see the three endnotes in Breton 1988: 1535). Probably without being aware of Babinski's participation in the 'scientific' construction of borderline characters (the play elaborates on the distinction between acceptable sexual 'inversion' and 'perversion', which leads to sexual abominations), Breton fell under the spell of the latent hysteria enacted by these feral and seductive femmes fatales who pile up sapphism and sadism in their bloodthirsty rituals. Breton concludes that Blanche Derval's beauty excused her character's moral failings: '… this character, too alluring to be true, should never be obliged to submit to a show of punishment which, moreover, she denied with all her splendour' (Breton 1960: 49).

This long preamble was not a detour: it paves the way for the psychological delineation of Nadja as another of these fascinating but unhinged *détraquées*. Curiously, despite his medical training, Breton mistook a woman who was obviously falling deeper and deeper into psychosis for a sublime hysteric – under his gaze, even – a misadventure that was not unknown to Freud.

Breton's ambivalence appears earlier in the narrative when he admits his fascination for the statue of Étienne Dolet in the middle of Place Maubert, immediately wondering whether he is not 'ready for psychoanalysis', a 'method' he then strongly qualifies: '… a method I respect and whose present aims I consider nothing less than the expulsion of man from himself, and of which I expect other exploits than that of a bouncer' (Breton 1960: 24). Describing Freud as a 'bouncer' (*huissier*) is not very flattering, even though surrealism shared the ambition to expel subjectivity from itself. Psychoanalysis, already in 1928, is accused of having not fully unlocked the secret of dreams, and of having added inhibitions, or, more precisely, of having failed to make a positive and dynamic interpretation of parapraxes – here Breton's punning becomes untranslatable: '… qu'elle n'occasionne pas simplement de nouveaux manquements d'actes à partir de son explication des actes manqués' (Breton 1988: 653). The French for *Fehlleistung*, 'acte manqué', is sent back to psychoanalytic doctrine, with the insinuation that it betrays in its very semantic form the method's grave limitations.

However, it was Freud's general impact that led Breton to trust the spontaneous production of language as a key to unlock the secrets of the unconscious. Breton acknowledged this derivation in the *Manifesto of Surrealism*:

> Quite busy as I then was with Freud, and having been familiarized with his examination methods that I had somehow used with patients during the war, I decided to obtain from myself what one seeks to obtain from them, that is a monologue flowing as fast as possible and upon which the critical mind of the subject makes no judgment whatever, letting it be unhampered by any reticence so it may render *spoken thought* as exactly as possible.
>
> (Breton 1988: 326; English translation, 1969: 22–3)

Freud's name and his inspiration are perceptible throughout the surrealist manifesto of 1924. Breton was also aware that a whole world separated psychoanalysis understood as a clinical practice from surrealist experiments aiming at abolishing the borders between sleep and waking life, art and life.

In October 1921, Breton had met Freud; the experience left him severely disappointed. In his 'Interview with Professor Freud' of 1922, first published in *Littérature* and then in *Les Pas perdus* in 1924, the year when surrealism was launched, he gives a curt account of the meeting. Breton provides a snide physical description: Freud looks like 'an old man without elegance who receives in the poor consulting room one would expect from a local doctor'. The article concludes ironically by quoting Freud's tepid endorsement: 'Happily, we have great faith in the young' (Breton 1996: 71). The discrepancy between Freud the man and Freudian ideas would weigh on Breton's attitude over the following years.

In March 1928, *La Révolution surréaliste* published Breton and Aragon's manifesto extolling the 'Invention of Hysteria'. The text celebrated the fiftieth anniversary, so dating the invention from 1878, a date that could only refer to Charcot. They could have gone back further in history, but Charcot's concept of hysteria was hailed as 'the greatest poetic discovery of the late nineteenth century' (in Richardson and Fijalkowski 2001: 143).[1] Quite logically, this homage to Charcot's view of hysteria rejected Babinski's theory that reduced hysteria to 'suggestion' or 'pithiatism'. However, Charcot was praised less for the theatrical scene at La Salpêtrière, in which he exhibited patients before a fashionable crowd, than for having created the conditions for the vulgarization of hysteria. Freud was not spared. Breton and Aragon opposed his conservatism to what they found admirable in Charcot's set-up: the fact that La Salpêtrière's interns would regularly sleep with their beautiful hysterical patients: 'Does Freud, who owes so much to Charcot, remember the days when, according to testimony from those still alive, the Salpêtrière house doctors would confuse their professional duty and their propensity for love when, come nightfall, the patients would either meet them outside or welcome them into their beds?' (in Richardson and Fijalkowski 2001: 144). Freud would have been horrified by the insinuation that he associated with that unruly crowd. The living poetry embodied by female patients and young interns sleeping together culminated in the 'passionate attitudes' photographed by Charcot. In these images, stunning half-undressed women in curious poses indicated the possibility of a 'convulsive beauty'.

In 1928, the two leading members of the surrealist group had thus provided their *ad hoc* definition of hysteria; it rejected any pathologization, and objected to any form of medical treatment. The text looks indeed like a manifesto with its block capitals, not reproduced here: 'Hysteria is a more or less irreducible mental state characterized by its subversion of the relations between the subject and the moral world by which it believes itself to have sprung in practice, beyond any systematic delirium. This mental state is founded on the need for a reciprocal seduction, which explains the hastily accepted miracles of medical suggestion (or counter-suggestion). Hysteria is not a pathological phenomenon and can in every respect be considered a supreme means of expression' (in Richardson and Fijalkowski 2001: 145, translation slightly modified). Thus Breton and Aragon insisted upon the quasi-normalcy of a state seen as a limit-experience. For them, hysteria also ruled out a 'systematic delirium', by which they mean classical paranoia. The phases of the classical hysterical crisis would lead to a 'superb aura' in a magnificent theatralization before subsiding by a 'simple resolution in everyday life' (in Richardson and Fijalkowski 2001: 144). Hysteria, identified with a mystical and erotic ecstasy, taps fundamental artistic impulses. Adding its erotic salt to the humdrum of everyday life, hysteria proves that the main surrealist ambition, which is to merge dream and reality, or poetry and life, is not a delusion.

In this pamphlet, Breton and Aragon bid farewell to their former master Babinski, for whom hysteria was a mimetic disease, an affection of 'suggestion' that could be eradicated by simple counter-suggestion. The concept of hysteria as simulation has to turn into poetry and writing. For the surrealists, simulation was a roundabout way of going back to Aristotle's *mimesis* while avoiding any 'realism'. This appears explicitly in a text Breton wrote with Éluard in 1930: *The Immaculate Conception*. In the section 'Possessions' the two poets recreate the discourses of debility, mania, general paralysis, interpretive delirium, and precocious dementia (Breton 1988: 848–63; English translation, Breton and Éluard 1990: 47–77). The introduction to this section, written by Breton, discusses the amphibology of the word 'simulation'. Breton links the technical meaning of 'simulation' in psychiatry, especially for war neuroses, with a critique of traditional poetic forms. An older and conventional poetry should be replaced by stylistic imitations of various types of psychotic speech: 'This is to say that we offer the generalization of this device and that in our eyes, the "attempts at simulation" of diseases that land you in a jail might advantageously replace the ballad, the sonnet, the epic, the nonsense rhyme and other now totally obsolete genres' (Breton 1988: 849; Breton and Éluard 1990: 49). The verbal production of the insane and those of poets are linked because they follow the same laws of composition, the same rhetorical patterns, the same tropes and stylistic devices. This general rhetoricity left room for a vision of another reality.

The surrealist idea was that a new beauty, created out of the ruins of ancient representations, would connect them to the dream world. What matters for Breton is that dreams in general provide considerable aesthetic freedom while avoiding any moral concern. In *Nadja*, after Breton has analysed *Les Détraquées*, he compares the powerful impression the play made on him with an even more disturbing dream he had. The dream's climax was an image of a moss-coloured insect about 20 inches long falling into Breton's throat, after which he pulled the hairy legs out of his mouth. Meditating on the nauseating disgust the memory still triggers in him, Breton reflects on the porous borders separating dreams and waking life:

> Since the production of dream images always depends on at least this double play of mirrors, there is, here, the indication of the highly special, supremely revealing, 'super-determinant' – in the Freudian sense of the word – role which certain powerful impressions are made to play, in no way contaminable by morality, actually experienced 'beyond good and evil' in the dream, and, subsequently, in what we quite arbitrarily oppose to dream under the name of reality.
>
> (Breton 1960: 51)

Here, Breton slyly introduces the Freudian concept of 'overdetermination', the idea that each element of a dream means several things at the same time, with often contradictory meanings. ‘Overdetermination’ entails positing an extramoral site for dreams: because of their plurality of meanings, these images are beyond good and evil. Breton in *Nadja* argues that avant-garde poetry will change life by introducing a deliberate confusion of the domains of dream and reality. The idea had already been developed in the *Manifesto*: ‘The mind of the man who dreams is fully satisfied by what happens to him. The agonizing question of possibility is no longer pertinent. Kill, fly faster, love to your heart’s content. And if you should die, are you not certain of waking up from the dead? Let yourself be carried along, events will not tolerate your interference. You are nameless. The ease of everything is priceless’ (Breton 1969: 13, translation slightly modified). The ‘otherness’ of dreams is such that one must acknowledge that they belong to a different realm in which moral issues have no relevance. Which does not mean that dreams are worthless fantasies, on the contrary, or that one should not attempt to think the world of dreams and of reality together. Breton adds: ‘What reason, I ask, a reason so much vaster than the other, makes dreams seem so natural and allow me to welcome unreservedly a welter of episodes so strange that they would confound me now as I write? And yet I can believe my eyes, my ears: this great day has arrived, this beast has spoken’ (Breton 1969: 13). The conflation of the two states, the waking state and the sleeping state, leads to a redefinition of reason and of reality: reality has to be replaced by ‘surreality’. One type of people who testified to its impact on their bodies is the group of those called ‘hysterics’ by doctors at the end of the nineteenth century. Surrealism had launched a praise and a defence of hysteria as a poetic mechanism, but this soon turned into a praise of paranoia.

This took place after the young Catalan painter Salvador Dalí joined the group and systematized psychic disorder, raising it to the level of an aesthetic credo. ‘Our epoch is dying of moral skepticism and spiritual nothingness. … I am thinking of you, youth exuberant with gay generosities, youth of neo-paganism guided by a monstrous utopian idea bloody and sacrilegious. I am thinking of you, companions, comrades of nothingness!’ (Dalí 1998b: 303–4). While Dalí’s painting *The Lugubrious Game* was praised by Breton for its ‘hallucinatory’ quality, (Breton 1992: 308–9) the dissident Georges Bataille took it as a new paradigm, but presented it differently. In December 1929, *Documents* published Bataille’s essay on the painting, in which he developed the idea of castration as a critical concept. Emasculation would have been depicted by Dalí in its very parody, via the shocking figure of a man who has shitty breeches. Nevertheless, Dalí, who had chosen Breton’s camp, refused to allow Bataille to reproduce the painting. He then attacked Bataille directly, calling him 'cretinous' and 'senile'; and, moreover, because Bataille's misreading derived from a wrong interpretation of Freud (Dalí 1998b: 117). In furious controversies that paved the way for the emergence of Dalí's paranoid-critical method, Bataille, Breton and Dalí reproached one another for misapplying Freudian ideas.

The Freudian source of these ideas stands out clearly in the text in which Dalí exposed his discovery, 'The Moral Position of Surrealism' (22 March 1930). Aligning himself with Breton's *Second Manifesto*, Dalí explained that next to going into the street with a revolver in hand and shooting people at random, his proselytizing activity aimed at propagating the 'violently paranoid will to systematize confusion' (Dalí 1998b: 110). Freud's ideas had been watered down, he argued, it was urgent to restore their 'rabid and dazzling clarity'. He mentioned that under a painting of the Sacré-Cœur he had written that at times, he has spat on his mother's portrait. The deliberate provocation was not taken lightly by his family. The general attitude corresponded with a systematic attempt at 'demoralization' similar to that of Sade. The point was to launch a method of seeing reality differently, and this he called 'paranoia': 'The particular perspicacity of attention in the paranoiac state must be insisted upon; paranoia being recognized, moreover, by all psychologists as a form of mental illness which consists in organizing reality in such a way as to utilize it to control an imaginative construction. The paranoiac who believes himself to be poisoned discovers in everything that surrounds him, right up to the most imperceptible and subtle details, preparations for his own death. Recently, through a decidedly paranoiac process, I obtained an image of a woman whose position, shadow and morphology, without altering or deforming anything of her real appearance, are also, at the same time, those of a horse' (Dalí 1998b: 112).

At the time, the surrealist interactions with psychoanalysis turned more aggressive when Breton entertained the suspicion that in the *Interpretation of Dreams* Freud had plagiarized other theoreticians of dreams. In the summer of 1931, as he was drafting *Communicating Vessels*, Breton read the French translation of the *Interpretation of Dreams* and took twenty pages of notes in a schoolboy's exercise book. When he reached the spot where Freud criticizes Delboeuf about 'Theories of Dreaming', his attention was alerted, especially when Freud stated that there was a link between dream activity and paranoia. Breton wrote on the right-hand side of the page: 'Theories of dreams. 1. "The whole psychical activity of the waking state continues in dreams". (Delboeuf) (Very insufficient) Dream = Paranoia.' The left-hand side has: 'Theories. Delboeuf. Dream-paranoia. Valéry: "The dream goes on"' (in Hulak 1992: 155). Breton was reading section E of the *Interpretation of Dreams* (Freud 1961: 75–8), in which Freud establishes a resemblance between dreams and paranoia: 'If I may venture on a simile from the sphere of psychiatry, the first group of theories construct dreams on the model of paranoia, while the second group makes them resemble mental deficiency or confusional states' (76). This sentence struck Breton so much he copied it twice. Then he checked the references, writing: 'Volkelt's *remarkable* sexual symbolism'. He added on the left-hand side: 'Volkelt, quoted by Freud *without references (?)*' (in Hulak 1992: 154). This led to a personal attack that wounded Freud deeply.

Breton apparently believed that Freud had omitted to mention Volkelt's book because he had borrowed more than what transpired in the remarks of the *Traumdeutung*. In Breton's reconstruction, Volkelt would have inspired the entire theory of sexuality in dreams: 'Freud himself, who seems, when it concerns the symbolic interpretation of the dream, just to have taken over for himself Volkelt's ideas – Volkelt, an author about whom the definitive bibliography at the end of the book remains significantly mute – Freud, for whom the whole substance of the dream is nevertheless taken from real life, cannot resist the temptation of declaring that "the intimate nature of the subconscious (the essential psychical reality) is as unknown to us as the reality of the exterior world", giving thereby some support to those whom his method had almost routed' (Breton 1990: 11; see also 1992: 109). Thus Freud would have stolen the idea of sexuality in dreams from an obscure writer (Freud 1961: 83–4). Moreover, Freud had to be taken to task for falling into the trap of dualism and idealism since he opposed dreams and reality to one another as belonging to radically different realms.

Breton's ferocious critique relied less on dialectical materialism than on the post-Kantian theories developed by Schopenhauer about prophetic dreaming or 'second sight'. For Breton, the main axiom is that reality is a single undivided continuum: dreams belong to it and keep a productive interaction with everyday life. Breton writes: 'Freud is again quite surely mistaken in concluding that the prophetic dream does not exist – I mean the dream involving the immediate future – since to hold that the dream is exclusively revelatory of the past is to deny the value of motion' (Breton 1990: 13). To prove Freud wrong, Breton presented the interpretation of a dream he had on 26 August 1931, a dream in which a tie is called 'Nosferatu'; predictably, it revolves around surrealist issues. Contradicting Freud's idea of an 'umbilicus' or the unknowable core of dreams, Breton aims at exhausting the contents of his dream by a thorough examination of its images and associations (Breton 1990: 45). He leaves few details out, but even when he rewrites Freud's principles of condensation and overdetermination in a materialistic language inflected by Marx and Lenin, he omits glossing the fact that throughout his dream he clutches a loaded gun – no doubt aimed at Freud.

Freud defended himself from insinuations of plagiarism by pointing out that Volkelt's name was only omitted in the French translation of 1926; it was present in the original German text. A second letter accounted for the missing reference. Volkelt's name had been dropped by mistake after the third printing. The French version was based on a later version (see Breton 1990: 149–55). Freud refuted Breton's hypothesis of his prudishness on matters of sexuality when Volkelt had been more explicit about sexual symbols in dreams. The third letter ended with a barb; Freud pretended not to understand surrealism at all: 'Although I have received many testimonies of the interest that you and your friends show for my research, I am not able to clarify for myself what Surrealism is and what it wants' (see Breton 1990: 152). Freud tried to reduce Breton's paranoid reading to hysteria. 'What it wants' thus meant: 'What do you want from me?' This echoed his current preoccupation with femininity. Freud had returned to surrealism a feminized version of itself, a Gallic version of *Was will das Weib?* Breton, eager for a male-to-male confrontation, noted gleefully Freud's contradictory responses in the flurry of successive letters. Freud attempted a miserable payback by denying any artistic value to surrealism. Finally, Breton quoted Wittels' book on Freud's pugnacious and jealous style: 'I knocked him to the ground because he knocked me to the ground' (see Breton 1990: 154 n. 7). Breton may have indeed 'touched on a rather sensitive point' (see 155).

The irony was that Freud and Breton were elaborating similar strategies of power and containment at the same time. Freud, who was forced to exclude first Jung and then Adler, ended up choosing a 'Committee' of selected and trusted disciples whose task was to protect the orthodoxy of psychoanalysis. The committee was made up of his most loyal followers, Ernest Jones, Karl Abraham, Otto Rank, Hanns Sachs and a few others (see Grosskurth 1991). The elect were given special rings by Freud and often behaved like a secret society. While Breton never enforced any dogmatic orthodoxy, there were certain practices that had to be condemned in the name of the group: for instance, journalism was to be avoided, as Philippe Soupault learned the hard way; long novels were suspicious, as Louis Aragon discovered quite early; the theatre was not a proper mode of expression, as Antonin Artaud later discovered. Even film had to be scrutinized, which led to the campaign against Jean Cocteau after he had produced *The Blood of a Poet* and was mistakenly considered as a fellow-traveller of the surrealists. However the Bureau of Surrealist Research had the aim of recording verbal and visual experiments, but never turned into a central committee denouncing dissidents.

Nevertheless, *Communicating Vessel*s did oppose Freud and Breton, both caught up in a paranoid struggle for mastery. Their endless dispute revolved around missing annotations, faulty bibliographies, deliberate misquotations, issues of literary ownership and intellectual propriety. Facing the case of President Schreber, Freud had claimed that he had succeeded where the paranoiac failed; Breton was to prove that a paranoiac poet could succeed where the psychoanalyst had failed. Freud was caught up in a strange textual net, writing apologetically to rectify the picture, and finally rejecting the whole business of the avant-garde as not being serious enough. However, when he met Salvador Dalí in London in 1938, Freud appeared more receptive to 'the young'. Freud liked Dalí, still a fellow surrealist at the time of *Communicating Vessels*, but by then long since excluded. Surrealism had moved abruptly from a strategy that promoted hysteria to a strategy that took paranoia as a weapon and a new mode of vision.

If we can easily understand why paranoid mechanisms are exemplified by a man imagining himself poisoned, this method of guided hallucination was not so new: its predecessor can be found in the poetics of Arthur Rimbaud when the 'systematic deregulating of all senses' generates wild, teeming and incoherent images. Dalí adds that the process has to turn more 'violent' or 'intense' so as to yield three, four, or even thirty different images. In *The Rotting Donkey*, Dalí, no doubt stung by Bataille's account of his work in terms of castration anxiety, pushes his thesis further by collapsing conventional systems of representation and pure paranoid delirium. He goes back to his example of a woman who is at the same time a horse, and a lion's head, explaining: 'I challenge materialists to examine the kind of mental crisis that such an image may provoke, I challenge them to examine the even more complex problem of knowing which one of these images has a greater number of possibilities for existence if the intervention of desire is taken into consideration, and also to investigate the more serious and more general problem of knowing whether the series of representations has a limit or whether, as we have every reason to believe, such a limit does not exist, or rather, exists solely as a function of each individual's paranoid capacity' (Dalí 1998b: 116). The reversal of perspective is obvious: whereas paranoia seemed to open a door into another kind of visual perception, it now turns into a regulating principle that replaces the Marxist idea of a 'material world' as a basis. The material world is just one type of simulacrum, which provides a sly way of debunking Bataille's 'base' materialism. Since reality is de-multiplied in a series of hallucinatory figments, there is no need for a foundation in matter, whether clean or base, obscene and dirty.

Dalí chose Breton against Bataille, but both camps criticized in Freud the domination of a dualism that kept pitting the principle of pleasure and the principle of reality against each other. In order to incorporate Freud's insights into a monist discourse, Bataille had started from the materiality of the body, with its attendant notions of excess, waste and excrement, while Breton and Dalí took reality as made up of oneiric simulacra; these, in their turn, were underpinned by a universal and productive desire. This debate proved formative for Lacan, who came into contact with it just as he was completing his doctoral dissertation on paranoia. As Roudinesco has shown, it was the impact of Dalí's *Rotting Donkey* that allowed Lacan to break with the classical psychiatric theories of personality and constitution and to revisit Freudian metapsychology.[2] At the time, Lacan was translating Freud's 1922 article on 'Certain Neurotic Mechanisms in Jealousy, Paranoia and Homosexuality' into French. In it the thesis underpinning the analysis of Schreber is developed: the root of all paranoia is the return of a repressed homosexuality. In a case of a jealous delirium observed by Freud in a heterosexual patient, the delusional attacks followed successful sexual rapports between the man and his wife. By inventing imaginary male lovers that generated delirious recriminations, the husband facilitated the projection of his desires facing these men. But Lacan's model at the time was surrealism, much more than Freud. Just then Lacan contributed to a collective essay on 'Inspired Writings' of 1931, in which the authors analyse the psychotic ramblings of a teacher hospitalized at Sainte-Anne. Their description of the formal components of a grammar of mad utterance pays homage to surrealism, since the authors quote the first *Manifesto of Surrealism* and look for a model of interpretation in Breton and Éluard's imitations of individual styles of typical delirium in *The Immaculate Conception* (in Lacan et al. 1975: 379–80).

Thanks to the convergence of interests among Bataille, Dalí, Breton and Lacan, the second decade of surrealism tended to be dominated by the concept of paranoia, much as the first had been by automatism and hysteria. Breton's most comprehensive prose synthesis, *Mad Love*, from 1937, reaffirms his belief that desire is the mainspring of all our dreams and actions. He still makes a place for paranoia, because desire, no longer structured by hysteria but by the call of an Other source of inspiration, is marked by paranoid features. Thus in the fifth section of

Mad Love, he reopens Freud's *A Childhood Memory of Leonardo da Vinci* before expounding the principle of paranoiac criticism or critical paranoia. The vulture hidden in the Virgin's dress had been seen by Oskar Pfister only after Freud had analysed its role and relevance. Once an interpretation generates a new image in a painting, it will not go away, even if proved wrong (Freud's identification of a vulture was triggered by a mistranslation) – it will remain there, hovering between objectivity and subjectivity.[3] Visual hallucinations can be shared whatever one's opinions about the divide between madness and sanity. Whereas hysteria invests a mutual seduction in order to reach the truth of desire, paranoia articulates a system of signs whose pseudo-objectivity hides its flimsy foundations. The force of desire appears as the source of what had been shared, even momentarily. The extravagant gestures enacted by hysterics were pathetic attempts at aesthetic expression; these were staged differently by paranoia. Paranoia launched a violent aggressive discourse shared by a dedicated group of like-minded experimenters, in a movement that tended more and more towards political confrontation and utopian assertion.[4]

Notes

1 The text is written in small capitals throughout. One finds an English translation of parts of this manifesto in Roudinesco 1990: 6–7.
2 See Roudinesco (1990: 110–12) for an account of their meeting, which had been instigated by Lacan, as well as Roudinesco 1997: 31–2, for a general assessment.
3 As noted by Breton in *L'Amour fou*, in 1992: 753.
4 This entry condenses and revises a passage from my *Cambridge Introduction to Literature and Psychoanalysis* (Cambridge: Cambridge University Press, 2014), pp. 95–106.

4 Utopia: the revolution in question

Georges Sebbag

Being modern and avant-garde, the Futurists in Italy advocated a national revolution while those in Russia wanted social revolution. Whereas the Dadaists of Zurich were sweeping away everything – modernity, the avant-garde and the revolution included – the Berlin Dadaists adhered to a revolutionary position. Apart from its 1920 Dada season, surrealism is evidently a modern, though not an avant-garde, movement. The history of the surrealist movement is the history of testing the concept of revolution. The surrealists would reject reductive political reason and not venture down the path of revolutionary insurrection. Increasingly, they trusted the utopian imagination, in accordance with the collective life of their free association, an association marked by the stimuli of passional motivations and novel practices.

'Revolution first and always!' The surrealists appropriated the word 'revolution' in autumn 1924 when founding their magazine *La Révolution surréaliste*; to the public they opened a Bureau of Surrealist Research and sought a 'new Declaration of the Rights of Man'. Such initiatives bespoke a nonconformist group impelled by a philosophical project and agitated by existential turmoil. When Aragon, Artaud and Breton proclaimed the surrealist revolution, they intended, above all, to work towards a revolution of the mind.

In August 1925, however, prompted by the colonial war in the Moroccan Rif, the surrealists placed political revolution on their agenda. With the communists of Clarté, the mystical philosophers of Philosophies, and the Belgians Camille Goemans and Paul Nougé of Correspondance, they signed the resounding declaration 'La Révolution d'abord et toujours!' The title plays on two different temporalities, namely the urgency of the revolution and permanent change. On the one hand, a Leninist-style watchword: *Revolution first*, in the knowledge that this would bring about a change in society, auguring the emergence of a new humanity; on the other hand, a sort of advertising slogan: *Revolution always*, which simultaneously intertwines a Heraclitian awareness of immanence with the indefinite expectation of a future revolution. The text was mainly penned by Aragon, who tried as best he could to reconcile the Leninist revolution of the editors of *Clarté* with the surrealists' revolution of the mind. Condemnation of the colonial war in Morocco meant denouncing the Fatherland and the Army. Anti-colonialist, anti-militarist and anti-patriotic watchwords, including a 'call for desertion' evoked in a footnote, could only cheer the communists of Clarté. However, throughout the tract there is a wavering of sorts. At the beginning, it states that the era 'is singularly lacking in seers' and that the world's conflicts outstrip 'simple political and social debate'. Presented side by side at the end is the surrealist formula, 'We are the revolt of the mind', and the communist one, 'We are not utopians; we conceive this Revolution in its social form alone', not to mention a third formula envisaging 'bloody Revolution' as the expression of revenge or resentment.

A list of twelve names (Spinoza, Kant, Blake, Hegel, Schelling, Proudhon, Marx, Stirner, Baudelaire, Lautréamont, Rimbaud and Nietzsche) emphasizes that Marx, rubbing shoulders with the federalist Proudhon and the anarchist individualist Stirner, is far from being the privileged inspirer of 'Revolution now and forever!' Above all, this collation of names, which gives priority to philosophers (even if Blake, Baudelaire, Lautréamont and Rimbaud defend the colours of poetry), reveals the revolution of the mind defended by the surrealists. One part of the tract, deemed to be the most scandalous, gives a clue to the twelve names that in one way or another appeared as the precursors of surrealism: 'We are undoubtedly barbarians since a certain form of civilization sickens us. … we are avowed insurgents against History. It's the Mongols' turn to set up their tents on our squares.' This is a direct reference to Maurice Barrès, the author of *Sous l'œil des barbares* (Under barbarian eyes), whom Aragon greatly admired. It should be remembered that, akin to a Fichte or a Stirner, Barrès called barbarians all those (and they were legion) who shamelessly sought to diminish the Ego and sacrifice the Ideal or Beauty. Let's not forget that the anarchist Barrès of *Le Culte du moi* (The cult of the self) was also a partisan of Proudhon, and that Kant's categorical imperative served as the connecting thread of his novel *Les Déracinés* (The uprooted). In August 1925 Aragon was playing cat and mouse with Barrès: sometimes flouting him: 'We are undoubtedly barbarians since a certain form of civilization sickens us'; sometimes finding him appealing: 'It's the Mongols' turn to set up their tents on our squares', thus reverting to the formula of the narrator of *Under Barbarian Eyes*, looking out over Paris, over 'that immense plain where the barbarians set up their tents'.

'Revolution Now and Forever!' is exemplary. A surrealist tract cannot be reduced to its political dimension. Never mistake the surrealist group for a political groupuscule, however revolutionary. Lasting several months, the attempt by the surrealists and the communists of Clarté to group together also ended in failure. The project to publish *La Guerre civile*, an amalgam of *Clarté* and *La Révolution surréaliste*, would not happen. At the beginning of 1927, André Breton, a new adherent to the French Communist Party (PCF) assigned to a cell of gas workers, would endure only three months as a militant.

The surrealists found themselves on the horns of a dilemma. The choice was between affiliation with the PCF and the independence of their own movement. If they proclaimed the proletarian revolution, they had, *ipso facto*, to renounce the surrealist revolution of the mind. In 1930, Breton and Aragon, having just broken off relations with Desnos and Leiris in particular, prudently called their magazine *Le Surréalisme au service de la Révolution*. Such concessions change nothing. The surrealists would pursue their activities as before. In 1932 Aragon and Sadoul, however, took the plunge to rally definitively to the PCF, thus renouncing their past and their surrealist identity.

Capitalism is more revolutionary than communism

Within the context of the grouping together with Clarté and individual adherence to the PCF, the positions of Pierre Drieu la Rochelle and Emmanuel Berl may be illuminating. A collaborator on *Littérature*, a witness during the Barrès trial, editor of the pamphlet 'Un cadavre' (A corpse) contra Anatole France, Drieu was a close friend of Aragon's. In 1927 he dedicated a short story to Breton in *La Suite dans les idées* (One idea leads to another), together with the important essay 'Le Jeune européen' (European youth) in which the author, sensitive to decadence and allergic to nationhood, calls for the creation of a United States of Europe.

In August 1925, in *La Nouvelle Revue française*, Drieu warned Aragon and the surrealists against an alliance with the communists: 'You fall into the trap and bellow "Vive Lenin!"' This immediately earned Drieu a sharp reply, a letter of farewell from Aragon. At the start of 1927, Drieu and Berl felt the need to make common cause and to emit a cry of alarm. The situation in Europe and throughout the world seemed unsettling. Not unlike the Viennese satirist Karl Kraus, solo editor of the newspaper *Die Fackel* and author of the play *The*

Last Days of Mankind, they resolved to deliver a 'political and literary notebook' to the public called *Les derniers jours* (The last days).

Berl and Drieu availed themselves of the concept of revolution but their conclusions differed from those of the surrealists. *First thesis*, common to both: the bourgeoisie is dead while capitalism is robust and tenacious. In fact Berl would write in rapid succession *Mort de la pensée bourgeoise* (The death of bourgeois thinking) and *Mort de la morale bourgeoise* (The death of bourgeois morality). *Second thesis*, specific to Drieu: capitalism pulls the rug out from under the feet of communism; of the two giants, capitalism is the more revolutionary; only it can realize communism. *Third thesis*, dear to Drieu: 'There are too many fatherlands'; capitalism is incompatible with nationalism; the United States of Europe must be established. Berl's conception of revolution was not a million miles from the surrealists' revolution of the mind: (1) The revolution is a miracle or pure event. (2) It is the object of a categorical imperative: 'I want the Revolution for its own sake, gratuitously.' (3) It ought to run counter to mechanization. (4) It is expected to be a form of *social marvellous*. Berl attempted to avoid Marxist schemas; in speaking of *the marvellous* he was gesturing towards the surrealists.

Strengthened by his analyses of the innovative and revolutionary nature of capitalism, Drieu could express himself without beating about the bush. In 'Troisième lettre aux surréalistes sur l'amitié et la solitude' (Third letter to the surrealists on friendship and solitude), he speaks at length about himself and the surrealists, his main criticism being linked with their political engagement. First, he makes various remarks about the quest for friendship, of the group or the community, which at times brings to mind Petrarch's *On the Solitary Life* and seems to announce Maurice Blanchot's analyses of the 'unavowable community'. Drieu claims to have been attracted by 'two groups alone … in which one can think and be enthused': the 'Action Française group' and the 'community of surrealists'. But today the surrealists are the only worthwhile interlocutors he knows; the only feasible friendship is that of Breton and his friends. 'Living constantly in your proximity for eight years now, I've always compared my ideas to yours. … I all but concern myself with you alone. I almost only chat with you. … the time is coming when we will be of the same mind, perhaps'. Drieu makes it clear to Breton and his friends that they have taken the wrong track. In adopting Hegelian-Marxist dialectic they have become untrue to themselves, betraying the discoveries of *The Manifesto of Surrealism* and *A Wave of Dreams*: 'I'd like to know exactly what relation can exist between Hegelianism and the psychological givens you based surrealism on. I think these givens subtended a philosophy entirely different from Hegel's, and put you on your guard against the conservatism and inaction forming its basis.'

Drieu didn't fail to point out the ambiguities adherence to the Communist Party elicited. Three formulas give a good account of the hard-hitting, well-documented analyses of the editor of *The Last Days*: (1) 'Surrealism was about revelation, not about revolution.' (2) 'You've left the path of the truth and taken the path of the century's lies.' (3) 'Thought outstrips the dialectical moment. Someone has to remain in the lighthouse, above the ebb and flow of the tides.'

Artaud's integral revolution

Antonin Artaud quit the surrealist group during the meeting of 23 November 1926 devoted to the question of joining the PCF. In May 1927 he was violently attacked by the five signatories of 'Au grand jour' (In broad daylight) for his absolute idealism, his indifference towards politics, and his phobia of materialism. While reproaching Artaud for confining himself to a revolution of the mind, Aragon, Breton, Éluard, Péret and Unik went so far as to judge his literary activity as unworthy of the mind: 'he has always chosen the most derisory of objects in which nothing essential to the mind or to life was at stake'. Sentence is passed: 'Today we've spewed that scoundrel up.' Artaud was quick to respond – the following month 'À la grande nuit ou le bluff surréaliste' (In total darkness, or the surrealist bluff) appeared. In this relatively clear text, the political revolution appears as a negligible quantity while the surrealist revolution of the mind that Breton and Aragon are on the point of abandoning or pretend to deny is described as an inestimable adventure.

Artaud argues that the whole basis of his quarrel with the surrealists revolves 'around the word revolution'. He rejects the Revolution because: (1) Lacking influence, the surrealists will be marginalized in the revolutionary process. (2) The communists' demands will be incompatible with the surrealist spirit. (3) Viewed from the absolute, 'seeing power pass from the hands of the bourgeoisie into those of the proletariat' isn't of the slightest interest. (4) The revolutionary who relies on 'things, on their transformation', to wit on materialism, adopts 'the attitude of an obscene brute, a profiteer of reality'. (5) Any wish to act on the social or material level is profoundly useless, as 'integral pessimism' warns us. (6) Lastly, surrealism, synonymous with revolt or absolute revolution, is dishonoured by humbling itself before 'a de facto revolt' calling for an eight-hour day or the struggle against the cost of living.

The author of *In Total Darkness* goes even further in speaking of his person and the surrealist adventure. Weighing his own existence against the advent of the revolution, the latter appears external or totally foreign to him: 'But what does all the Revolution in the world mean to me if I contrive to remain eternally sorrowful and miserable within my own charnel house?' He then traces the outlines of an authentic revolution, one which ought to be internal and solipsistic, he believes: 'Let each man consider naught beyond his profound sensibility, his intimate self – that for me is the viewpoint of the integral revolution.' If genuine revolutionary forces existed, then rather than working for a readjustment of salaries they would throw the 'current foundation of things' out of kilter; they would change 'the angle of reality'.

Refreshing the memory of Breton and Aragon, Artaud permits himself to redefine surrealism as a revolution of the mind which strives to provoke a 'displacement of the spiritual centre of the world', a 'breaking up of appearances' and a 'transfiguration of the possible'. The decentring of the mind challenges the legislation of reason, the breaking up of appearances escapes the impostures of reality, the transfiguration of the possible gives the imagination carte blanche. Artaud had, of course, shared these three objectives with his surrealist friends since 1924. The author of *L'Ombilic des limbes* (The umbilicus of limbo) is thus able to continue without fear of contradiction, stating that with surrealism 'the whole of concrete reality changes its garb or shell' and that 'the world no longer holds', or there again that with surrealism 'the treasures of the invisible unconscious' become palpable, 'guiding speech directly, with a single impulse'. The notions of the unconscious, automatism and nominalism are far from being a dead letter in Artaud's mind.

Lastly, Artaud refutes the idea of an organic development or a logical necessity which inevitably drives surrealism into the arms of Marxism. In his opinion, surrealism does not come within the framework of ordinary logic any more than it does within the apparatus of the Hegelian dialectic. He sees only duplicity or bad faith on the part of the surrealists when they combat logic with illogic and at other times reject freedom in the name of necessity: 'Speak to them of Logic, they will respond Illogic, but speak to them of Illogic, Disorder, Incoherence, Liberty, they will respond Necessity, Law, Obligation, Rigour.' Persuaded that the members of the surrealist group were not men of action, he predicts setbacks for them in their political tribulations. To close this debate opposing the revolution of the mind to political revolution, Artaud hastens to add that for the true revolutionary, 'individual freedom is a greater good than any [political or social] conquest'.

In August 1927, Artaud persisted and in *Point final* (Matter closed) asked: 'Why has Breton foregone the surrealism of the early days, pure surrealism?' In the face of the sectarian deviation he observes, Artaud attempts to go deeper into this crucial issue. He lets on that for him surrealism, this attempt 'to revolutionize thought in the sense of the absolute', had been a lifeline at a time when he saw no way out for him than death or madness. Surrealism taught him to believe once more in his own thought processes and to be content with the lucubration of his brain. The surrealism of the early days had been capable, 'albeit with an extremely unstable and subtle sense of balance', of introducing a revolution 'in the very functioning of thought'. Without giving in to the phantasms of a pure metaphysics or a deceptive idealism, it managed to create a domain at the margins of reality, a 'sort of vibrant density' characteristic of 'thought taking wing'. After surrealism, abstraction itself possesses a body and 'enters through different doors'. In any event, Artaud did not intend to call off this revolution of the mind, which had given him so much and which he is henceforth to experience in solitude: 'In essence the Revolution is spiritual. … A sort of cosmic respiration traverses the different states of a thought process whose only object is the Absolute. … There is not much hope that I now shut this door onto eternity. … While waiting I champ at the bit. … I can suffer alone'.

How could André Breton, the group's prime mover, have abandoned an integral surrealism? Artaud appeals here to a memory stretching back to the Bureau of Surrealist Research. Breton had confided to him that he wouldn't attend the debates on action and revolution due to concerns of an intimate nature. A few remarks follow on this non-participation in a political project: (1) Breton had judged the absolute nature of love to be superior to any kind of 'common revolutionary endeavour'. (2) The disappointment experienced in this 'personal Absolute' has even precipitated him towards communism; without this disappointment 'the face of surrealism was changed'. (3) At the time Breton recognized 'the value of absence, of isolation'. (4) One perceives the road travelled by Breton and his friends, who have exchanged an 'impotent despair' for an 'optimism of abdication'.

In conclusion, Artaud asserts the need for a solitary quest. Since the surrealist group now abandons the 'superior reality' of the 'innermost depths of the head' or the 'intervals of thought', it is time to proclaim that the 'veritable revolution' is an 'individual affair'. 'The imponderable demands a self-communion which is only rarely met with in the limbo of the individual soul.' The revolution is resolved in solitude. A solitude which, let it be said, also occupies a certain place in *Le Paysan de Paris* (Paris Peasant), the first part of the 'Introduction to the Discourse on the Paucity of Reality', and Drieu's 'Third Letter'.

Charles Fourier or the release from revolution

At the end of 1929 Breton had yet to read Hegel seriously and only knew Marx second-hand. In the *Second manifeste du surréalisme* he made use of Hegel as a screen or guarantee. Although he adhered to historical materialism, he scarcely envisaged swapping surrealism for Marxism.

From 1936 to 1939, in symmetrical fashion, André Breton and his polycephalous surrealist group and Georges Bataille and his acephalous community would evade the war in Spain on the political front. The first, returning enthused from the Canary Islands and outward bound for Mexico, did not know how to cogitate the blooming and then failure of the revolution in Catalonia. The second, fascinated by the corrida and a frequenter of the brothels of Barcelona, failed to arrive at the coexistence, in his mythic and tragic conception of history, of the Siege of Numantia and the civil war in Spain.

In 1941, in Marseilles, André Breton, Victor Brauner, Óscar Domínguez, Max Ernst, Jacques Hérold, Wifredo Lam, Jacqueline Lamba and André Masson participated in redesigning the deck of cards, which they renamed 'the Marseilles deck'. To them it seemed vital to loudly reaffirm their values in those disastrous days. This pack of cards is a *summum* of the mythology and concepts of surrealism. The Flame, the Black Star, the Bloody Wheel and the Lock – these four new emblems have as their meaning Love, the Dream, Revolution and Knowledge. Three extraordinary insurgents or personages chart the course of the Revolution: the Genius Sade, the Siren Lamiel (the strange libertine of Stendhal's novel), and the Magus Pancho Villa (the Mexican guerrilla). These three ardent or sombre figures seem to have supplanted revolutionaries like Robespierre or Lenin.

In 1945, immersed in reading Fourier, Breton began to put the lid on Marx. He was now convinced of three things: (1) The inventor of the phalanstery had the philosopher's stone at his command. (2) One day it would be necessary to try this remedy. (3) The 'ingenuous doubt and exigency' set to music by Fourier ousted or 'forced from cover' all the platitudes of socialist, communist and even revolutionary dogma. Utopia was clearly taking over from political revolution.

To backtrack a little. In 1799, Charles Fourier was scandalized by the arrogance of the philosophers and theologians who, from Plato to Rousseau, brandished their moral doctrines and played one system off against another, amassing a minimum of 400,000 volumes of vain and useless remarks. Notwithstanding their ostentatious disagreements, the philosophers, the most recent of whom advocated Enlightenment or Ideology, took turns in carrying the *sensations of apperception* or the *perfectibilization of perfectibility* to a point of fanaticism or, there again, were at pains to defend the virtues of virtue. In fact they all converged on the same one-track mentality, according to which humanity would find itself at its apogee after acceding to civilization. However, according to Fourier, in the series of the five ages of humanity – Eden (which persisted among the good savages of the Pacific islands and corresponded to Rousseau's first state of nature), savagery, patriarchy, barbarism and civilization – the fifth age did not in the slightest signify a successful break or decisive instance of progress. While here and there he took the opportunity to borrow something from Plato, Descartes, Leibniz, Rousseau or Condillac, Fourier was furious with the philosophers because in their own ways they condoned almost all the evils of civilization.

Against them he had three main charges to bring: (1) Those who, like Montesquieu and Rousseau, prescribed a new constitution or social contract, were on the wrong track since political revolution could only lead to a bloody stand-off, as in 1793. (2) They were wrong in advocating economic liberalism because the realm of commerce, interposing itself between production and consumption, increased the number of merchants, enriched speculators or investors, fomented bankruptcy and financial panic, and brought misery to farmer and artisan alike. (3) They quibbled about all sorts of details but didn't attack the central scourge of a civilization in the grip of indigence and double-dealing, oppression and carnage, the unsettled state of the climate and epidemics, all this leading to a curious apportioning of happiness since, of any eight individuals, for one of them to be happy seven others had to be unhappy.

What Fourier imagined and described was a society of luxury and abundance, a free and harmonious association which allowed the free expression of the twelve innate human passions on which, contrary to philosophers in thrall to reason, he wagered everything. In first place were the desires of the five senses, the five passions individuals felt in their bodies, the five 'luxurious' (*luxiste*) passions which obviously implied a prodigious expansion of material riches. Among them, the gustatory passion, or *gourmandise*, was a perfect example of refinement, to which all those living in Harmony would add their grain of salt. Falling somewhere between gastronomy and dietetics, this passion, far from being reduced to gluttony, gave rise to an inventive, savant research known as *gastrosophy*.

Next came the four group desires, the four affective and relational passions of the soul. On the one hand these four *groupiste* passions turned, *in major key*, on the group guided by honour or ambition, and on the other, on the band of friends, and *in minor key* on the one hand on the group of love and on the other on the familial group. Even if the familial passion was the least free of the group passions, it was understood that the four passions in question could only truly take off in freedom.

Lastly, after the five *luxiste* and four *groupiste* passions, which took to the wing in abundance and in freedom, it being understood that they were etiolated in civilization, there came the three 'serial' (*sériiste*) desires, three passions amalgamating soul and body, three mechanizing and distributive passions reshuffling all the cards of the different groups, three passions deemed to be depraved in civilization, in which they were repressed. There were, then, three passions organizing sympathies or antipathies and arranging them in series: (1) The *cabalist*, a passion involving intrigue and rivalry, the play of discordant accordance, a serious-minded ardour mobilizing the groups and the series around subtle disagreements or tenuous differences. (2) The *composite*, a passion involving enthusiasm and infatuation, the play of concordant accordance, a blind ardour accomplishing feats of prowess thanks to a distribution in subgroups relating to a compartmental choice of tasks and functions. (3) The *butterfly*, a passion involving variation and change, relying on alternation in work and in love, a 'zapping' or ludic activity favoured in particular by short sessions permitting individuals to flutter or flit from one pleasure to another.

Just as the luxurious and group passions thrived in the context of abundance and freedom, the sole purpose of the serial passions, which split members up into age brackets and series, groups and subgroups, was distributive justice. Furthermore, a clarification is called for: obviously the twelve passions would be pulled hither and yon if they weren't deployed in a fan shape around the pivot of unity, harmony being nothing but the unification of a multiplicity of series, a diversity of characters and an infinity of distinctive traits or passional nuances. Fourier was barely understood during his lifetime, even though he had the good fortune to be joined by a few friends and disciples. In January 1893, the first resurrection of Charles Fourier was announced by Maurice Barrès in *L'Ennemi des lois* (The enemy of laws). For publishing an article casting aspersions on the ability of students at the Saint-Cyr military academy to command, André Maltère, a young teacher and the novel's hero, is sentenced to three months in prison, which wins him the admiration of two young women. While in Sainte-Pélagie Prison he begins studying the doctrines of Saint-Simon and Fourier with one of them. The lively, didactic exposé of Fourier's life and work is vibrant with sympathy for the author of the *Théorie des quatre mouvements*.

The novel has a Fourierist fragrance; it describes an intellectual and amorous quest which ends in a free union *à trois*. The three rebels create 'a laboratory of sensibility' in a sort of alfresco phalanstery.

During the summer of 1945, Fourier resurfaced in America. André Breton, in exile in the United States since 1941, went to Reno to divorce and remarry. While visiting the American West, notably various Indian reservations, he wrote the *Ode à Charles Fourier*. He recalled that early one morning in 1937 a fresh bouquet of violets had been placed on Fourier's statue in Paris. Into his long poem Breton didn't hesitate to insert some of the Besançon thinker's ideas and even a fragment of his writing. Systematically comparing the twelve passions with the tragic reality of the era or to the sacred time of the Hopis, Breton not only grants Fourier 'the reed of Orpheus' but appeals to his 'light', a light 'standing out clearly against the greyness of ideas and aspirations today'. Acclaimed and addressed familiarly in the *tu* form throughout the poem, the Christopher Columbus of Harmony henceforth belonged to the surrealist gesture. In 1950 the enlarged edition of *The Anthology of Black Humour* devoted an introductory note to him. In 1953, the utopian was received with open arms by the surrealists during the game 'Ouvrez-vous?' (Would you open the door?).

The great collective consecration arrived in December 1965. Entitled *L'Écart absolu* (Absolute deviation), after the radical method adopted by Fourier, the eleventh International Exhibition of Surrealism hoisted the colours of the inventor of the 'museum orgy' and gave thanks for his speculative and imaginative ardour. Fourier's resolutely *active* doubt consigned Descartes's hyperbolic and yet *passive* doubt to the dustbins of oblivion. The star turn of the exhibition was *Le Consommateur* (The consumer). Designed collectively, this immense object, both manikin and scarecrow, golem and robot, was assembled by Jean-Claude Silbermann. The great padded figure, with a washing-machine belly and TV-screen head, combined with a wedding dress and the car number plate HT/110QT (phonetically *Achetez sans discuter*, namely 'Buy without a second thought'), crowned with klaxons and encompassed by interstellar bleeps, condensed different aspects of consumer society: home economics and the conquest of space; cars and technocracy; the mass media and brainwashing. How was it possible to confront a society of production that edified its empire on consumption and leisure? Such was the question posed in the wake of Fourier by the surrealist group, not long before May 1968. Another collective work, the *Désordinateur* (Discomputer) identified ten critical points in this euphoric society. In the exhibition catalogue, '*L'Œuf fait nix* (The egg nixes; phonetically the French also gives us *le phénix* (the phoenix)), by Robert Benayoun is ironical about the achievements of cybernetics: 'A boxwood sewing egg has more memory than a computer.'

In April 1967, the surrealists, having seemingly definitively swapped the dialectician Hegel for his contemporary Fourier, once again honoured the visionary in baptizing their new magazine *L'Archibras*. The proletarian revolution was just a memory.

A collagist community

In 1945, in *La Poésie moderne et le sacré*, Jules Monnerot intended to show that modern poetry, as represented by surrealism, was consonant with the most archaic sacred of primitive religions or the profoundest of secular religions. Posing the question of the nature of the surrealist group, Monnerot rejected the words 'band', 'clan' or 'sect', instead proposing the English word *set*. But while this term was apt for 'an accidental union without either obligation or sanction', it could hardly be applied to a group based on 'elective affinities'. In fact the surrealist set would, without arriving at that point, ideally tend towards the forming of a *Bund* (a league), this German word being opposed to both a contractual society (*Gesellschaft*) and a community of blood (*Gemeinschaft*). How might the surrealist group be defined? Was it the 'communism of genius', as a surrealist sticker had claimed? Did it relate to a 'secret society', as Breton had suggested in *The Manifesto of Surrealism*?

We shall immediately dismiss the literary or artistic denominations of cenacle or coterie, but also the label of an avant-garde, which presupposes that the group would be a cultural figurehead, or indeed that in connivance with a revolutionary organization its destiny would be to guide the people. The surrealist group, without being detached from society, was autonomous. Above all, it was a passional community of the Fourierist kind, feeling all the passions of human nature, *luxiste, groupiste* or *sériiste*. A free association of strong individualities, the surrealist group was a polycephalous community consisting of stand-alone individuals but also of duos, trios or even quartets. Georges Bataille defined himself in relation to this polycephalous model when he founded the secret society Acéphale and the College of Sociology.

The surrealist group subscribed to three types of collage: (1) Formal and material collage (scattered elements united in a new contiguity). (2) Concubinage or amorous collage (intertwined bodies, associated minds, combined desires as in Fourier). (3) Temporal collage (supervening of coincidences, magnetization of *durées*, or durations). All the same, this collagist community was to vary: after painting *Au rendez-vous des amis* (Rendezvous of friends) in December 1922, Max Ernst would rework the group portrait in his photomontage *Au rendez-vous des amis 1931*.[1]

These collagists met almost daily in the café. They launched inquiries, devoted themselves to games, undertook experiments, devised magazines, drew up tracts, prepared exhibitions. They drifted around the streets. They weren't far from inventing a utopia of everyday life. How did they unite without overly disuniting? How did they think two at a time or even many at a time? This was a concrete utopia that each surrealist group put into practice *there and then*, with notable differences, in Paris, Brussels, Prague, London, Tenerife, New York, Mexico, Saint-Cirq La Popie, Chicago and elsewhere.

Because it was not organized as a revolutionary avant-garde surrealism didn't seem soluble in the political revolution. However, a new question was now posed: was surrealism, which advocated poetry 'made by all', to dissolve itself in the democracy of the overall majority?

Notes

Translated from the French by Paul Hammond.

1 The latter work is more commonly known by the title given to it by the Museum of Modern Art in New York: *Loplop Introduces Members of the Surrealist Group* (trans.).

5 The Marquis de Sade and revolutionary violence

Michael Richardson

The Marquis de Sade is an exemplary figure for the surrealists, exemplary to the point of myth. But exemplary, and mythic, in what senses? In some ways the myth was born from a will to demythologize: to divest his character of the demonic sheen that had accrued to it during the nineteenth century, but without rehabilitating him or making him acceptable. Sade's value indeed lay precisely in the fact that he was unacceptable, that he both embodied and refuted the unacceptable nature of existence itself, as well as in his refusal to allow the world to dictate what he should be.

Invocations of Sade permeate surrealism. From Dalí and Buñuel's film *L'Âge d'or* (1929) to Jean Benoît's extraordinary enactment of his testament at the opening of the *Exposition InteRnatiOnal du Surréalisme* (Eros) in 1959, the surrealists have given us powerful tributes to the spirit of the Divine Marquis that testify to his importance. Sade's presence in numerous artworks by Hans Bellmer, Man Ray, André Masson, Jacques Hérold and many other artists is evident in multifarious ways as they engage with Robert Desnos' insight that 'Sade considered love and its acts from the perspective of infinity' (Desnos 1978: 134).

Jean Benoît, however, is the surrealist artist who has identified with Sade's spirit most profoundly and his 'Execution of the Will of the Marquis de Sade' at the home of Joyce Mansour on 2 December 1959 represents the apogee of his – and surrealism's – engagement with Sade.[1]

Yet nothing about Sade is simple and for the surrealists above all he was a supremely ambivalent figure. If he was, as Apollinaire described him, 'the freest spirit that ever lived', this was so only in a particular, almost ironic, way.

The surrealists had been aware of the importance of Sade from early on, alerted by Apollinaire that there was more to him than the legend implied. He was frequently mentioned in passing with respect in early texts by Breton and Aragon, and Robert Desnos, writing in 1922, recognized in him 'the first philosophical and vibrant manifestation of the modern spirit' (Desnos 1978: 133).

Serious attention was not really paid to him, however, until the mid-twenties, at the time the surrealists were making overtures towards the Communist Party, and it was also as a revolutionary that they primarily saw him. Yet, as we look back we have to wonder if the attraction towards Sade in part represented a retreat, or a hesitation, from the communist conformism already making itself felt and that would soon result in Stalinism. Sade's work now seems even to constitute a thoroughgoing refutation of the possibility of social revolution, at least in the terms sought by the Communist Party. This was even apparent to some at the time, notably André Masson, in his assertion that the surrealists needed to develop a 'physical idea of revolution',[2] a revolution that would combine social change with bodily and mental liberation. Masson seems to have drawn this notion from Sade, although he didn't invoke him at the time.

We owe it to Annie Le Brun to have developed this revolutionary significance, separating Sade from Robespierre and Saint-Just – for both of whom in different ways the 'end justifies the means' – asserting that for Sade in contrast it is the means and *only the means* that can justify the end. Violence is a fact of nature that cannot be ignored, but it should never be exercised other than as an expression of the passions. Moreover, as Le Brun expresses it, Sade shows that 'there are no ideas without body and no body without ideas'. She adds: 'Sade also shows that behind any social or political system, behind any construction of this type, the relation to power equally reflects conceptions of the world influenced by our desires, that even social thought is linked with erotic conceptions of the world. He thus implicitly shows that our political choices are completely determined by our erotic sense (Le Brun 1989: 31). This seems to be the foundation of a Sadian sensibility and it deeply affected surrealism.

Of course, Sade lived in revolutionary times and was a supporter of the French Revolution, however conditionally. Yet, whether we consider Sade's espousal of the Revolution to be principled or opportunist, we have to take into account his courageous stand against capital punishment. This latter fact in particular drew the surrealists' attention, revealing that his popular reputation only told part of the story. It was as a moralist that they overwhelmingly regarded him. But what are we to make of Sadian morality?

Despite the homages paid to Sade in surrealist work, and the fact that Maurice Heine and Gilbert Lély, the two people who have perhaps been most instrumental in setting the record straight about the importance of his work, were both linked with surrealism, no clear sense has so far emerged of precisely what position Sade holds within the surrealist firmament. However, the surrealist who has most extensively examined the significance of Sade's work for surrealism has been Annie Le Brun.

Her preface to his *Œuvres complètes* is an impressive work that had been translated into English as a separate volume and does much to dispel the myths around Sade's ideas as she takes issue with some of the more fanciful attempts to make Sade 'a philosopher like any other'. Yet while her understanding of Sade, and her analysis of his work, seems sound, I have difficulty in accepting the consequences she draws from her analysis as far as surrealism is concerned. Indeed, in her will to get to the core of what Sade is actually saying, she seems at times to have taken leave of her critical faculties, even to have been possessed by him, so strongly does she extol Sade's work.

Le Brun asserts that the essence of Sade's thought is contained in this quotation: 'My way of thinking, you say, cannot be approved. What does that matter to me? A person is really mad if he adopts a way of thinking for the benefit of others! My way of thinking is the fruit of my reflection; it is critical to my existence, to my organization. I am not able to change it; and if I was, I would not do so.' This makes Sade, in Le Brun's view, 'absolutely surrealist, imagining his way of thinking as a metaphor for his relationship with the world' (1989: 145). However, there is something troubling in this quotation for if, on the one hand, such intransigence in the face of prejudice is to be applauded, on the other hand it suggests a rigidity of thinking, asserting that only what has resulted from his own thinking has value, which he won't change no matter how compelling the evidence against it.

Indeed, far from being the absolute surrealist she insists he is, Sade comes over to me – even from her own account of him – as radically separated from surrealism in some very fundamental ways: he appears to deny love, community, desire, and the otherness of being, indeed everything that concerns affectivity with other humans. Le Brun would deny the latter two, but although she sees a strong affinity between Sade and Rimbaud nothing seems more alien to Sade than Rimbaud's assertion of fundamental otherness: for Sade the *I* is not other but is nothing but the *I*, which is simply there and requires no justification or seeking out. She also sees Sade as being engaged in the surrealist project by which 'man discovers within himself the power to become everything he is not' (144), something which again links with Rimbaud.

She thus speaks of the critical origin of poetry in Sade as 'plunging its roots into the ferocity of a desire which, for want of ever being able to be satisfied as desire for the Other, becomes desire to become Other' (144). I don't, however, see how desire *for* the Other can be separated from desire to become Other. If one doesn't recognize the Other as the object of desire, how could one even think of *becoming* Other? Elsewhere, indeed, Le Brun insists that the great quality of Juliette, Sade's most fully formed character, is that, far from desiring to become Other, she is constantly and consistently herself: 'Juliette studies absolutely nothing, assimilates nothing, and does not alter in any way at all. From one end of the story to the other she is splendidly herself' (1990: 189). How can these statements be reconciled?

But also I entirely fail to see Sade as a poet of desire, as Le Brun argues. She says that he was the first person to ask the question, 'What is desire?' (1990: 119). But if he did how did he answer it other than by negating it? Indeed, isn't the negation of desire essential to the whole argument he makes about existence? Sade appears to want to reduce himself to his most elemental state, one of pure energy, that rejects everything constituted by human experience. In asserting the sovereignty of the ego so forcefully in this way, however, Sade can allow no place for the other. His heroes are isolated beings and in the end this is their tragedy: their experience is theirs alone and doesn't touch others. There is no communication, no communion, no poetry,[3] only a community of sovereign beings, Olympian gods ruling a sterile universe.

Le Brun seems to lend support to this in the revelation she discovers into Sade in the expressions of four birds of prey she sees in a New York zoo. This indeed seems an apt association, but can one imagine anything more distant from desire than the expressions of predatory birds which view weaker creatures as fodder for their own sustenance?[4] They act out of pure contingency, their predation determined entirely by their natures. This may correspond with the demeanour of Sade's heroes, but it manifestly excludes desire, which is a human attitude, one that is almost certainly tied in (we don't entirely need to concur with Bataille to assert this) with our awareness of death, an awareness that underwrites our need for *communication*. As purely sovereign beings committed to the life instincts, Sade's heroes deny this *awareness* of death, as Le Brun asserts. But in doing so they also have to deny desire, which would certainly get in the way of their pure sovereignty, because desire is a response and an aspiration to an *object* as a response to some perceived *lack*. It is not a pure sensation, existing apart from what is desired. Sade's libertines may aspire to the implacability of the volcano. This is a vain hope, however, since their only approach to it is through the edifice they construct due to their cultural accumulations. They are ultimately no more capable of attaining the energy surge of the volcano than any other humans: they can only be its victims. Faced with its force they are as helpless as those they treat as prey in the Castle of Silling.

Le Brun extols the fact that Sade had no interest in death. Again he is utterly consistent: since his characters, as they aspire towards pure contingency, either live or die with no anxiety permeating either state. But how can this be consistent with surrealism? Wasn't the experience of the First World War with its meaningless sacrifice of so many lives a determining element in the constitution of surrealism? Wasn't one of their first impulses to ask whether suicide was a solution? No indifference to death there. Moreover, doesn't the first manifesto proclaim that 'surrealism will usher you into a secret society, which is that of death', a secret society that nevertheless functions against death. This insight was developed more incisively in the second manifesto, which defines the aim of surrealism as being to aspire to the supreme or sublime point which exists where, inter alia, life and death are no longer perceived as contradictory. It therefore seems bizarre to berate Bataille as Le Brun does for his obsession with death and to use it to decry his 'mysticism', setting it against Sade's 'atheism'. But if Bataille was a mystic by this criterion, then surely so too was Breton. Indeed, we should remember that Bataille's statement about eroticism being the assent of life even in death, which she criticizes, was quoted with approval by Breton in his introduction to the Eros exhibition of 1959.

This leads into a further problematic. Sade's thoroughgoing and uncompromising atheism could hardly fail to impress the surrealists; indeed, it was one of the things that most strongly attracted them to him. But even here his thinking seems ultimately incompatible with surrealism and even to reveal a vast caesura.

Le Brun seems to clarify this point as she lauds his integral atheism as his fundamental attitude. One has to respect Sade's courage in the context of his time for insisting so trenchantly and uncompromisingly on an elemental atheism. But how well does this really play in today's world?

I have difficulty, for instance, in seeing how this integral atheism differs from the sort of intolerantly positivistic and vulgar atheism of such contemporary figures as Richard Dawkins. First, such an 'integral atheism' goes against the surrealist watchwords of 'absolute doubt' and 'absolute divergence'. More than this it actually undermines the essential characteristics of the atheism that underlies surrealism, which does not deny the *existence* of God but reduces it to insignificance. For instance, what is Breton's invocation of the myth of the Great Invisibles if not an engagement with the notion of the gods, but gods devoid of any quality as deities and reduced to beings who are as indifferent to our existence as we are to theirs?

More than this, however, to promote an integral atheism would be to invalidate all of the interest the surrealists have shown in non-Western religious beliefs and practices; it would be to deny the manifest correspondences between surrealism and aspects of Gnosticism, Buddhism, Taoism or Sufism (belief systems that can all be viewed from particular perspectives as atheist). Sade's critique of religion – powerful though it is – is almost entirely determined by a reaction against Christianity and from any surrealist perspective it surely pales beside Marx's perception that 'religious suffering is at one and the same time the *expression* of real suffering and a protest against real suffering'. Here surrealism seems closer to Marx than to Sade, in acknowledging the essential place that the notion of a god (and religion) occupies in the human mind and acting critically against it. It is surely this 'real suffering' that has to be addressed in any religious critique and not metaphysical speculation about the existence or non-existence of a deity. Recent years have shown us the persistence and insidiousness of religious belief against which any sort of 'integral atheism' – itself a form of 'fundamentalism' – is powerless. Isn't it arguable that it has been one of surrealism's merits to reject such an alibi and while rejecting the notion of belief in itself to seek to understand the vital impulses that lie behind it?

Furthermore, Sade seems to accept without question the materiality of the world as the only reality. His attitude is rigidly empirical and almost even positivistic. He may exalt the imagination, but only as a projection of what exists; the creative force of imagination that gives it the possibility to transform the world – which surrealism derived from alchemy and Romanticism – seems absent from his work. The *force* of imagination, admittedly, is the driving motive of Sade's world, but it is a compensatory imagination, one making it possible to exist in a hostile environment rather than having the possibility to transform that environment.

Thus, while Sade's strength is precisely to be able to stand so far outside of the human as to see it in all its animal nakedness, in doing so doesn't he also divest us of our very essence? Sade effectively utilizes this imaginative force to replace culture, giving back to experience its immediacy. But can human beings exist in such immediacy? Wouldn't it be to condemn us to extinction? Sade was perhaps the first to offer us an image of our ultimate unimportance when he noted that the disappearance of the ant would probably have severe consequences for life, but the disappearance of the human would make no difference at all. This is an important revelation, especially for our ecologically conscious times, and we should thank Sade for raising it. But the problematic it raises can hardly be resolved by our renouncing our humanity and the culture that has made it possible. Human beings, finding themselves alone in the world, doubtless needed to develop culture in order to survive in a predatory universe.

Culture has made us the masters rather than the victims of the world. Perhaps the price that had to be paid for this mastery is too great, and this is what makes Sade's interrogation so vital. But to give it up would still be to invite our own destruction. It is perhaps significant that Sade's heroes need to retreat to an inaccessible castle, one impermeable to all external threats, not simply that posed by human laws, but also by nature itself. They retreat, furthermore, to a *castle*, the human defensive construction par excellence, and not into the wilds of the deep forest.

Contrary to Sade's worldview, everything leads us to believe that human beings could not survive in a world of pure predation – it is why we separated ourselves from nature and constructed culture. If culture is our achievement, it is also our curse – the basis of the evil we have inflicted on the world – and perhaps it will ultimately destroy us. Yet the alterative Sade offers seems only to lead to our own annihilation as human beings.

What Sade explicitly attacks is the law rather than culture, but the law is what makes culture possible. He is usually seen as embracing evil, but in a sense he abjures it, or even denies that it exists. What he celebrates is not evil but crime. If evil exists for him, it appears to be precisely located within the law, which is really what he finds unacceptable. The law is evil for Sade because it tries to control human passions, which is wrong because these passions were given to us by nature and therefore we should not be condemned for following them.

For Sade crime is thus not a transgression of the law, but a moral refusal of its authority. It is even tempting to compare Sade with St Paul and to see this as a displacement of Pauline revelation: where Paul rejected the law in favour of Christ's love, Sade does so to favour crime.

Moreover, there is no room for pity or indeed any sort of human sympathy, in Sade's universe. Perhaps a world of pure predation might be preferable to the world we currently live in, but it would be a world without the human. Ultimately, however, even Sade draws back from this option: the very fact that he writes, and so addresses his fellow humans, asserts the culture he would otherwise reject.

Despite all this, what makes Sade important is that his obstinacy in pursuing his arguments to their extremes opens up an abyss that is present within the sensibility of each and every one of us. And here Le Brun is undoubtedly right to perceive that above all he provides a thoroughgoing critique of the forms of tyranny and totalitarianism that dominated the early twentieth century. Notwithstanding his reputation, no serious consideration of his work could conclude that it has any link with totalitarian ideology, or indeed with any ideology at all. As Le Brun emphasizes, Sade refuses all generality: each being has reality only in its particularity. This is the great moral lesson Sade teaches: providing a person remains within their own particularity and never ventures into generality, their actions – no matter how extreme – cannot be judged, because they are only acting in accordance with their natures. It is only when they identify with others, so sacrificing their particularity and mingling in the general, that they become tyrants. Thus, on the face of it Shakespeare's Macbeth or the actual figure of a Stalin might appear to have Sadian characteristics. They might have the capacity to glimpse the Castle of Silling but their taste for power, and their paranoia, would inevitably consume them from within and ultimately destroy them before they could take a step closer. A Hitler on the other hand would become lost in the foothills on the way, because he placed an ideal (the thousand-year Reich) above his own particularity. All violence, for Sade, must be committed in passion and be disinterested. It can serve no cause, not even one's own sovereignty, because if it did it would cease to be sovereign and reveal one's weakness. The violence of Sade's heroes is directed towards the weak and defenceless, pitilessly and remorselessly. But it is also a challenge, demanding that they cease to be weak and rise up against oppression. And because this violence must be disinterested; it cannot be indiscriminate. The 'sadists' are engaged in a battle against weakness (not against the weak as such). They do not hate their victims (this again would be a sign of weakness and disqualify them) any more than they pity them.

However, is it possible for human beings to live within the particularity of being? Are we not fundamentally and irrevocably social beings who need to relate ourselves to the general in order to survive? In fact, couldn't Sadian morality even be seen as the basis of the neo-liberal agenda that has polluted human relations over the past thirty years: Margaret Thatcher, indeed, might be seen in many ways as a Sadian figure with her contempt for the weak and unsentimental view that everyone should simply 'pull themselves up by their bootstraps'? Thatcher's vision may have been bourgeois, lacking the grandeur of Sade's, determined only by opposition to the vapid 'socialism' against which it provides an equally vapid instrumentalism that would have struck Sade as mediocre. In essence, however, her vision was the same in its rejection of ideology and of society. Her famous phrase 'there is no such thing as society' even directly echoes Sade. This reflection must give us pause, and cause us to question whether rejection of generality is sufficient to avoid tyranny. If we can say that Stalin and Hitler, and perhaps the majority of twentieth-century tyrants, are precluded from the Sadian universe, there are many that weren't. How about Idi Amin, Jean-Bédel Bokassa, Sese Seko Mobutu or Alfredo Stroessner? None of these men were impelled by ideology or concern with the general. Even more so than any of them, Augusto Pinochet seems to have been motivated by an almost Sadian will to impose particularity against any form of generality. Indeed, would not Pinochet or Thatcher be welcomed with open arms into the Castle of Silling?

Sade is remarkably consistent in his thinking, but it is a consistency that is relentlessly reductive and entirely undialectical and this ultimately tarnishes his work. Moreover, he does not escape historical contingency: his freedom is the sovereignty of the absolutist king, turned upside down and thoroughly subverted, but ultimately just as sterile. His value is that he offers us a challenge, not a remedy. His 'philosophy', when examined closely, seems to be risible and I find Annie Le Brun's unqualified enthusiasm for it perplexing. She seems almost to see him as a universal genius having an incomparable insight into human existence rather than, as he surely was, a disenfranchised aristocrat imbued – principally because of incarceration and the vindictiveness of others – with an acute insight into human limitations. But he had little appreciation of the impact of social conditions and so assumed that weakness can be overcome through a sheer effort of will and projection of the imagination.[5]

This ultimately is incompatible with surrealism, which constituted itself as a moral community concerned with a collective quest that would break down the very foundations of the predatory ego that Sade is so keen to shore up. Le Brun is very critical of Bataille, but he seems to have a much greater insight into the implications of Sade's thought than she has. While Bataille was fascinated by Sade, he never succumbed to his influence and was always acutely aware of the distance that separated them. In many ways they may even be seen as polar opposites. Bataille undoubtedly identified with Sade in the intransigence of his thinking and the will to go to the extreme. He was always conscious, however, that this had to be regarded as a challenge and not as a consecration. As he insisted, '[t]o admire Sade is to betray his thought.'

Nor is Breton's position towards Sade as uncritical as Le Brun presents it. Breton was careful to define Sade as 'surrealist in sadism', but this is as much a limitation as a sanctification. Elsewhere he commends Sade as representing the 'nadir' of the tradition of courtly and romantic love of which surrealism is the 'zenith'. Both of these examples situate Sade as *outside* of surrealism proper but constituted within it as a dialectical element that surrealism has sublated. Breton insisted that all of the ancestors he invoked were imperfect from a surrealist perspective. The only exception is Lautréamont and this I think is above all because 'Lautréamont' is brought into question by Isidore Ducasse in writing *Les Poésies*, in which contradiction becomes manifest: having built up his sovereign being in Maldoror, Ducasse is impatient to knock him down in *Les Poésies* as he brandishes good against evil in a way that brings both into question. Having none of Ducasse's taste for paradox Sade treats himself seriously even in his irony and black sense of humour.

While, therefore, it is not difficult to see the ways in which Sade is an attractive figure for surrealism, he is also intensely problematic. He may still stand as the perfect emblem for surrealist revolt. His value also lies in the unsparing and uncompromising character of his critique – one might almost say defenestration – of the human condition, but he offers nothing that indicates an alleviation of it, merely a retreat that in the end denies the very humanness of that condition.

Notes

1 The pretext for Benoît's intervention was the fact that at his death the provisions of Sade's will were entirely ignored.
2 Masson first put this idea forward during a surrealist meeting of 23 January 1925; see Thévenin 1988: 114.
3 Le Brun insists that Sade has to be read as a great poet. Perhaps. But I tend to agree with André Pieyre de Mandiargues that Sade has no 'feeling for poetry [which] he must consider a useless and contemptible thing' (1971: 330).
4 This association reminds me of one of the most chilling moments I have witnessed in a film: in Andrzej Wajda's *Landscape after a Battle*, set in a concentration camp after the liberation, in which in their desperation two friends begin to see each other not as friends but as potential food.
5 André Pieyre de Mandiargues makes a telling point that in *Philosophy in the Boudoir*, the valet Augustin is sent out of the room before the reading of the revolutionary tract, being told 'this is not for you' (1971: 331). There seem many incidents in Sade's life indicating that he had contempt for the working classes.

6 'The speaking flame': the Romantic connection

Michael Löwy

Surrealism is the most striking and the most fascinating example of a Romantic current in the twentieth century. Of all the cultural movements of the era, it has carried the Romantic aspiration to re-enchant the world to its highest expression. More than any other it has also incarnated, in the most radical fashion, the revolutionary dimension of Romanticism. The revolt of the mind (spirit) and the social revolution, the imperatives to change life (Rimbaud) and transform the world (Marx): these two polar stars have oriented the movement since its beginnings, driving it in the permanent search for subversive cultural and political practices.

What is Romanticism? It has been reduced to a literary school of the nineteenth century, or to a traditionalist reaction against the French Revolution – two propositions found in countless works by eminent specialists in literary history or the history of political thought. In our view it is something much broader and deeper: a structure of sensibility irrigating all fields of culture, a worldview which extends from the second half of the eighteenth century to the present, a comet whose incandescent 'core' is the revolt against modern industrial/capitalist civilization, in the name of certain social or cultural values of the past. Nostalgic for a lost paradise – real or imaginary – Romanticism opposes itself, with the melancholic energy of despair, to the quantifying mind of the bourgeois universe, to commercial reification, the platitude of utilitarianism, and above all, to the *disenchantment of the world*. While some of the Romantics are backward-looking, regressive and/or reactionary (like Coleridge and Friedrich Schlegel in their old age), others – from William Blake to Ernst Bloch – are emancipatory, utopian and/or revolutionary: their aim is not a return to the past, but a *detour* by the past towards the future. It is to this revolutionary variant that the surrealist movement belongs.

The surrealists were not 'influenced' by Romanticism, as an empty vessel that is filled with a cultural content. In their struggle against bourgeois rationality and capitalist civilization, they used Romantic ideas, notions and images as tools to develop their own revolutionary vision. Breton and his friends had never hidden their profound attachment to the Romantic tradition of the nineteenth century – whether German (Novalis, Arnim), English (Gothic novels) or French (Hugo, Pétrus Borel).

Before discussing the interest surrealists had in some Romantic writers, and in some essential Romantic notions, let's try to assess the fundamental relationship of the surrealist movement with the Romantic culture. What does Romanticism mean for the surrealists? In their eyes the petty academic approach which made it a 'literary genre' is despicable. Here's how Breton put it in his conference given in Haiti on 'The Concept of Liberty of the Romantics' (1945):

> The image of Romanticism imposed upon us by scholars is a *falsified* image. The use of national categories and absurd pigeonholes which only separate literary genres serves to impede the consideration of the Romantic movement as a whole.
>
> (Breton 1999b: 218)

In fact, Romanticism is a worldview – in the sense of a *Weltanschauung* – which cuts across nations and eras:

> It must be observed that Romanticism, as a specific state of mind and *mood* whose function is to everywhere instil a new general conception of the world, transcends those fashions – very limited – of feeling and speaking which were named after it … . Through the swath of works produced by or deriving from it, notably through Symbolism and expressionism, Romanticism imposes itself as a *continuum*.
>
> (Breton 2008: 1029)

Surrealism clearly places itself within this long temporal continuity of Romanticism as 'state of mind'. Criticizing the pompous official celebrations of the centennial of French Romanticism in 1930, Breton comments in the *Second Surrealist Manifesto*:

> We say that this Romanticism, of which today we are willing to conceive ourselves as the tail – *but a very prehensile tail* – by its very essence, even in 1930, remains uncompromising in its negation of these bureaucrats and their festivals; its century of existence is only its youth, which has been wrongly called its heroic epoch, and can

> only honestly be taken for the first cry of a being just beginning to make its desire known through us.
>
> (Breton 1969: 153, translation modified)

One can hardly find, in the twentieth century, a more categorical proclamation of the actuality of Romanticism …

One should not draw the conclusion, from that explicit allegiance, that the Romanticism of the surrealists is the same as that of the poets or philosophers of the nineteenth century. Through its methods, its artistic and political choices, its way of life the surrealist movement *invented* something radically *new*, which fully belongs to the culture of the twentieth century, in all its dimensions, and cannot be considered a simple re-edition, or even worse, an imitation of the first Romanticism.

First of all, the surrealist reading of the Romantic heritage is *highly selective*. It is a bold attempt to actualize the latent revolutionary moments of the Romantic writers, sometimes reading them 'against the grain'. What attracts surrealists to the 'gigantic facades of Hugo', to certain texts of Alfred de Musset, Aloysius Bertrand, Xavier Forneret and Gérard de Nerval is, as Breton writes in 'The Marvellous against Mystery' ('Le merveilleux contre le mystère'), the will to 'emancipate man totally' (Breton 1995: 2). It is also, as he emphasizes in 'The Political Position of Art Today' (1935), in 'a good number of Romantic or post-Romantic writers' and artists – like Borel, Flaubert, Baudelaire, Daumier or Courbet – the 'completely spontaneous hatred of the bourgeois type', the 'will to absolute non-compliance with the ruling class', whose domination is in their eyes a sort of leper against which – if one wishes to save the most precious human acquisitions from being stripped of their meaning and contributing only to the daily-worsening debasement of the human condition – it is no longer enough to brandish the whip, but one day we must apply the branding iron (Breton 1992: 422).

The same is true for the German Romantics. Breton did not ignore the 'fairly confused but ultra-reactionary doctrine' espoused by Novalis in his essay *Europe, or Christianity* (1799), or the hostile position Achim von Arnim took against the French Revolution. But that did not prevent their works – as well as those of Karoline von Günderrode and Bettina Brentano – veritable lightning stones (*pierres de foudre*) – from shaking the foundations of the bourgeois cultural order, through their questioning of the separation between real and imaginary. Breton was fascinated by Arnim – almost ignored in France, barely known at all in English-speaking lands and considered a minor writer in Germany – whom he saw as having a more brilliant imagination than any other in his time. Moreover, Arnim was the first, almost one century before Rimbaud, to conceive of the poet as a *Seer: Nennen wir die heiligen Dichter auch Seher* ('Let us name the sacred poets also seers', quoted in German by Breton 1999a: 99).

Their thinking thus took on a profoundly utopian/subversive dimension, as for example when Novalis, in his philosophical fragments, 'reclaimed as his own what was the magical postulate par excellence – and he did it under a form which barred any restriction on his part: "It depends upon us that the world must conform to our will"' (Breton 2008: 51). In the *Dictionnaire abrégé du surréalisme*, written in 1938 by Breton and Éluard, there is an entry on Novalis, with a quotation by Albert Béguin, a French historian of Romanticism: 'For Novalis … the perfect consciousness, obtained in ourselves by an interior transformation, at the same time transforms the universe' (Breton 1992: 825) – an insight that has obvious analogies to the surrealist project.

Surrealists were also interested in German Romantic philosophers, such as Schelling. In a footnote to the tract of 1925, 'Revolution First and Always!', written by the surrealists, together with the communist thinkers of the journal *Philosophies*, Schelling is named, together with Kant, Hegel and Marx among the philosophers favoured by the signatories (Richardson and Fijalkowski 2001: 95–7 and 213). Recent research by Georges Sebbag (2012) documents the importance of Romantic philosophers such as Schelling and Fichte for the surrealists. The most striking example is Louis Aragon's *Paysan de Paris* (1926), where Schelling appears as a philosopher moving a colourful hoop with a magic wand: 'he spends his life playing with what he calls the wheel of becoming [*la roue du devenir*]' (Sebbag 2012: 355).

Schelling's philosophy of nature (*Naturphilosophie*) was an important source for Aragon. Many surrealists were attracted to the Romantic magical and poetical approach to Nature, as a radical alternative to the positivist, productivist and utilitarian one of bourgeois industrial society. This is particularly the case with Breton, but his sympathies were with Johann Wilhelm Ritter, author of *Physics as Art* (1798) rather than Schelling, rejected as 'opportunist' (Breton 1999a: 94). However, the most important Romantic philosopher of nature was, for Breton, once more, Novalis. The German poet believed that all living creatures, vegetal, animal or human, share a common substance, which for him, as for Heraclitus, is fire. The surrealists seemed to share this viewpoint: in the *Shortened Dictionary of Surrealism*, in the entry for 'Flame', one finds the following quote: 'The tree cannot become but a flourishing flame, the human being a speaking flame, the animal a walking flame (Novalis)' (Breton and Éluard 1992: 811). In the conflict between the human machine and Nature, surrealists would always side with the latter, as in Max Ernst's famous painting *Airplane Swallowing Garden* (*Jardin gobe avions*, 1935).

Next to the French and German Romantics, surrealists shared a fascination for the English (Romantic) Gothic novel. According to Breton, never, as in their writings, 'has the principle of pleasure taken its revenge so manifestly on the principle of reality'. In the novels of Horace Walpole, Ann Radcliffe, Matthew Gregory Lewis, Charles Robert Maturin (to which we could add Mary Shelley) – these true 'observatories of the inner sky' – one reaches the 'the point where human reason loses its control', because they are manifestations of 'the innermost emotion of a human being' that is 'unable to externalize itself within the confines of the real world' (Breton 1995: 13). A few years after Breton's death, Annie Le Brun published a powerful surrealist celebration of the English *roman noir, The Castles of Subversion* (1982).

As we saw above, the cultural protest against modern bourgeois civilization is a central component of the Romantic worldview. This *Zivilisationskritik* is one of the key notions of the Romantic culture that will be reinterpreted in revolutionary terms by the surrealists. The opposition of the surrealist movement to modern capitalist civilization is neither reasonable nor moderate: it is radical, categorical, irreducible. In 'Revolution First and Always!', the founders of surrealism proclaim: 'Wherever Western civilization reigns, all human attachment but that motivated by self-interest has ceased, "money is the bottom line". For over a century, human dignity has been reduced to the level of exchange-value. … We do not accept the laws of economy or exchange, we do not accept the slavery of work …' (Richardson and Fijalkowski 2001: 95).

This critique of modern bourgeois society often refers, in a typically Romantic way, to a precapitalist past, when human dignity still existed; when it was not reduced to a commodity, and human relations were not yet limited to what Carlyle – a Romantic critic of modernity much admired by Marx and Engels – called the *cash-nexus*. However, unlike backward-oriented Romantics, the surrealists aimed not at the restoration of the past, but at a revolutionary transformation of society, beyond capitalist slavery – a radical social and political option that over the following decades led them to support the Communist Party, then the Trotskyist Left Opposition, and finally, the anarchists.

Several years later, remembering the very beginnings of the surrealist movement, Breton observed,

> At that time, surrealist refusal was total, absolutely unable to let itself be channelled into the political arena. All the institutions on

> which the modern world rested, as the First World War proved, were aberrant and scandalous in our eyes.
>
> (Breton 1969: 265, translation modified)

The Romantic poets' and philosophers' critique of the dominant form of rationality is also the object of a surrealist reformulation. The main philosophical targets of the surrealist attack on Western civilization were abstract and narrow-minded rationalism, bourgeois realist conventions, and positivism in all of its forms. In the *First Surrealist Manifesto* (1924), Breton denounced the attitude which is shown in the banishment, 'under the guise of civilization, under the pretext of progress', of anything that hints at the chimerical; faced with that sterile cultural horizon, he affirmed his belief in the omnipotence of dream. One of the most significant alternatives to the shallow bourgeois rationality is, for the surrealists, a quintessential premodern way of thinking (celebrated by Romantic poets like Percy Bysshe Shelley): *analogy*. According to Breton, the key to release us from the mental prison is 'the free and limitless play of *analogies*' (Breton 1972: 200). The analogical method, revered in ancient times and the Middle Ages, has been since then 'crudely superseded by the "logic" method, which has led us to the present dead end'. It is the first duty of poets and artists to 're-establish it in all its prerogatives', emancipating it of its spiritualist parasites (Breton 1978: 282, translation modified). Many surrealist games, from the 1920s till today, are inspired by the principle of analogy.

The search for an alternative to Western civilization has remained present throughout the history of surrealism – in the 1970s a group of French and Czech surrealists went so far as to speak of a 'surrealist civilization' (see Bounoure 1976).

As we have seen, the Romantic critique of modernity is based on precapitalist cultural and social values. The surrealists shared this Romantic passion for premodern traditions but, again, in a selective way compatible with their revolutionary commitment. Unhesitatingly, the surrealists would draw from alchemy, the Kabbala, magic, mythology, astrology, art from Oceania or the Americas, and Celtic art. All their activities on this terrain are aimed at exceeding the limitations of 'art' – as separate, institutionalized, ornamental activity – in order to enter the limitless adventure of the re-enchantment of the world. Nevertheless, as revolutionaries inspired by the spirit of the Enlightenment, of Hegel and above all of Marx, the surrealists were the most resolute and uncompromising enemies of the values at the core of Romantic reactionary culture: *religion and nationalism*. As the *Second*

Manifesto states: 'Everything must be done, every method must be utilized to destroy the notions of family, nation, religion' (Breton 1969: 128, translation modified). At the gates of the lost surrealist paradise can be found, in flaming letters, that well-known anarchist inscription: Neither God nor master!

Let us for the remainder of this chapter examine three key notions that illustrate this surrealist reinterpretation of 'archaic' or precapitalist elements: *myth, magic* and *primitive arts.*

Among the Romantic strategies for re-enchanting the world, *myth* occupies a special place. At the marvellous intersection of multiple traditions, it offers an inexhaustible reservoir of symbols and allegories, ghosts and demons, gods and vipers. There are many ways to dig for that dangerous treasure: the poetic or literary reference to ancient myth, the 'learned' study of mythology, and the attempt to create a new mythos. In the third case, the loss of religious substance in myth transforms it into a profane image of re-enchantment, or rather, a non-religious way to regain the sacred.

In his 1800 *Discourse on Mythology*, one of the most visionary 'theoretical' texts of German Romanticism, Friedrich Schlegel imagined a new mythology, which would be no pale imitation of the past, but would radically distinguish itself by its very nature, by its spiritual texture so to speak; while the former immediately reconnects to the closest and most lively things in the world of sensation, the latter must be made, by contrast, from the 'deepest depths of the mind' (*tiefsten Tiefe des Geistes*). Coming from that internal source, the new mythology would thus be produced by the mind from itself; this explains its elective affinity with idealist philosophy (Schlegel here is thinking primarily of Fichte), itself also created 'from nothing' (*aus Nichts entstanden*). Coming from the depths, that mythopoetic interiority cannot accept the limits imposed by rationalist reason; it is the realm of 'whatever forever evades consciousness' of 'the beautiful disorder of the imagination' and 'the original chaos of human nature' (Schlegel 1984: 235–6). That's not to say that it ignores the exterior world; the new myth is also 'a hieroglyphic expression of surrounding nature under the transfiguration of the imagination and of love' (239). It's difficult to avoid the conclusion that Schlegel, in these passages, intuitively identifies the domain that Freud, a century later, would attempt to crown with the category of the unconscious.

Concluding this astonishing text, saturated with fulgurant intuitions and seeming to announce now psychoanalysis, now surrealism, Schlegel turns his eye towards the future. One day, human beings will rediscover their divinatory power (*divinatorischen Kraft*) and greet the golden age, 'which is yet to come'. 'This is what I mean by the new mythology' (Schlegel 1984: 242). In situating the golden age in the future, not the past, Schlegel transfigures myth into utopian energy and invests mythopoetics with a magical power.

One hundred and fifty years later, the surrealists would blow anew upon those embers, illuminating the dark heart of the cave with their aid. For Breton and his friends, myth was a precious crystal of fire; they refused to abandon it to fascist mythomaniacs. In 1942, at the worst moment of the war, Breton believed more than ever in the necessity for a counter-attack in this domain: 'Faced with the current conflict mobilizing the world, the most difficult minds are coming to admit the vital necessity of a myth opposable to that of Odin and various others' (Breton 1994: 75).

In a 1937 text, 'Limits Not Frontiers of Surrealism', Breton first suggests that surrealism must be assigned the task of 'the elaboration of the collective myth of our time', whose simultaneously erotic and subversive role would be analogous to that played in the eighteenth century, just before the French Revolution, by the Gothic novel.

The importance of myth, to the surrealists, lies also in the fact that it constitutes (along with the esoteric traditions) a profane alternative to the grip of religion on the non-rational. It is in this sense that we must interpret Breton's remark – taken as a provocative and iconoclastic image – in the dedication of a copy of *Mad Love* sent to his friend Armand Hoog: 'Let's demolish the churches, starting with the most beautiful, so that no stone rests upon another. Then will live the New Myth!' (Beaujour 1970: 22).

In the *Prolegomena to a Third Manifesto or Not*, Breton asks (and asks himself) the question, 'To what extent can we choose or adopt, and impose a myth, in relation to the society we judge desirable?' (Breton 1972: 288–9, translation modified). Everything thus seems to indicate that for him, myth and utopia are inseparable; if they are not identical, they are at least linked by a system of communicating vessels which assures the passage of desire between the two spheres.

The second of surrealism's key notions for the reinterpretation of precapitalist elements is magic. In his book *L'Art magique*, Breton defined magic as 'the whole of human operations having as their goal the imperious domination of the forces of nature through the use of secret practices of a more or less irrational character'. It 'implies protest, even revolt'; pride too, in its assumption that man 'controls' (disposes of) the forces of nature. Religion, in contrast, is the domain of resignation, begging and penitence: 'Its humility is total, because it leads [man] to pray for his very unhappiness to the power which has refused to answer' (Breton and Legrand 1991: 27).

The sacred, in its religious, hierocratic, clerical, institutional forms, can only inspire, as a system of authoritarian prohibitions, an irrepressible desire for *transgression*, profanation and desacralization on the part of the surrealists, through irony, scorn or black humour. Sacrilege or blasphemy are the highest forms of politeness when faced with holy monsters.

Breton borrowed the concept of *magical art* from the archetypical Romantic poet Novalis. It was that 'very great Romantic spirit' who chose those words to describe the art form he hoped to promote, both rooted in the past and shot through with a 'strong tension toward the future':

> In the sense in which he [Novalis] understood them, one could expect to find not only the quintessential product of a millennium of experience, but also its supersession owing to its conjunction into a being of the most brilliant lights of the mind and heart.
>
> (Breton 2008: 49)

For Breton, all art originated in magic; he proposed the designation of *specifically* magical art for that which 're-engenders to some degree the magic which engendered it'. What did the ancient magician and the modern surrealist artist have in common? In his inquiry into magical art, Breton declared that they 'both speculate on the possibilities and the methods of *enchanting the universe*' (Breton 2008: 74, 114).

In assessing the surrealist interest in magic, one should take into consideration its historical background: in pre-industrial times it had been condemned, persecuted – the witch-hunts! – and banished by institutional religion, which had in its place imposed the holy, the sanctified, the venerable as separate and inviolable realms. It had been subsequently effaced by capitalist/industrialist civilization, which rejected or systematically destroyed whatever was not calculable, quantifiable or capable of being transformed into merchandise. The enterprise of the total *disenchantment of the world*, which, according to Max Weber, characterizes bourgeois modernity, has driven from human life not just magic, but everything that might escape the rigid and narrow-minded confines of instrumental rationality.

If magic attracts the attention of the surrealists with an irresistible strength, it's not because they want to control the forces of nature through ritual acts. What interests them in so-called 'archaic' magical practices – as with alchemy and other Hermetic arts – is the immense *poetic charge* borne by these activities. That charge – in the explosive sense of the word – helps them to sap the established cultural order and its shallow positivist conformity, while pursuing their enterprise of *poetic re-enchantment of the world.*

The same is true, *mutatis mutandis*, of primitive art, the third key interpretative notion that links surrealism and Romanticism. The attraction of 'primitive' or 'savage' cultures is a recurring theme in Romanticism, where it can inspire, as for Jean-Jacques Rousseau in his *Discourse on the Origins of Inequality* (1755) – an essay which can be considered, to a certain extent, as the founding document of Romanticism – the revolutionary critique of modern civilization. Marx and Engels did not hide their admiration for the egalitarian, democratic way of life of those still living at the stage of 'primitive communism', like the indigenous peoples of North America. Engels was greatly inspired, in *The Origins of Family, State and Private Property* (1884), by the work of the American Romantic anthropologist Lewis Morgan, whose writings celebrated the free and interdependent universe of peoples, represented by the Iroquois Confederacy. Here is a passage from Morgan's work, cited by Engels, and in turn quoted by Breton in his conference on Romanticism in Haiti (1945):

> Since the beginning of civilization, the accumulation of wealth has become so enormous, its forms so diverse, its application so extensive and its administration so skilful in the interests of the property-owners, that this wealth has become, in the eyes of the people, *a force impossible to master* .... Democracy in its administration, fraternity in society, the equality of rights, and universal education will inaugurate the next, superior stage of society .... *This will be a revival – but in a superior form – of the liberty, equality and fraternity of the ancient gentes.*
>
> (Breton 1999b: 268–9)

Still, the early surrealist interest in primitive civilizations was not limited to their ways of life, but was also, and more significantly, focused on the spiritual quality of their artistic works. Oceanic art represents, according to André Breton – in his famous 1948 article 'Oceania' – 'the greatest effort ever to account for the interpenetration of mind and matter to overcome the dualism of perception and representation' (Breton 1995: 172). He goes so far as to suggest that the surrealist path, at its beginning – that is, throughout the 1920s – 'is inseparable from the seduction, the fascination' exercised by the works of the indigenous peoples of the Americas, the North Pole, or New Ireland. Why such a strong attraction? Here is the explanation proposed by Breton in the same text:

> The marvellous, with all its assumptions of surprise, luck, the fulgurant vista of something other than what we can fully grasp, has never, in plastic art, known the triumphs which it is afforded by such high-quality Oceanic objects.
>
> (Breton 1988: 838; English translation, 1995: 173)

The extraordinary charge of *subjectivity* in primitive arts also seduces the surrealists. Here's what Vincent Bounoure – surrealist and expert in primitive arts – has written regarding the surprising flash, the 'piercing rays', of the eyes of Oceanic figures:

> The power of subjectivity (the *mana* of old-fashioned ethnological vocabulary) expressed by the gaze: there is no reality to which Oceania had been more sensitive. Such an incitement was completely lacking in Greece – Hegel ceaselessly reproaches [Greece] for its marble eyes, the vacant stare of its gods. It's quite remarkable that the expression of the gaze had suggested to the Oceanic peoples the use of methods foreign to the art of sculpture, powerless by itself – always according to Hegel – to express the interior light. Oceania had innumerable materials at its disposal to intensify that strength. Inserted in the orbit of the eye, cowries, seeds and berries, pearls and shell each in turn animate the Oceanic subjectivity.
>
> (Bounoure 2001: 204)

The surrealist Romantic empathy with precapitalist 'primitive' cultures is one of the reasons for their categorical opposition to colonialism, from their denunciation of the French war against the Berber resistance led by Abd el-Krim (in the Rif Mountains of North Africa) in 1925, to their support to the right of desertion from the colonial war in Algeria, in the famous 'Manifesto of the 121' (1960). Colonialism was, in their eyes, the despicable attempt by the Western imperial powers, to impose, by brutal military means, the mercantile capitalist way of life and reactionary Western religions on the indigenous peoples, repressing or destroying their rich and 'magical' cultural world.

Surrealists have drawn upon Romanticism to develop their own understandings of humanity's relation to the natural world, the relation of microcosm and macrocosm, the unity of thought and action, the supreme value of poetry. We have focused here on myth, magic and the primitive arts, but one could also analyse the surrealist interest in dream, mad and/or sublime love, objective chance and the marvellous, as manifestations of this unique reinterpretation of the Romantic tradition – a tradition that drew its strength from the resources of the non-rational (which doesn't mean 'irrational'), the premodern, and the enchanted dimensions of life and culture. However, in all these examples, surrealism radically renews the Romantic poetical approach, infusing it with a radical, subversive and emancipatory spirit.

7 Dada

Krzysztof Fijalkowski

Ever since the New York Museum of Modern Art's landmark exhibition *Fantastic Art, Dada and Surrealism* of 1936 it has been commonplace to group Dada and surrealism together as a complementary, even binary, pair of early twentieth-century movements whose attitudes challenge or disrupt the usual models of avant-garde modernity. This perception of kinship, though rarely promoted by Dadaists or surrealists themselves even among those who had participated in both, has the convenience of identifying two historically and geographically adjacent outbursts of scepticism and freedom, rooted in the alienation generated by the First World War. In particular, the initial emergence of surrealism in France (the main focus of what follows, though the relation is not so clear elsewhere) cannot fully be understood without taking account of the experience of its immediate predecessor, Paris Dada. But this pairing also risks conflating all kinds of complex issues in rather misleading ways. Above all, the popular notion that Dada was driven by an anarchic and overwhelmingly negative urge (that it is purely 'anti-art', for example), from which surrealism salvaged a positive but dogmatic ethos, does serious disservice to both parties.

Taken as a whole, Dada is by definition gleefully incoherent, as the competing narratives of the origins and meanings of the movement's name suggest.[1] Not only did its individual members often take pleasure in contradicting themselves,[2] but also, while each Dada group enjoyed its own specificity, its participants – often moving and communicating freely between these groups – tended to hold quite discrete, even divergent views, part of the reason why Dada circles could be so explosive and short-lived. Dada's drastic promotion of absurdity, together with its disdain for the rational systems behind the ideologies of power, makes it tempting to see it as a model for an antithetical and ungraspable refusal of philosophy, while its resistance to universals means that no stable concepts find a place within it. Dada's challenge is to undermine all of consistent system or rationale; as such its identity seems ith the denial of any fixed and plausible philosophical position. ra's *Dada Manifesto 1918*, for example, mimics the language of logic to undermine the possibility of a single logical position:

> I am writing a manifesto and there's nothing I want, and yet I'm saying certain things, and in principle I am against manifestos, as I am against principles .... I'm writing this manifesto to show that you can perform contrary actions at the same time, in one single, fresh breath; I am against action; as for continuous contradiction, for affirmation too, I am neither for nor against, and I won't explain myself because I hate common sense.
>
> (1977: 3–4)

The rejection or parody of logic, however, doesn't merely expose the absurdity of its system; it also ridicules the idea that thought has a goal or outcome.[3] Can Dada itself be said, then, to possess a coherent philosophy? On the contrary, perhaps, its use of strategies of irony, humour and absurdity ('everybody knows that Dada is nothing', Tzara insists (Motherwell 1989: 246)) effectively inserts a self-reflexive or self-destructive mechanism to prevent its actions from even beginning to constitute one.

Yet at the same time we might also see the ability perpetually and in every situation to pose questions as Dada's fundamental operation: in particular, to interrogate every basic and given value, judgement or belief. In the visual sphere alone, Francis Picabia's flouting of the demand for artistic prowess or style, John Heartfield's reassignment of the artist as 'engineer', or Marcel Duchamp's insistence that neither artist nor artwork are necessary and sufficient conditions for the 'creative act', all force complex and challenging adjustments in the categories of art and aesthetics that continue to tax audiences a century later.[4] Raoul Hausmann's identity as self-appointed 'Dadasoph' is an only half-mocking indication that the category of knowledge itself is part of this attitude: that Dada constituted a 'state of mind' rather than a movement (Breton 1996: 74). It thus proposes a kind of metadiscourse in which every text, image or performance obliges audiences to doubt or reframe assumptions about the medium and contexts as well as its content. In this way, Dada's significance might be to put the fundamental task of philosophy itself into operation in a paradoxical and divergent way.

The issue here, though, is not the philosophy (or anti-philosophy) of Dada but to identify those aspects of Dada relevant to the thought of surrealism. Most first-generation Parisian surrealists passed through

Paris Dada, many finding it a formative but less than satisfactory experience that would soon lead them to dismiss it, claiming that it 'was never seen by us as anything more than the vulgar image of a state of mind that it in no way helped to create' (Breton 1996: 74). Globally, however, different surrealist groups had distinct attitudes to Dada, indicating that the path from one to another was by no means a logical and necessary move: while Belgian surrealism, for instance, emerged directly but rather gradually from a distinct Dada phase in the early and mid-1920s, and future Czech surrealists were interested in aspects of Dada throughout the 1920s without ever embracing explicit Dada positions, the Serbian surrealist group (very nearly as old as the one in Paris) owed nothing to the significant Dada activities happening elsewhere in the Balkans.

Despite these variations, and with some justification, Paris remains the paradigm for the Dada–surrealist axis. Notoriously fractious and complicated, the short-lived but highly visible Paris Dada group (active principally between 1919 and 1922) was driven above all by the energy of Tzara and Picabia, inflected by (and sometimes in tension with) the interests of the set of young French writers around the journal *Littérature*, an alignment that soon degenerated into arguments, recriminations and shifts of position. Yet despite this apparent incoherence, a large majority of the key players of Paris Dada went on to constitute what soon became the far more stable first surrealist group (all, significantly, poets): Louis Aragon, André Breton, Robert Desnos, Paul Éluard, Benjamin Péret and Philippe Soupault, with René Crevel joining shortly afterwards. Of the artists, Man Ray and Marcel Duchamp, arriving late at the party since their earlier activity had largely been as the proponents of New York Dada, would also be drawn into surrealism's orbit,[5] while Max Ernst, the leading figure of Cologne Dada, reached Paris in 1922 (André Masson and Joan Miró were the only major first-generation surrealist artists not to have arrived by way of Dada). Of the key Paris Dadaists, only Picabia and the writer Georges Ribemont-Dessaignes rejected the new movement.[6] Even Tzara, whose quarrels with other Paris Dadaists and Breton in particular left him isolated throughout the remainder of the 1920s, would eventually become a significant member of the surrealist group in the 1930s.

If these facts may be clearly established, the intellectual relationship between Paris Dada and the surrealism that emerged gradually but in a distinctive way through the so-called *mouvement flou* of 1922–24, leading to the publication of Breton's first surrealist manifesto and the journal *La Révolution surréaliste* in late 1924, are more open to interpretation. It would be convenient to view this as a sequential espousal and then rejection of Dada by its core French participants, who then replaced it with a new movement. Michel Sanouillet, the major historian of Paris Dada, even leans towards reading French surrealism as an iteration of, rather than substitution for, Dada (1965: 431–2).[7] The surrealists themselves, however, would insist that the intellectual components of surrealism were largely in place *before* the encounter with Dada and Tzara's relocation to Paris at the start of 1920. The significance and impact of psychoanalysis (about which Dada remained sceptical) should not be ignored; the defining surrealist practice of automatic writing was instituted in the spring of 1919, when Breton and Soupault wrote *Magnetic Fields*. The discovery of Lautréamont's writings had been made as early as 1917, with extracts from his forgotten *Poésies* also published in early 1919. Two of the key reference points for surrealist painting, meanwhile, also predated Dada and owed nothing to it: Giorgio de Chirico and Picasso. For Breton the two movements were not so much causally related as 'in correlation, like two waves each covering the other in turn' (Breton 1993: 44, translation modified).[8]

Seeking to distance themselves from their immediate Dada past, surrealists would retrospectively emphasize their affinities with certain 'natural Dada' figures, above all Breton's friend Jacques Vaché. For the young French poets, Vaché's prestige lay above all in his unique capacity for a refusal of the world's compromised values. Vaché's apparent suicide in January 1919 sealed the status of this genial and larger-than-life figure whose nonchalant irony and sarcasm made him disdain all literary or artistic activity in favour of his notion of 'umour': 'the sense of the theatrical (and joyless) pointlessness of everything' (Breton 1993: 18). Only rarely would surrealist pessimism lead this far, but a taste for a certain strand of dry, provocative and deliberately disorienting humour would survive in French surrealist production – and provide a keynote of Belgian and Czech surrealism – that can be traced running through Dada as well. While it is far more reasoned and coherent, Breton's first manifesto, for example, retains some playful elements reminiscent of earlier Dada manifestos: hyperbole, random typography snipped from found print sources, or the deliberate variety of writing genres ranging from dictionary definition to self-help manual to prose poem. If Breton's second manifesto is more polemical and politically oriented, these 'Dada survivals' are one reason why the earlier text is more accessible and widely read. Humour with an echo of Dada's laughter is a key feature of the poems and prose of Benjamin Péret or Salvador Dalí; Aragon's provocative essay style of the mid-1920s is more knowing and polished but full of sarcasm and satire, as are the polemics by Crevel and other contributors to *La Révolution surréaliste*. An ironic, acidic humour first tested in Belgian Dada-related experiences became the default drive behind much of the writing emerging in Belgian surrealism for example, from its earliest days to its late twentieth-century survivals, and again in Czechoslovakia from the 1940s right up to the concept first developed in the 1990s by the AIV circle in Brno of 'azure humour' (Ingr et al. 2012).[9]

This strand of refreshingly acerbic humour, traceable back to Vaché and other Dadaists (such as the provocations of the poet, critic, dandy and amateur boxer Arthur Cravan), is not quite congruent with Breton's more theoretical and literary category of *humour noir* developed in the 1930s, but it is arguably just as central to surrealism's armoury.[10] But aside from its roots in the convivial wit of everyday life and relationships common to both movements, we could also begin to distinguish the specific functions of this humour for Dada and surrealism. For Dada it lies above all in the rejection of categories and certainties, and in the repeated and provocative signal to a perplexed audience that nothing can be taken for granted – a mode that in the line from Zurich Dada to Paris Dada also has clear links to the cabaret tradition of ribald performance and satirical comment. For surrealism it is the tendency, rather like a model of an atomic particle, to draw contradictory ideas around a central core of playful and aggressive drives held in explosive but fertile tension. For both, however, this humour is above all a work on *language*, in its widest sense, as evidenced in a pair of founding moments: Hugo Ball's cacophonous performative sound poetry ('jolifanto bambla o falli bambla') and Breton's *phrase de réveil* ur-image, described in the first manifesto, of a man cut in two by a window. Puns, wordplay, neologisms or jokes all have their place in both movements, visible most clearly in Duchamp's writings. There is nevertheless a contrast between surrealism's conviction that language – free from ideological constraints and the vehicle of unconscious or desiring impulses – can express 'the actual functioning of thought' (Breton 1969: 26), and Dada's fundamental scepticism about its certainty or stability. Overall, Dada's penchant for aggressive absurdity gave way in surrealism to the unexpected but productive logic of nonsense: the work of Lewis Carroll, a reference point for surrealists from Aragon in the 1920s to Jan Švankmajer in the 1970s and 1980s, exemplifies this interest (and Robert Benayoun would publish an anthology of nonsense in 1957).[11]

Surrealism also learned a particular attitude towards an audience from the experience of Paris Dada. Far from being limited to the avant-garde's usual targeting of a highly restricted and specific public, Dada in all of its forms wished to reach broad, even mass audiences. Through its strategic co-opting of the mass media and presentations in venues the size of the Salle Gaveau (with a 1,000-seat capacity), under Tzara's impetus Paris Dada clearly saw itself not as a progressive movement in art and literature but as a social and cultural force with a far wider critical remit. While surrealism would eventually find the idea of trying to reach mass audiences problematic (navigating the tensions between its hope for an alignment with communism and its desire for 'occultation'), the location of the movement on a much broader plane than any of its contemporaries is one of the reasons why it is a mistake to see surrealism as an avant-garde project. Paris Dada, like Dada manifestations elsewhere, drew its energy and appeal from the dynamos of confrontation, scandal, shock and aggression, and likewise hatched, perfected and broadcast its intellectual positions through volatile tension and contest rather than careful argument. Surrealism too, particularly in its early years, was not averse to courting scandal or participating in outbreaks of affray, and in seeing its critical viability tested on the street as much as on the page, even if the intention here was ethical rather than provocation for its own sake; it would remain unafraid to advertise its position at the antipodes of all conventional wisdom. One might even read surrealism's attraction to the Hegelian dialectic as in part a more formal echo of Dada's insistence that new ideas emerge and develop through tension and conflict, but it is also possible to speculate here on the extent to which surrealism really expected, on a day-to-day basis at least, to attain the Hegelian resolutions of the 'point suprême', drawing at the same time, if at a more subterranean level, upon the shifting, playful and emergent energy of Dada's constant disbelief.

This harnessing of tension and conflict common to the thought of both movements is one of the reasons why we cannot read Dada as a purely negative, destructive and pessimistic force, answered by surrealism as a positive, constructive and optimistic one. For one thing, Dada always contains at least a germ of affirmation ('a little yes and a big no', to borrow the apt title of George Grosz's autobiography). While surrealism too contained strong strands of pessimism ('we are never pessimistic enough', as Breton claimed),[12] Dada's promotion of incoherence and negativity is also, at one level, an acknowledgment that they assert a strand of existence itself, as the culmination of Tzara's anti-logic tirade of 1918 expresses clearly (and in a way that begins to anticipate the first surrealist manifesto): 'Liberty: DADA DADA DADA; – the roar of contorted pains, the interweaving of contraries and of all contradictions, freaks and irrelevancies: LIFE' (1977: 13).[13] Dada pessimism is never purely negative: its function is above all to assert that complete – or even partial – knowledge is not possible. True, Dada could often be cynical where surrealism might be ready – sometimes against best judgment – to place its faith in other causes.[14] But Dada's pessimism is also linked to a wider malaise found everywhere in Europe, a zeitgeist stemming from the social and political debacle of the century's second decade and which led, for example, to Dada-like activity right across the whole of Central and Eastern Europe, reaching Russia and even Japan, in some cases predating Dada itself.[15] Dada's apparent transience – burning brightly but quickly, with nearly all formal group activity limited to the period 1916–22, and in stark contrast to surrealism's extreme longevity (from around 1924 to the present day) – can also partially be explained by its grounding in this zeitgeist.

Clearly, the experience of Paris Dada *was* significant in the formation of surrealism in France, and yet there is also the probability that in more global terms the spirit of Dada was both historically determined and inevitably short-lived.[16] Since, as we have seen, not all surrealist groups passed through a Dada stage, the deeper significance of Dada for surrealism may lie less in Dada as such, than in its powerful model of a *collectivity* – the ability to think and act in concert, even at the risk of interpersonal tensions – rather than an expedient alignment of individuals. Though previous avant-garde movements promoted the ideal of group activity, with the exception of Futurism none conceived of it as an integral ethical community (even if Dadaists would probably have been scornful of this suggestion, and no promise of a Dada ethics is imaginable), lived and experienced as an 'all or nothing' commitment. In Berlin Dada the positions of Grosz and Heartfield, who were both early members of the German Communist Party, suggest more coherent political attitudes and action – though one should note that the majority of Paris Dadaists, reliant on what Tzara, Picabia or Ernst told them, knew little about this at the time. The rhythms of debate, dissent and expulsion in most international surrealist groups, often considered a measure of their dogmatism and hierarchy, are really an index of their rigour and significance, which stems from Dada experience. Dada and surrealism, then, are both at some level all-embracing, ethical projects: never a matter of preference, style or expediency, but an intense immersion and engagement in a collective adventure.

Paris Dada's lesson, however, also lay in the dynamic composition of that first group, its passions, thoughts and modes of action. Again, though other modernist circles notably combined a range of media (especially poetry and painting), Dada's heterogeneity was of a different order. If the stability of text was undermined by strategies of performance, found language, manifestos or absurdity, the idea of painting or sculpture was challenged on all sides by collage, mechanical and technical drawing, appropriation and Duchamp's discovery of the ready-made;

photography, film, theatre, music, even dance, leaking one into the other, all became part of Dada's armoury. Surrealism in turn embraced this crossdisciplinarity and heterogeneity, deliberately avoiding fixed styles, promoting fertile exchanges between media and freely experimental attitudes towards all forms of expression, extending its enquiries into almost every arena of thought and action, and never shying away from its own inherent otherness. Rather as Adorno, late in his life in his Aesthetic Theory, described the heterodox, the 'ugly' or the discordant as forms of critical, resistant and unassimilable expression offering glimpses of freedom in an otherwise alienated world (1997: for example 45ff.), divergence and heterogeneity in Dada and surrealism bear less on a restless will to experiment and diversify than on the need to maintain a critical and mobile thought in which knowledge is perpetually in a state of revelation or becoming. For Dada, this heterogeneity meant that no concept of aesthetics was possible; surrealism in contrast uses heterogeneity as the very basis for a new aesthetic theory based on confrontation of categorical difference: the oft-repeated phrase borrowed from Lautréamont, 'as beautiful as the chance encounter on a dissecting table of a sewing machine and umbrella', releases an idea of beauty from what first appears to be arbitrary encounters, reinserting it into the realm of imagination and desire in the everyday world.

This in turn reveals further distinctions. Where Dada tended to assert an epistemological break from its peers and predecessors, usually rejecting any alliances, surrealism remains open to tracing affinities with certain historical or contemporary currents of thought. Dada's heterogeneity of action and thought is fundamentally irrational, resisting attempts at structure; for surrealism, in contrast, it points not away from systems of thought in their entirety (surrealism is not anti-rational as such, does not oppose cogent thought or the prospect of models and theories, even as it mounts a vigorous critique of dominant philosophical paradigms), but towards dynamic, emergent and plural forms of reasoning: a community of reason that can make room for – in fact privilege – forms of thought and aspirations to knowledge such as magic, analogy and poetic insight now largely banished from the repertoire of Western thinking. For surrealism, such figures as Freud, Charles Fourier or Sade showed the way into realms of non-reasoned thought and action that operated on the expanded and emergent logics of analogy, intuition and the structures and impulses of the unconscious, but these systems of knowledge are extended outwards towards every other sphere of action and experience in the world. Surrealism's embrace of alterity means that each object (and hence each subject) contains the possibility of its otherness, but arguably Dada's playful refusal, and sometimes cruel mockery, of all categories and objects helped make this thought possible.

Plunging willingly into what Georges Hugnet would call the adventure of Dada, those who became the founding figures of surrealism quickly realized that while Dada's spontaneous and anti-rational stance was refreshing and no doubt cleansing, in itself it was ultimately unproductive, limited and even (like much contemporary 'alternative' popular culture) repetitive and open to recuperation: its fragmented revolt lacked discrimination. The role of the fragmentary in Dada production, typified by Ball's disintegrating language games or Arp's torn-paper collages from 1916 onwards, points to how Dada often celebrated and proliferated its own ruins amid the shattered territories that were the legacy of the First World War. At one level, then, surrealism's subsequent task was an archaeology of these shards, expeditions among the wreckage to discover what still remained intact, or had been preserved from previous epochs through having already been buried. But, for many surrealists – notably those in Central and Eastern European locations where the task was to build rather than demolish – the work of shattering was largely over. Surrealism's future alliances with former Dadaists tended to be with those less inclined towards Dada's leaning to a fugitive irrational and its attendant hollowness. But it would continue to make place for a grain of Dada in its thought, with Picabia, Vaché and especially Duchamp all granted room in its constellation. The latter's place of honour, despite his refusal to formalize his membership, seems especially significant, suggesting that it was above all the cerebral, playful and non-reductive phase of Dada that surrealism would prefer to prioritize. Seen from the outset by Breton as a harbinger of original ideas, in many ways the surrealist artists would prove rather more conventional practitioners than Duchamp, while his executive role within the movement remained above all that of (in Breton's phrase) a 'benevolent technician', overseeing exhibitions, generating ideas and maintaining just the right balance between gravity and levity.

Once the recriminations had receded, Dada would eventually be seen by many surrealists as a necessary but youthful moment of revolt, insufficient in itself to satisfy surrealist aspirations for revolutionary change. More than this, we might also be tempted to read Dada as a stage in the savage infancy of surrealism, or even think of it as in a sense acting as one part of surrealism's id, stowed away, acknowledged and paid due respect even if it would be unproductive once again to unleash it. Breton's anxiety over the violence that threatened to erupt among participants in the experiments into hypnotic trances between late 1922 and early 1923 (sometimes viewed scornfully by critics as a loss of nerve, as though the urge to preserve one's friends from harm is somehow a betrayal) indicates clearly the distance already marked between Dada and the movement that would become surrealism a year or so later. Only in rare instances – such as Antonin Artaud's howls of anguish, or the moments of despair and appeals for incendiary violence among the Romanian surrealists in the wake of the next war – would that negative energy seem to be breaking to the surface again.

Notes

1 See for example the account in Richter 1965: 31–2. This incoherence makes the kinds of generalization that follow here problematic: for each assertion, one might find at least one instance that contradicts it.
2 As Francis Picabia famously suggested, '[i]f you want to have clean ideas, change them as often as your shirts' (1960: 1).
3 'Dada, recognizing only instinct, condemns explanation *a priori*', wrote Breton; his earlier text 'For Dada' emphasizes the way in which Dada both seeks nothing and denies knowledge ('Two Dada Manifestos' and 'For Dada', in Motherwell 1989: 202–3). 'Everybody knows that Dada is nothing', Tzara himself would offer in 1922 (Motherwell 1989: 246). Marcel Duchamp, on the other hand, would eventually take issue with the idea of opposing knowledge when his aim was rather to withdraw from such problems altogether: 'the word "anti" annoys me a little, because whether you're anti or for, it's two sides of the same thing. And I would like to be completely … nonexistent, instead of being for or against' (interview with Francis Roberts, 1968, cited in Parkinson 2008b: 109).
4 See Duchamp 1978. Arguments have also been made for Duchamp's philosophical position as expressing a version of nominalism; see Girst 2014: 128.
5 Duchamp made several journeys back to Paris from 1919 onwards, but before 1921 these would all be relatively brief visits.
6 Ernst's signature painting *At the Rendez-Vous of Friends*, painted soon after his arrival in France, gives a glimpse of the hybrid and imaginary nature of the prototypical surrealist group he had just joined: while Tzara and Picabia are notably absent, Cologne Dada members – Baargeld and Arp (the latter would eventually work with the surrealists) – are included among the phalanx of French poets; but so, more intriguingly, are Dostoyevsky and Raphael.
7 Sanouillet specifically characterizes surrealism as 'Dada without the laughter', though as we shall see this view can be challenged on both counts.
8 This set of radio interviews, made in 1952, is a particularly useful, if retrospective, source on the interrelationships between the two movements in Paris (see §§2–5).
9 The term 'azure' is adopted in English translation to distinguish it from the connotations of 'blue' humour.
10 The two categories must nevertheless have some degree of overlap, since Breton's *Anthology of Black Humour* includes Vaché, 'the very spirit of humour' (Breton 1997: 293).

11 Carroll, along with other literary proponents of nonsense such as Swift, had already featured in Breton's *Anthology of Black Humour*.
12 Author's interview with Guy Flandre, Paris 1988.
13 Compare this to the final lines of Breton's first manifesto: 'This summer the roses are blue; the wood is of glass. The earth, draped in its verdant cloak, makes as little impression upon me as a ghost. It is living and ceasing to live that are imaginary solutions. Existence is elsewhere' (1969: 47).
14 For instance the French surrealists' endorsement of ex-USAF bomber pilot Garry Davis's 'world citizen' campaign in 1948–49, a well-intentioned but increasingly compromised initiative in which they would soon lose confidence.
15 See the wide range of Dada-style practices across Central and Eastern Europe described in Janacek and Omuka 1998. If a form of Dada taking root in Europe and beyond can be seen as an historical inevitability, this raises a question: would surrealism too have emerged regardless, given that it too arises in so many places? The corollary of this thought is that what's also called for is a kind of anti-history, focused in reverse on where and why Dada and surrealism precisely *did not* emerge.
16 Breton, looking back many decades later, saw his first commitment to Dada in 1919 in these terms: 'Dada … found itself to be that which responds to a form of contemporary necessity, which is historically to *connect*, in order to *overcome*, certain predominant objections emerging … on all sides' (1993: 64, author's emphasis).

Part II
Key concepts

8 Community at play

Raymond Spiteri

Poetry must be made by everyone. Not by one.

Isidore Ducasse, *Poems*

One frequent misunderstanding regarding surrealism is to see its goal as a new, more authentic form of self-expression that reveals the truth of one's individual identity. This view regards the writers and artists associated with the movement as heir to the notion of Romantic genius: the belief that original poetic or artistic expression was the domain of exceptional individuals. Expression is important to surrealism. As Breton said, it is concerned with the 'problem of human expression in all its forms' (1969: 151). Yet this problem harboured a collective dimension that not only goes beyond the bounds of self-identity, but engenders new modes of collective belonging and community. 'Self-expression' was thus never the issue. The various historical incarnations of surrealism as an organized movement – first and foremost in Paris around the figure of André Breton, but equally in the numerous regional offshoots in Belgium, Czechoslovakia, Britain, Japan, Latin America and elsewhere – have in common the formation of a group around a set of shared ideas and experiences. This community is also a model for a broader political programme: that the experiences at the heart of surrealism can be shared with people outside the inner sanctum of the group. Consequently, surrealism sought to link questions of artistic or poetic expression to the more expansive goal of collective social transformation. In this chapter I consider the role of community in the surrealist enterprise. Community, for surrealism, has a double aspect: on one hand, it addresses the dynamics of the movement's collective identity, particularly the role of imaginative endeavour in the constitution of movement's collective identity; on the other, it entails a belief that the repressive structures of society – family, country, religion – can be overthrown and replaced by a new, non-hierarchical mode of sociability.

A critique of individualism was already evident in the writings of two important precursors of surrealism, Arthur Rimbaud and the Comte de Lautréamont (Isidore Ducasse). Rimbaud took his distance from his Romantic precursors in 'The Letter of the Seer'. His claim that '*I* is another' (Je *est un autre*) distanced the authorial 'I' from the source of poetic creation, exemplified by his claim that he 'witnessed the unfolding of my thought' (Rimbaud 1986: 9). In identifying the authorial self with otherness or alterity, Rimbaud highlighted the movement of affect as an integral aspect of poetic experience. Similarly, in *Poésies* Ducasse called into question his identity as an author by discounting the poetic intemperance of his earlier *Les Chants de Maldoror* (written under the pseudonym Lautréamont). The divorce of the authorial self from the source of poetic creation is also apparent in automatism: writers were 'modest *recording instruments*' who maintained a passive relation to the impersonal automatic 'murmur' (Breton 1969: 28). In this way automatic writing discounted the role of talent or genius, thus making the practice of poetry accessible to all. This conformed to the frequently cited dictum 'poetry must be made by everyone, not by one' (Lautréamont 1978: 279).

In following in the steps of Rimbaud and Lautréamont, the surrealists were aware of the risks they faced. Rimbaud had abandoned poetry; Lautréamont's work was greeted with indifference, forgotten after his premature death until rediscovered by the surrealists. The intoxicating images revealed through surrealism harboured the risk of madness, particularly if pursued in isolation; here the role of the group was to provide a buffer against the threat of an irrevocable loss of identity.

At one point in the *Manifesto of Surrealism* Breton introduced the image of a castle. He imagines 'a rustic setting, not far from Paris', where his friends – he includes a list of current surrealists – 'are living here as permanent guests'; Francis Picabia and Marcel Duchamp come to visit, while 'Picasso goes hunting in the neighbourhood'. Here the 'spirit of demoralization has elected domicile in the castle, and it is with it we have to deal every time it is a question of contact with our fellowmen, but the doors are always open'. This image of the castle can be taken as emblematic of community in surrealism. Although it constitutes a world apart, outside the laws of the city, it is not conceived of as exclusive: its doors are always open. Yet the dynamic of gender is also in play: the male occupants are 'masters of women, and of love too' (Breton 1969: 17) – a point I will return to later in this chapter.

If this castle was an imaginary place, it had its counterpart in the Bureau des recherches surréalistes, the office the surrealists opened in October 1924. This office, decorated with a mannequin suspended from the ceiling, a shooting target and a painting by Giorgio de Chirico, appeared on the cover of the first issue of *La Révolution surréaliste* as the setting for the three collective portraits of the surrealist group. For our purpose, the most important is the photograph of Robert Desnos in a hypnotic trance, surrounded by the surrealist group who listen attentively as his utterances are carefully transcribed by Simone Breton (Figure 1).

Desnos, along with René Crevel and Benjamin Péret, was one of the key participants in the exploration of somnambulistic trances by the surrealists in 1922 (Breton 1996: 89–95; Crevel 1932). Crevel participated in a mediumistic trance while on vacation on the Normandy coast; he then demonstrated the technique to the surrealist group one evening, initiating an enthusiasm for trances as a 'collective undertaking' (Crevel 1932: 185). Although not all participants were able to fall into a fugue state – Breton, Paul Éluard, Louis Aragon and Max Ernst never succumbed – all were astonished by the sleepers' remarkable ability to generate striking poetic images and enter into dialogue with the spectators.

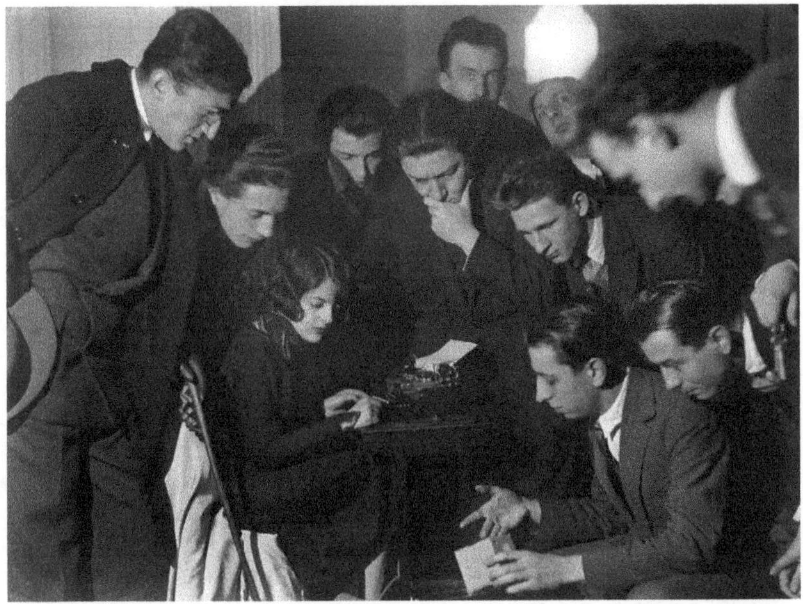

Figure 1 Man Ray, *Waking Dream Séance*, 1924. (© Man Ray Trust/ADAGP. Licensed by Viscopy, 2015.)

In 'The Mediums Enter', his account of the *époque des sommeils*, Breton offers the first definition of surrealism as 'a certain psychic automatism that corresponds rather well to the dream state', and relates the experiments with hypnotic trances to the discovery of automatic writing in 1919 and the recording of dream narratives – a position he would reiterate in the *Manifesto* (Breton 1996: 90–1; 1969: 19–29). In this context Man Ray's photo serves to document this process: it emphasizes the collective dimension of the experience, offering evidence of the source of poetic inspiration in states where rational consciousness appeared absent. Breton would later stress this collective aspect of surrealist practice; addressing the revival of automatic writing and interest in dreams in 1922, he notes:

> Everything that concerned any of us was daily put on the table and gave rise, for the most part, to very animated, very cordial discussions (rivalries arose only later). I believe I can say we put into practice a true collectivization of ideas, without individual reservations. … No one sought to keep anything for himself. We all looked forward to enjoying the fruits of our mutual *gift,* of what we had *shared.* And indeed, nothing at the time was more fruitful.
>
> (Breton 1993: 56)

Games played a similar role of affirming a sense of collective purpose:

> Games, too, were very popular with us: written games, spoken games, which we made up and tried out on the spot. It was perhaps in these games that our receptivity was constantly regenerated; at least they sustained the happy feeling of dependence we had on each other.
>
> (Breton 1993: 57)

Breton went as far as to affirm Jules Monnerot's comparison in *La Poésie moderne et le sacré* of the surrealist group with a 'Bund' as 'group whose members are joined only by bonds of choice' (Breton 1993: 56; Monnerot 1945: 72–3).

Although automatism remained the founding principle of surrealism, collective games helped to enhance the dynamics of the movement: valued not only as a mode of relaxation, but also a form of research; their results carefully documented and preserved, and frequently published in surrealist reviews. These games took various forms – the evaluation of places or figures; dialogues or question-and-answer sessions; experimental research into irrational knowledge; the fabrication of 'exquisite corpses'; 'one into another', and so on – but they were also a means to reinforce the collective identity of the group.

One of the most vivid examples of a collective game is the exquisite corpse. In this game, which could be played using words or images, one person would begin a phrase or drawing on a piece of paper, which is then passed to the next participant, folded so that the preceding contributions could not be seen (Breton 1972: 289). The result was a collective work whose significance was greater than the sum of its individual parts (Figure 2).

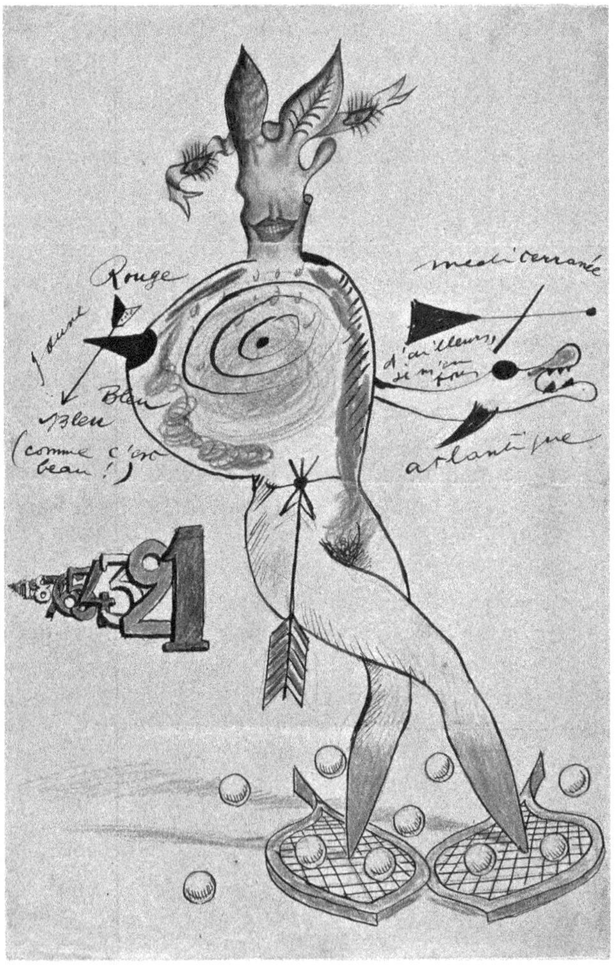

Figure 2 Yves Tanguy, Joan Miró, Max Morise and Man Ray, *Cadavre Exquis.* (Digital image © (2015) The Museum of Modern Art/Scala, Florence; © Yves Tanguy/ARS; © Successió Miró/ADAGP; © Man Ray Trust/ADAGP. Licensed by Viscopy, 2015.)

In 'The Exquisite Corpse, Its Exaltation' (1948) Breton would acknowledge the significance of these games: 'they were stamped with a uniquely collective authority', 'endowed powerfully with that power of *drifting with the current* which poetry should never undervalue' (Breton 1972: 290). Indeed, this 'collective authority' is a theme that runs through surrealist games. Emmanuel Garrigues has noted Breton's comment in the *Second Manifesto of Surrealism* about the role of games in the 'pooling' (*mise en commun*) of thought: collective games had 'brought out into the open a strange possibility of thought, which is that of its *pooling*. The fact remains that very striking relationships are established in this manner, that remarkable analogies appear, that an inexplicable factor of irrefutability most often intervenes, and that, in a nutshell this is one of the most extraordinary *meeting grounds*' (Garrigues 1995: 18; Breton 1969: 178–9). Playing games generates a new mode of sociability in which the resources of thought (image, word) are pooled into a common fund.

Surrealism retained an enduring interest in games. In 1954 Breton would devote an important essay to games, emphasizing their communal character which 'specifically appeared to strengthen the relationships that unite us, promoting awareness of our desires and what they could have in common' (Breton 2008: 883). He drew on Johan Huizinga's *Homo Ludens* to establish the link between play, poetry and community: 'to see in poetry the human realization of the ludic demand at the heart of the community'. Play and poetry were two faces of freedom: to abandon either would undermine 'the best in man' (Breton 2008: 884).

The communal character of thought was also at issue in the debates on the political question. If surrealism began as a 'means of total liberation of the mind' (Nadeau 1968: 240), by mid-1925 it had assumed a more social form, and the surrealists began to align themselves with the French Communist Party (PCF). This orientation was not without its critics within the movement. The stakes are most clearly exposed in an exchange in November 1926 during collective deliberations over membership in the PCF. Asked to state his attitude to joining the PCF, Antonin Artaud declared: 'I refuse to consider anything on a social and economic level, as I have no insight on this level, and no one can force me to think about something that does not enter my mind. … I refuse for the moment – undoubtedly because I am incapable of so doing – to consider questions fundamental to my interior debate apart from myself.' Éluard responded: 'Artaud speaks about exercising thought for himself; this is a counter-revolutionary attitude because thought is for everyone' (Bonnet 1992b: 21). At issue was the collective nature of thought: for Artaud it was a question of individual experience, while for Éluard, speaking for the surrealists, there was a collective dimension to thought. Since they were unable to find common ground with Artaud on this point, he was excluded from the movement.

Surrealism repeatedly attempted to situate itself beyond art to participate in an aesthetic revolution that would incorporate a concrete political dimension, even if this fell short of direct political action (Spiteri 2015). One manifestation of the position was the fabrication and interpretation of objects, which once again demonstrates the collective dimension of surrealist endeavour. Breton initially formulated the principle of the surrealist object in his 'Introduction to the Discourse on the Paucity of Reality', where he recounted his dream of a small book-object, but the fabrication of actual objects only took place in the early 1930s (Breton 1999a: 16–17; Dalí 1998b: 237–8). Objects became the focus of collective activity, a means to reinforce the *esprit de corps* of the group during a period of pronounced tension over the movement's political position (Thirion 1975: 283–6). The December 1931 issue of *Le Surréalisme au service de la Révolution* published the initial results of the surrealists' activities; the role of object would be a recurring theme in Breton's writing of the mid-1930s, including the books *Communicating Vessels* and *Mad Love*, and culminating in the 1936 *Exposition surréaliste de l'objet*.

One of the first objects was Alberto Giacometti's *Suspended Ball* (Figure 3). According to Salvador Dalí, although *Suspended Ball* still employed 'means peculiar to sculpture', it demonstrated 'all the essential assumptions' of 'objects functioning symbolically', which 'depend solely on everyone's loving imagination and are extra-sculptural' (Dalí 1998a: 232). He described *Suspended Ball* as a 'wooden ball marked with a feminine groove' suspended by a violin string over a 'crescent whose wedge merely grazes the cavity'; however, this object provoked a powerful response in the viewer, who 'feels instinctively compelled to slide the ball over the wedge, but the length of the string does not allow full contact between the two' (Dalí 1998a: 233). The importance of the object was twofold: it not only impelled the viewer to action, but the emotion it generated was shared by its audience: 'everyone who has seen the object function has felt a violent and indefinable emotion, doubtless having some relation to unconscious sexual desires. This emotion has nothing to do with satisfaction, rather with irritation, the kind provoked by the disturbing perception of a *lack*' (Nadeau 1968: 188). The important point here is the role of *Suspended Ball* as a shared experience. It is not merely the individual beholder activating the object, but the role of the work when witnessed collectively: the two (or more) beholders sharing this

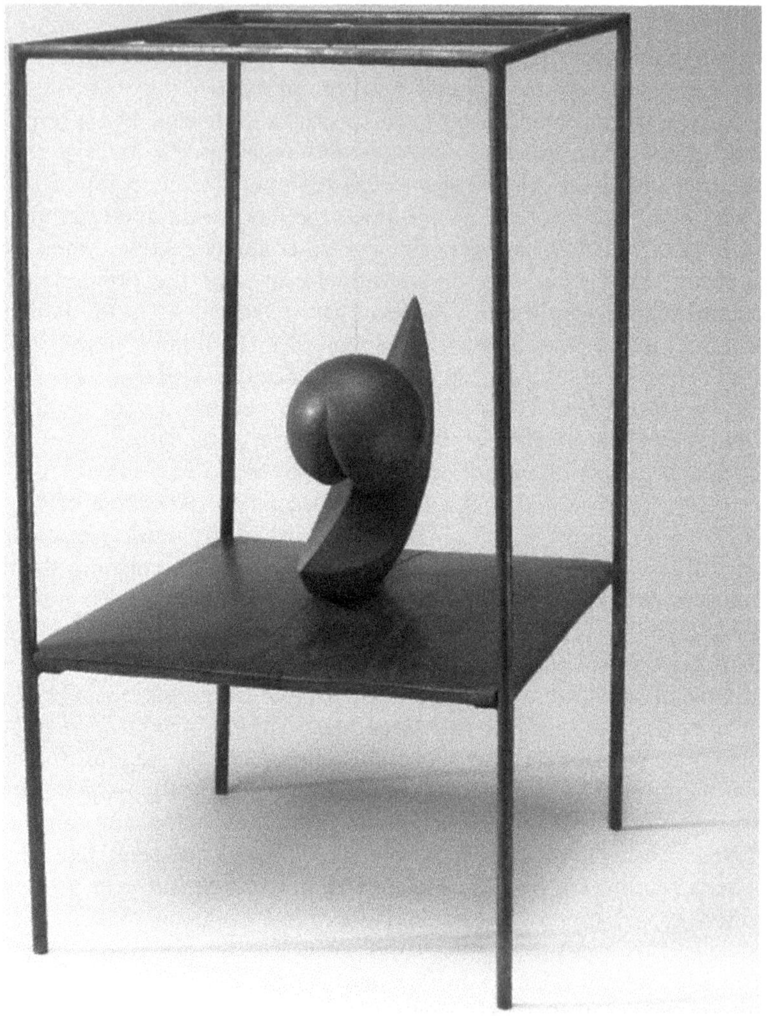

Figure 3 Alberto Giacometti, *Suspended Ball*, 1930–31. Wood, iron and string, 60.4 cm × 36.5 cm × 34 cm. Musée nationale de l'art moderne – Centre Georges Pompidou, Paris. (Photo © Centre Pompidou, MNAM-CCI, Dist. RMN-Grand Palais/Philippe Migeat; © Fondation Alberto et Annette Giacometti. Licensed by Viscopy, 2015.)

'violent and indefinable emotion'. This emotion touches on the experience of community in surrealism.

Allied to the surrealist object was the notion of objective chance, the found object or chance encounter that answers a pre-existing necessity.

According to Breton, the pursuit of this goal required an 'openness' that 'keeps me in mysterious communication with other open beings, as if we were suddenly called to assemble' (Breton 1987: 25). Here chance functions as the catalyst of community: the openness to chance is not only an openness to other beings; it is an openness to alterity itself. To demonstrate the character of this intervention Breton described a visit in Giacometti's company to the Saint-Ouen flea market. Here they discover two objects that obscurely answer their shared desires: an enigmatic metal half-mask, purchased by Giacometti, and a handcrafted wooden spoon that Breton buys (Breton 1987: 28). For Breton the wooden spoon, which had an odd, shoe-shaped rest at the end of the handle, answered his desire for the Cinderella ashtray he once asked Giacometti to fashion. In Giacometti's case the discovery of the mask helps resolve the formal structure of *The Invisible Object*, a sculpture he was struggling to complete.

The found objects here play a 'catalysing role' to overcome the 'paralyzing affective scruples' that frustrated the realization of the task (Breton 1987: 32). Significantly, this role is only fully realized in a collective situation, where the object mediates the desires of the other: since Breton and Giacometti discovered the objects together, the found object does not simply respond to individual desire, but to their combined desires:

> I observe in passing that these two discoveries Giacometti and I made *together* respond not just to some desire on the part of one of us, but rather to a desire of one of us with which the other, because of particular circumstances, is associated. I claim that this more or less conscious desire … only causes a discovery by two, or more, when it is *based* [*axé*] *on typical shared preoccupations.* I'd be tempted to say that the two people walking side by side constitute a *primed* electrostatic inductor. The found object seems to me suddenly to balance two very different levels of reflection, like those sudden atmospheric condensations whose effect is to make conductors out of regions that were not so before, producing flashes of lightning.
>
> (Breton 1992: 701; 1987: 32–3, translation modified)[1]

The important point here is that the shared discovery of the object engenders a collective experience. It is not that the object has the same value for Breton and Giacometti – they actually respond to different objects – but the act of discovery establishes a shared experience of community. Events that in isolation would appear accidental become meaningful when experienced in common, creating a feeling of 'sympathy' between members who share 'this sudden dazzling combination of phenomena' (Breton 1987: 34–5).

One question to pose here is: to what degree is this a gendered relation? The catalytic role of the found object occurs in a homosocial context, between two men. It is perhaps no coincidence that the section on the found object in *Mad Love* is followed by the 'Night of the Sunflower', which describes Breton's fateful encounter with Jacqueline Lamba – the woman who embodies his desire. Indeed, Breton returns to the theme of the relation between surrealism and desire later in *Mad Love*, in a section that describes the ascent of Mount Teide in Tenerife. As Breton and Lamba ascend the volcano they are engulfed by cloud, so that they 'are at the unformed interior, prey to the hasty notion … of something that can be "cut with a knife"', which leads Breton to reflect on the role suggestive textures (such as clouds or old walls) play in resolving the 'whole problem of the passage from the subjective to the objective' (Breton 1992: 753; 1987: 85–6). Like the intervention of a chance event, '[t]he novel association of images that the poet, the artist, the scholar brings forth are comparable in that they take some screen [*écran*] of a particular texture.' This screen appears as an answer to desire:

> Every life contains these homogenous patterns of facts, whose surface is cracked or cloudy. Each person has only to stare at them fixedly in order to read his own future. … There – if his questioning is worth it – all the logical principles, having been routed, will bring him the strength of that *objective chance* which makes a mockery of what would have seemed most probable. Everything humans might want to know is written upon this screen in phosphorescent letters, in letters of *desire*.
>
> (Breton 1992: 754; 1987: 86–7, translation modified)

Up to this point Breton has presented this screen as an individual phenomenon; he next links the individual experience to collective experience. He draws on the example of paranoia (as theorized by Dalí) to note that the image revealed in the screen is communicable. Although two individuals may interpret the same 'spot' differently, each according to his or her desire, it is possible to transmit this interpretation, which constitutes the basis of communication:

> Therein resides a deep source of communication between beings that has only to be disengaged from everything that is likely to unsettle or overlay it. Real objects do not exist just as they are: looking at the lines that make up the most common among them,

> you see surging forth – without even having to blink – a remarkable *riddle-image* which is identical with it and which speaks to us, without any possible mistake, of the only *real* object, the actual one of our *desire.*
>
> (Breton 1992: 754–5; 1987: 87–8)

In other words, the object of desire is not a specific or concrete object, but the affective movement between individuals; moreover, this movement is the basis of a sense of community.

One of the strange aspects of this section is the ephemeral presence of Lamba. Whereas Giacometti participates as an active, named agent in the section on the *objet trouvé*, Breton does not explicitly name Lamba within the book.[2] She acts as an unnamed presence, implied by the use of plural pronouns in the Mont de Teide section. In part this is related to the theme of reciprocal love in this section, which Breton described as 'a system of mirrors which reflect for me, under the thousand angles that the unknown can take for me, the faithful image of the one I love' (Breton 1987: 93). Where the object plays an explicit role in the homosocial relation between Breton and Giacometti, mediating their desire to form a fraternal bond, with Breton and Lamba this bond is no longer contingent on an object; rather, reciprocal love is based on a relation of immanence, where each person acts as the mirror reflection of the other's desire. In contrast to the homosocial community configured by external mediation, the heterosexual community of lovers represents an ideal state of pure immanence.

This points to a blind spot in Breton's writings regarding not only the status of feminine experience, but also the dynamics of power between the sexes. Indeed, following Eve Sedgwick (1985), it could be said surrealism perpetuated patriarchal power relations based on masculine rivalry, in which women functioned as objects of exchange among the male members of the group. Yet the feminine also functioned as a figure of difference within surrealism: an encounter with alterity that harboured the potential to escape the logic of the same and transform the world. This problem is characteristic of modernism, but within surrealism these two levels act in a mutually reinforcing way: not only is the heightened affirmation of sexual difference necessary to negotiate the threat of same-sex desire within the homosocial relations of the surrealist group, but it is predicated on the marginalization of female agency and the insistent imagining of the female body as a series of fetishistic part-objects. In terms of community, this logic is played out in the oscillation between utopian and dystopian modes of sociability: either the phalansteries of nineteenth-century utopian socialist Charles

Fourier, or the dystopian republic of crime found in the writings of D.A.F. de Sade.

In a sense reciprocal love, with its valorization of sexual difference, represents a limit to the thought of community in surrealism. Indeed, the implications of this limit are obliquely addressed by Jean-Luc Nancy in *The Inoperative Community*, where he takes up Georges Bataille's notion of the 'absence of community' to deconstruct an understanding of community based on 'an absolute immanence of man to man' (1991: 3). In place of a notion of community based on either nostalgia for a lost original communion or the self-reflection of the absolute subject, exemplified by communism, Nancy rearticulates a notion of community based on the finite 'co-appearance' of singular beings.

In developing this trajectory, Nancy responds to Maurice Blanchot's discussion of literary communism in *The Unavowable Community*. Blanchot looks back to the struggles of the interwar period when the surrealist group acted as 'the loved or hated prototype' of a new type of group that assembled around the 'ideal community of literary communication'. The surrealist interest in the aleatory, chance and the fortuitous encounter allowed a few reader-witnesses to assemble around a 'fragile event' that, 'due to the misunderstanding peculiar to singular existences', permitted them 'to recognize the possibility of a community established previously though at the same time already posthumous'. In a characteristic gesture Blanchot offers and withdraws this fragile event, comparing it to 'the very ordeal of effacement writing demands' (Blanchot 1988: 21).

For Blanchot and Nancy the work of art exemplifies the experience of finitude at play in the inoperative community. Crucial here is Blanchot's understanding of the significance of the artwork in an encounter with the limits of language, what he calls unworking (*désœuvrement*), rather than the communication of a message. In this context Nancy describes the work of art as a tracing that exemplifies 'the limit, the suspense, and the interruption of its own exemplarity' (Nancy 1991: 79). This opens the possibility of community based on a mode of communication as unworking that exposes singular beings. The artwork does not reflect the immanent essence of community, but exposes singular beings to the limit of language.

Glimpses of this inoperative community appear in the ruined facade of the subject constructed by surrealism. This is not to claim that surrealism prefigured the inoperative community, although unworking dramatizes the relation between surrealism's contribution to art or literature and the experiences documented through those works. More importantly, it suggests how to understand the community at play in surrealism. While immanence was the major mode of surrealism, exemplified by Breton's celebration of reciprocal heterosexual love, there is also a counterpoint that remains unthought: the role of failure, insufficiency and the formless, which constitutes an alternative community founded on the experience of *désœuvrement*.[3]

Notes

1 The description of lightning recalls Breton's discussion of the surrealist image in the *Manifesto of Surrealism* as 'the fortuitous juxtaposition of the two terms that a particular light has sprung, *the light of the image*, to which we are infinitely sensitive. The value of the image depends upon the beauty of the spark obtained; it is, consequently, a function of the difference of potential between the two conductors' (Breton 1969: 37).

2 Lamba's identity can be inferred from biographical facts mentioned in the book, such as Breton and Lamba's marriage. Breton also included a photograph of Lamba.

3 Research for this chapter has been supported by an FHSS Research Grant, Victoria University of Wellington.

9 Otherness and self-identity

Michael Richardson

Identity will be convulsive or will not be.

Max Ernst

In recent years themes of otherness and self-identity have been in vogue, engaged with in myriad ways in cultural and art historical debates, and have entered everyday discourse via identity politics and lifestyle choices. Some of these debates and activities may – probably subconsciously – be drawing on surrealism, although as they do so any surrealist specificity is generally lost as the ideas are taken in directions alien to or even contrary to what has been at issue for the surrealists.[1] This chapter therefore looks at the background to the surrealists' engagement with questions of otherness and identity in theory and practice.

It was during the First World War that André Breton had two experiences in this respect that perhaps more than anything determined his attitudes for the rest of his life and in many ways constitute the starting points of surrealism. This first emerged from his friendship with Jacques Vaché, a young man contemptuous of everything and already embodying the spirit of absolute revolt that Breton would continue to extol until the end of his life, providing one of the building blocks for the establishment of surrealism. In the first *Manifesto of Surrealism*, Breton would enigmatically write that 'Vaché is surrealist in me.' This statement effected a double displacement: it effectively announced an overcoming of death (Vaché, having died in 1919, still lived within Breton) while destabilizing Breton's own identity (he was, in a sense, *both* André Breton *and* Jacques Vaché). This complex play with otherness, displacing the self into the other and vice versa, will characterize Breton's early writings and open up a thematic that will come to underlie the surrealist attitude and be explored in numerous ways not simply in surrealist writing and artworks but also in terms of lived experience.

The second experience occurred towards the end of the war when he treated a shell-shocked young soldier who had come to believe that the war was a fantasy concocted by politicians. Behaving with extreme recklessness, yet never having been wounded, he explained that 'the make-believe shells could do no harm, the apparent injuries were only makeup and, moreover, under cover of asepsis, no one undid the bandages to make sure. He also maintained that the corpses removed from the operating tables at night were distributed around the fake battlefields' (Breton 1993: 21).

These two experiences made Breton aware of the instability of what we regard as 'reality', suggesting that it was constituted by more layers than is generally recognized, certainly in positivist and rationalist ways of thinking. They also undermined the sense of the self, especially the idea of it constituting a unique entity as promoted by Enlightenment notions of individuality. Furthermore, they revealed that our sense of identity is neither determined nor constant but precarious, and this from many different perspectives. This insight only served for Breton to accentuate anti-individualist strands already latent in certain nineteenth-century French cultural traditions and given its most explicit and emphatic exemplification in Rimbaud's revelation that the '*I* is another'. Rimbaud's challenge to positivist and Enlightenment notions of the individual as underwritten by the Aristotelian 'laws' of identity, would be further brought into question as the surrealists encountered Ducasse's *Poésies*, with its demand that 'poetry must be made by all, not by one'.[2]

Breton's experiences during the war also fed into more widespread feelings about the nature of personality as revealed by Freud's research, especially the notion of the unconscious. During this period, and apparently quite independently of any particular concern with psychological theories, this theme was being explored most profoundly in the artistic sphere by Marcel Duchamp. Duchamp's deliberations would lead among other things to his creation of his *other* personality of Rrose Sélavy in 1919, something that would also directly flow into nascent surrealism, gaining a third presence, or shadow, that came to be added to this persona as the poet Robert Desnos also assumed Rrose's identity, adding further complexity to this communicative ensemble. Rrose Sélavy cannot be considered Duchamp's alter ego, above all because 'she' is not an 'ego' at all but more of an emanation, an embodiment of the life spirit itself ('éros, c'est la vie') manifesting itself *through* Duchamp. Her persona is so complex as almost to defy discursive language, standing as 'she' does for the celebration of life, life considered in the sense of the *disponibilité* that would become so important to surrealism; life as an availability to all that surrounds us and that refuses the everyday rules and duties that weigh us down.

This sense of *disponibilité*, going as far in Duchamp's case as the refusal of sexual destiny, offered a challenge not simply to the stable notion of personality but also to the relationship between the individual and the society in which he or she existed. It refused all ties of a sentimental or conventional nature, recognizing only relations that would be affective and voluntary in principle. The individual therefore had no express obligation to the social situation to which he or she had been consigned. Thus the surrealist watchwords – borrowed from anarchism – of 'no master or god': any ties due, as of right, to family, church or country were to be rejected. This sensibility would also be extended to the basis of the surrealist group itself, which would endure, or not, only on the basis of affective relations as a community of friends. Collaborative practices and games, like the 'exquisite corpse', often drew upon the effacing and interaction of individual sensibilities into a collective outcome.

This refusal of enforced ties would also be extended to one's own person, leading many surrealists to place their own selves in question. Philippe Soupault was one of those who had a penchant for carrying this challenge into everyday life. There are numerous anecdotes recounting occasions when he might, for instance, knock on the door of a random house and enquire whether Philippe Soupault lived there, or ask passers-by in the street if they were Philippe Soupault (Nadeau 1968: 15). Meanwhile Max Ernst would soon come to invoke his totemic other, the bird-man Loplop, which he inserted both into his own life story and into his artworks, as a revenge against the nature of the world, transforming a childhood terror represented by a threatening nightingale into a relatively benign confrère.[3] This questioning of personal identity was further informed by Aragon's and Breton's reading of Hegel and Schelling, philosophers who in different ways emphasized the communicative rather than singular nature of our sense of being, marked by the famous question 'Qui suis-je?' which opens Breton's *Nadja* and in which Breton dissolves his own identity into his surroundings as he asserts that who he is depends upon whom he is haunting or whom he is pursuing.

Long before Foucault announced the 'death of the subject' or Barthes proclaimed that the author was dead, then, the surrealists had implicitly taken both notions for granted. Indeed, an essential element of surrealism's coming into being was precisely the recognition that Enlightenment individualism had ceased to be a tool of human emancipation and had assumed increasingly oppressive aspects. Self-identity, as the culmination of the Aristotelian 'law of non-contradiction', could therefore not be assumed but needed to be subjected to a rigorous interrogation, an emptying out. This impulse led Breton and Soupault to the discovery of automatism as they created a composite character from their respective contributions to compose the founding surrealist text, *Les Champs magnétiques* in 1919. This putting into practice of Rimbaud's perception that 'it is incorrect to say "I think", one should say "I am thought"',[4] at first disconcerted its authors but soon came to be recognized as the starting point for a new sensibility. It was gradually realized that Ducasse's demand for a poetry made by all was not a poetic flourish but a declaration of war against the univocity of self-identity. In surrealism it would be tested over the coming years by the period of sleeping fits and games of collective creation and challenge like the game of truth. These experiments would lay the foundations from which the surrealists would variously question their complex relations with other people and the world.

It is also against this backdrop that we should understand the developing internationalism of surrealism. Profound hostility towards nationalism of any sort went back to the earliest days of Dada and the surrealists were not slow to declare that for them 'France no longer exists' (in Richardson and Fijalkowski 2001: 96). Moreover, the interest they sustained for non-European art forms, which they had increasingly come to see not merely as the equal of European works but as containing an aesthetic that challenged time-honoured assumptions of Western superiority, was reinforced by an early interest in Oriental philosophies, nourished by readings of René Guénon in particular.[5]

The crucial event, which deepened and gave a political edge to these deliberations, was the decision of the French government in 1925 to send troops to Morocco in support of Spanish efforts to suppress the revolt by the Berber peoples in the Rif Mountains. Uniting with the Communist Party, the surrealists aligned themselves unequivocally with the Rif and called upon French soldiers to desert. This identification with other cultures was also fed by increasing awareness of colonial abuses, witnessed at first-hand by Paul and Gala Éluard in company with Max Ernst as they journeyed through Southeast Asia over the course of 1924.[6] As Robert McNab has convincingly shown, Ernst brought back this experience with him – whether consciously or not – incorporating the landscape of Cambodia, notably that of the ancient temples of Ankor Wat, into his apocalyptic visions of a European landscape in process of decomposition in his paintings of the 1930s and 1940s like *Europe after the Rain II* (1940–42).

However, neither the Éluards nor Ernst actually wrote or, seemingly, even spoke, about their experiences. Jacques Viot, who later made several trips to Oceania as agent for the art collector Pierre Loeb, was not so reticent, writing coruscatingly about colonial pillage in two books, *Déposition de blanc* (1932) and *Malaventure* (1933), in which he asserted that: 'There is only one means of colonization, that is against the colonized.' But Viot also recognized a fundamental gap between modern perceptions and the needs of indigenous people who live in an 'enchanted castle' we can never enter but only destroy. The experiences of the Éluards, Ernst and Viot were instrumental in deepening the surrealists' political perception of the world and their recognition of the importance of the anti-colonial struggle, which was to culminate in their protests against the enormous and prestigious Colonial Exhibition held in Paris in 1931. The surrealists, with support from the Communist Party, called for a boycott of this celebration of what they called 'colonial piracy' and organized their own counter-show, 'The Truth about the Colonies' (see the tracts in Richardson and Fijalkowski 2001: 185–8).

The experiences of Éluard and Ernst in the tropics, combined with the surrealists' fascination with the work of Guénon, doubtless also lay at the root of the 'Orientalist' phase that surrealism underwent during 1925. This short-lived episode, which at first seems at odds with the increasing politicization of the movement, but which on closer examination will be revealed as a complementary aspect of it, was initiated by the 'Letter to the Dalai Lama' published in issue 3 of *La Révolution surréaliste*, an issue that announced 1925 as representing 'the end of the Christian era'.

As Marguerite Bonnet has insightfully argued, this phase represented an essential passage for the surrealists, by which they immersed themselves in the tropes set up by nineteenth-century Orientalism without being seduced by its exoticism. Recognizing that this 'Orient' was a pure construction having no necessary relation with a geographical place, the surrealists were able to utilize it as a myth both to situate themselves as *alien* to their own Occidental culture and to help them to define their own complex cultural relations with actual non-Western cultures. This 'Orient' was a state of mind that could embody any opposition to the Western culture the surrealists had come to despise, a state of mind that incorporated Russia and Germany into its trajectory; the former for having initiated communist revolution; the latter for its challenge to French rationalism and English empiricism. As Bonnet writes, 'The Orient therefore had no true reality. It was just a word offering a vague image enabling a resolutely Manichaean opposition to come into effect: the Occident, absolute evil/the Orient, absolute good' (1980: 416). It was, in a sense, Baudelaire's 'anywhere, anywhere out of this world', but politicized and divested of Baudelaire's sense of spleen. The myth was an essential complement to the reality of the actual

Orient brutalized by colonialism, as witnessed by the Éluards and Ernst. But it was also characterized by the stirrings of revolt in China (where one of the most momentous strikes in the history of the workers' movement occurred in 1925), Indo-China and India, not to mention the aforementioned Rif rebellion which the surrealists directly supported. As they insisted in a tract: 'The Orient is everywhere. It represents the conflict between metaphysics and its enemies, who are also the enemies of freedom and contemplation. Even in Europe, who can say where the Orient isn't? In the street, the man you pass bears it within him: the Orient is within his consciousness' (in Richardson and Fijalkowski 2001: 213).

Engagement with other cultures was also extended as surrealism developed beyond Western Europe to have considerable impact in Eastern Europe, Japan, Latin America and Egypt. Significant surrealist groups emerged in Serbia and Japan as early as 1925, in Czechoslovakia in 1934, in Egypt in 1936 and Romania in 1940. Each of these groups had their own distinctive qualities and a concern to put into effect a critical surrealism that would address social and cultural issues in their own local situations rather than simply mimicking the surrealism that had emerged in Paris. This internationalization (also promoted by the number of non-French surrealists in Paris) inevitably inscribed surrealism with a strong sensitivity towards issues of cultural differentiation and otherness, subsequently disseminated around the world through the exchanges of texts and works between groups in journals and exhibitions.

In addition to engagement with philosophical and experiential issues around otherness and a growing appreciation of the socio-political and cultural issues relating to the relationships between societies, there was at the same time a growing awareness of the sociological and anthropological implications of the modernism of which surrealism – if often unwillingly and under protest – was inescapably a part. As James Clifford (1981) has shown, surrealism and French anthropology both emerged during the same period and they embarked along paths that for the most part existed in parallel but often converged. This convergence became an at times uneasy collaboration in the journal *Documents*, edited by Carl Einstein and Georges Bataille between 1929 and 1931, in which Bataille and Michel Leiris published essays that explored the otherness of one's own human body (even its alien quality). Bataille's contributions were the most scandalous, as he developed his notion of base materialism through essays on the divergences of nature, the big toe and in several entries in the Dictionary included in *Documents*, most famously his definition of 'formless' pouring scorn on the delusions upon which human self-esteem is based.

Leiris's most important contribution was an extraordinary essay, 'The "Caput Mortuum" or the Alchemist's Wife', in which what is at issue is nothing less than the otherness of god as a reflection of the emptiness of human identity. Leiris, who was training to be an anthropologist at the time and would become one of France's leading human scientists, was haunted by the absence at the heart of his own sense of identity. This led him to participate in the major French anthropological mission Dakar-Djibouti, led by Marcel Griaule (1931–33).[7] As he was to recount in his archivist diary, published in 1934 as *L'Afrique fantôme*, he was attracted to this expedition to Africa precisely to escape himself and to encounter the 'other', only to experience an ever more profound engagement with the 'otherness' of his own self. He would explore this theme throughout his work, but most coruscatingly in his four-volume work *Le Règle du jeu* which, taking its lead from Breton's *Nadja*, engages in an extended and unsparing examination of his own sensibility and is less an autobiography than an anthropology of the self.

If Leiris sought to escape his sense of self through travel, the Egyptian surrealist Georges Henein, described by Sarane Alexandrian (1981: 67) as a 'wayfarer of two worlds', was acutely aware of the fundamental otherness that lay at the root of his own identity from his childhood, as a French-speaking Egyptian from a Coptic diplomatic family constantly in process of relocation. For Henein there was no given identity he was seeking to escape. He was more concerned to explore the nature of his in-betweenness: between the Orient and Europe as a French-educated colonial subject in a predominantly Islamic land.

For other surrealists themes of otherness were explored by taking their own bodies as objects of examination and transformation. Claude Cahun, for instance, taking a lead from Duchamp, transformed herself into an androgynous personality first through the assumption of her name (she was born Lucy Schwob) and then through her photographic work, by which she delved into different aspects of her persona in a way that corresponds with Breton's and Leiris's anthropological examinations of their sensibilities. Going to an even greater extreme, the painter and photographer Pierre Molinier documented a whole personal mythology in which he becomes his own 'other', transforming himself not so much into an androgynous character as into someone who was simultaneously male and female, but also simultaneously both himself and not himself, able to desire and make love with a being that was external and internal to himself.

Antonin Artaud's assertion of the 'body without organs', later taken up and rather trivialized by Deleuze and Guattari, was another extreme example of this attempt to think one's own otherness, or even dissolution, that was specific to Artaud's own psychosis and sense of disassociation, but also gave voice to a sense of personality disorientation that was more generalized within the surrealist milieu and linked in with Bataille's notion of the formless and Roger Caillois' explorations of mimesis in the insect kingdom.

Artaud's personality, unstable at the best of times, meant that the spectre of madness was never far away, and when he was diagnosed as medically insane and incarcerated between 1936 and 1947, the treatment he suffered only increased the disassociation of his personality, something he explored in writings and drawings that give us a more profound insight into the turmoil and instability that lie at the heart of our own being than most of us would wish to admit.

Other surrealists who explored the 'other side of being' and have been able in return to give us rigorous accounts of their experiences were Leonora Carrington and Unica Zürn. Carrington, fleeing traumatized and disoriented to Spain after Max Ernst's arrest by the Gestapo in 1940, was incarcerated at the behest of her family, and gave a compelling account of her experience in her narrative *Down Below*. Carrington's extreme suffering was of fairly short duration and she was thankfully able to recover a relative stability, but Zürn's anguished state, as recounted with equal compulsion in *The Jasmine Man*, was of extended duration and only ended with her suicide in 1970.

As they reveal the fragility of the ego when faced with traumatic experiences, these distressing examples also bear witness to the determination of that same ego to recount, make sense of and utilize those experiences for what they have to tell us about the nature of being in a more general sense. In this respect, the experiment conducted by Breton and Éluard in 1930 to simulate states of madness assumes particular significance. These were undertaken as part of the project of *The Immaculate Conception*, an attempt to give an account of the phenomenology of the life process in poetic form. Breton and Éluard write, in their preface to the 'Possessions' section of the book:

> If I can successively cause the richest person in the world, and the poorest, the blind and the hallucinated, the most fearful and the most aggressive, all to speak through my own mouth, how can I accept that this voice, which is after all mine alone, comes to me from regions that are even temporarily condemned, regions to which I, like most of mankind, must despair of ever gaining access?
>
> (1990: 66)

This universalizing of thought processes, while retaining the specificity and complexity of individual expression, lies at the heart of the surrealist determination to penetrate to the centre of what constitutes being in its most extended sense, and in which our notions of self are always mediated by our relations with our various others.

Numerous other, albeit less dramatic, examples could be given of the slippage of personality in surrealist activities, artworks and writings. It was not something unique to the surrealists but can be seen as part of a continuity that can be traced back into literature and immemorial folk tales of doubling. The uncanny nature of shadows, doppelgängers, twins and so on has always raised issues about the constitution of our being and inspired wonder, but what drew the surrealists to this theme was less the uncanny aspect of such doubling, which generally inspires terror, than what it revealed about their own sense of indetermination about what actually constituted their own being and their relationships with what surrounded them.

This concern extends beyond the living as such to engage also with the material world. This was revealed during the 1930s especially in the interest the surrealists took in mannequins, something that became a central theme in the major international exhibition they organized in Paris in 1938, which contained among its exhibits a whole avenue of mannequins made up in complex ways by different surrealists. René Crevel (1986; see also 2015) had earlier written a remarkable text in which the mannequin is imagined as a being more living than the living, breathing humans that surround it. In this text, Crevel destabilizes the distinction between living and dead matter, something that again is a persistent theme in surrealist work, explored most extensively in the films of Jan Švankmajer, in many of which objects take a revenge upon humans as they assert their place in the world. Objects, as Švankmajer expresses it, contain within themselves the memories of what occurs around them and they actively participate in those events; they are not mere mute witnesses of them.

The history of surrealism, from its foundation as a reaction to the carnage of the First World War and its rejection of the received ideas of Western culture, combined with its collectivist and internationalist ethos, has led the movement into multiple engagements with issues of otherness at both a theoretical and practical level that might be seen as having fed into contemporary debates about identity and self-definition. The urge behind surrealist exploration of these fields, however, seems to have a fundamentally different basis from more recent concerns.

In the early twenty-first century, modern communications have made other ways of thinking accessible to us that were previously inconceivable and may make surrealist explorations of issue seem banal. However, this very accessibility comes with its ow It can lead to a crisis of identity, in which one loses oneself in the ve otherness that was once denied, a warning against which Lautréamont issued more than a century ago. The major importance of the surrealist engagement with otherness – in all its various forms – reminds us that, while our being may be more complex and layered than Enlightenment notions of the self were prepared to accept, it nevertheless aspires to an autonomy that is strengthened by the multiple transformations to which it is subject. The surrealist view may treat being as mutable and in constant transformation, but it still retains an essence that is not diminished by its multiple encounters, both with itself and with its others, which are simultaneously part of one's own self and yet not part of it. In this it is the contrary of the plurality of being sought by modern identity politics, which leaves the self adrift in a welter of otherness.

Notes

1 A notable, but far from unique, example of this is the work of Cindy Sherman, whom Annie Le Brun accuses of being among those who shamelessly plagiarize surrealist artists to create 'the most derisory gender reversals pitiably reflecting nothing but themselves' (2008: 192).

2 Ducasse, in his *other* guise (as Maldoror, authored by Lautréamont), appears directly to contradict Rimbaud: 'If I exist, I am not another' (Lautréamont 1978: 189). The slippage in Lautréamont's language here, as always, is, however, complex, marked by the condition, 'if I exist …'. Maldoror demands autonomy, refusing to acknowledge 'this ambiguous plurality in myself'. This is a refusal of any sort of mental oppression and he is here railing against sleep and dreams as well as against the Creator ('My subjectivity and the Creator, that is too much for one brain'). This 'other', then, is not the unknown part of oneself invoked by Rimbaud, which is still to be discovered and which connects us with others, but rather the umbilical cord that ties us to origins and denies our independence of action. This alerts us to a fundamental difference between surrealist concerns with identity and those of more recent debates. For the surrealists, the ego is not split: there is no plurality of being resulting in a fundamental alienation that needs to be overcome or explored. On the contrary, the breaking down of the individual self is effected in order to constitute a greater integration, in which one's autonomy (to act and to feel) is not reduced but rather amplified.

3 For Ernst, this totemic association with birds had deep roots, going back to his childhood memory of Hornebom, a pet cockatoo, which died the evening before the death of his sister who, he believed, appropriated the bird's spirit.

4 This perception coincides with some anthropological findings among non-European peoples. For instance Akira Okazaki (1986), in his ethnographic work among the Gamk of South Sudan revealed how they would never say 'I had a dream', but something like 'a dream ate me' (Okazaki expanded his

discussion on this issue in his doctoral thesis, Okazaki 1999). This suggests that a reappraisal of the surrealist relation to the unconscious is called for, because this sense of otherness implies that the consciousness of the world (as an active force and not as some form of collective archetype) is acting through the individual in a manner that would be revelatory if we had sufficient awareness of the message that is being conveyed.

5 Guénon in fact was one of only two people actually invited to join the surrealist group (the other was Raymond Roussel); both refused (see Breton 1996: 82–3).

6 McNab's (2004) enthralling account of this journey documents the effect it had on the evolution of surrealism.

7 The Dakar-Djibouti expedition would be documented in issue 2 (1934) of the surrealist-dominated journal *Minotaure*, but nevertheless marks a point of fundamental fissure between surrealism and anthropology, for the latter was complicit, and even in many respects openly supportive, of the colonialist endeavour that disgusted the surrealists. This tension is written into Leiris's account in often disturbing ways.

10 Poetics

Michael Richardson

Surrealism might be said to have been born from an uncomfortable encounter between poetry and war. In fact this is one of the ways the most famous surrealist image might be interpreted: the surrealist dissecting table being the place upon which the meeting of the sewing machine of war and the umbrella of poetry occurred.

The First World War was certainly a determining feature in the lives of those who, a decade after the declaration of hostilities, would unfurl the banner of surrealism, an act that was itself a declaration of war against the society that had initiated the carnage. The reaction of the future surrealists to the war was, however, very different from that of other poets and artists who experienced it. They had little interest in denouncing the slaughter or telling of their own experiences, as did the British war poets, or in documenting its devastating social effects, like the German expressionist and *Neue Sachlichkeit* artists. For the most part, the future surrealists were just as disgusted by the war as their British and German counterparts. Nevertheless, they went beyond this primary response to see it as bringing the nature of existence, and reality itself, into question. It impelled them not to engage with the effects of war but to go beyond them, to create a poetics that would be the basis of a new society incapable of initiating such horrors. The specific nature of surrealist poetics has, however, incurred little critical commentary. The aim of this chapter, therefore, will be to trace out some discussions and disagreements internal to surrealism to provide a backdrop against which surrealist poetic attitudes may be considered.

For André Breton, Louis Aragon and Philippe Soupault the effect of their war experiences was to impose a need to question their own existence within the world as well as their relation to their immediate society. As poets, they were, of course, imbued with what they had been taught by their nineteenth-century forebears, who had already taken some steps in this direction. Baudelaire, Rimbaud and Mallarmé were the giants, but many others provided a dazzling springboard from which surrealism could take off. Nerval, Forneret, Bertrand, Jarry and Cros had all given indications of a new poetics which surrealism would take up and develop. It would not be until after the war, however, that the young poets would find the dialectical key to unlock the Symbolist door and reveal the treasures that lay beyond it. This would be provided by the discovery first of the derisive text of *Les Chants de Maldoror* by the 'Comte de Lautréamont' and then, most crucially, by *Les Poésies*, written by the same author but published under his own name, Isidore Ducasse, and bringing the former text into question. *Les Poésies*, not poetry but supposedly a preface in aphoristic form to a never written collection of poetry, showed the surrealists that the real task of the poet was not to write poetry but to discover its source. Furthermore, Ducasse gave them the intellectual ammunition they needed in order to renounce the idea of the poetic gift being a property of the individual: they would make Ducasse's call for a poetry to be 'made by all, not by one' a mantra. Thus, poetry, for the surrealists, had a particular sense. It did not mean writing verses, but implied a total sensibility, one that embraced the whole of life, that would indeed constitute a poetics, even a philosophy, of living.

Of course, another crucial element in this evolution was the passage through Dada. Dada's dynamism and its negation of traditional values of respect provided a further counterpoint to Symbolist poetics, causing Breton above all to question the extent to which his immediate mentors, Apollinaire and Valéry, remained within them. Pouring scorn on any form of poetics, along with everything else, Tzara, as a Dadaist, advocated the arbitrary cutting up of texts taken at random from newspapers as a means of producing poetry. This renunciation of rational modes of thinking led to an emphasis on bodily expression: 'thought,' insisted Tzara, 'is made in the mouth'.

When it reached Paris, the virulent anti-art rhetoric of Zurich and Berlin Dada was nevertheless tempered by the poetic aspirations Breton, Aragon and Soupault had grown up with. From the very first, Paris Dada was more interested in interrogating than in rejecting artistic traditions. Giving their journal the ironic title *Littérature,* the first surrealists (still Dadaists – or even 'pre-Dadaists' – though they may have been) were taking up as a battle cry the distinction drawn by Paul Valéry between poetry and literature, while plumping unequivocally for the former. *Littérature* was thus still invoking established literary figures like Apollinaire, Valéry and Gide even as it embraced the nihilism of Dada.

In Paris, therefore, Dadaist negativity did not undermine the need for poetry but rather became the starting point from which surrealism would seek to cleanse traditional poetry of its extraneous matter (i.e. literary effects and rhetorical flourishes), thus making new approaches possible. The step from Dada to surrealism was a short one for the poets of Paris Dada and without their realizing it at the time this step had already been taken by Breton and Soupault in 1919 when they wrote together *Les Champs magnétiques* following a method of automatism (writing spontaneously with no preconceived idea of what they were aiming at) that would provide one of the foundation stones of the surrealist attitude, famously providing the basis of the dictionary definition of surrealism given by Breton in the manifesto of 1924: to express 'the actual functioning of thought'.

The essential quality of automatism was to assert a direct relation between perception and representation, refusing any need for an intermediary agent to effect the passage from one to the other. This was effected through the primacy of the image, defined by Pierre Reverdy as 'a pure creation of the mind' (quoted by Breton (1969: 20)). Such images were born from the juxtaposition (and not comparison) of distant realities, revealing their affinities and so undermining the realist view of the integral autonomy of different phenomena (the famous Aristotelian 'law of identity'). 'Poetry' was founded in just such a task and thus provided it with its essential quality for the surrealists and against 'literature', rejected for being confined within its mode of expression and acting not as a dynamic element of the world but rather as an intermediary between the world and our experience of it. Thus the crucial distinction Tzara, now as a surrealist, would later draw between a 'means of expression' (literature) and an 'activity of the spirit' (poetry) (Tzara 1981: 261).

As noted earlier, the surrealist 'negation' of the Dadaist negation was effected most significantly through Lautréamont/Ducasse. Where Rimbaud had recoiled before the implications of his plunge into the poetic vortex, Ducasse, having published his ferocious and disorientating *Les Chants de Maldoror* in 1868 as a culmination of Romantic themes, annulled his own engagement with 'evil' by writing *Les Poésies* celebrating the 'good'. In so doing he effectively crossed the threshold to a surrealist poetics by means of a rigorously dialectical method that undermined the dualism of good and evil that was the basis of rationalism. Ducasse's call to order was the stepping stone surrealism would utilize to determine its own poetic direction: precisely to discover the place where dualisms are dialectically broken down and thus cease to be perceived as contradictions.

Unlike Ducasse's rigorous taking apart of established forms, however, automatism functioned – at least in the beginning of the movement –

by means of a spontaneous burst of energy, a 'holocaust of words', as Georges Bataille would later felicitously call it, which was given a programmatic sense in the *Manifesto* of 1924, in which it was assigned the task of revealing 'the actual functioning of thought …' (Breton 1969: 26).

The application of automatism was by no means as simple as Breton and some of the earliest surrealists believed, however, and it has remained contentious even within surrealism, with surrealists in Belgium and Czechoslovakia above all expressing severe doubts about this formulation. For Breton himself, even though he was to accept that the history of automatic writing had been a tale of 'continual misfortune', he never lost the belief that it provided a means to, 'definitively purge the literary stables'. However, while, as Aragon said, it revealed to them 'a power they didn't know they had' (1990: 12), how that power might be utilized raised considerable difficulties.

In 'Notes on Poetry', a text composed with Paul Éluard and published in *La Révolution surréaliste* in 1929 (issue 12: 53–5), Breton sought to establish the distinctive features of a surrealist poetic as he and Éluard saw it. This was a 'correction' of part of a text published by Paul Valéry under the title 'Literature', in which Valéry put forward propositions he saw as forming the basis of the modern poetic attitude. Breton and Éluard made their correction of this text in accordance with Ducasse's dictum that good cannot be exchanged for evil, making it necessary to undermine an erroneous proposition, thereby freeing the underlying concept concealed within it. Valéry's modernism, derived and extended from Symbolism, has to be put to the test.

If, in Valéry's poetics, the Symbolist aesthetic is taken to its logical conclusion, in which classicism returns to frame the Romantic imagery, the surrealists sought the opposite path: to lay bare symbolism so that its underlying disorder of the sensibility could be released. Valéry saw poetry as an artificial construction, held together only by a tenacious will, a testimony to mankind's highest aspirations and a celebration of the most exalted sentiments of life. But it is also extremely fragile, and its survival at all in the modern world is something of a wonder. It exists, then, practically by default in a world that has no need of it. As such it needs protecting. For Breton and Éluard this is sentimental nonsense: poetry is as natural to mankind as breathing; it requires no subtle development or careful construction: its existence itself provides a testimony to its vitality and it embodies not a celebration but a revolt against the world as it is. Far from being precious it is perfectly integrated into everyday life. So for Valéry, 'Poetry is a survival.' For Breton and Éluard, 'Poetry is a pipe.'

This is emphasized in the correction of the very first statement. Where Valéry had written (1985: 88):

> Books have the same enemies as man: fire, humidity, wild beasts, time; and their own content.
>
> Completely naked thoughts and emotions are as feeble as naked men. One must therefore dress them.

Breton and Éluard corrected (89):

> Books have the same friends as man: fire, humidity, wild beasts, time; and their own content.
>
> Completely naked thoughts and emotions are as strong as naked women. One must therefore undress them.

Where Valéry reveals his Enlightenment formation, by which culture must rise above brute nature and bring it under control, for the surrealists culture is simply one manifestation of nature and is given no privileged status. The distinction rationalism makes between culture and nature is broken: poetry is returned to its natural state. From this perspective poetry becomes the expression of the body and mind at one with the world. Equally the surrealists accept unreservedly the temporal and even ephemeral nature of poetry, at least to the extent that Breton and Éluard refuse to place the value of poetry within a realm that stands apart from or above the historical process.

More specifically, where Valéry had defined poetry as 'a feast for the intellect', Breton and Éluard insisted that it was a 'debacle of the intellect', debacle being defined as a 'stampede, but a solemn and coherent one; an image of what should be, of a state in which effort is no longer of any importance'. And where Valéry had defined perfection as 'hard work', the surrealists corrected, '"Perfection" is laziness.' No doubt both meanings of this ambiguous statement were intended: it requires no effort to achieve perfection; but to achieve it is to remain unresponsive to what is still to be achieved. Surrealist poetics thus accepts incompletion, not for its own sake but because the notion of an achieved work is refused. This, again, is in accordance with the essential and temporal nature of the poetry they sought, one that would not be an object of contemplation, a glimpse of an unattainable ideal, but would enter into a relation with the world, having meaning only as part of a dynamic process. As Breton and Éluard explained: 'a poem is always completed – it can't be at the mercy of the accident that terminates it, which is to say the form by which it is given to the public'. In the same way, where Valéry posits the subject as essential to the poem, for Breton and Éluard the poem *is* the subject and a successful poem can only be one in which there is no separation between form and content. Breton and Éluard also reject calculated construction, refusing to make any concession to musical composition: 'Never, never, never, has the human voice been at the basis of poetry.'

Surrealist poetics can be summarized, as distinct from those of Valéry, in terms of these oppositions: it is natural and real, not artificial and fictive; it is direct and spontaneous, not elusive and deliberate; its harmony responds not to the consciously constructed symmetry that determines Western musical composition, but to the – often discordant – inner rhythms of human existence. For Valéry poetry satisfies a human need for greatness and sanctity although this very endeavour represents a vain attempt to encapsulate a perfect form. For Breton and Éluard, on the other hand, the form is always perfect, indeed must be so, since inspiration is always familiar. What matters therefore is neither form nor content, but a content which is at one with its form. Furthermore, where for Valéry the idea of the poem is textual, for Breton and Éluard poetry does not inhere in the text but extends out of it.

Breton and Éluard's correction of Valéry's text gives us an unequivocal statement of the first principles of surrealist poetics. It does not, however, address the difficulties that lie within the surrealist poetic attitude itself and which have been subject to debate among the surrealists. These difficulties revolve principally around the understanding of automatism.

The most consistent and coherent critic of Breton's idea of automatism has been Roger Caillois. Caillois joined the surrealists in 1932 precisely because he was drawn to the possibilities automatism had to go beyond literature to a realm in which social and cultural phenomena would be treated, whether on a creative or scientific level, with absolute rigour. He left the surrealist group in 1934 disillusioned, not with surrealism, but with what he considered to be other surrealists' complacent attitude whereby they did not face up to the consequences of their own research (see his 'resignation letter' in Caillois 2003: 84–6). At the root of his dispute was a complex understanding of the function of poetry.

From the first text he wrote as a surrealist in *Le Surréalisme au service de la Révolution*, Caillois declared his intention to penetrate and lay bare the sociocultural determinants of what we call poetry (Caillois 2015). Later texts such as 'Les Impostures de la poésie' (1944) divest this intention of any ambiguity. Where Breton regarded inspiration as always familiar,[1] for Caillois poetry was a form of scientific activity, although one with its own determinants.

The differences between Breton and Caillois came to the fore two decades after Caillois left the group. In 1959 Breton published another set of 'Notes sur la poésie', written this time in collaboration with Jean Schuster, which are again a 'correction' of another text, this one by Caillois.

Caillois' original 'Art Poétique' had been entitled 'negative confession of the poet' and published in 1950 as a preface to a volume of poems by the Catalan poet José Carner, but he had revised the text and published it separately as *Art Poétique, ou confession négative*, together with a commentary, in 1958. It was the latter text Breton and Schuster 'corrected'.[2]

By presenting *Art Poétique* as a confession before Osiris, Caillois was almost inevitably attracting Breton and Schuster's ire: 'the poet has no need to exonerate himself before any judge'. However, they fall into a trap here, because this is a *negative* confession, in other words not a confession at all (one 'confesses' what one *hasn't* done).[3] But it is with the fourth statement that we really see the gulf between the protagonists. Caillois had written:

> Mankind's dreams and deliriums have found a place in my poems, but to receive there a name, a form and a sense. I have ordered their confusion. I have stopped their flight. They are fixed in my words.
> (Caillois 1978: 74)

Breton and Schuster's corrected:

> Mankind's dreams and deliriums have culminated in my poems. It hasn't been for me to make them state their name; proteiform, they take on several meanings. I have respected their disorder. I have given free course to their flight. My words bear witness to their perpetual metamorphosis.

At first view there seems a clear line of demarcation: where Caillois seeks to limit the poet's powers and to bring poetic material under control, Breton and Schuster extol the unrestrained imagination and its power to transform reality. The matter is not so simple, however. By refusing to accept any ordering of confusion Breton and Schuster are reducing the poet to a sort of conduit, untouched by the material passing through him. This goes beyond the notion of a 'modest recording instrument' to detach the poet from the poem, making any transformation of the sensibility impossible. How is the poet to escape from a state of passivity, at the mercy of what he works with? Caillois is actually raising here a complex conundrum that Breton and Schuster either refuse to see or seek to elide. If Caillois calls for fixity, he does so to grasp an essence inherent in the materials that ordinarily remains concealed. In this process the experience of the poet is brought to bear on the materials to hand and his own sensibility is transformed through the transformation to the materials. Caillois is actually closer in this statement to the Breton of the *Second Manifesto* who demanded the transformation of being 'into a jewel neither of ice nor of fire'.

For Breton and Schuster, the poet creates as a spring prepares fresh water: it is a natural process requiring no effort by the spring itself. Caillois denies this equation, locating the role of the poet further down the chain, as the water fecundates the land. However, we might question Breton and Schuster's identification at source: spring water is obtained only through a complex purifying operation which requires a particular type of 'sensitivity': water that falls from the sky does not purify itself.[4] And automatism, for Caillois, is a process to encourage such sensitivity – it is a means to gain access to and to utilize the raw material of the mind. Breton, on the other hand, apparently deceived by the seduction which the initial experiments with automatic writing had over him, always tried to legitimate the idea of the involuntary act of poetry even in the face of abundant evidence that poetry could only emerge from a reflective response to the world. So mesmerized was he by this initial excitement, that Breton never seems to have been able to question the poet's relation to the material. The issue was not one of spontaneous creation but rather of the authenticity of unconscious reflexes. This is abundantly apparent in surrealist poetry, which achieves its highest forms when it is manifestly *calculated*, albeit in ways that may be infinitely complex, relating to the relation between conscious and unconscious reflexes. It is even true of Breton's own work, the best of which weaves complex webs of meaning that could not have emerged spontaneously.[5] Indeed, did not Breton often speak of the difficulty he had in writing, the words only coming to him reluctantly?

This was an issue that also concerned Paul Nougé, the major theorist among the Belgian surrealists. Like Caillois, Nougé recognized a disjunction between poet and material that made the idea of spontaneous creation unviable. He thus refused the unbridled lyricism invoked by Breton: '… if words allow themselves to be handled, it is with the help of infinite carefulness. One has to welcome them, listen to them before asking any service of them. Words are living things closely involved with human life. Let someone try to retain certain "properties" to the detriment of others, and they immediately take their revenge' (Nougé, quoted in Matthews 1976: 108).

Moreover, for Nougé the relationship between poet, poem and audience also had to be taken into account. Poetry was analogous to a game of chess, in which writer and reader seek to outwit one another. But the pieces in the game, words, also have their own integrity. Nougé appears directly to challenge Breton: 'one notices at this very moment that it was the blind cult of spontaneity, of unrestricted "expression", that bound the writer almost inevitably to the worst mental servitude' (Nougé, quoted in Matthews 1976: 108). For Nougé authentic poetry must never be arbitrary: it involves a moral imperative inherent within poetry itself. This necessitates a 'transcendence of approbation' whereby a need is realized that 'expresses the fact that everything is possible for man and for the universe' (Nougé 1980: 164). This in turn entails an experiment in the transmutation of reality. Thus, as Nougé insists, 'the poetic problem is inseparable from the moral problem' (161). This moral problem is in turn tied in with the question of automatism and also lies at the heart of the disagreement between Caillois and Breton.

Caillois had been attracted to surrealism because he saw automatism as a means to destroy 'literature'. At the same time, he rejected the practice of automatic writing, something he abhorred as being precisely a literary indulgence of the sort surrealism ought above all to bring to ruin. Caillois spoke not of automatic writing, but of 'automatic thought'. He was concerned to oppose the vaunted 'liberté d'esprit' of rationalism with a 'necessité d'esprit'[6] constituting a sort of science of lived experience, a phenomenology of imaginative processes, in which the dynamic aspects of affective life are given prominence. The determinants of human freedom set by the mind needed to be penetrated not in terms set by liberalism, but on the basis of the demands made by the mind's own aspirations. This involves an exploration of the relation between internal stimuli and external motivation and vice versa. It would not be a question of an invocation of hidden forces, be they conscious or unconscious.

Like Nougé, Caillois saw the poet as closer to the artisan, testing his materials and creating with care and respect. Breton and Schuster explicitly reject this, objecting that they do not observe 'disrespect in the workshop of the artisan'. Disrespect for what? They continue: 'I have picked up a wood shaving to praise the curve, the colour and the quality.' This seems rather condescending: the poet can recognize in wood shavings what the artisan's utilitarian approach ignores or excludes. Fair enough, perhaps: the poet is not seeking to satisfy an existing market as is an artisan (although this may be debatable), but this proviso aside, is not the sensibility of the artisan analogous with that of a poet? Indeed, aren't the best artisans – who don't create to sell – poets? Isn't this even the meaning of poetry being made by all? There is some legerdemain in Breton and Schuster's correction, because what Caillois had written was: 'I have observed the same respect [i.e. for his materials] in the artisan's studio.' They are therefore turning this around, interpreting 'respect' as 'submission'. The dialectic involved, so complacently invoked by Breton and Schuster, is properly contained in Caillois' own statement, for respect, in the sense in which he is using it, implies no submission to what is existent, but rather a refusal to see things *other* than as they are: the poet, like the scientist as well as the artisan, must be committed to truth of expression, which indeed is precisely the basis of automatism: no artifice, only methodical precision (what Ducasse called 'practical truth'). Breton holds onto the banner of revolt but for Caillois and Nougé this is not the issue. They see established forms as epiphenomenal and not worth worrying about: their poetics is elsewhere. The transformation by which poetry is created is not a matter of technique or lack of it, but the result of a decisive purification – the decisiveness that results in the purity of the spring as against a fetid pool in which water stagnates. For Caillois, as for Nougé, automatism is an aspect of consciousness that needs to be provoked by the poet: poems do not come ready-made.

This concurs with the aim towards objectification we see in the best surrealist creative work. Against the arbitrariness of the sign, which Nougé identified as the enemy of surrealist endeavour, surrealism sought a *systematic irrationality* that would provide the platform for a poetics based on the fusion of objective and subjective states.

Thus surrealist poetry as a whole is almost always visually concrete. We find very little use of sound as was so common in Dadaist poetry. Even when sound is utilized it is in a very concrete way, as in the later poems of Artaud, in which human language dissolves into something that is more than language without ceasing to be language: a communication with the world through the ritualistic use of sounds coming from elsewhere. Similarly, Gherasim Luca, a unique poet who established a special relationship with language, constructed in dialogue with the sound of words, coaxes them – in a form of automatism that complies with the arguments of Caillois and Nougé – to reveal hidden correspondences in a way similar to the technique Raymond Roussel used to construct his novels. Luca plays with them, enchants them, gets them to give up their secrets. One of the few surrealists to have an interest in reading his poems aloud, he does so not to communicate but to allow his audience into this coaxing practice: a process of seduction as a prelude to love. This is an intimate setting in which the listener is drawn into complicity with the tearing apart of the signification of words, allowing them to be reborn in new forms.

This relation of intimacy and secrecy is a surrealist characteristic. As Breton wrote, 'poetry is made in bed like love' (Breton 1999a: 149). It is thus, in a profound sense, a love poetry to be experienced between lovers. This should be stressed: it is to be experienced between them, not addressed to a lover in epistolary form: its value lies in recognition of this complicity: the beloved's glance at a moment of pure intimacy. As such this complicity lies centrally in the surrealist will to 'change life'. Poetry is the science of the loved relation, defined here in its widest possible sense, concerned with the encounter between the temporal and the ineffable, is also a fundamentally 'impossible', but not utopian, aim.

In demanding poetry with 'practical truth' as its aim, Ducasse was banishing, along with all subjectivism, any form of personal poetry that expressed inner emotions and feelings. 'The science I am establishing', he told us, 'is a science distinct from poetry. I am not writing the latter. I am trying to discover its source' (Lautréamont [Ducasse] 1978: 281). If consideration of surrealist poetics has been obscured by the initial conception of automatism to which Breton tenaciously but not very convincingly held, Caillois seems closer to giving us a definition that better describes surrealist practice: 'To poetry belongs the concrete science of the concrete facts of nature' (Caillois 1978: 246).

Notes

1 Of course, the surrealist conception of the role of the poet (which unites Breton and Caillois) was drawn from Rimbaud: 'I say that the poet must be a *seer*, must make himself a *seer* …'. This relation of the poet with the shaman is very different from the ethnopoetic ideology that has emerged especially in the US seeking to integrate poet and shaman, since for surrealism poetry is a temporal activity not exempt from cultural determinants.

2 Caillois published 'Art Poétique ou confession négative' as a plaquette in 1958 and reprinted it in Caillois 1978: 65–87. The response of Breton and Schuster was published in the review *BIEF/Jonction surréaliste*, no. 7, July 1959 (see Breton and Schuster 2008).

3 It is strange that Breton didn't recognize this, given that a decade earlier, in *Arcane 17*, he had spoken the formula 'Osiris is a black god', linked as it is to the negative confession, the aim of which is not redemption but annihilation of one's individual self in contact with universal awareness, represented by the god as the sun.

4 The two aphorisms are the following:
Caillois: I have often worked for a whole night and, as dawn is announced, have only a single word to show for all my work. At other times, in periods

. leisure, laziness and distraction, my finest verses are born without even ,ny knowledge. I recall that for water the path from the rain to the spring is both arduous and uncertain. I have not maintained that I am like the spring and able to produce pure water by miracle, but rather to be like the earth and the clay. I filter like one, collect like the other. Verses surged forth at the finish (1978: 80).

Breton and Schuster: Work? Pain? Unknown. I have recalled that for water it was an easy, unquestioned course from rain to the spring. I have presented myself as a spring, producing pure water naturally. Verses surged forth from the very first.

5 In a well-known incident recounted in *L'Amour fou*, Breton speaks of the catalysing effect of finding, in company with Giacometti, two objects at the flea market, but their significance is revealed to him only later, through a process of reflection. The spontaneity that impelled them to purchase these objects was only the beginning, not the end, of the poetic process.

6 This, indeed, was the title of a book he wrote while a member of the surrealist group, which would not be published until after his death, in which he first set out his ideas (see Caillois 1981).

11 Objective chance

Raihan Kadri, with Michael Richardson and Krzysztof Fijalkowski†

In theoretical terms surrealism is constituted both as an epistemology and as a set of practices. The surrealist movement, throughout its long history and its many participants, has developed its epistemological means with the aim of provoking revolutionary change in life and in the world. Yet, while it has been extremely influential and its philosophical notions are highly developed, in many ways perhaps constituting some of the defining characteristics of modern experience, its theoretical origins and orientations have rarely been critically evaluated and remain relatively obscure. Today, surrealist ideas tend to be understood largely through those figures, such as Freud and Hegel, who were the major influences on them and often in terms which may in some respects be seen as having been imposed by some of their more well-known sympathetic critics (Georges Bataille and Walter Benjamin particularly come to mind) or often by such unsympathetic and even overtly hostile thinkers as Albert Camus or Jean-Paul Sartre.

The substantial body of theoretical work in which participants like André Breton, Louis Aragon and Antonin Artaud engaged during the formative years of the movement, however, has rarely been seriously taken into account.[1] In these writings can be found the evolving ideas that were to constitute the many well-known watchwords for which surrealism became, and remains, an attractive and inspirational enterprise: liberty, revolution, imagination, desire, convulsive beauty, the marvellous. These were never mere platitudes or invocations. There was an axis around which these surrealist ideas turned and in this essay we will examine one of its more difficult yet defining elements: objective chance.

As it took form within surrealism over the course of the late 1920s and 1930s, objective chance can be seen to be concurrent in its evolution with the development of surrealism, which advanced well beyond the basic experiments in automatism and evocations of anarchistic revolt characteristic of the *mouvement flou* period of the early 1920s.

The idea of objective chance can also be seen as the main thread, an almost connective tissue, running through Breton's three key theoretical works from this period. In *Nadja* (1928), *Les Vases communicants* (1932, *Communicating Vessels*) and *L'Amour fou* (1937, *Mad Love*) the idea of objective chance gains an ever more sophisticated articulation.

In the interviews conducted by André Parinaud in the 1950s, Breton would claim that 'philosophically, objective chance – which is nothing more than the geometric locus of these coincidences – seemed to constitute the knot of what for me was *the problem of problems.* I was trying to clarify the relations between "natural necessity" and "human necessity" and correlatively between necessity and freedom' (Breton 1993: 107). In order to understand the surrealist view of objective chance, these conceptions of necessity have to be unpacked to see how they correspond with one another. We also need to understand surrealist views of subjectivity and objectivity, of unconscious and conscious thought, of poetic life and mythical life and of desire and love. Objective chance became the locus through which the surrealists were able to situate a principle of agency. Far from the passivity that Sartre, for instance, ascribed to surrealism, the notion of objective chance represents an acceptance of the fact that we have a responsibility for the world while also contributing to the production of the beautiful.

During the war, Breton identified objective chance – along with Rimbaud's derangement of senses and the notion of black humour – as one of three 'continuing' paths of surrealism (in a 1942 interview with Charles Henri Ford, included in Breton 1993). Here he refers to objective chance as 'the place where natural necessity and human necessity are reconciled, the peak of revelation, and the pivot of freedom' (Breton 1993: 187).

From chance to objective chance

The elevation of chance to the level of a methodological principle had already become apparent in some of the earliest surrealist and proto-surrealist texts, such as Aragon's *Les Aventures de Télémaque* (1922) and *Une Vague de rêves* (1924) and Breton's 'The New Spirit' (1922, in Breton 1996: 72–3). This focus was largely an extension of their interest in Freud and the investigation of the unconscious. The surrealists rejected the notion that there is a rational and ordered reality that can be understood and accepted purely in terms of its appearance, as extreme forms of positivism might insist. Chance is one of the key elements that tend towards destabilizing such a rationalist sense of order. Aragon opens *Une Vague de rêves* by identifying himself directly with it: 'And then I grasp chance within me, I grasp all of a sudden how I surpass myself: I *am* chance, and having formed this proposition I laugh at the thought of all human activity' (Aragon 2011: 13–14).

Chance thus became part of the surrealist vocabulary, and the willingness with which the early surrealists were prepared to surrender themselves to it is evoked at the beginning of the second part of *Paris Peasant*, as Aragon muses before paying the visit to Breton that would result in their impulsive decision to take a midnight stroll in the Buttes-Chaumont park in company with Marcel Noll:

> During those marvellous, sordid times, I almost invariably preferred the times' preoccupations to my own heart's occupations, and lived a chance existence, in pursuit of chance, which alone among the divinities had shown itself capable of retaining its authority. No one had preferred charges against chance, and some were even reinvesting in it with a great absurd charm, going so far as to place a few infinitesimal decisions in its care. So I let myself go.
>
> (Aragon 1971: 127)

Breton similarly recounts how willingly Marcel Duchamp would leave himself open to the vagaries of chance by 'toss[ing] a coin in the air while saying, "Tails I leave for America tonight, heads I stay in Paris." *No* indifference involved' (Breton 1996: 97). Less dramatically Breton too would leave himself open in this way. He recounts, for instance how in his youth in company with Jacques Vaché in Nantes they would establish a phenomenology of cinema by which they would drop into any cinema they happened to be passing without consulting the programme in order, through the chance elements, 'to experience the only *absolutely modern* mystery' by surrendering to the cinema's 'power to disorient' (in Hammond 1991: 81–2). For Breton, more specifically, it was the street that was his 'true element: there I could test like nowhere else the winds of possibility'. In the same text, he also speaks of leaving the door of his room in the hotel open 'in hopes of finally waking beside a companion I hadn't chosen' (Breton 1996: 4).

The revelation of chance allowed for the realization of unconscious desires, or perhaps of desires that were not even unconscious but that only come into existence through the operation of chance. This answered the determination of the surrealists not to be mere poets, concerned with the productions of texts, but to act under the imperative, drawn from Lautréamont, that 'poetry must lead somewhere' (Breton 1996: 47). This realization also lies at the basis of Breton's famous invocation at the beginning of *Surrealism and Painting* that 'the eye exists in its savage state' (1972: 1). This may be the starting point, but

Breton is not content to remain there. He takes issue with the idea that the eye is concerned only with what is immediately before it. It may also be directed inwards, seeking out what is not apparent and prepared to have its apparent perceptions challenged. Thus, the 'human sensibility is capable of conferring an entirely unforeseen distinction upon even the most vulgar-looking object; none the less, to make the magic power of figuration with which certain people are endowed serve the purpose of preserving and reinforcing what would exist without them anyway, is to make wretched use of that power. In fact it constitutes an inexcusable abdication' (Breton 1972: 4).

Such assaults on positivist assumptions of the primacy of immediate perception would characterize early surrealist experiments and experiences, extending from their initial interest in automatism, which in itself implied a surrender to chance. Developments towards *objective* chance began with the formal creation of the surrealist movement near the end of 1924. The major work that followed its formal inauguration was concerned with investigating and theorizing how the vicissitudes of chance do not preclude responsibility in forming knowledge, human connectivity, and participation in political action.

The theoretical foundations of objective chance

While the tenets of objective chance were effectively delineated and illustrated through 1920s works like *Nadja* (especially the first part) and *Le Paysan de Paris*, the formal term 'objective chance' was not taken up until the early 1930s, when the surrealist movement had entered a significantly different, more ideological, phase. The term first appears in *Les Vases communicants* where Breton makes a specific link with a formulation he draws from Engels according to which 'causality cannot be understood except as it is linked with the category of objective chance, a form of the manifestation of necessity'. He adds: 'the causal relation, however troubling it is here, is real, not only because of its reliance on reciprocal universal action but also because of the fact that it is noticed' (1990: 91–2).

There is something curious about these citations. When preparing Breton's complete works, Marguerite Bonnet and Étienne-Alain Hubert failed to discover their source (which Breton does not give) despite extensive enquiries (see Breton 1992: 1367–8). Nevertheless, the quotations do seem to correspond with the essence of Engels' discussion of the relation of necessity and chance in *The Dialectics of Nature* and *Ludwig Feuerbach*. Engels' source was Hegel, drawn from passages in the *Encyclopaedia Logic*, in which the 'objectivity' of chance is discussed (although not in so many words). Neither Hegel nor Engels, however, appear to have coined the actual phrase 'objective chance', which seems to be Breton's own formulation, drawn from his own personal experience and the experience of surrealism as a whole as much as from his reading of the philosophers and so it appears to represent a development of the intimations he found in Engels and Hegel.

What is crucial here is the linkage of chance and necessity. In Hegel chance is opposed to what is necessary; as contingent it is whatever within a being does not depend on that being but on something else. But by rising above the merely contingent to assume an objective form chance opens up the realm of freedom, defined by Hegel as its recognition in necessity. The need to elicit 'the necessity that is hidden under the semblance of contingency' (Hegel 1991: §145; 219) is one of the essential steps along the path leading to the realization of a notion of freedom that goes beyond mere freedom of choice. The contingent is a part (but only a part) of the actual: 'this *externality* of actuality implies that contingency (as immediate actuality) is essentially what is identical with itself only as *positedness*; but this positedness is equally sublated, it is an externality that is there. Thus it is *something-presupposed*, whose way of being is at the same time a *possibility*, and is destined to be sublated – i.e. to be the possibility of an other: the *condition*' (§146; 219). It is this 'externality of actuality' that Breton seems to have perceived as 'objective chance'.

Yet, while Hegel and Engels may have been the influences Breton acknowledged in forming the idea of objective chance, it is important to recognize how the idea extends logically from surrealism's fundamentally anti-rationalist epistemology. The surrealists' philosophical pessimism drew upon a broad theoretical lineage – the 'modern evolution', as Breton called it in 1922 – that comprised just as much poets like Lautréamont and Rimbaud as other philosophers, like Heraclitus and Nietzsche.

The invocation of Nietzsche may surprise the reader here, as current studies of surrealism rarely acknowledge his major influence. Surrealist theory is too often reduced to an attempt to reconcile Freud and Marx but Nietzsche was an acknowledged presence for many surrealists, notably Ernst, Masson and Simone Breton, from early on. Even if not acknowledged as such, we can also discern this influence in the writings of Aragon and Breton.[2]

It is an influence that perhaps first needs to be sought through Rimbaud's demand for a decentring of the subject, combined with a derangement of senses. Nietzsche explored similar themes, especially through the idea of *amor fati*, as developed in *The Gay Science* and

Ecce Homo. Amor fati underlies Nietzsche's conception of the world. There was for him no template of the universe to be adopted. Positivism and mechanistic theories are shown the door: nature is not a clock; it does not function mechanically. Rather, 'Nature, appraised by art, is no model. It exaggerates, it distorts, it leaves gaps. Nature is *chance*' (Nietzsche 1998: IV §7; 46). Love (*amor*) and necessity (*fatum*) are linked in a way that has obvious ties with the discussion we have encountered between chance and necessity in Hegel and Engels, and we can see here the root of Breton's determination to clarify the relations between 'natural necessity' and 'human necessity'. Nevertheless we should be careful not to conflate the notions. The two words *amor* and *fatum* – and above all, their conjunction – need to be understood in terms of Nietzsche's own thinking, which means that we have to take care not to mix our fortuitous and familiar notions into them.

In Nietzsche's understanding: *Amor* is to be understood as *will*, the will that wants whatever it loves to be what it is in its essence. The supreme will of this kind, the most expansive and decisive will, is will as transfiguration. Such a will erects and exposes what it wills in its essence and so enacts the supreme possibilities of its Being.

Fatum is to be understood not as an inscrutable, implacable and overwhelming reality, but as the rotation of a need that unveils itself in the awestruck moment as an eternity.

Amor fati, then, is the transfiguring will to belong to what within being is most *among* beings. There is a *fatum* that is unpropitious, disruptive and devastating to the one who merely stands there and lets it overwhelm him. On the other hand there is also a *fatum* that is sublime and constitutes supreme desire to the one who appreciates and grasps the fact that he belongs to his own fate insofar as he is a creator, that is, one who is ever resolute:

> *Sum, ergo cogito: cogito ergo sum.* Today everybody permits himself the expression of his dearest wish and his dearest thought; hence I, too, shall say what it is that I wish from myself today … . *Amor Fati*: let that be my love henceforth! I do not want to wage war against what is ugly. I do not want to accuse; I do not even want to accuse those who accuse. *Looking away* shall be my only negation.
> (Nietzsche 1974: §276; 223)

The connection between *amor fati* and objective chance is further strengthened by what Gilles Deleuze perceives in his analysis of the difference between Nietzsche and Mallarmé when it comes to chance:

> The number-constellation is, or could be, the book, the work of art as outcome and justification of the world. (Nietzsche wrote, of the aesthetic justification of existence: we see in the artist 'how necessity and random play, oppositional tension and harmony, must pair to create a work of art' – *Philosophy in the Tragic Age of the Greeks.*) Now, the fatal and sidereal number brings back the dice throw, so that the book is both unique and changing. The multiplicity of meanings and interpretations is explicitly affirmed by Mallarmé but it is the correlate of another affirmation, that of the unity of the book or of the text which is 'as incorruptible as law'. The book is the cycle and the law present in becoming.
>
> (Deleuze 1983: 32–3)

Close as Mallarmé and Nietzsche are in many ways, Deleuze shows how the resemblances between them remain superficial because Mallarmé always understood necessity as the abolition of chance.

This critique of Mallarmé (who had been an early influence on Breton's poetry) is a useful way of understanding Breton's ultimate rejection of Symbolism and the move into a mature surrealism. Breton would say, 'I don't know of anything more childish than Mallarmé's concern with postponing publication (until he had "applied some shading") of one of his texts he had just read aloud and was afraid might have been too readily understood. Such a distillation can only lead to self-dissolution' (Breton 1995: 6, translation slightly modified). The fear of contingency in Mallarmé's attitude reveals the limitations surrealism would find more generally within Symbolism.

Thus the evolution from the surrealist movement's original pursuits, dominated by automatism, into its more mature philosophical orientation, centred on objective chance, can be understood through the terms offered in the essay of 1936 from which this quote comes, 'Marvellous versus Mystery'. For Breton, mystery is 'an end in itself, intentionally injected – at all costs – into art as into life, [it] looks not only like a cheap trick but also like an admission of weakness, of jadedness' (Breton 1995: 6). Mystery is thus antithetical to the surrealists' pursuit of the *marvellous* – an abandonment to 'the only source of communication between men'. This communication only occurs when life and art are perceived as one, when art is not something slipped (injected) into the current of life, but is inseparable from it. Thus the surrealists' concern to dismantle the idea of individual genius: artistic creation is not a property of the individual but arises from an immersion of the artist in a universal flow of which objective chance is the evidence.

Mallarmé's poem 'A Throw of the Dice Does Not Abolish Chance' most fully exemplifies the Symbolist collapse into mystery as it surrenders itself precisely to what Hegel called the 'merely contingent'. For Hegel, if we have understood him correctly, the dice throw is precisely what *does* abolish chance, as it makes it actual and thus reconciles it with necessity. This perhaps also determines what we can speak of as objective chance, constituting as it does the 'dice roll' that both determines meaning and action from within the encounter and simultaneously opens up further avenues for new encounters. In this respect, Maurice Blanchot seems fundamentally mistaken in interpreting Breton's 'dice roll' as being directed against any 'passer-by' (Blanchot 1993: 414–5). Breton is rather waging war against himself, placing his bet on his opponent, in order to be 'responsible for my own defeat' (Breton 1999b: 12). The encounter does not designate a new relation, as Blanchot states, because the relations are already contained within the determination of the encounter. Chance in surrealism is therefore not the 'indeterminate that indetermines' (Blanchot 1993: 415) that Blanchot claims it is. The stake lies in the way Breton comports himself, steps forward on the field of the present, breaking the mental deadlock between action and non-action. Surrealism's sense of unity is thus not the projection of a transcendent absolute or ideal – in either the Hegelian or the Mallarméan sense – but rather a terrain, a space for encounter offering the possibility of a realization of the supreme point at which contradictions are resolved.

Although Breton seems to have drawn the idea of objective chance intuitively from Hegel via Engels while also drawing in a no doubt unconscious way on Nietzsche's notion of *amor fati*, in the fact that transcendence is denied we may find its actual source in the cosmology of Heraclitus, in which all things are an 'exchange for fire, and fire for all things'. If all things are constantly passing through fire, then both the reconciliation between necessity and chance sought by Hegel and the love of fate extolled by Nietzsche become coherent and help us to perceive its underlying basis. According to Bruce Baugh, surrealist negation is a 'spurious infinite' in which 'a series of negations and surpassings extends *ad infinitum* and thus is not truly "dialectical"' (Baugh 2003: 56). Yet, the refusal of transcendence is not a denial of resolution; rather it demands that each negation and surpassing needs to be tested by means of the passage through fire. For Breton and the surrealists the notion of objective chance becomes comprehensible not through philosophical speculation, but as a result of actual encounters experienced in the course of their own lived lives.

Identity and the encounter

The emphasis on automatism in surrealism's foundation, underlined by Breton in the dictionary definition given in the first manifesto (as an expression of the 'real functioning of thought'), has tended to overshadow the second, philosophical, part of Breton's definition, that surrealism 'is based on belief in the superior reality of certain forms of previously neglected associations' (Breton 1969: 26). What is particularly significant about this statement is that this 'superior reality' is not pre-existing, but occurs through 'associations'. These associations are specified as the 'omnipotence of dream and the disinterested play of thought'. If dream is omnipotent and the play of thought disinterested, then automatism cannot, as critics have often assumed, express, or give access to, a personal unconscious. Rather, it serves to reveal these neglected associations. This is precisely where objective chance – with its focus on the encounter – comes in. The encounter was largely understood in terms of the tension between different forms of necessity: as Breton explained in the quotation given earlier from the *Entretiens*, in which he drew a distinction between 'natural' and 'human' necessity, as between necessity and freedom. Michel Carrouges argues that surrealism's specificity lies above all in its confrontations between subjectivity and social and material conditions, offering a synthesis of subjective and objective states emerging from the network of meetings and 'interferences' between them: 'Objective chance is the whole of those phenomena which manifest the invasion of everyday life by the marvellous' (Carrouges 1974: 180). In its day-to-day relations, and in particular in its constant and expectant quest for new encounters with objects, places and individuals, surrealism would come to be characterized above all as a documented enquiry into the matrix of facts and coincidences whose meanings demand to be unravelled.

While Aragon's *Paris Peasant* found in such facts evidence of a 'modern mythology' taking shape at every step in the urban environment, Breton's *Nadja* treats the tangible signs of this network of the marvellous with more caution, emphasizing their enigmatic and fleeting character. In the latter case, these signs were revealed largely through the person of Nadja, the magnetic but troubled young woman whose apparent powers of premonition and catalysis both fascinate and unsettle Breton, at the same time questioning and destabilizing the writer's identity. The powers of revelation triggered by Nadja, even if they test credulity, occur within the everyday external world.

Breton tells us he is concerned with facts whose intrinsic value is unverifiable due to 'their absolutely unexpected, violently fortuitous character, and the kind of suspect ideas they provoke … which may belong to the order of pure observation, but which on each occasion present all the appearances of a signal …, which when I am alone permit me to enjoy unlikely complicities, which convince me of my error in occasionally presuming I stand at the helm alone' (Breton 1960: 12–13).

This is where we again need to question Blanchot's understanding of objective chance as the 'indeterminant that indetermines' (1993: 415). Blanchot writes:

> In the relation thus offered neither [Breton nor Nadja] encounters what they encounter: André Breton is for her a god, the sun, the dark and lightning-struck man close to the sphinx; for him she is the genie of the air, inspired-inspiring, she who always departs. (1993: 417)

If these expectations are unrealized (or unrealizable), and aren't such expectations to an extent contained within all relationships, don't they still have a resonance that justifies them? That 'Nadja should also be Mlle D. who makes idle, tiresome remarks' (417) doesn't necessarily mean that she isn't the genie of the air, or that 'misunderstanding' was the essence of the encounter, as Blanchot assumes. The encounter does not take place in isolation. Nadja appears to Breton at a critical moment in his life and even if – a big if – she is no more than a projection of his need, her presence, as Blanchot acknowledges, partakes of the marvellous as a chance happening determined by necessity. Yet for Breton the encounter is far more than an 'interruption' for the writer who 'receives and retains, without knowing, for his part, whether the silence … would be deprived of all communicable reality' (Blanchot 1993: 417). We should also bear in mind that we can't really know what the encounter meant for Léona Delcourt, the troubled young woman who described herself to Breton as 'Nadja', since our understanding is filtered almost entirely through Breton's perceptions. Even if she actually thought of him as 'a god, the sun, the dark and lightning-struck man', this may have been her reality of him, and not necessarily a desired one: a response to feeling overawed in the company of a man who we know could be quite intimidating. If we now know something of her tragic fate, we have no way of knowing the extent to which the encounter with Breton contributed or did not contribute to her ultimate destiny. Breton recognized the possibility that 'the magic that Nadja surrounded herself with was the mind's compensation for the heart's defeat' (Breton 1993: 108).

For Breton, however, the objective chance that gave rise to an intense encounter lasting for just ten days would mark him profoundly and have an effect on his subsequent relationships, as recounted in his later narrative works (*Communicating Vessels*, 1932, *Mad Love*, 1937, and *Arcane 17*, 1945). In *Mad Love*, Breton speaks of the particular texture of a screen upon which the phrase we need to hear will sound (Breton 1992: 753; 1987: 86). 'There – if his questioning is up to it – all logical principles having been routed, all the potency of *objective chance*, as it makes light of probability, will be encountered. Everything we might want to know is written on this screen in phosphorescent letters, in letters of *desire*' (Breton 1992: 754; 1987: 87, translation modified).

This gives evidence of how surrealism considers reality to be layered, in such a way that events occur not so much on the basis of cause and effect but due to an underlying necessity that can be revealed through an openness to its structures. Breton's idea is partly drawn from medieval notions of analogy and correspondence with which the surrealists engaged from early on. In this passage he might even be seen as invoking the Nietzschean notion of eternal return and this helps to affirm our view that the notion of objective chance owes as much to Nietzsche's *amor fati* as it does to Hegel's explorations of the relation of chance and necessity. In any event, the surrealist idea of objective chance emerges from intimations with deep roots in the history of thought that have most often been concealed by the rationalist view of manifest reality as that which is always present to the senses. It is the concept that, perhaps more than any other, underscores surrealism's claim to constitute a philosophy of living.

Notes

† This text has been created by us from notes left by Raihan at his death. Parts of his text were relatively well-formed, but others, especially towards the end, were extremely fragmentary. We have had to try to intuit his meaning and as far as possible to retain his style of writing while developing the half-formed aspects of his argument. We hope we have been able to convey at least the essence of what he wanted to argue – MR and KF.

1 Georges Sebbag (2012), however, has recently taken a major step towards redressing this gap.

2 Breton would include Nietzsche in his *Anthology of Black Humour*, and in the collective game 'Ouvrez-vous?' of 1953, in which participants have to state whether or not they would open the door to each named historical figure; for Nietzsche Breton answers 'Yes, through defencelessness (a state of trance)' (Breton 1999b: 1101).

12 The chance encounter: language, and madness

Michael Stone-Richards

> In this primitive that modern man bears within, to which surrealism gives expression, the uncanny [*l'insolite*] unleashes the *feeling-of-other-presence*. ... The phenomenology of the feeling-of-other-presence cannot become constituted except by recognizing all that such a phenomenology owes to the clinical descriptions produced by psychiatrists ...
>
> Jules Monnerot, 'L'Insolite', in *La Poésie moderne et le sacré*

The encounter with madness in surrealism is one marked by the caesura of war: between the Great War of 1914–18 and World War II, 1939–45. The Great War, in which a number of future surrealists participated, produced 'this madman who did not believe in the war' as commemorated in the inaugural work of surrealist experience, the proto-surrealist narrative (*récit*) 'Sujet [Subject]', composed by André Breton in 1918, a text and experience which Breton will recall throughout his life. This text also marks the encounter of language and madness in surrealist experience. Thematically, 'Sujet' nominally recounts the narrative of exceptional bravery of a soldier willing to sacrifice himself although recognizing that in the larger scheme of things he is no more than a guinea pig:

> Would that, with the aid of God, I may one day become war-hardened. ... Suited to the greatest social zeal [*dévouement*, also self-sacrifice], I was destined to be the experimenter's guinea pig. Still, today, unless they persuade me otherwise, I shall perhaps make the sacrifice of my reason to the human species.
>
> (Breton 1988: 24)

This, however, is before it is realized, Breton later informed us in his interviews with André Parinaud, that the man in question did not believe in the war and thought everything about the war was but a theatre, a spectacle to order:

> War, you announce, while in make-belief the official placards and the call of trains arrange themselves. As to that simulation of farewell to which the bit players at the stations are given, as soon as I ignore the scene I bet that they reintegrate their foyers. This forced emulation: no proceedings of high note took place, – Jaurès would appear to me without my mistaking him for his ghost. It is indeed a question of life and death for Paris.
>
> (Breton 1988: 24)

Breton's contemporaneous letters to his close friend – and future physician – Théodore Fraenkel, contain many examples of notations and transcriptions of patients' conduct, writings and conversations as he encountered them at the Neuropsychiatric Centre of Saint-Dizier where he was a voluntary psychiatric intern in 1916. During this time, Breton begins to familiarize himself with Freud as reported in Emmanuel Régis's *Précis de psychiatrie* (third edition, 1914) and subsequently in Régis and Angelo Hesnard's considerable book *La Psychoanalyse des névroses et des psychoses* (1914), and it was precisely the question of what type and model of experience and attention (*troubles de l'attention* was the clinical term used) he was encountering in his patients that was determinant for his intellectual development, and it is, too, this question, this phenomenology of attention and alterity, which fascinated him in the phenomenon of the psychoses. Particularly revealing are some of the passages that Breton copies from clinical books which he is reading in order to convey his excitement to his then close friend Fraenkel who observes in his *Carnet V* (19 August 1916): '[Breton] in his hospital for madmen is moved and horrified to see the insane as greater poets than himself' (Fraenkel 1990: 56). In his letters to Fraenkel he argues for the continuities between *troubles de l'attention* and the figures and prosodic movements which structure poetry (cf. Bonnet 1988a: 26–36 and 98–114; and 1992a: 115–35). In this light, a work such as 'Sujet' represents the beginning of a distinctive encounter, namely, the encounter between language and madness, for which, in 1916–18, there was not yet available any definitive model of comprehension for the young not-yet surrealist even as he would be confronted with surreality, that is, surrealist states, language and utterance where, in the words of Henri Ey, 'experience is marked by the infiltration of dreamlike constructions into waking and ordinary thought' (see 1983: 83–7). From this kerygmatic encounter between language and madness in the medium of a fluid surreality there will emerge what, drawing upon an inflection from Stanley Cavell, may be characterized as *an original shape of madness* in surrealist thought and experience wherein speech, coterminous with the powers of imagination, finds itself subjected, unmoored, and in movement away from the framing powers of intentionality – in other words, the automatism of thought in dream-like movements. This language-based approach to madness will be the mark of the original shape of madness made available by the surrealist encounter with alterity in conditions of war.

The other moment of the caesura might be Paul Éluard's response to the distressed, emptied psychotics and borderline cases encountered in Dr Lucien Bonnafé's experimental psychiatric hospital in Saint-Alban (Lozère), a sobering, humanizing experience from Éluard's direct encounter resulting in the poems and later portraits published as *Souvenirs de la Maison des fous* (1946). Everything about this title bespeaks simplicity, even a post-surrealist simplicity, all the more so when compared with the textual work of *L'Immaculée conception* jointly composed by Éluard with Breton and published in 1930. Consider, for example, this passage from 'Essai de simulation de la démence précoce', which it is known from the Musée Picasso manuscript was written by Éluard:

> The woman here an arm on her stony head of pralines which leave from here without one being able to see in clearly because it's a little more of noon here leaving from the laughter in the teeth which extend throughout the palace of the Danaides which I caress with my tongue without thinking that the day of God has arrived – music at the head – for the little girls who mourn the seed and whom one looks at without seeing them cry through the hands of the Graces on the window of the fourth floor with reseda and cat that the fronde takes in the rear and the feast day.
>
> (Breton 1988: 859; English translation, Breton and Éluard 1990: 69)[1]

All the by now accustomed hallmarks of surrealist language are present: rapidity of image movement, fluidity of image and concomitant dematerialization of matter; rapid and unforeseen juxtapositions; absence of causal connectivity working with and against the presence of grammatical and thus *logical* markers of connectivity, etc. It is not a work of particularity or lived experience but is rather concerned with the putting into movement of the structural aspects of a language, of experience as *Erfahrung* rather than *Erlebnisse* (lived). Where *L'Immaculée conception* is a work of research – at once linguistic and dramaturgical – predicated upon the power of language to evoke as well as project certain borderline or psychotic states, a work of deep process of generation and fabrication – complex in rhythms, imagery, tone, address, dramas of situations and liminality – *Souvenirs de la Maison des fous* is marked by a steady, earned simplicity in the voice of address, a poetry of *Erlebnisse* and so a poetry of the direct rather than the structural, an attempt to convey an interiority, even the blocked interiority of the subject, rather than exteriority: direct observation, perceptual stability, and empathy as the principal embodied mark of moral psychology, and everywhere humility confronted with distress, physical collapse, mental disintegration, the recognition of the profound apathy of the poems' subjects, in a situation where life itself has slowed as if to make visible the appearance of nothingness – 'Le monde est nul' (the world is null, empty, nothing, voided) is the title of the first division, while a poem devoted to a small and beautiful woman sees the loss of focus in her eyes as dispossession as 'I look at/ The faint day pleasurelessly marry her vague eyes', and then another poem concludes with the simple declaration: 'She no longer speaks she no longer eats.' (One can scarcely imagine any subject in *L'Immaculée conception* not part of a hyper-machine for the production of speech.) When published with the graphite portraits made by Gérard Vulliamy, Éluard's son-in-law, the language of inertia and psychic entropy of the poems of *Souvenirs de la Maison des fous* assume the status of a full encounter with the face of madness. From the opening poem ('Buried shaking within their shroud/ Women of chalk women of soot/ … Their own image eternally alone'), the face as image and medium is a key aspect of the working of this sequence of poems, all the more so as built into the comprehension of these poems, each of which addresses a woman, is that Éluard is the surrealist lyric poet par excellence, the poet of the celebration of female beauty. The world of mental collapse – 'Crushed weighed down fit for ageing …/ Fish were leaving from all the oceans' – is figured not simply through the body but activated through the reciprocity of the encounter with the face. Of course, there are genres, pictorial and otherwise, dealing with *maisons des fous* (for example, Goya), the direct engagement with the face of madness (for example, Géricault), but there are few writers or thinkers able to encompass – who have traversed – the linguistic and affective economies of Éluard from *L'Immaculée conception* to *Souvenirs de la Maison des fous* and whose work thereby may leave us with complex continuities and aleatoric movements rather than mere renunciations.

Underlying Éluard's no less than Breton's trajectory are acts of witnessing, imaginative engagement, and an ethical refusal of ready-made thought which serves as a pretext for locking people up. In so doing the surrealists welcome the availability of what Éluard following Heraclitus speaks of as a thought *common to all*, without which no ascription still less language of madness could make sense. It is a form of engagement predicated upon a thinking of *experience* in surrealist sensibility where the poetic and the aesthetic are understood as forms for the realization, construction and comprehension of limit-experience, which we shall characterize initially as that mode of experience in which there is always present an enigmatic and thus resistant element or core in subjective appropriation, the result of which is a pushing towards psychic unbinding from an environment or object. The madness recorded in the *Souvenirs de la Maison des fous* is qualitatively different than that in *L'Immaculée conception* principally in the difference between *Erfahrung* and *Erlebnisse*, or between structure and particularity, between language as such and a particular body. In all cases the monologues, the drawings and writings of these marginalized persons connected with surrealism – 'Sujet', Nadja, Artaud, etc. – are processes of mediation as well as encounters with and negotiations of *im-mediating experience*, hence the problematic for surrealism no less than for the history of thought lies in the terms in which the discourses inaugurated by surrealism should be placed, 'To speak of madness – in what language?' (Felman 1985/1987: 17).

Surrealism and a philosophical anthropology of madness

> In speaking and writing something mad occurs: the true conversation is a pure play of words.
>
> Novalis, 'Monologue', 1798

Following earlier generations of commentators on surrealism, such as Ey, Sartre, Monnerot and J.-B. Pontalis all the way to the work of Vincent Bounoure and Vratislav Effenberger in *La Civilisation surréaliste*, it needs to be plainly stated that surrealism is a philosophical anthropology. Its thinking of madness is part of its anthropology, that is, its thinking of *what is common to all*. The expression *what is common to all* is, of course, taken from Heraclitus and it is part of a developing use of Heraclitus by the surrealists, in part spurred by Solovine's French translation of the Heraclitus *Fragments* published in 1931, but it is present most tellingly in the jointly composed *L'Immaculée conception*. According to the introduction written by Éluard to the division of the work called 'Les Possessions' (written by Éluard, as the manuscript reveals), the practice of writing deployed by the two authors did not aim to produce a pastiche of clinical language, but rather to show that 'the mind of the normal man *poetically* laid out is capable of reproducing in its broad outlines the most paradoxical and the most eccentric verbal manifestations, [and] that it is within the power of the mind in this poetic state to submit itself voluntarily to the principal delirious ideas without experiencing a lasting disturbance [*trouble durable*]' (Breton 1988: 848; Breton and Éluard 1990: 47). In other words, the linguistic powers of this madman who did not believe in the war from 'Sujet' and Breton's encounter with the derangement of the war neuroses is the subject of human poetic creation and the aim of the new kind of prose *work* called *L'Immaculée conception*. Éluard's statement speaks of a poetic capacity or power, that *poetically* man becomes capable of a certain kind of identification, which identification, one presumes, must in turn be that of poeticality, an enlarged sense of being. Very soon, voice comes to be the means for this enlargement (Celan 1988: 58–60), a voice, furthermore, removed to a capaciousness beyond itself – the question of place – through another identification, this time with what is common, *le commun des mortels*:

> If I may successively allow to be spoken through my own mouth the richest as also the poorest being in the world, the blind and the hallucinated, the most fearful as also the most menacing being, how should I admit that this voice which is, ultimately, mine alone, comes to me from places even provisionally condemned, from places to which, in the lot common to all mortals, I must despair of ever having access?
>
> (Breton 1988: 848–9; Breton and Éluard 1990: 48)

If language is here conceived in terms of *Erfahrung* it is then not the expression of an individual but of what is possible as such, and how, asks Éluard, can anything that belongs to the nature of language itself as such (*le commun des mortels*) be condemnable, and why should it not be permissible to explore new forms of access to 'the richest as also the poorest being in the world'? Finally, in 1935, Éluard, for himself and Breton, writes a preface for the Japanese translation of *L'Immaculée conception*, wherein he condenses the developing presence of Heraclitus in saying that sustained reflection on the possibilities of thought, 'la pensée commun à tous' (the thought common to all), will reveal all hierarchy amongst men as vain; instead, 'To be two in destroying, in constructing, in living, that is already to be all, to be the other to infinity and no longer oneself' ('Note à propos d'une collaboration,' in Breton 1992: 564; Breton and Éluard 1990: 23). This compact of plural voices along with the sense of movement – of place, of voice, of subjection – is the experience, poetically achieved, which underwrites, says Éluard, the possibility of 'a poetic philosophy which, without ever making language subject to reason, leads, however, one day to the elaboration of a true philosophy of poetry' ('Note à propos d'une collaboration,' in Breton 1992: 564; Breton and Éluard 1990: 23). The inversion, from *philosophie poétique* to *philosophie de la poésie*, is intentionally pointed by Éluard. By this inversion he intends to show how what is given is not only continuous with but itself makes available philosophical reflection in a movement shadowing the terms of Hegelian *Aufhebung*: the movement of destruction and construction, of two into a third to infinity, wherein one is no longer *one-self* (think of this as a naturalization, as it were, of the psychotic phenomenon of hearing voices), the movement of lived measure (passing through the measureless) which bears witness to the primary significance, if not insight, of *L'Immaculée conception*, which is not so much the simulation of the language of madness (the question of what Breton and Éluard mean by 'hypersimulation' remains open) as the recognition that madness is the human anthropological condition. This helps one to understand the demand by Breton and Éluard to recognize 'the reality of this madness and affirm its existence latent in the human mind' (Breton and Éluard 1991: 163; Breton and Éluard 1990: 25), which is to say that Breton and Éluard accept the thesis that the risk of madness is constitutive of what it is to be human. This is the anthropological claim of the surrealist researches into the conjuncture of language, madness and expressive measure, which partakes with Freud and subsequently Lacan in the elaboration of an original shape of madness. When Lacan writes that 'he does not assume who wishes it the risks which envelop madness', or, 'He does not become mad who wishes it', it could well be thought that the statements target certain Romantic, bohemian or even surrealist attitudes; but Lacan restates the same anthropological insight about the necessary latency of madness (*folie*) as a condition of human existence when, in the same essay on 'Propos sur la causalité psychique,' he observes that

> [f]ar from it being then that madness is the contingent fact of the fragilities of [man's] organism, *it is the permanent virtuality of an open fault in man's essence ....*
>
> And the being of man, not only cannot be understood without madness, it would not be the being of *man if he did not carry in him madness as the limit of his liberty.*
>
> (Lacan 1966: 176, my emphases)

Henri Maldiney in his great work *Penser l'homme et la folie* will express this insight with acute simplicity: 'Il n'y a de psychose que d'un existant' (There's no psychosis save for one who exists) (Maldiney 1991/1997: 13). For Éluard and Breton the philosophical formulation available to them for this anthropology – a formulation which also made available a certain way of thinking – came through Heraclitus but also from Hegel, the Hegel of the *Philosophie de l'esprit* (in Véra's translation as read by Breton and Éluard), where Hegel writes that it is precisely because man can think himself that he has the *privilege* of madness per se: 'It is to man alone that it is given to think himself in this state of complete abstraction of the self. It is what, so to speak, makes possible the privilege of madness' (Hegel 1867: 382–3; English translation, 1971: 128).

The *Manifeste du surréalisme* (1924), codifying the practices and positions collectively developed between 1922 and 1924, and so preparing the surrealist experience for transmission, opens with an account of the fragility of belief in life itself, a belief so fragile that it requires powerful and repeated acts of imagination, the ultimate psychic source of which is childhood. Within four paragraphs of the opening account of imagination and childhood we learn, almost by a surprise, an indirection, that '[t]here remains madness [*Reste la folie*], "the madness that one locks up".' If there is from the inaugural encounters definitive of surrealist experience a phenomenology of alterity (Monnerot's *sentiment-de-présence-autre*/feeling-of-other-presence) and a related experimental epistemology, there is, too, another aspect of the discourse of surrealism, namely, an anger at, and a refusal of, the prevailing social constraints for *talking about* madness which cannot but touch upon the values and sought-after performative identities pursued by the surrealist group. *They locked up Baudelaire; they locked up Sade, Nietzsche*, etc., declares Breton after learning of the incarceration of Nadja. This is *the madness that one locks up*. It is the rhetoric of refusal, and its facility, its glamour, one may say, which has shaped much of the reception of the surrealist approach to madness and obscured its moral seriousness, along with the seriousness and analytic imagination that enabled a great historian of psychiatry such as Henri F. Ellenberger (1970: 837) to comment that '[h]ad Breton taken his medical degree and remained in active psychiatry, he could very well, with [his] new methods, have become the founder of a new trend of dynamic psychiatry.' It is the same poetic and anthropological seriousness present in a great poet such as Paul Celan, whose own apprenticeship in surrealism is in danger of being lost, when he asks: 'Can we now perhaps find the place [*Ort*] where strangeness [*das Fremde*] was present?' (Celan 1988: 51), which is to say, the place from which the human voice – language – begins in alterity, always close to madness. In a range of thinking, from Breton's encounter with the patients of the war neuroses and later Nadja, up to Éluard's encounter with the face of madness, and all the way to

Artaud's psychotic collapse and disintegration after his visit to Ireland in 1937 and the experiences recounted in Leonora Carrington's *Down Below* and Unica Zürn's *The Man of Jasmine*, the varied languages of surrealist culture allow one to grasp the extent to which madness (*folie*), a philosophical and not a technically clinical term (such as insanity or psychosis), is a continuum of experience, 'the well-known absence of frontier between *not*-madness and madness' (Breton 1988: 741; English translation, 1960: 144) marked by the unworking of language and the withdrawal (the *retrait*) of reason, that is, the withdrawal of the sociality or visibility of thought. When in the experience and performance of madness perception becomes destructured or disordered this is not to be grasped as a function of the narrowly neurological, that is, the organic condition, but is instead a hermeneutic phenomenon, that is, a function of the relations between existents and their psychic historicities, from which it may be understood that there is nothing in the mad that is not also and already present in the sane; rather, in the experience of madness all is become a system marked by intensity, repetition and *compulsion* as elements of dreamlike constructions enter the perception of the world. The language and discourses of madness in surrealism – chance encounter, the passage from voice to language, alterity, the moment of the violence of passion in perception – foreground such an anthropology and an experimental epistemology with significant implications that have until now largely been ignored in the literature.

Note

1 Translations of the French are throughout my own, but citations of English translations are given, if available, for reference.

13 Dream: a manifesto of the manifest dream

Georges Sebbag

Published in autumn 1924, Louis Aragon's *Une Vague de rêves* (*A Wave of Dreams*) and André Breton's *Manifesto of Surrealism* seemed like two manifest dream manifestoes not overburdened with Freudian interpretation. The dream narrative was a surrealist conquest which followed in the footsteps of Zhuang Zhou, Diderot, Grandville, Hervey de Saint-Denys, Jarry and Bergson. Dream notation was a surrealist duty, almost, performed most notably by Breton, Leiris and Aragon. After 1945, the contribution of the Romanian surrealist Dolfi Trost and the critical eye of Roger Caillois underlined the importance and the necessity of debating the dream.

D'Alembert's dream

In 1769, Diderot used his encyclopaedist friend D'Alembert for dramatic purposes in *Le Rêve de d'Alembert*. The philosopher sought to convince the mathematician that there was only a difference of degree between inert matter and living beings: one could pass seamlessly from a marble statue to a being of flesh and blood. The animal, which has organs with vibrating cords that oscillate and resonate long after being tweaked, may be compared to a harpsichord endowed with sensibility and memory. Man, who possesses self-consciousness, is both harpsichord and musician; he is affected as an instrument and he is conscious of what he plays. Faced with this theory of a single substance, of a universal sensibility, of a nature which produces many changing forms, the sceptical D'Alembert goes to bed.

D'Alembert's sleep is restless. He speaks out loud as if continuing his dialogue with Diderot. Surprised by his words, his friend Julie de Lespinasse starts noting them down. Disturbed by what she takes to be ravings, she summons the doctor, Bordeu. From time to time D'Alembert awakens, then dozes off again. In the end the ideas emitted by D'Alembert, and completed by Bordeu, permit the revelation of Diderot's intemperate philosophy: it is impossible to distinguish between waking and sleeping. Besides, one can perfectly well philosophize while sleeping and rave while being awake: there is no difference in thought processes between a wide-awake Bordeu and D'Alembert dreaming. The researches of the surrealists overlap with Diderot's enquiry into the dream. In autumn 1922, René Crevel, Robert Desnos and Benjamin Péret experimented with hypnotic sleep. They spoke, they were questioned, they scribbled down a few words or drawings. The results were carefully gathered, as in the protocol adopted by Diderot which turned Julie de Lespinasse into the secretary of the séance. There are even similarities between D'Alembert dreaming and Benjamin Péret slumbering. Both evoked an unknown world invaded by eggs and plants and succumbed to an excess of the giggles.

In the *Manifeste du surréalisme*, focusing on imagination and the dream, André Breton would exclaim, 'When will we have sleeping logicians, sleeping philosophers?' His wish has been fulfilled. Diderot's dreamer may be considered the first sleeping philosopher. One might also invoke the Taoist Zhuang Zhou who, after dreaming that he was a butterfly, did not know upon awakening whether he was a man dreaming he was a butterfly or a butterfly dreaming he was a man.

Diderot was born in 1713. At an early date André Breton observed that the initials of his signature simulated the figure, '1713': *AB = 1713*. Henceforth Breton identified himself with the year 1713. During his exile in New York, he made an object-poem entitled *Portrait of the Actor AB in His Memorable Role, the Year of Our Lord 1713*, in which phrases, objects and images form a system relating to 1713. In particular, he included the birth of Diderot but also the marriage of the blind mathematician Saunderson, the inventor of a calculating machine that Diderot described in *Lettre sur les aveugles* (Letter on the blind). Each of our five senses has an original input. Thus, the blind Saunderson made use of touch to come up with the calculations and demonstrations about the solid objects he had confected. Someone born blind may excel in geometry. Nevertheless, the empiricist Diderot observes in *Lettre sur les sourds et muets* (Letter on the deaf and dumb) that the mind collects its impressions as a single entity, in a synthetic manner, while language takes time to detail all these touches by expressing them successively: 'Our mind is a moving machine, which we are perpetually copying.' In their philosophy of the dream, the surrealists would retain two lessons from Diderot: his experimental approach and his conception of life, dream and mind as something continuous. There is continuity in the dream, to be sure. The disjointed impression the dream can give

is only apparent. On 20 October 1760, Diderot wrote to S
'There is nothing disjointed in the head of a man who d
that of a madman.' After *L'Esprit contre la Raison* (The
reason), René Crevel would claim open kinship with Di
Clavecin de Diderot (Diderot's harpsichord), he would criticize humanism, realism and idealism, all three of which have recourse to metaphysical reason. As Crevel said amusingly, 'The idealist refuses to be the harpsichord that allows itself to be played.' Here, metaphysics can no longer rhyme with music.

Philosophy of the dream

For Freud the dream was the royal road when it came to acceding to unconscious ideas and desires. Starting out from the manifest dream, one could go back, thanks to the method of free association, as far as the latent dream. The manifest dream appearing absurd, it was important to interpret it, to find meaning in it. The surrealists didn't agree. For them, the dream was not a means but rather an end in itself. The dream was manifested and fulfilled in the manifest dream. In the surrealist enunciation of the dream Aragon (2011: 30–1) detected an unusual approach: 'for the first time since the world began, when André Breton writes down his dreams they retain the characteristics of dreaming in the telling'. This led the author of *Une Vague de rêves* to designate eleven presidents of the Republic of the Dream – from Saint-Pol-Roux to Freud, by way of Picasso and Chirico – and to evoke each of the twenty-nine surrealist dreamers. In a lyrical flight of fancy he also suggested the unfurling of dreams and the bewildering power of images: 'In a bed at the moment of falling asleep, in the street eyes wide open, with all the apparatus of terror, we were shaking the hand of phantoms. … O phantoms of fickle gaze, children of shadows, wait for me, I'm coming and already you turn away. … O great Dream … take hold of me for the rest of my life, take hold of me for all lives, rising tide whose foam is flowers'. Surrealism had the feeling it was nothing save what it dreamed. And when it awoke, given the paucity of reality in reality itself, it saw to it that the marvel of surreality stood revealed.

Modern philosophy is based either on the Cartesian *cogito* or on the transcendental ego of Kant. According to Descartes, I may doubt external reality but I cannot doubt that I think when I doubt. As it is, reflexivity is not the prerogative of consciousness – the dreamer also undergoes the experience of it. On 2 January 1928 the dreaming Morise asked himself if he was dreaming or if he was awake:

'I imagined I was dreaming, perhaps.' On 18 June 1937 the dreaming Éluard dreamt he was not dreaming and amassed material indications to prove it. He dreamt he was in bed at a late hour, that he couldn't get to sleep, that he got up in the dark, that he fell down in the corridor, that he crawled into Nusch's bedroom, that he went to sleep. Next he dreamt that he awoke with a start because Nusch had coughed, that he attempted to call her name, that he felt blind, dumb, paralysed, that he probed the parquet floor to check where he was. He was safe; in fact he was in bed.

There is no break between day and night, but continuity instead. Hervey de Saint-Denys undertook to direct his dreams. For Alfred Jarry, there were neither days nor nights; life was a continuum; there was only hallucination or perception; accustomed to directing his thoughts, Sengle, hero of the novel *Les Jours et les nuits* (*Days and Nights*), made no distinction between 'his thinking and his acts or his dreaming and his waking life'. Breton (Breton 1969: 14) recalled that at the moment of retiring each day Saint-Pol-Roux used to place this sign on the door of his country house: THE POET IS WORKING. He also confessed that he readily identified with the insomniac Maldoror desperately awaiting daybreak: 'My greatest desire is to make mine the admirable sentence of Lautréamont: "Since the unmentionable day of my birth, I've sworn implacable hatred towards the somniferous bed-boards"' (Breton 1996: 4, translation modified). In short, the surrealist dreamt night and day and was awake day and night.

The surrealist philosophical project, elaborated by Aragon and Breton, was based on three principles. The *first*, subjectivist, solipsistic and immaterialist, prolonged the speculations of Berkeley and Fichte. To be is to perceive, to be is to be perceived. All is in me, the world is spirit. The *second*, intuitionist, imaginist and oneiric, echoed Novalis, Schelling or Bergson; mind is creative imagination, intellectual intuition, thinking via images. Consequently, it was important to describe the modern mythology that was taking shape and to use the 'astounding image' without restraint. The *third*, nominalist or linguistic, under the auspices of Berkeley, Condillac and Jean Paulhan, that one cannot think without words, without a syntax and without the odd platitude. These three principles combined an integral idealism, a wave of dreams or images, and an absolute nominalism.

Definitive dreamers or sleeping logicians, the surrealists went in quest of a philosophy of the dream and the image. By day as well as by night they hoisted the colours of the imagination. The dream, connective tissue of images and of shots in a film, was the stronghold and perhaps even the source of the imagination. Aragon, Breton and their friends quickly understood that there were as many surrealist images in their dream narratives as in their notebooks of automatic writing. The motive force of automatism transports and transforms images. Surrealist paintings were not fixed – they were simply in freeze-frame. Following the example of Chirico's metaphysical pictures, they pulsated with life, condensed an image and fixed a moment of eternity.

In 1844, in *Un autre monde* (Another world), subtitled *Transformations, Visions, Incarnations, Ascensions, Locomotions, Explorations, Peregrinations, Excursions, Stations, Cosmogonies, Phantasmagorias, Reveries, Frolics, Jests, Whims / Metamorphoses, Metempsychoses, Apotheoses, and Other Things*, the illustrator Grandville invented the philosophy of disguise. As he saw it, the universe is a puppet theatre, an opera house, a vast music hall in which, onstage as in the stalls, the animal parodies the human, the human apes the vegetal, the vegetal plays god, the god has something of the puppet, the puppet mimes the artist, the artist takes himself for an instrument, and so on. Grandville urged the Hegelian philosophy of history to give way to a philosophy of imitation, a society of the spectacle, a ferocious battle between disguises and doubles, animate and inanimate objects, living and imaginary creatures. It is known that Walter Benjamin related the jests and whims of Grandville to the wonderland of the universal exhibitions and to commodity fetishism. In actual fact the illustrator from Nancy had merely to draw on the dramaturgy of the dream image. Grandville, illustrator of *La Musique animée* (Animated music) and of *Les Fleurs animées* (Animated flowers), is the first painter of the *animated images* of the dream.

Which mischief-maker leads the dance? The illustrator or the writer? The pencil or the pen? That is the question posed in the introduction to *Un autre monde*. For Grandville, the answer was not in doubt. Image, pencil and illustrator opened the ball and gave the signal for the waltz or the roundelay to begin. The draughtsman was no longer the simple illustrator of a sacrosanct text, he was the inspirer of it. Henceforth, he would take the lead and make his presence felt. By means of maps, emblems, figures, symbols, enigmas, rebuses, signs, posters, labels, portraits, landscapes and other kinds of framing he would allow a new connecting thread to unwind, he would sustain a different mode and rhythm of reading. Such, moreover, was the teaching of the dream in which words counted for very little with regard to the dramaturgy of the images. Such would be the bias of the comic strip and the cartoon film. Such would be the perspective of film editing in which sight competes on an equal footing with hearing.

Shortly before his death, on 17 March 1847, Grandville sent two drawings to *Le Magasin pittoresque, animated* drawings, so to speak, because they were clearly based on the transformation of an initial object and had to be looked at in a dynamic descending line.[1] The first, *Visions et transformations nocturnes* (Nocturnal visions and transformations) (the *wayside cross* is transformed into a *fountain*, which metamorphoses into a judge's *cap* and the *scales* of justice) or *Crime et expiation* (Crime and atonement) (a huge, terrifying eye pursues a murderer), is akin to a nightmare. The second, *Promenade dans le ciel* (Taking a turn in the sky), not unlike a reverie, describes a cascade of transformations in the firmament: a crescent moon, humble cryptogram, umbelliferous plant, parasol, bat, winged bellows, bellows, bobbin with a skein of thread, four-wheeled cart pulled by three fiery steeds, canopy of stars.

It is curious to note that three weeks before his death André Breton did a series of *animated* or *automatic* drawings keeping to the same principle of an initial object, the difference being that the surrealist stressed, in his meandering line, the continuity of the mark-making. In Grandville as in Breton the previous shape served as a dynamic, analogous motif to the one that followed.

Leiris, Trost and Caillois

In March 1922 *Littérature* published three of Breton's dreams, in October three of Desnos's and in December one of Breton's. With *La Révolution surréaliste*, this would turn into an avalanche. December 1924: Chirico (one dream), Breton (three), Renée Gauthier (one), Michel Leiris (six, under the title of 'The Land of My Dreams'), and lastly a speculative text by Crevel about the dream and sleep, evoking a painting by Chirico in passing. April 1925: Max Morise (one), Antonin Artaud (three), Paul Éluard (six), Pierre Naville (two), Raymond Queneau (one), Jacques-André Boiffard (one), not to mention three children's dreams. July 1925: Morise (one), Leiris (four). October 1925: three old poems by Chirico ('Hopes', 'A Life', 'One Night') in which dream visions and *pittura metafisica* were combined; Leiris (five), Morise (three). June 1926: Marcel Noll (two), Leiris (one). October 1927: Aragon (one), Naville (one). March 1928: Morise (one). In addition there appeared, in 1929, in the Brussels-based magazine *Variétés*, two dream narratives by Georges Sadoul, along with an iconography of the dream.

The most assiduous in writing down his dreams, Michel Leiris would include them in his *Journal* all through his life. He would publish more than a hundred in 1961. On 15 March 1925 he ended his dream with this opportune play on words: 'Nadia, naïade noyée' (Nadia, inundated naiad). Language, autobiography and dream were freely combined. His

Glossaire (Glossary), which included assonant entries like 'RÉVOTION – solution de tout rêve' (Revolution – solution to every dre or 'SUICIDE – idée sûre de sursis' (Suicide – reliable idea of reprieve, was potentially nourished by day and night alike. Leiris, the definitive dreamer, never forgot that the dream freighted stupefying images and finely chiselled words.

The Romanian surrealists would expressly support the idea that the dream, the wellspring of life, was manifested exclusively in the manifest dream. Diurnal residues, the latent dream and Freudian interpretation were denounced as being false trails, useless detours or abstractions. In revolutionary terms, the reactionary content of certain diurnal residues ought to be opposed, even. Dolfi Trost (1916–1966) insisted on the following points: (a) the dream that is inherently erotic is not the object of censorship; (b) it ends in a nightmare that triggers awakening; (c) it expresses a *current* desire and not a past one; (d) as it bears its interpretation within itself, it is useless to resort to analogy; (e) it is tautological: 'The dream is the dream and nothing but the dream' (Trost 1947: 6); (f) it can only be conceived from a poetic point of view; (g) it tends to advance towards '*perfect* madness'; (h) the dream and madness both belong to the world of stars and planets; and (i) thought is as logical in the dream as it is in wakefulness.

Trost constantly repeated that the manifest dream was erotic in itself and that there was no need to interpret it. However, as an analyst, he advocated in *Vision dans le cristal* (Vision in the crystal) the recourse to objective chance in order to interpret the seven erotic dreams of a woman. Each dream fragment was confronted with a few lines from a manual of sexual pathology he had opened at random (14).

From 1956 onwards, Roger Caillois developed a number of critical ideas about the dream. In his masterful groundbreaking book *Le Surréalisme et le rêve*, Sarane Alexandrian would pass severe judgement on Caillois's method as being too rationalist. In fact, even Caillois's titles – *L'Incertitude qui vient des rêves, Puissance du rêve*, 'Prestige et problème du rêve' – appear to respond to surrealist preoccupations. While Breton introduced his *Discours sur le peu de réalité* (Discourse on the paucity of reality), Caillois discoursed on *The Uncertainty That Comes from Dreams*. Surrealism was defined philosophically as the belief in the 'omnipotence of the dream', while Caillois bowed in turn before the *Power of the Dream*. Finally, when speaking of the prestige and problem of the dream, one was inclined neither to reject nor reduce it.

Caillois distrusted dream dictionaries and Freudian interpretation. The dream hides nothing and does not repress very much; there is no message to decipher, then. Far from being struck by the irrationality or the phantasmagoria of the dream, Caillois invokes his own dreams in which a debauchery of logic, reflection and commentary reigns; certain of them, moreover, are devoted to solving crime mysteries. Above all, Caillois focuses on the hallucinatory power of the dream, on the feeling of absolute reality and of fatefulness experienced by the dreamer, who seems crushed by his destiny, compared to the man who is awake, who seems to float in a more serene and gentle world. Whereas Breton perceives the paucity of reality in reality, Caillois encounters the excess of reality of sleep and the dream. This is why he considers that the dream necessarily instils the metaphysical uncertainty in us that ancient Chinese writers had detected, a doubt Cartesian philosophers believed could be overcome. The lesson of the 'rationalist' Caillois is that it is rationally impossible to state that I do not dream when I am awake and that my dream is illusory when I am asleep.

From Zhuang Zhou and Diderot the surrealists borrowed the notion of dormant philosophizing. In Grandville they discovered the animated painting of images. In Hervey de Saint-Denys they saw a dream experimenter. Like Bergson they thought that the plane of the dream is much more extensive than that of action. While they saluted such studies of Freud's as *The Interpretation of Dreams* and *Delusions and Dreams in Jensen's 'Gradiva'*, they nonetheless developed their own philosophies of the dream, which involved a series of postulates. (1) There is porosity between the nocturnal and the diurnal; the dream and the waking state are two communicating vessels. (2) Objects and persons undergo metamorphosis in the dream; they follow the more or less collision-bound trajectory of an animated cartoon; they seem carried away as in a comedy film; objects and persons live, perish and are reborn. (3) The dream can be inventive and favourable to dormant philosophizing. (4) An urban *dérive* fulfils the equivalent of the trajectory of a dream. (5) Surrealist automatism brings the animated painting of the dream into the light of day. (6) The dream does not remind us of the past but of the future; surrealist works are souvenirs of the future. (7) Whereas images metamorphose in the space of the dream, events are magnetized in the temporality of wireless time, outside the linear course of history.

Notes

Translated from the French by Paul Hammond.

1 The two drawings by Grandville would be published in *Le Magasin pittoresque*, no. 27, in 1847, under the title of 'Two Dreams by J.J. Grandville'. The drawing *Crime et expiation* was reprinted in*Documents*, no. 4, September 1929, with a commentary by Georges Bataille.

14 *Amour fou* – mad love

Dawn Ades and Michael Richardson

Mad love – *amour fou* – is the surrealist concept, or notion, that has probably gained the greatest popular currency, so much so that when it is spoken about it is usually in ways that would not be recognized by the surrealists. And apart from Breton's account of a 1930s ecstatic love affair, which he chose to call *L'Amour fou*, we don't very often find the term in surrealist work, and other surrealists like Benjamin Péret and Alain Joubert have preferred to speak of 'sublime' or 'absolute' love.

Mad love is difficult to pin down and there are probably as many concepts of love in surrealism as there are surrealists. We find quite divergent notions about love apparent in the work of Joë Bousquet, Octavio Paz, André Pieyre de Mandiargues, Gherasim Luca, Nelly Kaplan, Joyce Mansour to name just a few . . . . What is extraordinary is the persistence of love as a theme throughout surrealist work. Perhaps all we can do within the limitations of our discussion is trace a trajectory of how they came – or how Breton came – to the idea of mad love.

Perhaps we should begin by considering how love came on to the agenda as a major surrealist preoccupation, since it doesn't seem to have been there from the beginning. Love is hardly a Dadaist concern and it doesn't seem to have played a significant part in the gestation of surrealism.

No, they started off with attitudes more typical of the avant-garde of the time: a refusal of conformity and a determination to live according to their desires, committed to open relationships and free love without examining the consequences.

Yet there is within surrealism, from the very outset, a questioning, or a doubt, not simply about the reality of the world, that positivist world that assumes that the perceptible realm is all that exists, but also of one's own presence within the world. And, in 1924, along with the first issue of *La Révolution surréaliste*, they issued a series of 'calling cards', one of which declares that 'if you love LOVE, you will love SURREALISM'.

We know that at the time Breton and Aragon were immersed in reading Hegel and Schelling, whose theories were in many ways instrumental in problematizing issues about personal identity that had been brewing within surrealist circles. Coming to these thinkers with little philosophical baggage, the surrealists were free to interpret them in their own terms. This philosophical encounter seems to have marked them above all with a realization that reality is not concretely present but is always mediated: something has existence not in itself but only by being recognized by its other. Thus it becomes almost axiomatic in surrealism that one's existence is always tied to some sort of a shadow. From this it follows that freedom is not freedom of choice but rather a matter of overcoming the alienation of being by means of placing oneself into harmony with necessity. This perhaps constitutes the starting point for their questioning of the nature of love.

So, love, sex and the erotic become fundamental preoccupations, not least in the ways they relate to each other, in a sequence of publications with dramatically different perspectives through the 1920s and 1930s which attempt to lay bare the theoretical grounds for their attitudes to love.

Breton's encounter with Nadja at the end of 1925 was a turning in the road whereby ideas in formation about personal identity and the elusiveness of the 'self' coalesce around the erotic relation and love itself, even if there is very little eroticism, and no mad love, at least from Breton's perspective, in the book he published in 1928.

But it gave a tangible recognition to the perception that our sense of self – and of reality as well – is to be found not within ourselves but only in relation to our surroundings and interactions with others. Nadja is the catalyst – whether in her own self or in what Breton projects on to her, we perhaps can't separate the one from the other – for reflections that until then were evanescent, implicit in the experiments in communication (automatism, sleep sessions and so on) and in what they had taken from their readings of Freud, Hegel and Schelling as well as – crucially – from their own sexual relationships. The disturbing apparition of Nadja seems also to provide a focus for responses to Rimbaud's demand for love to be reinvented, or the crisis in sexual relations announced by Villiers de l'Isle-Adam in *The Future Eve*.

Yes, this crisis seems to have become significant within discourse at the end of the nineteenth century, revealed not only in Rimbaud and Villiers, but also apparent in Nietzsche, Jarry, Lautréamont and many others, as well as in the sexology of Kraft-Ebbing, Hirschfeld and Havelock Ellis that had lain dormant for a couple of decades, awaiting Freud's detonation of the time bomb they had primed. Moreover, as the surrealists' own lives became more complicated so did belief in love as the supreme state of being become established as a principle, one to be both affirmed and questioned. Throughout the 1920s and 1930s interrogations of sex and sexuality and insistence on love alternate.

Sex comes first, with the *Recherches sur la sexualité* that begin on the evening of 27 January 1928 and continue on several dates until 6 May, in which the surrealists get together to discuss their own sexual behaviour (see Pierre 1992).[1] They appear to have started casually, as a game of truth prompted by a crisis in Breton's life, although when the first two sessions were published in issue 11 of *La Révolution surréaliste* they were given a scientific character, an approach following lines indicated by Hirschfeld or Havelock Ellis. Yet this was compromised from the beginning by the fact that no women participated.

We already see here a tension that frequently emerges in surrealist research between a will towards scientific objectivity and the personal determinations that have led to the research being undertaken in the first place.

A tension they didn't necessarily want to resolve …

No, not if it meant that the one would disqualify the other. So when Pierre Naville objected that the discussions should not be published unless given greater scientific objectivity, especially by involving women, Breton responded that this would inhibit discussion, allowing the men to hide their penchants behind literary sublimations, so defeating the whole object of the exercise (see Naville 1977*: 145–9).*

Which suggests that the *Recherches* resulted from Breton's personal crisis rather than being a particular group concern. Actually, in reading them there is a question of how seriously some of the others took them.

As scientific documents, Naville was right that they are seriously deficient. We are given no introduction, no setting of agendas or objectives, no foreplay, one might say. Breton just plunges in: 'A man and a woman make love. To what extent does the man take account of the woman's pleasure? Tanguy?' Which doesn't seem to please Tanguy: 'why ask me first?'

This focus on the physical aspect of sex remains pretty constant throughout the discussions, from which love, or any aspect of the emotional relationship with the woman (since all of the participants are men[2]) is almost excluded. Bearing in mind the Hegelian argument that reality is always mediated by relation with an Other, this separation of sex from love is curious.

*Yes, Breton insists that 'the whole point of this investigation is, in love, to establish what part belongs to sexuality' (*Pierre 1992*: 85–6). We should remember that at the beginning of 1928, he was in the midst of complicated amorous involvements involving a whole gamut of emotions. Three months earlier he had embarked upon a tortuous love affair with Suzanne Muzard, by all accounts an extremely sensual and sexually demanding woman. A month before he convoked the other surrealists to discuss sexuality, Suzanne had left him for the writer Emanuel Berl, with whom she was then in Morocco. This had followed a long troubling affair with Léona Delcourt (Nadja) and a painful rejection by the aristocratic ice maiden Lise Meyer. His marriage to Simone – who seems to have been as much a sister as a wife to him – was also coming apart. At the time, apparently still unbeknown to Breton, she was conducting an affair with Max Morise (the person charged with recording the sexuality discussions!).*

Simone accepted the surrealist principle of openness in amorous relations, but kept her liaison with Morise secret from Breton, who bitterly reproached her when he found out, considering that this secrecy (and not the affair itself) broke the pact of their relationship. In a letter to her cousin Denise Lévy of January 1926 she reflected upon a failed love affair with Roland Tual, as well as on Breton's various liaisons, that 'I've always noticed a strange and almost monstrous trait in me in regard to the most dominant concept of love, namely that I'd prefer to see a man I love be in love with a woman I esteem, in lieu of not loving at all' (S. Breton 2005: 238). The relations with Nadja and Meyer had not greatly troubled her, but she had no esteem for Suzanne Muzard, as she related in a later (September 1928) letter to Denise: 'Yet I know that this woman will do everything I've been careful to avoid doing, which is that she will try to monopolize him completely, at the expense of everything André represents in the world, of everything he is able to do' (S. Breton 2005: 241). For both Simone and Denise, the politically and socially revolutionary sides of surrealism were extremely important – even constituting an essential aspect of Simone's commitment to Breton – and she feared Suzanne was intent upon steering him away from it.

Breton does seem to have lost his head over Suzanne – if Nadja provided the catalyst for the surrealists to question issues of identity connected to the sexual relation, the appearance of Suzanne led to a crisis of sensibility that almost resulted in a complete break-up of the group. This truly was 'mad love', although not in the way that Breton would theorize it a decade later.

It was a period in which surrealism really concretized itself as a moral sensibility. A crisis followed, in which the surrealist group was torn apart, as the majority of his old comrades abandoned Breton. This split, generally attributed to political differences in the literature, was certainly as much about affective relations, as Breton was later to say himself.

Yes, Simone was too popular within the group for her break-up with Breton not to cause ructions.

At the same time, too, Breton's closest comrades, Aragon and Éluard, were in the midst of amorous crises of their own.

The extent to which sexuality troubles the mediated relation could hardly be more starkly illustrated and seems clearly to have been the motivation behind the Recherches *at a time when several of them were feeling bruised, and Breton himself was suffering from feelings of rejection and insecurity. Perhaps, too, this explains Breton's reluctance to involve women in the discussions – the issues were too raw.*

Yet several did object to the absence of women, which seemed to them ludicrous given the centrality in their discussions of the notions of reciprocity and equality in sexual relations. Aragon in particular held that as men and women had equal rights in 'physical love' the latter's absence invalided the discussion. From today's perspective, they reveal remarkable ignorance about female sexual responses.

We should remember that they were taking place when the notion of 'sexuality' – established by late Victorian sexologists and elaborated by Freud – was still in its infancy. What is most remarkable is how they address sex almost as a discourse, in some ways anticipating Foucault in this respect.

Still they have been strongly criticized in recent literature for the attitudes displayed towards homosexuality.

Yes, but we should be careful not to impose our own standards onto an earlier era, especially about something that has since been so radically transformed, notably by the advent of gay liberation and gay pride, as to be almost completely different from how it was understood in the twenties. Moreover, what they were discussing was not actually homosexuality but 'pederasty', a word – and indeed to a great extent a practice, since it involved a whole set of attitudes and values no longer associated with homosexuals – with no contemporary currency, making it very difficult for us today to understand what was at issue for them. In fact, at times they seem to be arguing at cross purposes, as if the meaning of the term had not yet been fixed.

To an extent the same thing must be true for the discourse about women. In scant evidence we have of how women responded to the *Recherches*, Marcel Duhamel recounts Youki Fujita saying that they just ought to get laid more often, while Georges Bataille tells us that surrealism had fascinated Colette Peignot but the *Recherches* repelled her, although he doesn't say why.

Youki Fujita's presence in the surrealist milieu actually provoked further moral soul-searching. At the time the girlfriend of Marcel Noll, she was the separated wife of the famous Japanese painter Fujita, from whom she had acquired expensive tastes. Noll was the group's treasurer and, desperate to satisfy her, he purloined the group funds. It didn't do him any good, as she rejected him for Robert Desnos, a contributory factor in the expulsion of Desnos from the group as he was accused of stealing her away from Noll. Noll himself vanished from the scene, never to be heard from again.

Thus the question that would appear in the following year's enquiry into love: how would you judge someone who went so far as to betray his convictions to please the woman he loves?

Love for the surrealists would always be – exclusively – affective. Issues around the idea of the encounter were also central to the surrealist attitude and tended to interpose between the sexual relation and love.

Actually, in excluding love (and in fact eroticism) from the *Recherches*, the participants seem almost to be prefiguring the distinction Bataille would later make between 'eroticism' as a fundamental human attitude and 'sexuality' as a purely animal instinct (might this even have been the basis of Bataille's assertion of this distinction?).

Another element is the profusion of extraordinary erotic texts that appear during 1928 and 1929. In this period we see the publications of Bataille's Histoire de l'œil, *Aragon's* Le Con d'Irène, *Desnos's* La

Liberté ou l'amour, *Péret, Aragon and Man Ray's* 1929 *and Péret and Tanguy's* Les Rouilles encagées, *as well as Dalí and Buñuel's films* Un Chien Andalou *and* L'Âge d'or.

And they issued a tract 'Hands Off Love' in support of Charlie Chaplin, at the time embroiled in a sensational divorce case. The first screenings of *L'Âge d'or* were also accompanied by a manifesto extolling love.

The version of the Recherches *published in* La Révolution surréaliste *ends with a note, 'to be continued' but instead it was replaced in the next issue with the* Enquiry on Love. *Was this a change of direction, or had the separation of sexuality and love been a temporary strategy responding to acute personal issues?*

The *Enquête* cast the net of interlocutors quite widely, including not only surrealists and fellow-travellers, but many writers and intellectuals and even magazines and reviews of all political complexions while the *Recherches* were confined to a small group of intimates, intended to debate sexuality through dialogues. The *Enquête* is more exploratory, seeking opinion rather than frankness.

The word love, amour, *is there qualified with an adjective, 'admirable', to lift it out of the associations rejected by the surrealists (filial, divine or patriotic love) and to make it clear that it concerns the total attachment to another human being, body and soul, as well as to contrast it with 'sordid life'.*

Yet the final question, asking whether one believes in the triumph of admirable love over sordid life, brings forth generally ambivalent responses, the most interesting of which is that of Maurice Heine, who points out that life is not necessarily sordid and love not necessarily admirable, but that the death of love would inevitably lead to making life sordid. Breton himself is one of the few to respond unequivocally in favour of admirable love, but does so only obliquely, in words 'signed' by Suzanne Muzard but under Breton's name.

There is something mysterious about this strategy. Are the words really Suzanne's, or are they those he wanted to hear from her? Suzanne herself was later to say that 'Breton overflattered his loves: he moulded the woman he loved so that she should correspond to his own aspirations and thus become, in his eyes, an affirmed value (in Jean 1980*: 190).*

Breton appears to have been attracted to women of contrary sensibilities, the composite of which would have constituted his ideal woman. Suzanne seems to have epitomized the ideal of the independent woman at the time: sensual and unfettered by conventional morality, but still imbued by the sense that woman's destiny is to be loved, indeed to be loved madly.

Perhaps a peculiarly French attitude, which we find in many films of the thirties.

Maybe not so much a French attitude as a specifically Parisian one, which women like Simone and Denise, coming from Jewish families in Strasbourg and with a strong German influence, don't share.

A feature of the surrealists' attitude towards women is that they assume an equality that isn't there. That is, that they treat women as equals, blind at many levels to the profound inequality that is so inbuilt into their social circumstances that they cannot see it. This shouldn't surprise us: no matter how critical of our circumstances we can never elude the standards of our time.

We are speaking as if the surrealists only ever comprised men as members of the group, and this was not the case. Women were always involved but rarely made their voices heard, at least, until the 1940s.

An incident from the affair with Nadja haunted Breton: her attempt to cause the car he was driving to crash by pressing her foot on his on the accelerator and trying to cover his eyes with her hands 'in the oblivion of an interminable kiss'. Needless to say, he tells us, he didn't yield to this desire but later realized that this was the test of love. Had his and Nadja's feelings been truly reciprocal – 'love in the sense I understand it – mysterious, improbable, unique, bewildering, and certain …' wouldn't they have chosen life?

Doesn't Breton himself say the contrary: 'I feel less and less capable of resisting such a temptation in every case'? Wouldn't the 'interminable kiss' precisely be the supreme moment when life and death are no longer perceived as contradictions, the motive point of all surrealist activity? Love, in surrealism is often in league with death, asserting life only in its relation to death. Isn't Bataille's perception that eroticism is 'assenting to life up to the point of death … eroticism is assenting to life even in death' a key here?

From Breton's perspective, perhaps. But if Nadja had loved him, would she have demanded such a token of esteem? Wouldn't death at that moment have been the triumph of sordid life over admirable love?

Maurice Blanchot (1993: 417) was later to note that '[i]n the relation thus offered neither [Breton nor Nadja] encounters what they encounter: André Breton is for her a god, the sun, the dark and lightning-struck man close to the sphinx; for him she is the genie of the air, inspired-inspiring, she who always departs.'

Suzanne Muzard would say that 'Love is a trap for lovers in quest of the absolute', something that, unlike Nadja, resolutely didn't interest her and perhaps, despite appearances, wasn't what Breton was really seeking.

Breton recounted that his vision of sexual desire took shape at eighteen years of age when viewing the paintings of Gustave Moreau, especially his representations of faces and eyes, and continued to haunt his image of the ideal woman and embody his notion of love.

Was he then always seeking the same woman, or himself? Or does what he was seeking go beyond such an inane correlation? What is striking is how different the various women he was involved with were, as though what he was looking for was some sort of composite, an image, in the medieval sense of a being who would come into existence through the process of being desired.

He addresses this early in *L'Amour fou*, written in 1934: in a kind of mental theatre he imagines two symmetrical rows, the men dressed in black and women in light clothes. The men would all be himself, the faces of the women only one face – that of the latest woman loved. This text was driven by the need to reconcile the idea of 'unique love' with prevailing social conditions, to prove that a solution was likely to be found outside the usual logical routes. Written a few days before the encounter he describes in ecstatic terms later in *L'Amour fou* with the woman who became his wife, he says that 'I've never ceased to believe that … love is the greatest purveyor of solutions of this kind, as well as being in itself the ideal meeting point and fusion of these solutions' (Breton 1987: 42, translation modified). Breton recognized a similar if less dramatic conception of the problem, that of 'love for a unique being' in the Romantic poets, Shelley, Nerval and Arnim. But perhaps for him it was more a question of a love that overwhelms all other considerations, is beyond reason.

Perhaps, therefore, 'mad love' isn't quite right, in that 'madness' requires reason to define itself against. Wasn't he rather searching for something outside the dichotomy between reason and madness?

'hich brings us back to the fact that love is not a matter of choice, nor even of attraction, whether mutual or not, but a confrontation with destiny, in which it is love itself that overwhelms the lovers, something Breton seems to perceive in *L'Âge d'or*, the only film, he writes, that exalts 'total love as I envisage it' (Breton 1987: 78).

In many ways, the final section of L'Amour fou, *written to his daughter to be read by her in 1952 when she will be sixteen, is the most extraordinary in the book, a paean to life at a time when he felt his own hanging 'by the slightest thread' (*Breton 1987*: 117) but anticipating the day when this Dawn (Aube), the product of love, will herself one day be 'madly loved'.*

For Breton, unique love is really a quest, a constant search rooted in the temporary magic of an encounter with a being in whom, each time, Breton placed his hope. Simone – Lise – Nadja – Suzanne – Jacqueline – Elisa – Nelly – Joyce, this procession of women loved by Breton, never exclusively but always responding to some imperative of his sensibility …

But we've been talking almost exclusively about Breton …

Yes, we should be careful not to congeal surrealism at a specific time and place, or tie it to the emotional needs of one person. Moreover, the surrealists have returned to look collectively at various aspects of the dynamics of love and the sensual relation in a range of enquiries issued over the years: the encounter (1933), striptease (1957), erotic representations (1961), eroticism (1971) and sensual pleasure (2004). Examination of the complexities of love runs throughout Buñuel's films, culminating in *That Obscure Object of Desire* (1978), in which the ambivalences of the amorous relation and the contradictory desires it unleashes are laid bare.

And Nelly Kaplan makes direct reference in her films, such as Plaisir d'amour *(1990), to the conflicts between male and female attitudes to love and erotic pleasure, often with considerable humour. She plays with gender stereotypes, as does Joyce Mansour in her poetry, and incorporates seamlessly in* Nea *(1976) scenes of same-sex desire.*

We should also say a word about Georges Bataille, in whose work we might find another notion of love, albeit one that is submerged and difficult to bring to the surface. The publication of Bataille's *Eroticism* in 1957 was a significant moment in the history of surrealism, concretizing certain ideas that had been implicit or half-formed for some time and inspiring the 1959/60 International Surrealist Exhibition, devoted to 'Eros'.

As noted earlier, Bataille's essential contribution was to make explicit the distinction between sexuality (as a pure animal instinct) and eroticism (as a play of human sensual experiences), and for the perception that the moment of orgasm offers us a glimpse of the supreme point of surrealist endeavour when momentarily life slips into death and contradictions are resolved.

But we are moving away here from the concept of mad love – there are so many attitudes to love within surrealism that we would need to write a whole book about them – and their histories – if we were to explore it properly.

Yes, and as we noted at the beginning, Benjamin Péret preferred to speak of 'sublime love', which differs significantly from Breton's mad love while Alain Joubert has recently criticized both notions from a surrealist perspective, preferring to speak of 'absolute love'. Joubert argues that neither mad love nor sublime love satisfies what is implicit within the surrealist demand, that is a transformation of being through the encounter with an other, a physical and spiritual union in constant metamorphoses. Breton, in contrast, remained content with the transformative possibilities of the encounter, contemplating the precipice and unprepared to plunge into the depths of an absolute love in which the individual identities of both lovers are dissolved. Péret, too, is dazzled by the precipice, which is implied by the use of the word 'sublime', and unlike Breton is still to some extent under the sway of a doomed Romantic desire for transcendence.

Perhaps we might leave the last word to Hegel, as quoted by Octavio Paz: 'Love excludes all oppositions and hence it escapes the realm of reason. It makes objectivity null and void and hence goes beyond reflection. In love, life discovers itself in life, devoid now of any incompleteness' (1996: 133).

Notes

1 They were resumed in 1930 and then continued sporadically and in a rather perfunctory way until 1932.
2 Women do participate in the later dialogues but not in a particularly enlightening way. The most interesting female intervention comes in the sixth conversation, from an anonymous 'Y' (who we believe is almost certainly Youki Fujita), but she really only asks questions rather than answering any.

15 Convulsive beauty

Krzysztof Fijalkowski

'Beauty will be CONVULSIVE or won't be at all.' With this decisive announcement André Breton closes *Nadja*, his account of a few weeks in late 1926 and early 1927 when a magnetizing but tragic encounter with Nadja (Léona Delcourt) leads to a declaration of love for an unnamed woman (Suzanne Muzard). There presides over both of these relationships, and over the book itself, a feeling of loss and unease mirrored by a repeated concern for a dissolution of his own sense of selfhood, yet in *Nadja*'s closing passage Breton chooses to transform this into a promise of what might strike the reader as an unexpected quality: beauty. Breton's works often begin with the expression of dense, difficult ideas and end with a crystal-clear statement that leads the text's questions elsewhere: thus, while *Nadja* finishes, in a slightly peremptory manner, with the assertion of the new notion of convulsive beauty, as if everything so far had been leading to it, this is answered in a key work of the following decade *L'Amour fou* (*Mad Love*) which begins by exploring the idea of convulsive beauty in all of its complexity.

With these two texts, Breton elaborates a concept that would remain largely his own, one that the rest of surrealism tended to take as read rather than challenging or directly expanding. But if the specific term 'convulsive beauty' is infrequently mentioned by Breton outside of these books, and rarely appears in the work of other surrealists, the affirmation in *Nadja* as well as *L'Amour fou* that beauty can *only* be convulsive asserts that, for him at least, any genuine idea of beauty must incorporate this convulsion.[1] By qualifying beauty as convulsive, Breton immediately hoists the idea out of dominant understandings of beauty, and into a set of associations that makes it available for correspondence with other key surrealist concepts and strategies such as automatism, the image, the marvellous (identified in the first manifesto as 'always beautiful, anything marvellous is beautiful, in fact only the marvellous is beautiful'; Breton 1972: 14), objective chance and love, situating it at the heart of surrealism's proposed resolution of opposing states.

Dramatic and oxymoronic, the term 'convulsive beauty' arises in a context that associates surrealist beauty with the unknown, with desire and with the promise of revelation. It is also, as the closing two pages of *Nadja* sketch out, characterized by tensions, by open-ended and dynamic but contradictory impulses. The passage in question is prompted by a quotation from Hegel that sets an apprehension of the world in terms of ethics, consciousness and communication: 'each man hopes and believes he is better than the world which is his, but the man who *is* better merely expresses this same world better than the others' (Breton 1960: 159).[2] The page marks a pause, then Breton continues:

> A certain attitude necessarily follows with regard to beauty, which has obviously never been envisaged here save for emotional purposes. In no way static, that is, enclosed in Baudelaire's 'dream of stone', lost for man in the shadow of those Odalisques, in the depth of those tragedies which claim to girdle only a single day, scarcely less dynamic – that is, subject to a wild gallop which can lead only to another wild gallop – that is, more frenzied than a snowflake in a blizzard – that is, resolved, for fear of being fettered, never to be embraced at all: neither dynamic nor static. I see beauty as I have seen you. … Beauty is like a train that ceaselessly roars out of the Gare de Lyon and which I know will never leave. It consists of jolts and shocks, many of which do not have much importance, but which we know are destined to produce one *Shock*, which does.
>
> (Breton 1960: 159–60)

This is an intricate passage, full of external references and repeatedly requalified in such a way as to make the argument of beauty feel unstable, prone to slippage or contradiction ('in no way static … neither dynamic nor static' yet 'a train [that] will never leave'). Breton moves between images relating to literature, nature and modernity to suggest a notion of beauty that is confrontational and oppositional (the Hegelian antecedent hints at dialectical processes at work) and for which a paradoxical quality of movement in immobility seems to be key. But this definition of beauty may also be seen as first of all personal and circumstantial. While 'I see beauty as I have seen you' seems addressed to the (unnamed) Muzard, whose intense but equivocal relationship with Breton was unravelling as he wrote the last sections of *Nadja*, there is also a specific anecdote in which he and his friends tried without success, on a platform of the Gare de Lyon, to prevent Muzard from leaving for Tunisia with the lover she chose in his stead (Sebbag 1988: §38). Against this lost encounter, convulsive beauty offers a concept through which even time and its events may be held and re-enacted, a promise for the future in what 'will be'.

One of the major achievements of surrealism over the course of nearly a century is to have redrawn our categories of perceptual and intellectual pleasure: in its wake new things have become fascinating and attractive that once were considered ugly or trifling. But if surrealism's attitude to these newly intensified objects is far from constituting an aesthetics, surrealists could remain alert to philosophy's engagement with these issues: Breton, for one, was an attentive reader of Hegel's *Aesthetics.*

Classical concepts of beauty are based above all on an appreciation of ideal human form and privilege symmetry, order and proportion; as they have been assimilated into the history of art, the qualities of beauty are inevitably asserted in the context of *reason*. Surrealism's interests, like those of many modernist movements, frequently lie at the antipodes of such ambitions: classical sculptures derided or disassembled (Dalí's *Venus de Milo with Drawers* of 1936), photographs of monstrous big toes by Jacques-André Boiffard, Joan Miró's gleeful scatology (*Man and Woman in Front of a Pile of Excrement*, 1935) or Benjamin Péret's riotous poetry of affray and miscegenated objects all aim, at one level, to oppose the very possibility of harmony, order, taste and the ideal, working on principles of rupture and anomaly rather than consensus. The journal *Documents* is particularly associated with this tendency to challenge aesthetic norms, privileging the lowly, the scattered and the formless. Other surrealist productions, especially in the visual arts, deal with the issue of formal beauty in more ambivalent ways. Man Ray's figure and nude studies, for example – not to mention his work as a fashion photographer – seem to aim to disturb rather than dismantle orthodox canons of beauty through unexpected juxtapositions, viewpoints or distortions mingled with an enigmatic, albeit now relatively conventional, eroticism. His illustrations for Paul Éluard's book *Facile* (1935) depict the naked body of the poet's wife Nusch, organized around verses drawing upon natural metaphors and the private language of intimacy that read like a caress rather than an affront to propriety.[3] Péret's consideration of beauty is likewise posited in terms of human bodies and affective relationships, and his introduction to the *Anthologie de l'amour sublime* poses true beauty as both something that best incarnates the desire of the viewer, and one in which one distinguishes between superficial, easily exhausted qualities and a profound, latent content linked to sublimation and love (Péret 1956: 70–1).

Where conventional ideals of beauty usually seek balance and plenitude, surrealism's beauty, as Breton's passage from *Nadja* indicates, is part of an engagement with ambiguous or shifting states, as a stake in a troubling dissolution of the self in the other (something that might move it closer instead to the notion of the sublime, generally seen as the polar opposite of beauty, awe-inspiring and fascinating at the same time).[4] In particular, the idea that such judgements and theories about cultural production might be used to shore up vested social interests (the patronage of 'high art' by dominant classes) or to carry political messages, well-intentioned as they might be (such as *littérature engagée*), is anathema to surrealism, which insists instead on the nature of the creative act as a connection to a profound, enigmatic and always renegotiated *revelation* in operation between the maker, the world and the viewer, independent of a work's formal qualities and aesthetic values. New categories of hitherto ignored expression – graffiti, pulp novels, esoteric knowledge, *art brut*, mathematical models, clinical reports – are re-evaluated by surrealism against or because of their apparently non-aesthetic qualities, while the aesthetic content of artworks (to which surrealists rarely apply the term 'convulsive beauty') generally remains without interest for the movement.[5]

For the French surrealists, these attitudes were partly informed by the experience of Paris Dada and its explicitly anti-aesthetic drive, notably found (in the visual sphere at least) in Francis Picabia's iconoclasm or Marcel Duchamp's campaign of nonchalance against taste; but sources such as the scurrilous grotesque of Jarry's Ubu, Sade's violence, Apollinaire's love of street conversations and *faits divers*, or Jacques Vaché's indifference to all cultural forms all played their roles as well. The most direct expression of the fascination and the problem of beauty informing early surrealism, however, is found in Isidore Ducasse's celebrated *beau comme* aphorisms from *Les Chants de Maldoror*, revelling in their collision of ultra-Gothic perversity and scientific detail: an owl 'as beautiful as a dissertation on the curve described by a dog as it runs after its master'; a vulture 'as beautiful as the law of arrested chest development in adults whose propensity to growth is not in proportion to the quantity of molecules their organism can assimilate'; and the tragic figure of Mervyn,

> as beautiful as the retractility of the claws in birds of prey; or, again, as in the unpredictability of muscular movement in sores in the soft part of the posterior cervical region; … and above all, as

> the chance encounter of a sewing machine and an umbrella on a dissecting-table.
>
> (Lautréamont 1978: 186 and 217, translation modified)

These lines, especially the final phrase, have been quoted and analysed too often to need unpacking in detail here: suffice it to note that, while they took on the quality of a heraldic motto for surrealism, in this last-quoted paragraph they refer not to a female protagonist but a sixteen-year-old boy who meets a violent end at the novel's climax, and they operate above all on the dissonance between the customary expectation of pleasure set up by 'as beautiful as …' and its answer with an image that seems as if it had been stolen from another, wholly inappropriate and often jarring or uncomfortable source. Surrealism is rife with recipes for *beau comme*, and Breton adds one in this vein on the very last page of *Nadja*, shortly before his definition of convulsive beauty: 'the human heart, beautiful as a seismograph'.

The power of surrealism's adoption of *beau comme* as an avatar of the notion of convulsive beauty comes in part from the repeated suggestion in Lautréamont's epithets that the attribute of beauty is forever in need of redefinition, and lies above all in the strategy of *comparison*, one in which every object, person, experience or state is linked to every other, their qualities available and transmitted to each other as if through poetic contagion.[6] Beauty, far from reassuring the onlooker, is disclosed as violent and unexpected: the structure of *beau comme* acts as a bridge between discourses (the scientific and the lyrical, the cultural and the natural, desire and its others), and its energy comes from the distance between its components, linking it to surrealism's conception of the bipolar image as laid out in the first manifesto, and in particular to the products of automatism. Henceforth, surrealist beauty is always marked by this paradoxical and adversarial staging: Dalí would write of 'the terrifying and edible beauty of Art Nouveau architecture', while Breton would describe his future wife Jacqueline Lamba on the occasion of their first meeting as 'scandaleusement belle' in *L'Amour fou*, the work in which his concept of beauty receives its fullest exposition.

The first section of *L'Amour fou* was initially published separately, as the article 'La Beauté sera convulsive' in issue 5 of *Minotaure* (1934).[7] It opens with a difficult and allusive discussion of the sovereignty of love, before moving to a consideration of beauty which is thus to be read in the context of this nexus of the mechanisms and objects of desire. Rather than offer explicit definitions, Breton develops an intricate and shifting discussion of beauty that moves to and fro across a network of ideas and themes within which the reader gradually understands the concept to be situated, through resonance and analogy rather than conventional argument. Once again, in terms evoking the final passage of *Nadja* (even down to another image of a train), the question of movement and rest, of the ambivalent, dynamic nature of beauty, is foregrounded from the outset.

> The word 'convulsive', which I have used to describe the only beauty which in my view should concern us, would lose any meaning in my eyes were it to be conceived in motion and not at the exact expiration of this very motion. There can be no beauty at all, as far as I am concerned – convulsive beauty – except at the cost of affirming the reciprocal relations linking the object seen in its motion and in its repose. I regret not having been able to furnish, along with this text, the photograph of a high-speed locomotive abandoned for years to the delirium of the virgin forest.
>
> (Breton 1992: 680; 1987: 10, translation modified)

Some of the same slippages Breton used in his discussion of convulsive beauty in *Nadja* return here – it is first identified as *not* in motion, or rather as no longer in motion, and then in terms of the tension between its motion and rest. This, however, is just the first of three intrinsic qualities of convulsive beauty that 'La Beauté sera convulsive' intends to map out, though the second and third feel less clearly identified.

Describing next the experience of observing rock formations in underground caverns (something we might read, a little simplistically, as evoking the idea of prospecting for chance images in the unconscious), the following passage, heralding a leitmotif of the book as a whole, introduces the theme of the crystal and its analogue coral, accompanied here by a photograph of each and echoing the natural and scientific language in both *Nadja*'s and *Maldoror*'s evocations of beauty. 'There could be no higher artistic teaching than that of the crystal. The work of art, just like any fragment of human life considered in its deepest meaning, seems to me devoid of value if it does not offer the hardness, the rigidity, the regularity, the lustre on every interior and exterior facet, of the crystal' (Breton 1992: 681; 1987: 11). The discussion of the crystal does not directly reference the concept of beauty, but the implication here gives a certain place to more conventional notions of harmony and symmetry, but with a strong ethical component – visibility, clarity, transparency in all senses of these terms, in addition to rigour and resistance – as well as evoking the idea of a precious, rare object that can only be unearthed and never deliberately created: 'Please understand', the paragraph continues, 'that this affirmation is constantly and categorically opposed, for me, to everything that attempts, aesthetically or morally, to found formal beauty on a willed work of voluntary perfection that humans must desire to do'. Beauty's autonomous nature is underlined in other texts too: Antonin Artaud would associate it with qualities of absence or obliquity: 'True expression conceals what it exhibits. … Hence true beauty never strikes us directly and the setting sun is beautiful because of everything else we lose by it' (1977: 53). Breton's text for the opening of the surrealist gallery in 1937 would identify the figure of Gradiva after which it was named as 'tomorrow's beauty [who] adorns herself with all the lights of the *never seen* that force most men to lower their eyes' (Breton 1993: 19). Beauty – convulsive beauty – is only discovered, never made, as the remainder of *L'Amour fou* would subsequently document in detail, a quality which thus keys it directly to surrealism's central and determining concerns with automatism, the unconscious and the image, and which at a stroke makes most of the canon of art's attempts at capturing or representing the beautiful appear irrelevant or futile.

To complement this sense of convulsive beauty's status as discovery or revelation Breton identifies a third quality, one that again provides a theme running throughout the book to come: beauty is not merely an attribute, some passive sheen or nucleus of an object; it is an active answer. 'Such beauty cannot appear except from the poignant feeling of the thing revealed, the integral certainty produced by the emergence of a solution, which, by its very nature, could not come to us along ordinary logical paths. It is a matter – in such a case – of a solution which is always superior, a solution rigorously fitting and yet somehow in excess of the need' (1992: 681; 1987: 13). *L'Amour fou* indeed has at its centre an encounter with beauty that is also an answer to desire, in the form of Jacqueline Lamba – an encounter foretold by an automatic poem Breton had written more than ten years earlier. Just as, once integrated into the book, 'La Beauté sera convulsive' begins to introduce the portents of the objective chance that will lead the poet's paths to cross with hers, Breton closes the essay (and thus the first section of *L'Amour fou*), in a direct return to the ending of *Nadja*, with a new declaration: 'Convulsive beauty will be veiled-erotic, fixed-explosive, magic-circumstantial, or won't be at all' (1992: 687; 1987: 19).

These categories of convulsive beauty are not easily mapped onto the qualities Breton had just laid out over the preceding pages, though a rule of three presiding over both structures hints that dialectical mechanisms are at work. But once more, against models of beauty emphasizing harmony and perfection, the common thread of this tripartite structure of convulsive beauty is above all the motor of tension and opposition, held in balance in an instant between one state and another. While there is no clear suggestion of an order of priority, the first category listed, *érotique-voilée*, seems the one most clearly anchored in Breton's concerns at the time. As we have seen, both 'La Beauté sera convulsive' and *L'Amour fou* are explicitly located within the consideration of surrealism's understanding of love and desire. The first direct mention of beauty in the text already makes this explicit:

> And it is there – right in the depths of the human crucible … that years ago I asked that we look for a new beauty, a beauty 'envisaged exclusively to produce passion'. I confess without the slightest embarrassment my profound insensitivity in the presence of natural spectacles and of those works of art which do not straight off arouse a physical sensation in me, like the feeling of a feathery wind brushing across my temples to produce a real shiver. I could never avoid establishing some relation between this sensation and that of erotic pleasure, finding only a difference of degree.
>
> (1992: 678; 1987: 8)

The 'convulsion' of surrealist beauty, its 'jolts and shocks', are thus first and foremost the shiver of desire, linking beauty regardless of the object in which it is discerned to its highest expression in the experience of erotic love. As Breton describes his first meeting with Lamba, this troubled motion is again linked to the concept. 'I had already seen her here two or three times, her coming announced before I saw her each time by an undefinable quiver moving from one pair of shoulders to the next, from the door of this café toward me. For me this motion itself, which, as it is disturbing to a common assembly, quickly assumes a hostile character, has always, whether in art or in life, signalled the presence of the *beautiful*' (Breton 1992: 714; 1987: 41). This palpable sense of sexual *frisson* explains Breton's insistence throughout his discussions of beauty in *Nadja* and *L'Amour fou* on a strictly personal viewpoint: 'as far as I am concerned'; 'I see beauty as I see you'; 'for me …'. Beauty operates for (it excites) the one who experiences it, for the one for whom it is a revelation and a solution, and as such no clear notion of a 'universal' surrealist beauty would make sense. The inherently erotic nature of convulsive beauty means that it can only be sensed and found, not discerned or ascribed.

Here we might locate the nature of beauty's convulsion itself, its character as a physical and, more specifically, bodily movement: an involuntary tremor announcing an 'automatic' nervous or somatic relation to external stimuli, just as a drop in air temperature produces a shiver, or trauma produces a shudder – a form of *seizure.* A convulsion, we might note, is itself characterized by a switching between two states, those of rest and excitation, and is experienced as a kind of violent flickering. Peter Bürger links Breton's adoption of the term to the French mid-eighteenth-century proponents of transports of religious ecstasy and miraculous healing, the *convulsionnaires*, a Jansenist sect already discussed in the context of surrealism by Louis Aragon (Bürger 2009: 38). But what the word suggests most strongly here is a connection to surrealism's interest in the physical manifestations of hysteria. In their celebration of the 'Fiftieth Anniversary of Hysteria (1878–1928)', published in issue 11 of *La Révolution surréaliste*, Breton and Aragon reproduced six of the famous late nineteenth-century photographs of female patients from the Salpêtrière clinic, in bed and dressed in nightgowns, adopting the 'attitudes passionnelles' characteristic of hysteria, alongside a review of the shifting definitions and imminent demise among clinical circles of the category of the illness. They arrived instead at a definition of their own:

> Hysteria is a more or less irreducible mental state characterised by the subversion of the relations established between the subject and the moral world to which he believes himself in practice to respond, beyond any delirious system. This mental state is founded on the need for a reciprocal seduction, which explains the hastily accepted miracles of medical suggestion or counter-suggestion. Hysteria is not a pathological phenomenon and can in every sense be considered a supreme means of expression.
>
> (In Richardson and Fijalkowski 2001: 145)

Contemporaneous with the writing of *Nadja* (whose eponymous heroine did not suffer from hysteria but was nevertheless a victim of mental illness), published only two months after this text, it is perhaps not too much of a leap to see this definition, notably its emphasis on the exchange between the subject and the outside realm, on attraction and seduction, on the 'supreme means of expression', as lending its powers to the emerging definitions of surrealist beauty in Breton's thinking of this period. Certainly the image of the female body giving in to a delirious spasm, read troublingly by the surrealists (in the face of the medical profession's equally problematic diagnoses) as a release of latent erotic drives, could not fail to strike readers of these surrealist texts as also inhabiting the notion of beauty's 'convulsion'.[8]

The use of documentary photographs to illustrate and validate the surrealist reception of hysteria is mirrored by the insistent presence of photographic images to accompany Breton's discussion of convulsive beauty, both in *L'Amour fou* and 'La Beauté sera convulsive'. While here as elsewhere in Breton's publications the use of illustrations, in particular photographs, serves both to support and destabilize the text in some complex ways, this time the effect is at least in part to suggest that the business of convulsive beauty relates above all to the realm of the visual, be this a more or less conventional ocular perception or surrealism's faculty of 'inner vision' – and indeed most of Breton's writing on beauty confirms this impression ('I see beauty as I have seen you').[9] 'La Beauté sera convulsive' is illustrated by several images, including three whose titles correspond to the three categories of convulsive beauty: Man Ray's *Veiled Erotic* (1933), in which the artist Meret Oppenheim stands naked behind the wheel of a printing press; *Explosive Fixed* of 1934, again by Man Ray, in which a flamenco dancer is caught at the moment of throwing her head back so as to transform her body with its outstretched arms into a horned, headless swirl of fabric; and Brassaï's *Magic Circumstantial* of 1931 in which a potato suspended in mid-air sprouts eerie aerial roots as though to suggest a cult object or (again) a horned head.[10]

These are well-known images, widely discussed elsewhere, and space does not allow detailed consideration of them here. But we can note the insistent presence in all three of ambiguous corporeal transformations and migrations (a female body sporting a handle-phallus, a headless dancer, a vegetable resembling a head), incipient eroticism (notably in the dancer's dress which takes on a distinctly vaginal appearance) and the sense of a ceremonial, perhaps even sacred or ritual context imbued in each photograph. The absence of a fourth photograph, that of a train abandoned in the jungle, is noted with regret by Breton in 'La Beauté sera convulsive', but indeed it turns up – or one very much like it – just a few issues of *Minotaure* later to illustrate Péret's article 'La nature dévore le progrès et le dépasse', vegetation spewing out of the cab and engine as though to reclaim the locomotive's power back for the living and unassimilated world. These images move, just as Breton's presentation of convulsive beauty had from the outset, between nature and modernity, between documentary and poetic modes, between the everyday and the sublime, between eroticism and its crisis. A footnote in *Nadja* recounts just such an instance of a beauty whose convulsion threatens to engulf or dissolve its protagonists, one of the most vivid – because both terrifying and believable – experiences ever recounted by surrealism:

> One evening, when I was driving a car along the road from Versailles to Paris, the woman sitting beside me (who was Nadja, but

who might have been anyone else, or even *someone else*), pressing her foot down on mine on the accelerator, trying to cover my eyes with her hands in the oblivion of an interminable kiss, wished that we might be extinguished, doubtless forever, save for each other.

(Breton 1960: 152, translation modified)

Notes

1 One might even note that in the end the term has proved more attractive to scholars and curators than to surrealists: see Hal Foster's *Compulsive Beauty* (1993) or the Centre Pompidou's celebration *André Breton, La beauté convulsive* (Breton et al. 1991).

2 According to Marguerite Bonnet, Breton found this aphorism in Benedetto Croce's *Ce qui est vivant et ce qui est mort de la philosophie de Hegel* (see Breton 1988: 1561).

3 Works such as these, of course, have frequently been read as once more supporting rather than challenging dominant visual ideologies around gender, though the question is far from straightforward.

4 One might also make a link between surrealism's negotiation of a beauty characterized by involuntary convulsion and Adorno's assertion of the terror that 'peers out of the eyes of beauty' (1997: 52). Adorno's commentary on Hegel's aesthetics emphasizes its sense that, for Hegel, beauty pertains not to balance but to tension (46).

5 In French, we might note, the very label of 'fine art', *les beaux-arts*, is already bound to the notion of beauty.

6 Breton would qualify the word *comme* as 'the most exultant word we have at our disposal' ('Signe ascendant'; Breton 1995: 106, translation modified).

7 References here are to the more easily accessible version in *Mad Love* (Breton 1987).

8 Adorno's aesthetics also characterizes the response to significant artworks in terms of a 'shudder' that takes the viewer by surprise: 'The shock aroused by important works is not employed to trigger personal, otherwise repressed emotions. Rather, this shock is the moment in which recipients forget themselves and disappear into the work: it is the moment of being shaken. The recipients lose their footing; the possibility of truth, embodied in the aesthetic image, becomes tangible' (1997: 244). Surrealism's great innovation, through the concept of convulsive beauty, is perhaps to have generalized this principle for the whole of experience, not just for art.

9 Here the 'wild' nature of convulsive beauty might also be linked to Breton's image of the eye existing 'in a savage state', at the opening of his essay 'Surrealism and Painting', first published in 1925.

10 Since two of these photographs substantially pre-date their publication in *Minotaure*, we might assume that it was Breton who established these titles and associations with convulsive beauty.

16 The object

Krzysztof Fijalkowski

Popular understanding of surrealism has usually confined its territory to domains beyond the physical: dream and the unconscious, myth and imagination, poetry and the image. From this it can be a short step to critiquing the movement – as some did from the beginning – as mired in idealism, escapism and mystification. But from the outset surrealists themselves took care to present their engagement not as an evasion of concrete reality, but as a more profound and dynamic apprehension of it, one that might recalibrate our relationship to everyday experience in the face of the social, intellectual and material structures that have left humanity bereft and imprisoned.

The *First Manifesto* opens with exactly this problematic: 'Belief in life, in what is so precarious about life, that is *real* life, being so much taken for granted, finally results in this very belief being lost. Man, that definitive dreamer, each day more dissatisfied with his fate, looks around with dismay at the objects he is propelled to use and that indulge his listlessness' (Breton 1988: 311; see also 1969: 3).[1] Freudian psychoanalysis had already raised this tension between the material and the immaterial as it probed the relationship between the hidden realm of latent desires and anxieties, repressed memories or deep-seated but invisible drives, and their outward and measurable manifestation as actions, behaviours or neurosis. Efforts to collaborate with communists and anarchists also situate surrealism, consisting predominantly of poets and artists, as a theatre of practical action, not vicarious contemplation, of concrete rather than abstract convictions, with at least part of its philosophical position anchored in the resolutely materialist thought of Marx and Engels.[2]

An intensified interest in the object from the early 1930s onwards, in critical texts, analytical games, documentary images and above all in a thirst for finding, making and displaying unexpected objects, may partly have been a riposte to those who viewed surrealism as a movement of aesthetes and idealists. Yet scholarship has only recently recognized surrealism's objects as a major research concern, for a time at least, of the movement itself when Breton announced that 'it is essentially on the *object* that the more and more clear-sighted eyes of surrealism have remained open in recent years', clarifying that in this context 'I take the word *object* in its broadest philosophical sense' (1969: 257–8).

But the word 'object' – in its English and French derivations stemming from the Latin verb *obicere*, to throw in the way or against, to obstruct – far from delivering the stable, compliant body we normally expect of it, designates an awkward and potentially unsteady concept with a number of distinct meanings and derivatives. As such, while philosophers have distinguished between objects as physical entities and as intellectual constructs, in general philosophy has had difficulty getting to grips with what, as Henry Laycock suggests, is so general as to resist definition in simple terms (Laycock 2010), and surprisingly few have tackled its problems in detail. Our commonplace sense of the word usually refers to physical entities, and most frequently to artificial bodies within a spectrum of things large enough to be seen, small enough to be held or manipulated; a degree of volume, resistance and stability over time is usually assumed (see for example Moles 1972). The term's conceptual value, however, should not be ignored. This is of concern in the investigation of objects of knowledge – including anything that can be brought to the mind – or with the pairing of the object with the subject in order to understand the relation between the self and its interactions. Considerations of the object frequently adopt this relational emphasis: linguistics distinguishes between syntactical objects and subjects, while taxonomy concerns itself with the naming, ordering and ranking of objects in order to grasp their operations within systems or classifications.

By and large, surrealism has been interested predominantly in the first of these categories – in physical, conventionally perceivable bodies, even if it tends by the very nature of its enquiries to destabilize and render ambivalent this physicality and status. For one thing (as in the sort of visual philosophy exemplified by René Magritte, for example, operating across the borders between object, image and language), it frequently points to problems posed by conventional distinctions between showing, designating or classifying an object and that object itself. Surrealism might also be seen as a vast and potentially limitless repository of both existing and possible objects: as representations in texts, artworks, photographs or films; as the focus for individual or collective analysis and games; as the subject of discovery, collection and interpretation through the category of the *trouvaille* or 'found object'; and lastly through the deliberate construction of new objects in which existing forms are either perturbed or combined in defamiliarizing ways (the *objet surréaliste* properly speaking). Taken as a whole, and in the light of a significant number of critical or poetic texts broaching the theme of the object, this multiple perspective produces a rather diffuse and speculative set of approaches rather than a concise and coherent theory. In each case, while the actual or potential materiality of the object in surrealism guarantees its pertinence, this object also tends to present an open, mobile category of being, one in process rather than fixed in its meanings: an enigma, a doorway.

While it rarely conceived or presented experimental activity around the object in conventionally philosophical terms, what is in play for surrealism can be seen as a branch of ontology, albeit one that never aims to construct a definitive system of knowledge, and in which the central problem is above all that of identity, whether of an object, an individual or a collectivity. This dynamic around problems of identity is summed up succinctly in another of Breton's opening lines, this time at the beginning of *Nadja*: 'Qui suis-je?' – an untranslatable play on words that asks not only 'who am I?' but also 'whom do I follow?': the focus of desire lies in the riddle of who each of us might be or become, in terms of an otherness that is always both real/concrete and imaginary/conceptual. The common accusation that surrealism objectifies what should be treated as a subject – above all the persons and bodies of women – tends to ignore the problem that while the very category of 'object' is multiform and constantly under negotiation, its fate is also bound to the subject in a flux of affirmations, negations and becoming.

This emphasis on an 'objective' seam within surrealism is testified by two major concepts. Breton's notion of objective chance emerged in the late 1920s as the matrix of external and internal forces in the relationships between subjective desire and objective (frequently object-borne) encounters. Black humour, another concept developed by Breton over the 1930s, was identified in its earliest iterations as *humour objectif*, a term originally coined (rather loosely) in Hegel's *Aesthetics* to designate how Romantic art forms were able to engage subjective values in external objects, and presented by Breton in the course of a lecture on surrealism and the object in 1935 in terms of 'the contemplation of nature in its accidental forms' (1969: 267). More circumstantially, the Czechoslovak surrealist group considered, in the pressurized years following the Second World War, replacing the very term 'surrealism' with that of 'objective poetry'. Objective chance, objective humour, objective poetry: all share (in English as in French, and to a degree in Czech) a triple meaning of 'objective' in a way that inflects the surrealism of the 1930s onwards with a particular set of priorities: to be object-like or invested in objects; to be rigorous and eschew prejudice; and to be oriented towards specific outcomes.

Surrealism's objects

From the outset, surrealist practice – notably automatic writing – produced representations of unfamiliar and destabilizing objects belonging to a world of fantastic literature, fairy tales or the bric-a-brac of dreams, that retained just enough of an echo of their more tangible everyday cousins to be believable (of which Lautréamont's oft-cited 'chance encounter on a dissecting table between a sewing machine and an umbrella' is no doubt the most familiar avatar). Freud in the *Interpretation of Dreams* had noted how the mechanisms of displacement and condensation could relocate objects to new contexts or produce hybrid forms; Breton described one such dream object, a book incorporating a wooden statue, recommending the production and circulation of dream objects to 'help to demolish those concrete trophies which are so odious, to throw further discredit on those creatures and things of "reason"' (1978: 26). Texts in *La Révolution surréaliste* frequently tested the charge generated by blocking and reassigning the original intentions of practical objects: 'Any discovery changing the nature or destination of an object or a phenomenon constitutes a surrealist act', declared the preface to the inaugural issue. A few pages later Louis Aragon's account of the Concours Lepine – an annual trade fair for inventions and gadgets – proposed that, in the light of its often ridiculous but startling results, invention itself 'can be summarized as the establishment of a surreal relationship between concrete elements and its mechanism of inspiration'. Such inventions – whether practical or preposterous – represented the point where philosophy met poetry since 'the concrete is the final moment of thought, and the state of concrete thought is poetry', where (in contrast to either scientific or 'vulgar' knowledge) genuine philosophy insists that objects and ideas be concrete not abstract. This triangulation between thought, inspiration and the concrete stands in opposition to categories of reality: 'since it denies the real, philosophical knowledge first and foremost establishes a new relationship between its materials: the unreal [*l'irréel*]' (Aragon 1924: 23). Such early texts show the object present from the outset as a key marker in surrealism's quarrel with established categories of reality and reason; by December 1926 *La Révolution surréaliste* was advertising a series of editioned surrealist snow globes and an imminent exhibition, catalogue and definition of surrealist objects.

That it took another five years before any such definition or display became possible suggests that either the time wasn't then ripe or, just as importantly, that the conceptual research the problem demanded had yet to reach fruition. For the Parisian group, the period 1926–30 was characterized by debates and quarrels around political adherence, social action and – above all for this particular issue – the status of surrealism's place and role in the everyday material world. By the end of the decade the movement had emerged as a much broader coalition of artists and thinkers as well as writers, but had lost much of its early, rather rose-tinted curiosity about, for instance, features of contemporary urban space like advertising and commodities (inherited from Apollinaire and de Chirico). The move towards communism brought with it an increased (if still partial) familiarity with the writings of Marx, Engels, Lenin and Hegel, whose thought began to impart surrealist texts with greater awareness of how political and economic realities underpinned the material world.

The object's place in a system of value and symbolic exchange thus became a central precept; at stake in this encounter was the question of utility. Rather than the ordered department store, Breton found in the disarray of the local flea market a privileged site for discovering an unexpectedly poetic meaning clinging to objects that had fallen out of current systems of function, value and exchange (as though to propose a kind of 'psychoeconomic' equation shadowing Marx's distinction between use- and exchange-value in the commodity): 'I go there often, searching for objects that can be found nowhere else: old-fashioned, broken, useless, almost incomprehensible, even perverse – at least in the sense I give to the word' (Breton 1960: 52). The interruption or deflection of an object's initial purpose and commodity value, then, provided the key to its rescue, unlocking something dormant within it. 'Here as elsewhere, the mad beast of *use* must be hunted down' (Breton 1972: 279, translation modified), Breton would write of surrealism's objects a decade later, with the French term *usage* indicating both utility and the sense of custom or convention. The homes of surrealists started to fill with flea-market finds alongside the books and contemporary or tribal artworks adorning the walls; Breton's studio at 42, rue Fontaine became the epitome of a surrealist domestic space crammed with things and resembling something between a *Wunderkammer* and an alchemist's lair.

The development of the concept of objective chance would inflect this interest into a more fully formed theory of the *trouvaille*, eventually defined in terms not just of its availability for reverie or wonder, but of its potential as a response from the external world to the inner workings of Eros. While this might be imagined as a generalization of anthropologist

Marcel Mauss's theory of gift exchange as social communication, for Breton the latency of any object as an emissary from the external world, cut free of the human agency that first plotted its destiny, is keyed not to social or ritual values but to deeper drives: 'any piece of flotsam and jetsam within our grasp should be considered a precipitate of our desire' (1972: 283). The fullest exposition of objective chance comes in Breton's *Mad Love*; central to it are two accounts in which the pursuit of objects portends the arrival of a lover – Breton's future wife Jacqueline – foretold years before in an automatic poem. The book's third section, first published in shorter form as 'Equation of the Found Object', is a detailed analysis of two discoveries made at Saint-Ouen market by Breton and the sculptor Alberto Giacometti: a carved wooden spoon and a slatted metal visor respectively (Breton 1987: 25–38). Giacometti is drawn to an ominous form that turns out to be part of a gas mask from the First World War. Its deathly intimations help Breton understand Giacometti's compulsion to obtain the mask as directly related to his current difficulties in resolving a major work, entitled precisely *The Invisible Object*. In it, the hands of an immobilized and elongated standing female figure reach out in a gesture of entreaty as if to cup the missing object of the work's title. But while this sense of absence or loss pervades both the work and its affective origins – Giacometti, like Breton, was suffering emotional distress in his personal life – it also marked the sculpture's process, where a sense of psychopathological blockage prevented the artist from completing the figure's face and bringing closure to the piece.

The encounter with the mask seemed to provide the missing element of a puzzle, overcoming trauma and enabling completion of the work (whose eventual head actually bore little resemblance to the find), prompting Breton to note that 'the finding of the object serves here exactly the same purpose as the dream, in the sense that it frees the individual from paralyzing affective scruples, comforts him and makes him understand that the obstacle he might have thought unsurmountable is cleared' (Breton 1992: 700; 1987: 32). Yet, despite Breton's optimism, the status of the 'found' object is not so easily assigned, given that the exchanges he has witnessed have to do with losing as much as finding, with absence as much as presence: *The Invisible Object* turned out to mark Giacometti's farewell to surrealism. Is the 'invisible object' here an intellectual enigma, present yet imperceptible – read as a gap – between the figure's hands (its alternative title is *Hands Holding the Void*)? Is it displaced to the mask, whose slatted visor closes off sight and invites inner vision? Is it the figure itself, the object of Giacometti's longing; or is he, fragile in his affective paralysis, *her* missing object? Things are complicated when we notice that some versions of the sculpture, including the one illustrated in *Mad Love*, place a conical form suggestive of a bird's head or animal skull on the platform beside the figure, echoing the deathly message of the mask and linking back to the troubling category of what the artist termed 'disagreeable objects', as though to return to the originary resistance of the *ob-ject*, the thing thrown against the senses.

Breton's account continues with a parallel analysis of *his* found object, a 'slipper-spoon' (its wooden handle ends in a miniature carved shoe that also becomes the spoon's 'heel') that he reads, in answer to Giacometti's mask under the sign of Thanatos, as a bearer of erotic and life-affirming motivations in the face of loss. The analysis takes two years, taking in fairy-tale narratives (Cinderella's slipper), psychoanalytic interpretation (gendered and erotic readings of the carving), biographical details and an eye for the minutiae of events and places. An earlier section of *Mad Love* had already linked the *trouvaille* to the categories of the marvellous and convulsive beauty, seeing the distance between an anticipated object of desire and its possible final form as a register of the object's potential for wonder and revelation, hoisting an elected item out of its mundane context: 'what is delightful is the dissimilarity existing between the object wished for and *the object found*. The *trouvaille*, whether artistic, scientific, philosophic or as useless as anything, is enough to undo the beauty of everything beside it' (Breton 1992: 682; 1987: 13, translation modified).

Breton's characteristic optimism that the signs of desire moving towards fulfilment can be offered to the individual by the gifts and objective encounters of the external world resonates through many surrealist representations and realizations of magnetized or perturbed objects, even if in many a sense of disquiet or humour comes to the fore. Jan Švankmajer, sensitive throughout his research to the object's secret lives, its tactile messages and capacity for betraying its owners, tracks the object between pathos, slapstick and fear in stop-motion animations such as *The Flat* (1968), in which a hapless protagonist is assailed on all sides by mere things. Jacques Bureau, a member of the wartime Main à plume surrealist group in Paris, invoked his incarceration in Fresnes prison in 1943 for a moving text intended for a special issue of a journal devoted to the object. 'The Nail' describes in intimate detail how a personal relationship with something found in a cell might open a dialogue when the customary relationship between subjects and objects is restaged:

> Speaking of objects is not easy. One must have lived with them outside the rules that tie them to us in misfortune. We keep them

> enslaved and they are, for us, devious enemies. We will need resolutely to strike up an understanding with them: to learn from them, and then teach them. ... We misunderstand the reality of the object because we live amongst too many of them, and give them divided attention. ... But live for weeks, months, every day, every night with just one of them, the drabbest and humblest of them. *Live alone for an entire four months with a nail*, and you will understand.
>
> (Bureau 2008: 252–3)

The idea that the object might enter into dialogue with the subject, becoming the focus for a process that combined chance, pleasure and revelation, had already come to a head within the Parisian surrealist group early in the 1930s, and here again Giacometti motivated its development. His tabletop sculpture *Suspended Ball* (1930–31), in which an incised sphere hangs from a cage in such a way that it could be made to rub along a recumbent crescent shape in a gesture simultaneously erotic and threatening, strongly affected the group. Noting the combination of concrete and psychosexual or dreamlike forces at work, Salvador Dalí proposed a collective game in which participants constructed informal assemblages from found materials and gathered them for analysis. The resulting Symbolically Functioning Objects were presented in issue 3 of *Le Surréalisme au service de la Révolution* – though they constituted only the first of six categories of what was now termed the 'surrealist object' (Dalí 1998b: 135). While *Suspended Ball* was seen as operating in the discipline of sculpture, an attraction of the Symbolically Functioning Object was its non-art status, closer to the everyday items from which it was composed than to plastic or aesthetic concerns, though surrealist objects would soon be presented in gallery contexts. Dalí's article comprised a theoretical text and brief interpretations, with the objects illustrated several pages further on. Made of diverse, often unassuming, materials – gloves, a shoe, a bicycle saddle, tobacco – their analysis, particularly in the case of Dalí's own explicitly sexualized assemblage, tended to point to anxieties and desires in ways that both keyed the results to psychoanalytic orthodoxy and tended to generate either rather limited and predictable readings, or else equivocal and uncertain ones. Breton himself would later declare his relative dissatisfaction with the results in comparison to the spark of the *trouvaille*:

> without hereby intending to formulate the least reservation over their explosive power or their 'beauty', I think I can say that they offer interpretation a less considerable scope, as might be expected, than objects that are less systematically determined in this

> direction. … No doubt in the end such objects, too specific in conception, too personal as they are, will always lack the astonishing power of suggestion with which some nearly ordinary objects by chance find themselves endowed.
>
> (1990: 55, translation modified)

The object in crisis

Notwithstanding this concern, the experiment helped trigger a trend for surrealist assemblage from the 1930s onwards, within the French group and further afield (especially in Belgium, Britain, Romania and Spain), and resulting in some of the movement's most iconic and immediate visual works. Surrealist exhibitions increasingly featured objects in their displays, eventually placing them in ambitious installations that gave the visitor the sense of stepping into a materialized dream. Exhibitions in Paris and London (1936 and 1937) devoted entirely to the object advertised the significance of the theme, and encouraged the extension of its scope and theorization, but also marked the beginnings of a process that saw what had initially been experimental or analytical activity tipped into the art market and – more worryingly – the domain of advertising and design. Shop window design, to cite but one discipline, would adopt 'surreal' juxtapositions of goods, mannequins and environments as a default style for the next decade. Not until much later, in the exhibition *L'Écart absolu* of 1965, would the Parisian group draw up coherent critiques of consumer society and its objects (by which time the fad for a 'surreal style' had itself become outmoded).

Located in the Galerie Charles Ratton, a space normally reserved for the display and sale of tribal artefacts, the *Surrealist Exhibition of Objects* of 1936 brought together well over a hundred exhibits. The presentation – works on the wall or atop plinths but most strikingly in glazed cabinets – deliberately mixed up the different categories of objects the small catalogue strove to distinguish: newly created surrealist assemblages sat alongside mathematical models, tribal carvings, found items and natural specimens. Just as importantly, the group developed an accompanying issue of the art journal *Cahiers d'Art* on the theme of the object, featuring photographic reproductions and several significant texts, in particular Breton's 'Crise de l'objet'. This essay begins by tracing parallels between key periods of poetic and scientific discovery – the height of Romanticism, for example, and the discovery of non-Euclidean geometry, 'an event which shook to its very foundations the edifice constructed by Descartes and Kant and "opened up" rationalism, so to speak' (Breton 1972: 275). The late nineteenth century, on the other hand, brought together the 'transcended contradictions' of Lautréamont and

Rimbaud alongside the development of a generalized geometry resolving Euclidean and non-Euclidean theories, resulting in 'a total disruption of sensibility by routing all rational habits, erasing the distinction between good and evil, expressing strict reservations about the hegemony of the *cogito*, and revealing the marvellous of everyday life' (275). Contemporary scientific and artistic thought thus share a relationship to the real:

> in either case, the real, confused for too long with given data, splinters in every direction possible and tends to become a component of the possible. By applying Hegel's dictum that 'everything real is rational, and everything rational is real', one may well expect to see the rational follow precisely in the footsteps of the real, and it is certainly true that, today, reason goes so far as to propose the continuous assimilation of the irrational, a process during which the rational is required to remould its own image constantly.
>
> (276)

The object, then (thus far not broached by the text but present in the accompanying illustrations of striking geological specimens) participates in a dynamic process in the history of sensibility whereby reality, reason and the rational unfold through a series of dialectical crises and resolutions. The crisis of the object portends a deeper (perhaps perennial but now fundamental) crisis of thought, brought to a height in the contemporary age's urgent 'desire to objectify' (277). Surrealism's own object interventions are cited as instances where irrational or unconscious disruptions of the concrete realm act as advance signals of the anxiety of contemporary intellectual life. Surrealism's objects, in Paul Éluard's phrase, participate in a 'physics of poetry', laboratory research in which the everyday forms in the 'hateful regime' of common sense are subjected to a stripping away of use and convention, playing upon the tension between contrary realities and their reconciliation so as to unlock 'latent possibilities' and concrete transformations (279). Whether found or made, these newly liberated forms 'succeed in achieving a separate identity simply through a change of role' (280).

The final French phrase Breton adopts here, *mutation de rôle*, indicates not simply a shift in purpose, but a 'change in job', a transfer of responsibilities: this object, no matter how much the markers of consumer and social utility encoded within it may have been scrubbed out, nonetheless continues to function – albeit now predominantly on a symbolic, affective and intellectual plane. This important distinction – that surrealism's objects don't so much aim to cancel utility as reassign it, blocking the customary and mercantile values inscribed in it in order to provoke a latent, non-rational purpose – had recently been echoed by other surrealists. Georges Hugnet's text 'L'Objet utile' in the previous issue of *Cahiers d'Art* insisted that 'there are no useless objects. Those that might seem so merely prove the poverty of our conception of the real': each object 'is a knowledge of the self in relation to the real. It functions as we do' (Hugnet 2005: 135). Roger Caillois, in the essay 'Spécification de la poésie', had already argued that utilitarian function is never a full explanation of the object's form: 'in other words the object always overflows the instrument. Thus it is possible to discover in each object an irrational residue determined amongst other things by the unconscious intentions of the inventor or technician' (Caillois 2015: 268). Claude Cahun's essay 'Beware of Domestic Objects', published alongside 'Crisis of the Object', began to sketch the role of the irrational in the politicized terms of labour and consciousness:

> we need to discover, manipulate, *tame*, make for ourselves irrational objects in order to appreciate the specific or general value of those we have in front of our eyes. This is why, in certain respects, *manual* workers would be better placed than intellectuals to grasp their meaning, if it were not that everything in capitalist society, including communist propaganda, did not turn them away from it.
>
> (Cahun 2002a: 540)

A notable inclusion in the 1936 Ratton show was Marcel Duchamp's ready-mades, differentiated from the *objets surréalistes* in the catalogue but clearly seen within the same body of enquiry. Though the first ready-mades predated surrealism by a decade, their action of deflecting utility by placing commercial objects in a gallery environment to induce a conceptual jolt in their value was read as an avatar of the surrealist object's challenge to use and exchange. The act of isolating and removing an object from its location, however, might function equally well in the framework of other approaches. Examining what he termed the *objets bouleversants* (disruptive objects) in Magritte's work, Paul Nougé stressed the object's subversive value in its separation from the world:

> Here the fundamental operation appears to us to be *isolation* and one might go so far as to suggest a kind of law: once isolated, the charm of an object is a direct result of its banality. ... Moreover, the subversive power of an isolated object is a direct result of the intimacy of the relations it maintained up to that point with our body, with our mind, with ourselves.
>
> (Nougé 1980: 239)

Changing the vision, position, scale or context of any daily object can provoke a fresh consciousness that might enable the individual to 'go where he has never been, feel what he has never felt, think what he has never thought, be what he has never been'.

The difficulty, certainly among many of the most successful surrealist assemblages, was the extent to which the surrealist object's role as a conceptual stake, as a harbinger of crisis, might speak louder than its power to disorient through the more transient mechanisms of humour and the absurd. Dalí's contribution to *Cahiers d'Art*, 'Honneur à l'objet', cites Plato, Socrates, Epicurus, Lucretius, Anaxagoras, Marx, Feuerbach and Chinese philosophy as character witnesses in a 'paranoid-critical' argument collapsing together several divergent concerns, a move that shores up an otherwise rather indistinct argument yet also destabilizes the philosophical underpinnings of the object world through proliferation. One of Dalí's contributions to the Charles Ratton exhibition was a *Monument to Kant* combining a base bearing an inscription from the *Critique of Practical Reason*, a tall scaffold displaying a number of fountain pens, and a bottle. The artist described another of his works in the show as a *machine à penser*, and though he was apt to appropriate philosophical ideas in a partial and unorthodox manner, the sense that each of his objects was intended to operate as a shifting nexus of conceptual reflection comes across repeatedly in his writings.

But what kind of 'crisis' do surrealism's objects enact or suffer? The implication of Breton's text is that the object's crisis is a physical manifestation of a deeper intellectual one, but the choice of vocabulary is significant. For one thing, it hints at the most obvious sense of material anxiety in recent times: the aftermath of the Wall Street Crash, a global financial crisis undermining consumer trade throughout the early 1930s in a way that highlighted everyday tensions between commodity, economy and labour. For Breton, a former medical student familiar with psychoanalytic theory, the idea of crisis would also have had echoes of a psychiatric emergency. Charcot's analysis of hysteria, for example, charts the stages of the *grande crise hystérique* as a sequence of individual crises, something medical science would define in terms of a pathological breakdown, whereas for surrealism this portent of imminent collapse heralds something more equivocal: a point of divergence (the word 'crisis' itself derives from the Greek for 'decision').

Dalí's repeatedly reviewed taxonomies of the object in his writings, like the revised lists of object categories issued by the group over the course of the 1930s, point to the object's role not just as a 'thought machine' but as an agent in an unfolding crisis of knowledge. Attempts by surrealists to classify and systematize the object ever more precisely ultimately have the reverse effect of blurring and rendering increasingly ambiguous the possibility of a coherent and stable order of objects as a system of knowledge, or as the material evidence of philosophy's desire for concrete determination. Just as potently, Dalí was liable to present the object as a lure for thought, dragging the mind away from manifest representations into the wormholes of tiny details. In this way, his analysis of a found nineteenth-century photograph of two women outside a shop immediately leads the viewer away from the main scene down to an apparently insignificant bobbin lying in the gutter, read by Dalí as a breakdown of the Kantian external object at the point where space becomes metaphysical (Dalí 1935). For surrealism, he seems to hint, the distinction between material phenomena in the external world and the qualities of the Kantian *Ding an sich*, unknowable and hidden from sight, becomes problematized and instrumentalized.

The object's ability to act as a lure for the subject, to draw it out in acts of ritual, memory, divination and sorcery, is given its most troubling expression in surrealism by the experiments conducted by the Bucharest surrealists in the midst of the Second World War, in particular Ghérasim Luca's *The Passive Vampire* – a narrative ruled and sometimes overwhelmed by 'objects, those mysterious suits of armour beneath which desire awaits us, nocturnal and laid bare, those snares made of velvet, of bronze, of gossamer that we throw at ourselves with each step we take, hunter and prey in the shadows of forests' (2008: 71). Drawing on the experience of a game in which players offered found items to each other, Luca traces the object's secret, sometimes malevolent, action on its finder or user. The heteroclite assemblages Luca makes, analyses and illustrates act as waymarkers on a journey into the hidden correspondences between desire, interpersonal relationships and a world in which forces beyond current dimensions of knowledge make us the victims rather than masters of their realm. Subject and object circle and act upon each other in the dialectic the Bucharest group termed 'knowing through not-knowing', a mutual assured destruction of all values and understanding. Decades later, Annie Le Brun would echo this reciprocal gamble of subject and object in the play of identity, chained together in an unfolding drama of shattering and becoming against the backdrop of the enigma of being:

> While the merely perceived object masks the void through its neutral presence or tends to be confounded with it, the privileged object imposes itself upon us as a touchstone of the void, acting to open up a horizon between interior psychic reality and external reality on which the threat of a separation that is overcome but not

> repressed becomes the guarantee of the freedom of play. … Never identical to itself, the object invites us to discover one by one the symbolically functioning pieces of the puzzle of our identity.
>
> (Le Brun 1976: n.p.)

Notes

1 Like many of Breton's books, the *Manifesto* begins with a complex, almost untranslatable, passage. Here, with 'Tout va la croyance à la vie qu'à la fin cette croyance se perd', he is playing upon a French proverb 'Tant va la cruche à l'eau qu'à la fin elle se casse' ('you'll break your jug if you keep throwing it in the water') which figuratively means 'Don't push your luck' or 'I can only take so much'. Breton is making a distinction between the unsatisfactory *real life* that is given to us and taken for granted, and the *true life* that becomes possible if we examine its foundation (see the discussion of this point in Breton 1988: 1344).

2 Complicating this position, though beyond the scope of this chapter, is the significance for surrealism of the thought of Berkeley, both as an antecedent of Hegel but also in his concept of 'immaterialism' (see Ades 1992: 132–5).

17 Black humour

Michael Richardson

It is not the least of humour's roles to cleanse the fields of the mind.

Aimé Césaire

I laugh at nothingness.

Georges Bataille

Surrealism is, no doubt more than any other cultural movement, the one that has made the most extensive use of humour. This is, indeed, a major part of its charm. Surrealist artworks frequently bring a smile to the face of the viewer in a way that is rare in the history of art, if one excepts the work of caricaturists like Hogarth or Daumier.

Nevertheless, surrealist humour is rarely comforting and often (although not always) inclines towards a shadowy realm that Breton would theorize as 'black humour'. It does not engage in wittiness or comic effect: there are no belly laughs here. One should not expect the sort of humour that serves as a counterweight to the human condition, allowing us momentarily to put aside our worries, or that gives us a sense of superiority over the misfortunes or inadequacies of others. Surrealism doesn't engage in the sort of wit that Hegel criticized in Romanticism, but works in the opposite direction; starting from what Hegel called 'objective humour', it tends to induce a feeling of discomfort even as it causes us to laugh. It arises from a determination not to take the world seriously and to treat our own position within it not as absurd but as strange and alien: it reminds us that we know nothing of why we are here or what purpose we are really supposed to serve. At the same time, it asserts that those purposes imposed upon us by society (above all as a result of loyalty to family, nation and church) are false and to be opposed. Humour in surrealism is always founded in a refusal of given conditions and as a revolt against whatever is imposed upon us.

This tactical dimension had already been established in surrealism's prehistory by Jacques Vaché, André Breton's wartime friend, when he spoke not of humour but of *l'umour*, a form of humour that falls short of the usual definitions. Vaché, who died in 1919, furnished Breton with many of the attitudes he would take with him in founding and maintaining the idea of the surrealist movement; indeed, by asserting that Vaché 'is surrealist in me', Breton underlined his importance as a continuing presence within surrealism. Vaché's *umour* is based on a principle of pure indifference, the assumption of 'the theatrical (and joyless) futility of everything' (in Hale et al. 1995: 216). This sense of futility was underscored by the ridiculousness of the world war into which Vaché, along with many of those who would constitute the first generation surrealists, had been inducted. As Breton tells it, during the war Vaché advocated wearing a uniform that was half French, half German, with equal proportions of provisions from each side (Breton 1997: 294). As contemptuous of those who protested against the war as he was of those who promoted it, Vaché upheld the virtue of total disdain, refusing to recognize the miserable reality into which such a choice had plunged humanity at the time.

Another significant and comparable influence was the example of Arthur Cravan, the audacious poet, dandy and boxer who challenged world heavyweight champion Jack Johnson to a match before vanishing somewhere in the Gulf of Mexico. Common to Vaché and Cravan was the belief that life generally was insufficiently important to be taken seriously. The only appropriate attitude in the face of it was a sense of derision: Cravan avoided being conscripted into the war by assuming different identities and becoming a 'deserter from nineteen countries'. For both men, the only choices open to humans of good faith were desertion and defeatism.

The attitude Vaché and Cravan upheld was comparable to but in some ways more radical than the contempt for the war mentality being displayed by the Dadaists in Zurich, Berlin and other places. For Vaché it was not sufficient to say 'no!'; it was more subversive to say 'yes!' One imagines that Vaché would have agreed with what Georges Bataille (who once desired to found a 'yes' movement to counter the Dadaist 'no') would later say about Dada: that it was 'not stupid enough' (quoted in Surya 2002: 72). Indeed, it seems to have been from what he learned from Vaché that Breton would soon perceive the inadequacy of the Dadaist attitude and be impelled to seek ways to go beyond it.

Yet, by 1919, as Dada was belatedly reaching Paris, Cravan and Vaché were apparently dead, both having taken their departure from this life in mysterious circumstances that may have evidenced their respective senses of *umour*. Vaché either killed himself in some strange ritual, or died in a banal accident as a result of a drug overdose. Craven set sail across the shark-infested Gulf of Mexico for Brazil never to be heard of again. Many and varied legends have grown up around his fate, although Roger Conover sets out convincing evidence that he did survive and returned to Europe, existing as a forger and assuming an elaborate succession of aliases that establish him as a master of *umour* (see Hale et al. 1995: 15–31).

If the Dadaists' rejection of a world that had descended into insane war was comparable in attitude to that of Vaché and Craven none went as far as they did in making a humorous attitude almost a mode of living. For all of their revolt against the way things were, the Dadaists did take the world seriously, at least in so far as their activity was directed against it, seeking to exasperate it through scandal and provocation, perhaps even wanting to shock it into awareness. Humour here became a weapon, a means of revealing the absurdity and brutality of a society that had degenerated to the extent of initiating a brutal and murderous combat. For the Dadaists all values needed to be brought into question; society had to be reorganized from scratch.

Nevertheless, there was one among the French Dadaists who went as far, if not further, than Vaché and Cravan: Jacques Rigaut. Rigaut considered life not 'worth the trouble of leaving' and took this sensibility of indifference to its logical conclusion as he treated suicide as the only legitimate vocation. But if Rigaut was contemptuous of life, he was equally so of death: suicide was to be a project, not a means by which to escape the cares of the world, something one prepared for and enacted irrespective of one's own state of mind. Having announced in 1919, therefore (when he was only 19), that he had condemned himself to death, the sentence to be carried out in ten years time, Rigaut did indeed kill himself in 1929.

In some ways Rigaut was a transitional figure who stands between Dada and surrealism in terms of humorous negation. For by the time Dada reached Paris its categorical negation was already beginning to fray at the edges and its sensibility would be put to the test through collective activities that gradually morphed into surrealism. Part of this adjustment came from a realization that the 'enemy' wasn't simply the society that had created the war; the malaise went deeper and demanded a response that would not simply challenge society as it then was but would interrogate the nature of existence itself and the reality that accrued from it. Humour could play an essential part in this examination, but to do so it needed to be extended beyond Dadaist refusal: it needed to bring into question existence itself, and one's own existence especially. The disinterested humour of Vaché, Cravan and Rigaut would play a crucial role here as Breton, Philippe Soupault and Louis Aragon, the 'three musketeers' who would be instrumental in founding surrealism, began to take stock of the crisis in consciousness Dada had revealed.

For all of its philosophical pessimism, and notwithstanding the fatality into which their attitude led Vaché, Cravan and Rigaut, surrealist humour is not morbid and rarely engages with the macabre. Indifferent to the struggle between life and death, the surrealist can assume a sense of ironic detachment from everyday concerns – whether those of an individual or those more general to society. Equally important, therefore, would be the more playful Dadaist humour of the globetrotting but at the time mainly US-based Marcel Duchamp and Francis Picabia. Their detachment from the war experience gave them the space to explore this feeling of indifference in less emotive ways as they respectively engaged in activity that 'was utterly gratuitous and spontaneous, that … never had any programme, method, or articles of faith' (Gabrielle Buffet, quoted in Richter 1965: 76). From this attitude resulted the ready-mades of Duchamp that scandalized New York's art world and changed the trajectory of modern art. For nascent surrealism, the examples of Duchamp and Picabia would add another element to the groundwork that was being undertaken and would provide the stimulus for the founding of the new movement.

The surrealist attitude also took inspiration from the contagious impact of slapstick film comedy which developed in France in the films of Max Linder and Louis Feuillade's Bout-de-Zan series, and reached its highest point in the Hollywood films of the twenties. Charlie Chaplin, Fatty Arbuckle, Buster Keaton, Harry Langdon, Larry Semon and Laurel and Hardy were all surrealist heroes, dispensers of what Petr Král (1984) would call 'custard pie morality' as they took revenge on the habitual world that surrounded them. The ethical message the surrealists discerned in these films would certainly play its part in the foundations of the movement and by the end of the twenties would feed its way back into Hollywood itself in the animated films of the Fleischer brothers, especially the early Betty Boop series. It assumed a still more derisive form with the coming of talkies, as W.C. Fields and the Marx Brothers were able to express verbally their scorn for society's moral strictures in terms that hardly differed from the surrealists own sensibility. For Antonin Artaud, the Marx Brothers' film *Monkey Business* (1931) adds to the notion of humour 'the notion of something disturbing and tragic, a fatality (neither fortunate nor unfortunate, but difficult to express) which slips in behind it, like the revelation of a dreadful illness on the face of absolute beauty' (Artaud 1976: 240). This tradition perhaps reaches its apex with the 1940s cartoons of Tex Avery like *What's Buzzin' Buzzard* (1943), in which two vultures spend the whole seven minutes trying to eat one another.

This humorous sensibility had something contagious about it, and Robert Benayoun recounts the shades in the expression of laughter among the surrealists he knew:

> André Breton's round and mocking laugh, silent or imperative and sometimes categorical.
>
> Marcel Duchamp's unhooked laugh, mechanical like an uncoupling of carriages.
>
> Benjamin Péret's dry laugh, lively as an easily sipped small white wine.
>
> Man Ray's resonant and throaty laugh, slightly out of tune.
>
> Tanguy's unhooked jaw laugh, as disturbing as a dislocating of the joints or an epileptic fit.
>
> Prévert's low and old man's laugh.
>
> Artaud's cataclysmic and petrifying laugh.
>
> Miró's urchin and uncouth laugh.
>
> E.L.T. Mesens's tidy, mischievous and wasteful laugh.
>
> Philippe Soupault's detonator laugh.
>
> [And so on.]
>
> (Benayoun 1988: 7–8)

This laughter, however, was not that of a complacent clique that ridiculed the commonplace world that surrounded them and took refuge in their disdain for it. It was closer to the 'joy in the face of death' identified by Georges Bataille, a laughter that affirmed one's own existence while recognizing its fragility and cruelty. It was this that qualified their humour as objective and disinterested, responding to Bataille's hatred for 'complacent laughter, the cliquish humour of the so-called witty'. He continues: 'Nothing is less characteristic of me than bitter laughter. I laugh innocently and divinely. I don't laugh when I'm depressed – and when I do laugh, I'm having fun' (Bataille 1992: 58).

The generalized refusal to treat existence with respect, and especially to refuse to take one's own existence seriously, implicit in the examples above, lies at the root of what Breton would define in the thirties as 'black humour'. He developed and refined this idea in compiling his *Anthology of Black Humour* during the second half of the 1930s, a time when 'humour' of the blackest and most serious sort was being inflicted upon the world with the emergence of fascism and Nazism.

In the book, Breton collected and presented texts by forty-five writers, chronologically organized, in which black humour is placed in evidence. Responding to his own taste rather than seeking to establish some sort of surrealist canon,[1] Breton begins with Jonathan Swift, including his renowned 'A Modest Proposal', in which he advocates that the children of the poor should be sold to the rich for food in order to alleviate their suffering, and ends with the surrealist poet Jean-Pierre Duprey, who offers us 'a spectrum of blackness that is every bit as diverse as the solar spectrum' (Breton 1997: 348). There is much more involved in black humour than the desire to provoke laughter. Many of Breton's selections, in fact, are not especially funny, and those that are, are tinged with disquiet, like Leonora Carrington's 'The Debutante', in which a young woman persuades a hyena to take her place at the debutante's ball.

In black humour, more than anything, death – and perhaps life itself – is a trick that is played on us all. Perhaps black humour's essence is contained in the joke recounted by Freud and quoted by Breton in his introduction: a condemned man being led to the gallows on Monday morning mutters 'What a way to start the week!' (Breton 1997: xviii). Death is here simultaneously denied and accepted in a way that affirms the surrealist refusal of what is presented to us as the reality of the world, in which we live and die to no purpose. A further quotation from Freud, also mentioned by Breton, underlines this sense: the ego 'refuses to be hurt by the arrows of reality or to be compelled to suffer. It insists that it is impervious to wounds dealt by the outside world, in fact, that these are merely occasions for affording it pleasure' (Breton 1997: xviii).

It was against this backdrop that Breton started to look into the theory of humour, finding a starting point in Hegel, who anticipates Freud in linking humour with the pleasure principle as it asserts itself against brute reality. For Hegel it is linked to the sublime: it 'doesn't resign itself but challenges, implying not only the triumph of the self, but also of the principle of pleasure, which thereby finds the means to assert itself' (quoted in Hubert 1992: 1758).

This 'triumph of the self' also, however, at the same time brings the self itself into question, for the pleasure principle implies that the self goes beyond itself to engage with the forces that surround it. For surrealists, human existence is not precisely absurd, but inharmonious, and this lack of harmony lies within ourselves: we have created a social reality out of kilter with our own aspirations and with the natural flow of the universe. Far from being worried by the apparent absurdity of the world, the surrealist embraces it as a weapon to expose the contradictions that lie within reality itself. Contrary to both the existentialists, who consider existence fundamentally meaningless, and the dramatists of the 'theatre of the absurd', who took pleasure in this very meaninglessness, surrealists tend rather to be overwhelmed by its surfeit of meaning. However, these are meanings that are in the main withheld from us as mere humans. The surrealists are thus more in accord with Isidore Ducasse when he asserted that '[n]othing is incomprehensible' (Lautréamont 1978: 270), a statement which, in its ambivalence and contradictory logic, encapsulates black humour in its broadest sense. Thus, perhaps, as Breton pondered in *Nadja*, life is a cryptogram inviting deciphering (Breton 1960: 112). And therefore the surrealists refuse the existentialist position, regarding the view of existence as absurd or nonsensical rather as a symptom of a sickness whose causes need to be investigated. As René Ménil noted: 'Humour is precisely the awareness of our diminished and restrained life as well as a revenge against this diminution and restraint and the triumphant cry of the liberated mind' (1996a: 162–3).

Here black humour, as enunciated by Breton, may be equated with the role of black bile in Hippocratic medicine, serving to counter the excessively phlegmatic character that modern society, under the sway of positivism and rationalism, has assumed. Raihan Kadri argues that '[h]umour enters the scene as a regulating force acting to break the deadly serious flow of imagination, putting one's existing perspective in the overall perspective of life. There, it can only see itself as incomplete, unresolved, as fragment. Humour works as a kind of reset button, a universal bullshit detector, bringing one back to philosophical pessimism and the need for revaluation' (Kadri 2011: 148).

Like any cure, however, a remedy contains within it a modicum of the sickness it seeks to treat. Breton's anthology itself had a tortuous trajectory that was redolent with a certain black humour. Conceived in 1934, it experienced many ups and downs before finally leaving the presses on 10 June 1940, the very day the Nazi troops entered and occupied Paris, and its publication was immediately prohibited. Finally published after the liberation in 1945, it received a curiously ambivalent reception from Raymond Queneau (a former member of the surrealist group whose own work is replete with a humour which had even been directed against the surrealists themselves in *Odile*, his *roman à clef* published in 1937), that is certainly not without its own blackness. Noting how the Nazis had given Parisians – along with the whole world – an appalling dose of black humour in action, he points out that 'the fight against Nazism didn't occur at the level of black humour. It needed tommy-gun shots and 10-ton bombs' (Queneau 1965: 194).

Writing in the immediate aftermath of the war, Queneau's hesitancy is perhaps understandable, but if we can recognize the mentality of Nazism as embodying black humour at an extreme, it is only so in a sense contrary to that advocated by Breton and the surrealists, as it treats itself with the utmost seriousness. Hitler's notion of the thousand-year Reich could indeed be said to constitute a supreme example of black humour that should be treated as nothing but a joke. The fact that he believed in it, and convinced other people to believe in it, makes it – and every other manifestation of Nazism, which never loses its seriousness – precisely an idea that has to be made a target of a black humour whose acerbity has to be such as to corrode such seriousness wherever it appears. Indeed, is not the Nazi Final Solution nothing but Swift's 'modest proposal' taken *in extremis*? The mentality that constituted fascism neither began with Nazism nor ended with the unconditional surrender of 1945. In so far as it persists as a poisonous presence in modern society, weapons need to be honed against it without complacency. No doubt the 'modest proposal' had little effect in preventing the suffering of the poor in eighteenth-century Ireland. It did, however, raise awareness of it and of our own complicity in it. If, therefore, black humour may be powerless to act against the sickness at the height of the fever, it can function as an effective preventative measure against its manifestation in the first place.

In this respect, the sense of demoralization that black humour inevitably promotes has to be seen as a positive force by the very means of its negation. Its ultimate target is solutions of any type. Alfred Jarry had already advanced pataphysics as the 'science of imaginary solutions', and Marcel Duchamp declared that 'there's no solution because there's no problem', evidencing a distrust of planning outcomes that would be prevalent within surrealism. Indeed, according to Aragon humour itself is precisely aimed against solutions: 'Humor is of the opinion that where there is a solution, there is no humor … Humor is the negative condition of poetry, which perhaps is ambiguous but which means that in order for there to be poetry humor must first get rid of antipoetry' (1991: 68).

Notwithstanding all of these influences upon it, though, the principal philosophical inspiration for black humour appears to have been Nietzsche, in whom, Breton asserted, '[h]umour has never attained such intensity, nor has it ever run up against stricter boundaries' (1997: 129). Breton is here discussing the strange letter to Jacob Burckhardt, which he includes in his anthology, that immediately preceded Nietzsche's complete breakdown. However, Breton seems more broadly to have in mind many of Nietzsche's late writings, like *The Twilight of the Gods* and *Ecco Homo*, in which intense insight is combined with delusion in a way that makes it difficult to distinguish between them. Could Nietzsche's madness and subsequent silence even be seen as a black joke he played on the world, a revenge against the bitter fate that marooned him (and along with him all of humanity) here? Indeed, isn't the use of the weapon of black humour itself not so much a sign of madness as an indication that one has recognized the madness of the world, and even of one's own collusion with it? In the receptivity to black humour there is an indication of one's own madness, at least in the sense of one's ill-adaption to the world. Nietzsche himself asserted the necessity of wisdom to be combined with laughter:

> To laugh at oneself as one would have to laugh in order to laugh *out of the whole truth* – to do that even the best so far lacked sufficient sense for the truth, and the most gifted had too little genius for that. Even laughter may yet have a future. I mean, when the proposition 'the species is everything, *one* is always none' has become part of humanity, and this ultimate liberation and irresponsibility has become accessible to all at all times. Perhaps laughter will then have formed an alliance with wisdom, perhaps only 'gay science' will then be left.
>
> (Nietzsche 1974: 74)

Laughter here is productive. It doesn't strive to amuse but to reveal. This revelatory quality is the essential feature Breton ascribes to black humour, causing him to berate Aragon in the preface of the book for what he calls his 'verbosity' in seeking to exhaust the subject, thus exhibiting what Breton calls a purely 'external view of humour' (1997: xv). At the time Breton was writing, of course, Aragon had long abandoned his own strictures against solutions and placed his faith in the Stalinist smooth talking of the French Communist Party. Raihan Kadri re-emphasizes Breton's point when he asks: 'When did Aragon stop being Surrealist?' He immediately answers his own question: 'When he stopped being funny' (2011: 148).

As Breton implies, the aim of black humour is to explore humour from within rather than from the outside. As such it becomes part of a surrealist methodology that took shape for Breton in the writings of the texts of the authors he includes in his anthology. The ultimate response to any situation is that given by the baboon 'Bosse-de-Nage' in Alfred Jarry's *Faustroll*: 'Ha Ha', without further exposition. Jarry describes how *ha ha* confounds identity, as well as materially referring to 'a ditched gap in a wall at the end of a garden path, an armed pit or military well into which chrome steel bridges may collapse …' (Jarry 1965: 22).

Is it not precisely into this ditched gap or armed pit that Nietzsche – along, perhaps, with his contemporaries Rimbaud and Ducasse – fell after completing the astonishing five books written in the last active year of his life? The last card of the tarot – the unnamed card that is both beginning and end and underlies all the others – is the Fool. Might we not in fact see Nietzsche, Rimbaud and Ducasse as embodying this figure of the Fool as they reached the point at which nothing more could be done or said than lapse into a silence that would perplex the world? In all three there is something definitive in their final works – even if Ducasse's *Poésies* was only intended as a preface, could he really have said anything more after having written it? – that inclines us to believe that in their last works they were all announcing their own humorous departures from a life whose resources they had exhausted and from which they could only disappear.

In so doing they provided us with a preface to the affirmation in the midst of a fundamental philosophical pessimism that underlies the surrealist attitude and gave rise to the notion of black humour that Breton recognized as an essential aspect of the surrealist armoury.

Note

1 The extent to which the *Anthology* represents a summation of surrealist humour rather than principally constituting an expression of Breton's personal preferences is thus open to question. Black humour should certainly not be seen as the exclusive type of humour we find in surrealism. Only seven of Breton's authors (Lichtenberg, Lewis Carroll, Alphonse Allais, Jarry, Apollinaire, Picabia and Péret) also appear among the thirty-nine Robert Benayoun includes in the other major surrealist anthology of humour (Benayoun 1977), evidencing the fact that surrealist humour has many facets.

18 The ecological imperative

Donna Roberts

The term 'ecology' was first used by the German evolutionary naturalist, Ernst Haeckel, in his *General Morphology of Organisms* (1866). He defined it as 'the entire science of the relationship of the organism to its surrounding external world, wherein we understand all "existence-relationships" in the wider sense' (Richards 2008: 9). Although the public profile of political-ecological thinking developed in the late 1960s and 1970s, the history of ecological discourse is much older, dating back to the evolutionary theories of the late nineteenth century that situated humans within and not outside of a natural schema, and, arguably, even further back to ancient metaphysical notions of the relative scale of human participation within a greater terrestrial and cosmic dynamic.

Although the key developments in surrealism pre-date the general rise of ecological consciousness in the twentieth century, the broadly political ideals of surrealism represent a critical vigilance that can be related to much of the more recent philosophical and political formations of ecological thought. Two of the clearest targets in André Breton's *Manifesto of Surrealism* (1924) were the blind faith in an idea of progress, ostensibly built upon the promises of technological advancement, and the Comtean view of the apparently ineluctable rise of 'scientific' man. Histories of European epistemology, such as that outlined by Michel Foucault in *Les Mots et les choses* (*The Order of Things*, 1970), have described how sympathetic and analogical relations between man and nature were superseded by the detached and differentiating thought that would come to define scientific method. In his *Discourse on Method* (1637), René Descartes affirmed the dualistic relation of humans to nature, and what now appears like the anti-ecological premise behind it, when he announced the scientific imperative behind the ambition to become 'lords and masters of nature' (Descartes 2000: 44). Breton expressed his concerns with the divisive method of scientific thought established by Descartes and Francis Bacon in the seventeenth century, and perpetuated in France by Auguste Comte in the nineteenth, as establishing the 'reign of logic' under which we still live (Breton 1969: 9).

In response, the surrealists pursued a radical epistemological shift that would reassimilate connective analogical and poetic thinking into the processes of knowledge. This would reinscribe humans within a more sympathetic continuity with nature, understood both in terms of inner and outer nature. In his book *Esthétique généralisée* (1962), Roger Caillois thus affirmed the ecological character of such a response:

> Man is not opposed to nature, he is himself nature: matter and life submitted to the physical and biological laws that govern the universe. They penetrate him, cross through him, organize him. He coincides with them, or, at least, they are not separable.
>
> (Caillois 2008: 822)

As well as exploring the complexities of the laws that govern them, the surrealists' affirmation of the continuities between man and nature can be seen as responding to dominant conservative ideas in political economy that naturalize principles of survival, accumulation and competition over other factors of life. Georges Bataille and Roger Caillois rejected the definition of man as essentially economic, and radically opposed the naturalizing of economic man developed by Herbert Spencer and his brand of social Darwinism in the late nineteenth century. Caillois, for example, transposes onto nature at large the surrealist affirmation of the Schillerean play drive and anti-utilitarian activity in general, and counters a restricted view of natural economic laws with a far more holistic one. Influenced by Marcel Mauss's notion of 'Total Man', Caillois rejects mealy economic principles as a naturalizing fallacy, as inadequate in understanding nature as the restricted view of man as one-sidedly rational, functional, and self-preserving.

Accepting Émile Durkheim's notion of man as essentially religious rather than economic, Bataille and Caillois analysed the sacred, non-utilitarian, elements of social life as those which bind and connect, rather than the profane dynamic which separates. Their critique of the naturalizing fallacy of 'restricted' economics is a major contribution to the refuting of the liberal dogma that has been powerfully renewed in recent decades, and upon which the anti-ecological hegemony of the corporate/industrial/military order has been built. In the 1970s, the anthropologist and radical ecologist Gregory Bateson would echo this critique of economic reductionism in terms of an ecological egalitarianism:

> We reduce ourselves to such caricatures as 'economic man', and we have reduced other societies and the woods and lakes that we encounter to potential assets, ultimately reducing them in still another sense as the prairie was reduced to desert, members of other groups to servitude.
>
> (Bateson and Bateson 1987: 141)

Like Bateson's interests, those of the surrealists in primitive modes of religious thought and the eruptions of the sacred within everyday life – in art, eroticism, collectivity – are a crucial factor in their counteraction of social, political, scientific, or economic views that reduce human life, and its relations with the natural world, to purely individualistic, molecular, and utilitarian functions.

Breton sensed in the increasing dominance of the scientific view the dangers of a gross reductionism: reducing non-scientific modes of thought, whether religious or mythological, to mere superstitions, and the poetic to the negative domain of the economically useless. Surrealist vigilance against such a reduction in values aligns the movement with an ecological critique of the current global order of market fundamentalism, which is sustained by the highly divisive principles of consumption and accumulation, and the exploitation of individuals, communities, and nature at large. The films of Czech surrealist Jan Švankmajer reflect these concerns. Discussing his work, Bertrand Schmitt defined this anti-ecological, consuming mania as a form of 'self-cannibalism': 'an absurd, irresponsible and suicidal end to which the modern world seems to want to condemn itself, by destroying, polluting and devouring, to the very last morsel, the ecosystem and resources that maintain life' (Dryje and Schmitt 2012: 334).

To an extent, surrealism's key concerns can be seen as a reconsideration of the very question of nature developed by the Enlightenment: further analysing humankind's place within, or distinction from, the natural world and how both liberty and necessity have a basis in nature. Surrealism addresses such questions in light of the subsequent developments in theories of the instincts, the relations of humans to nature at large, and the embodied mind as proposed by Darwin and Freud. It is through the legacy of their theories that the surrealists develop the Enlightenment dichotomy of nature and civilization outlined by Jean-Jacques Rousseau, with nature also considered in its internal human aspect, thereby extending the scope of a conflict to be reconciled on two fronts: intellect and instinct, nature and civilization. Within surrealism, nature is represented in manifold ways: it is disconcerting, paradoxical, destructive, erotic, unifying. It is both a poetic signifier of the correspondences that link mind and world and the signifier of a political-economic critique, one which challenges a restricted view of both external and internal nature and doesn't adequately account for the totality of the interrelations between them. Although surrealism did not develop with a consciously environmental or 'ecological' agenda, its concern to develop understanding of the relations between body, mind, and world are very close to what Bateson called an 'ecology of mind' (Bateson 1972).

Ecopoetics and the 'entangled bank' of surrealist art

The literary historian Jonathan Bate has proposed the category of 'ecopoetry' to define Romantic lyricism and its modern legacy. He traces the roots of modern ecological thought to Rousseau's account of the agony experienced by social humanity at the loss of a mythical, originary state of nature, one corrupted by social convention and municipal displacement. Bate considers the work of the Romantic poets to be largely a development of Rousseau's critique, as an exploration of both the subjective and political dimensions of a conflict originating in those epistemological shifts of the late Renaissance that placed humankind outside and above the realm of nature. 'Once you invent the category of the "human"', Bate notes, 'you have to make "nature" its Other' (Bate 2000: 35). This crucial move to separate 'Man' from 'Nature' is the crux of what Theodor Adorno and Max Horkheimer (2007) termed in 1944 the 'dialectic of Enlightenment'. Like their contemporaries in the Frankfurt School, the surrealists were very aware of the double bind that enables one form of progress at the risk of degeneration of others.

In *Mad Love* (1937), Breton presents an intimate reverie on love and the natural environment of the island of Tenerife. This fusion of love, nature, and the lyric imagination highlights how the surrealist sensibility is profoundly ecological in the non-dualistic relationship it conceives between humans and the natural environment. The surrealists' acknowledgment of the negative consequences of a rationalized separation from nature is at the heart of their opposition to the dualistic basis of modern scientific method. This is evidenced by a broad interest in the non-dualistic logic of 'primitive' cultures and through the influence of the Romantic tradition, wherein the reconciliation with nature is pursued through a poetic sense of the binding of subject and object – the individual with the non-human world – in which nature is experienced as a space of transformation and a force that dissolves boundaries.

Mad Love evokes such a transformative and unifying experience of nature. As an ode to erotic love, Breton's book also presents one of his most intense reflections on nature, and the mysterious and yet determining forces that bind us to it. His emotional reverie, bound to the object of his love, Jacqueline Lamba, is diffused into the 'impassioned landscape' of Tenerife, which is experienced as a synthesizing terrain (Breton 1987: 82). Breton's lyrical account of the island reflects what Bate sees as the significant role of poetic language within ecological discourse. Poetic language is, he writes, 'a special kind of expression which may effect an imaginative reunification of mind and nature' (Bate 2000: 245). Breton's text fulfils such a dynamic through the deep poetic logic of surrealism that traces the correspondences between human experience and the natural world.

Breton's fascination with the fauna of Tenerife entails a constant relay between subject and object, between the rapports of natural forms and the human imagination. *Mad Love* also resonates with the writings of the German Romantic naturalist and pioneer of ecological thinking Alexander von Humboldt, who studied the plant ecosystems of Tenerife en route to the Americas. The account of the island in his *Personal Narrative* was of legendary influence on the development of Darwin's thought and consequent ecological science. Like Humboldt, Breton describes the transition from the heady vegetation of the lowlands to the increasing scarcity of plants on the volcanic slopes of Mount Teide, and admires the ancient Dragon Tree of the Gardens of Orotava: one of the 'kings of the Jurassic fauna' which 'plunges its roots in prehistory' (Breton 1987: 73). If Humboldt's Romantic science of the interacting forces of nature and the influence of environment on organism provided the grounds for ecological systems, then *Mad Love* can be seen to incorporate another extensive aspect of Romantic thinking – that of the ecological relations of mind and nature – into a form of surrealist ecopoetics. Breton's pursuit of a general law of relations between subjective and objective worlds, what he called *objective chance*, can be understood, then, as a form of surrealist natural philosophy, which, like that of Schelling, assumes a continuity between the forces governing both mind and world: 'Only when they are observed and considered together shall we be able to determine the law according to which these mysterious exchanges between material and mental worlds are produced' (Breton 1987: 40).

In terms of the visual arts, a harmonizing between the human and the natural is central to the works of numerous surrealist artists, including Joan Miró, André Masson, Roberto Matta, Gordon Onslow Ford, Toyen, and Jacques Hérold. This frequently effects what Gavin

Parkinson has called a 'fusion' with the non-human elements of nature (Parkinson 2009: 262). The harmonious relations of human to nature are, however, not consistent throughout surrealism. Surrealist artists such as Max Ernst and Salvador Dalí often exploit an anxious or uncanny slippage between the realms of human and vegetal, mineral, or animal. In terms of recent 'post-human' and ecological thought, the interrelating of human and natural reveals the prescience of the surrealist imagination in grasping the most basic ecological premises of Darwin's thought on the continuities between humans and non-human life forms. Modern ecological thinking has developed a systemic logic, essentially based on Darwin's idea of the common origins of all organisms, as envisioned in Darwin's famous metaphor of entanglement: 'It is interesting to contemplate an entangled bank, clothed with many plants of many kinds, with birds singing on the bushes, with various insects flitting around, and with worms crawling through the damp earth' (Darwin 1859: 489).

While representing such an 'entangled bank' of nature, the surrealists' play with the boundaries of human and non-human reflects a Romantic manoeuvre that is infused with psychoanalytic and biological overtones pointing to the binary of Eros and Thanatos: the sublime dissolution of eroticism and, as outlined in Freud's *Beyond the Pleasure Principle* (1920), the deathly return to an insensate condition. In their zoological reimaginings of the evolutionary human, Ernst and Dalí, for example, draw on the biological uncanny in their depictions of human hybrids: the phylogenetic vegetal mass of Ernst's *The Horde* or Dalí's human/mantis archetype of atavistic sexual savagery, outlined in his *Tragic Myth of Millet's Angelus.* Such fantastical interpretations of the evolutionary, phylogenetic route that binds humans to the natural world take their logic from the bases of Freud's metapsychology in the theories of Darwin and Ernst Haeckel, as defined by Stephen Jay Gould (1977) and Frank Sulloway (1979). They have both analyzed how Freud adopted Haeckel's 'Biogenetic Law' (ontogeny recapitulates phylogeny) as an evolutionary maxim for the analogous development of the individual and its distant ancestral organic forms, transposing the law from the development of body to that of mind. Haeckel's law thus provided Freud with the phylogenetic axis of the developmental parallels between the primitive/child/neurotic, as well as the *bio-logic* of an otherwise metaphysical vision of every individual's rise from and return to primal organic indistinction: the ultimate origins and ends of the ecological journey.

This aspect of surrealist visuality arguably maintains a model of human/natural distinction if only in order to transgress it and to exploit the zoological or biological uncanny. In her study of the rise of biocentricism in modern art and literature, Margot Norris selected Ernst as a surrealist exponent of biocentricism, a tendency she defined as 'an interrogation of anthropocentric assumptions' (Norris 1985: 21). Norris defines the early twentieth-century image of the human/animal hybrid, such as that found in Kafka or Ernst, as a key transgression of the culture/nature division that she attributes to the influence of Darwin on 'the destruction of species as a normative category' (Norris 1985: 16–7). Ernst and Dalí thus exploit the cultural anxiety that followed Darwin's theories as they blurred the boundaries between the human and other natural realms – what John Ruskin (2010: 61) called Darwin's 'filthy heraldries'.

Another tendency within surrealist visual art, biomorphism, perhaps comes closer to a more properly ecological tradition of thought. Biomorphism, as Jennifer Mundy (2011) has discussed, has been described as an attempt to overcome the dualism between cultural and natural by exploring the possibilities of a plastic equivalent to natural processes and formations. As also noted by Hubert F. van den Berg (2006), biomorphism is reflected in the work of Hans Arp. Already disgusted with anthropocentrism as a Dadaist in Zurich and repelled by the mechanized horrors engulfing Europe, Arp sought a less Promethean vision of the human, and drew on medievalism and German Romantic *Naturphilosophie* traditions for ways of reintegrating the human within a natural world on a more conciliatory basis. Arp rejected mimetic representation because it reflected the Cartesian division of subject and object, man and world. Exemplified by his statement 'art is a fruit growing out of man like a fruit out of a plant' (Motherwell 1989: 222), Arp bridges the Romantic poetic, reconciliatory tradition with a nascent ecological consciousness that situates humans within the natural order, defining the creative human spirit as a trajectory of more general terrestrial, even universal, energies.

Dismal Darwinism and surrealist anti-anthropocentricism

Ever since Darwin changed the distinction between human and other organisms to one of degree not kind, ecologists have emphasized the need for a renewed sense of human humility. The surrealists' critique of rationalist and scientific hubris was at times inflected with an aggressive anti-anthropocentricism, emphasizing automatic and instinctual behaviour that cast doubt upon human exceptionalism. The 1930s periodical *Minotaure*, for example, represented human/bestial hybridity through the classical creature from the labyrinth. In his 1934 essay therein, titled 'The Praying Mantis: From Biology to Psychoanalysis', Roger Caillois (2003: 69–81) chose an even more disconcerting avatar of erotic and deathly human instincts in the praying mantis, aiming to 'restore' man to nature by a most disturbing route. Henri Bergson in *Creative Evolution* (1907) defined insects as the evolutionary opposite of the human, as the evolutionary pinnacle of instinct, and man of intelligence. Caillois collapses this distinction, and in comparing erotic and deathly impulses in humans and insects sets out a refusal to view nature (human included) as functional and utilitarian. As Claudine Frank has discussed, Caillois followed Nietzsche in arguing that life is not so restrictedly goal-oriented, and makes room for loss, risk, free play, and transformation. Caillois and the surrealists in general thus follow what Elizabeth Grosz has outlined as Nietzsche's elaborating of 'a small space of excess that functions outside natural selection, where life does not simply fulfil itself in surviving in its given milieu successfully enough to reproduce, but where it actively seeks transformation' (Grosz 2004: 11). Again, the surrealists' critique of a reductive utilitarian view of nature provides a forceful opposition to social-Darwinist arguments that use the natural sciences to legitimize human self-interest and competitive economic principles that present the main obstacles to ecological transformation.

In contrast to Caillois, Georges Bataille developed a view of human 'specificity' based on the human urge to distinguish itself from nature, which he saw as the original drama upon which civilization was built. In essays in the journal *Documents*, Bataille presented a dismal picture, envisaging human evolution as full of hubris and cruel tragicomedy. The human delusion of being beyond nature became central to the critical focus of *Documents*, and Michel Leiris aided Bataille in his contemptuous account of anthropocentricism. In his text, 'Spittle/Mouth Water', for example, published in the 'Critical Dictionary' of *Documents* in 1929, Leiris derides the supposedly divine status of human thought and reason by connecting its medium of oration to formless spittle, finally comparing man to a kind of cosmic phlegm. Closing his text, Leiris mocks any philosophical position that 'imagines a human being to be something – *something other* than an unmuscled, hairless animal, the spit of a delirious demiurge who roars with laughter at having expectorated this conceited larva, this comical tadpole who swells up into a demigod's puffy meat' (Leiris 1989: 35).

Leiris's anti-anthropocentricism shows how much Darwin's ideas that 'dethroned' the human from the top of nature's hierarchy influenced surrealism. To understand the relation of Darwin to surrealism we need to separate his ideas about the continuity of man and nature from the political-economic assumptions of social Darwinism, or the muddle of Darwinian ideas Morse Peckham called *Darwinisticism* (Peckham 1959). Darwin actually penned some extraordinary comments which would not have looked out of place in *Documents*, declaring in his *Notebook B*, for example: 'People often talk of the wonderful event of intellectual Man appearing – the appearance of insects with other senses is more wonderful, its mind more different, probably' (quoted in George Levine 2006: 116). While it would be erroneous to suggest some kind of 'Green' agenda within *Documents*, the aggressive anti-anthropocentricism of the periodical finds accord with an ecological drive to decentre Promethean human conceit in both instrumental reason and abstract logic and to delegitimize the destructive consequences of human exceptionalism.

Running throughout *Documents* is the general surrealist alignment with what Howard E. Gruber defined as Darwin's (then Freud's) 'consistent interest in the dethronement of reason and conscious will as the sole governors of human behaviour' (Gruber 1974: 69). This is reflected in the derision shown towards the human head in *Documents* – from Picasso's savage constructions, to shrunken heads, to ludicrous masks, to the critical mass of scorn poured on the *figure humaine* – by which Bataille and his team humiliate the old grounds for human distinction. Logocentricism is shown as a mere symptom of a deluded, monomaniacal creature that, through the fortuitous process of erection via the big toe, believes itself not only the paragon of animals, but also a form of divine incarnation. This derisive tendency within the surrealist milieu could be defined as a kind of *dismal Darwinism*, according with Darwin when he wrote: 'Why is thought, being a secretion of the brain, more wonderful than gravity a property of matter? It is our arrogance, it is our admiration for ourselves' (quoted in Lewins 2007: 250).

Roger Caillois, ecology of mind, and 'adventurous coherency'

The Pascalian concern with human mismeasurement – exemplified in Pascal's metaphor of man as the 'thinking reed' – is echoed throughout surrealism, and no more so than in Roger Caillois' writings on man. More pessimistic than Breton in his view of humankind, Callois' obsessive contemplation of stones and minerals – what he called his 'materialist mysticism' – was akin to a Buddhist recognition of human temporality and cosmic insignificance, seen as a momentary note within 'a cosmic movement of progress and decline' (Caillois 2008: 168). In this sense, Caillois reflects a kind of ultra-ecological perspective, akin to that established by James Lovelock in his Gaia theory, but one which considered humans merely an 'episodic species' doomed to extinction: 'As a member of a species, the human species which is late-coming, temporary, and transient – it will not even last as long as the dinosaurs lasted – I am doomed to error' (Caillois 1991: 149).

For Caillois, the division between humans and nature Cartesian dualism enacted in the late Renaissance involved a grave distortion leading to an arrogant mismeasurement of human status and singularity. Caillois' view of humankind was never flattering, and he frequently expressed a lugubrious and pessimistic derision of the anthropocentric outlook while insisting upon the greater integration of the human within the system of natural laws, as exemplified in the following statement:

> Man can less and less doubt that he is only an excrescence of nature, with which he remains co-substantial and to the laws of which entirely submitted. Yet he has been so successful in domesticating the energies within reach that he is naively persuaded that nature belongs to him, while he knows very well that it is he who belongs to nature and that he is an extension of it, far from having been parachuted in by some God.
>
> (Caillois 2008: 164)

Surrealism perhaps finds its strongest critical allegiance with ecological thinking in Caillois' work, not only in his anti-anthropocentricism and dim view of instrumental, dualistic reason, but also in his tendency towards what he called *generalized* thinking. By this he intended to build a broad picture, scientific and poetic at once, able to assimilate all the world's complex interrelations. Drawing on Max Scheler's ideas about the coherency of nature, man's participation in it, and the existence of a universal grammar, Caillois called his intellectual and creative ambition an 'adventurous coherency' (2008: 809). In his posthumously published book, *The Necessity of the Mind* (written in the mid-1930s), Caillois first used the image of the chessboard as a quasi-ecological metaphor for the coherency of the universe and the economy of its processes. Over the decades he developed his thinking around this image, and in 1970 described the board as analogous with nature at large, as 'an absolutely coherent extension' upon which 'there is no movement of any piece which does not have repercussions on the others and which does not more or less modify the general situation' (Caillois 2008: 560). This strict metaphor of the unity and interrelations of the world reflects an ecological emphasis in Caillois' keen sense of the natural order of things.

Caillois' implicit 'ecology of mind' bridges the ambitions set out by Breton to develop a reconciliatory method of thought with some of the most radical ecological ideas from the last fifty years. In their derisive anti-anthropocentricism, Caillois, Bataille, and Leiris present a startling case for both the continuities between humans and nature and the need to acknowledge the tragic dimension of their distinctions. Thus, combined with the political spirit to effect a transformation of values away from those that maintain social divisions amongst humans and stubborn ontological divisions between humans and nature at large, the key ideas of surrealism have many parallels with ecological critique, further maintaining the continuing significance of surrealism within critical debate.

19 Magic art

Bertrand Schmitt

There are many references to occult practices, 'traditional sciences' or magic within surrealist texts and declarations. From the 1924 *Surrealist Manifesto* onwards André Breton was already referring (albeit in a rather humorous and loose manner) to the 'secrets of surrealist magic art' (Breton 1969: 29). Some years later, in texts like the *Second Manifesto of Surrealism* (1929), *Les Prolégomènes à un troisième manifeste du surréalisme ou non* (1942), *Du Surréalisme en ses œuvres vives* (1953) or in the different studies written by Breton and collected in *Surrealism and Painting* (1928, republished in expanded form in 1965), we find allusions to alchemists or magicians (such as Hermes Trismegistus, Nicolas Flamel, Paracelsus, Eliphas Lévi or Albert le Grand), as well as to the Cabbala and high magic. In one of his studies of Max Ernst, Breton identifies the painter's *esprit-enfant* with that of 'the great arch-sorcerer himself, Cornelius Agrippa' (Breton 1972: 159). In another text, Breton spoke of Wolfgang Paalen's painting as having 'the feathers of that miraculous bird with iridescent plumage which appears in the *Chymical Marriage of Christian Rosenkreuz* and has the power to restore life' (Breton 1972: 78). The notion of 'magic art' within surrealism may therefore seem self-evident. Yet there are many ambiguities in the relations between art and magic. Do they share the same approach to the world? Do they use the same tools? How, moreover, could a magic that radically rejects any idealist, spiritualist, mystical or transcendent presupposition be envisaged if it were to remain consistent with the framework of the materialist thought within which surrealism had clearly established itself? So it ought to be made clear that what brings surrealism close to a particular conception of magic is beyond all else the use each makes of the principle of analogy. As an eminently 'non-rational' thought, magic interests the surrealists for the inventive, interpretative and poetic richness it offers reality. In the same way, magic appears as an 'operative' method, a direct means of intervention and transformation of that reality, which is similar to the way surrealism for its part views poetry and creation. Without needing to subscribe to the spiritualist presuppositions of some magical conceptions, the surrealists can thus use this approach to enrich their sensory arsenal, just as they use the psychoanalytical approach without necessarily subscribing to all of its postulates. This is what Breton developed in one of his most fundamental works.

At the end of 1957, the Club Français du Livre published an impressive work entitled *Magic Art* (*L'Art magique*). The richly illustrated book contained an important study by Breton accompanied by several notes and articles and ending with the responses to an enquiry sent to some seventy-six individuals, among them ethnologists, anthropologists, art historians, painters, poets and specialists in the occult sciences[1] who had been solicited by reason of their 'specific expertise'[2] and because they would be able to propose an 'authoritative view' about the immense and specialized, complex and disputed problem of the relations between art and magic. The work, published in a limited edition, quickly went out of print and became a genuine 'cult book', avidly sought after by connoisseurs and collectors (see Breton and Legrand 1991: 7 and 15).

It was intended to be the first volume in a series of five studies, written by different authors, each of which would be devoted to a different period, field or aspect of art. After this first volume devoted to magic art, a second, dealing with religious art should have been followed by two more on classical and baroque art, before concluding with a final volume summarizing the field of 'art for art's sake'. As the extent and heterogeneity of the different titles suggested, the series had not been conceived as a rational, systematic or consecutive history of art, nor even as a classical panorama of different artistic periods, but offered five open and shifting *visions*, in which the most prominent, singular and subjective approaches and perspectives would flourish. The authors and organizers of the collection were convinced that subjectivity was one of the *keys* that allowed the true nature and stakes of art to be revealed. In 1953, Breton therefore launched himself into preparing and writing what would be the last of his great theoretical texts, one that would represent, in his eyes, the 'work of a whole lifetime'. In support he relied upon notes and documents he had been compiling since the end of the 1930s and that he had completed later on, especially in the course of the visits he made during the summer of 1945 to the Hopi and Zuni Pueblo Indian reservations in Arizona and New Mexico (see Breton 1999b: 183–209). But in spite, or perhaps because of, the wealth, variety and abundance of the material at his disposal and as a result of a number of tangible and intellectual difficulties in defining and demarcating the sometimes ambiguous notions of 'art' and 'magic' precisely, work on the text stalled. The book, originally intended for publication in 1955 as the first volume in the series, finally appeared only at the end of 1957 as the last of the series to go to print, after André Breton had sought the help of the young surrealist Gérard Legrand in order to complete the complicated work (see Legrand's testimony, in Breton and Legrand 1991: 187).

Indeed, *L'Art magique* was presented as a universal history of art, entirely reassessed from the perspective, sensibility and thought of surrealism. The book went back to the earliest period of humanity, to the age of prehistoric parietal paintings, engravings and sculptures, then continued (in Legrand's words) by means of a 'perambulation' through different periods and geographical centres of art in order to reach the modern period and conclude with its most contemporary manifestations. The various chapters, organized chronologically but with a deliberately open approach that continually allows encounters and dialogue among the most diverse periods and locations, offered in a syncretic way examples of the arts of supposedly 'primitive' (Oceanic, Polynesian, Amerindian, Inuit) peoples, the art of antiquity (Egyptian, Etruscan, Greek) and Pre-Columbian, Khmer or Indian civilizations, that of the Celtic and Gaulish tribes, as well as some works chosen from the medieval period and the Renaissance (especially those of the Fontainebleau School), before tackling modern history, through Romanticism, post-Impressionism, Symbolism, expressionism and (to a lesser extent) cubism, to conclude in a projective way with a brief consideration of the 'magic directions of surrealism in art' (Breton and Legrand 1991: 252).

The selections made by Breton and Legrand were intentionally affective and partial, and were affirmed as such. In contrast to the usual 'canonical' histories of art, the two authors had effectively decided to overlook makers or periods which they didn't consider of any interest or had nothing in common with a 'magical' vision of art. Michelangelo, Raphael, Rubens,[3] Velásquez, Poussin, Rembrandt[4] and Vermeer, almost all the baroque and classical artists, but also some Romantics, like Delacroix, and many modern painters, beginning with Manet, Cézanne, Monet and Renoir, were thus rejected from their study, making way for artists who had sometimes been forgotten or judged of lesser importance (such as Paolo Uccello, Hieronymus Bosch, Piero di Cosimo, Mathias Grünewald, Antoine Caron, Giuseppe Arcimboldo, Michael Maier, Monsù Desiderio, William Blake, Gustave Moreau, Georges Seurat and Charles Filiger). The authors favoured a selection that allowed them to disclose and support an *essential intuition.* That intuition, which Breton expressed on many occasions, was that poetry – and by extension art in general – revealed strong analogies with several aspects of magic, as it had been practised since the beginnings of humanity. Just like certain magical practices, poetry aims in this way to highlight the hidden, but nevertheless *real*, links existing between subjectivity, the individual creator's desire and the cosmic rules that drive, order and harmonize the functioning of the universe. Like magical practices, authentic poetry and art don't aim so much to express the ephemeral, superficial and very soon obsolete *forms* of the human sensibility, but to recover the timeless, immemorial and essential *forces* that bind the human microcosm to the stellar macrocosm and that link them to one another. Like magical or alchemical practices, too, authentic poetry and art pursue a concrete and practical aim, by seeking to unveil, but also to comprehend, master and 'control', in a Promethean and demiurgic endeavour, hidden and occult forces, whether of a physical or psychic order, in order to restore the ancient 'alliance' and harmony that unites man with Nature. In this respect, rituals and magical practices seem related to certain religious rituals, which also aim to 'bind' people with natural and cosmic forces. But, unlike the latter, magic does not seek to attain this reconciliation by appeasing 'superior' forces or by trying to move or please the gods. On the contrary, magic is related to the free, proud and sovereign exercise of a power, a 'control' over 'superior' forces. It constitutes a 'revenge' that seeks to act through the direct appropriation of forces and powers capable of providing man with control. It could be said to relate to the 'theft of fire', in the Promethean revolt against the gods. As an expression of the excesses of desire and the strength of the imagination, magic, like art, is therefore a revolt against the subordinated state of things. Citing Dr Jacques Maxwell, Breton thus recalls that '[m]agic ritual is the expression of a strong will, affirmed in each detail of the ritual, tending to the subjugation of supernatural beings or the domination of natural forces ordinarily removed from mankind's empire' (Breton and Legrand 1991: 27). Breton immediately adds that 'magic implies protest, if not revolt, as well as pride', making it clear that magic, like surrealism, rests on an ontological and radical rebellion that rejects every form of the supplication, penitence, resignation or submission that are the marks of religions.

In the minds of Breton and the surrealists other important aspects also contribute to bringing magic close to the practice of poetry or art. Through the 'work' they conduct upon the unconscious and the drives that pass through the mind of the artist and creator (but also in the collective unconscious of society), artistic creation and poetic intuition act as so many 'exorcisms', allowing an externalized and *objectified* form to be given to the deadly or destructive drives and to certain obsessive ideas, in order to clear them out; just as shamanic practices and rites of sympathetic magic extract fatal and uncontrolled influences from the body and mind of the 'possessed', so as to enclose them symbolically in controllable objects. Like certain esoteric practices (the foremost of which is the alchemical quest), poetry and art also aim at a transformation, a *transmutation*, of the nature of the elements upon which they act, while provoking an internal and intimate transformation in the officiate or the disciple who launches onto this quest.[5] Thus Breton had written in 1929 in the *Second Manifesto of Surrealism*, 'I would appreciate your noting the remarkable analogy, insofar as their goals are concerned, between the Surrealist efforts and those of the alchemists: the philosopher's stone is nothing more or less than that which was to enable man's imagination to take a stunning revenge on all things' (Breton 1969: 174).[6] With this declaration, he reaffirmed the total confidence he placed in poetic intuition and in the force of the imagination, as a means of knowledge and 'revelation' (that is as 'hieroglyphic keys' capable of helping us decipher in an analogous or symbolic way the 'real functioning of thought'),[7] but also as practices able to act on reality, in other words to 'transform the world' and 'change life' at one and the same time. This was what Breton and the surrealists had repeatedly insisted on affirming when confronted with those militant revolutionaries who, blinded by the rational and utilitarian aspect of political action, were unable to see the practical and effective means by which art and poetry (which they considered merely entertaining or gratuitous acts), just like magic, could act as tangible forces and means to metamorphose reality.

It was therefore in order to try to show how throughout history art, in co-operation with ritual and magical practices, in direct interaction or as a delayed echo of them, had been able to accompany humanity in its desire for knowledge and control, for going beyond or metamorphosing reality, that Breton launched himself into the writing of *Magic Art*. The question the surrealist poet raises throughout the work could be summed up in this way: 'Does art have the *magical* power to change life?' Breton was not the first to pose this question. So, to justify his initiative and approach, he appealed to other poets who had opened up the path. At the beginning of his study, Breton therefore draws upon Novalis, who coined the term 'magic art'. 'Without being too arbitrary', he wrote, 'from the outset we will be able to enlighten ourselves with what a very great mind like Novalis thought about the topic. If he chose the words "magic art" to depict the form of art he aspired to promote, we can also be assured that he had addressed the necessary scales needed to consider his terms … . In the meaning he gave it, we can expect to find the product of a millenarian experience that is not only decanted but also surpassed' (Breton and Legrand 1991: 28). But, beyond Novalis, for Breton and the surrealists, all the essential names of modern poetry and art (that is, all the actors in the shattering of the sensibility that occurred after and in the wake of German Romanticism, giving birth to a modern vision of poetry and art) would share, whether consciously or not, this 'magical' vision.[8] For Breton, a particular form of modern poetry and art, based on a set of 'analogical correspondences' or that sets itself the task of seeking a universal symbolism, rediscovered the 'magical' language that was the property of art among primitive peoples as well as certain pantheistic or animist cultures and civilizations, before its rich and fertile vision was repressed by monotheistic religion. The last survivals of this ancestral vision had still nourished the art of the medieval period, through fables and superstitions. But the suffocating vision of Christianity, in alliance with incipient 'positivism' and 'scientism', rapidly combined to control minds more effectively and entail the almost complete disappearance of this way of feeling and thinking. And so the Renaissance, considered by so many to be an apogee and rectification of art after the darkness of the Middle Ages, appeared on the contrary to the surrealists as the beginning of a long decline. This transitional and ambivalent period was marked by an encyclopaedic desire for knowledge (and was in this respect close to the magic will to comprehend the world), but was also characterized by a withering and depletion of the ancient systems of interpretation of the universe, marking thereby the swansong of symbolic and magical thought and entailing the loss of the 'transmission of the legendary message' (Breton and Legrand 1991: 185) in favour of a progressive rationalization of thought and art. It would lead, a century later, to the most passive, closed and sterile classicism.

It was in order to counter the apparent regression and impoverishment endorsed by Christianity and the positivist rationalism that had dominated later nineteenth-century thinking that several 'modern' poets, following the lead of the Romantics, tried to situate magic at the centre of the dialogue they wove between the external world and their own internal and subjective world. Language became for them an active *Word*, a dynamic, fertile and fertilizing one able to act in a productive way on the world, through the new vision of the latter it offered, as a magic formula could do, thanks to the power of analogy, correspondences, image and symbol. In a interview with Claudine Chonez given in July 1948 for *La Gazette des lettres*, Breton made it clear that: 'As to the idea of a "hieroglyphic" key to the world, it more or less consciously existed before all high poetry, which can only be driven by the principle of analogies and correspondences. Poets such as Hugo, Nerval, Baudelaire and Rimbaud, or thinkers such as Fourier, share this idea with the occultists, and likely also with the majority of scientific inventors' (Breton 1993: 225). In *Arcane 17,* published some months earlier, Breton had already fastened on this aspect, when clarifying the links he considered to exist between esotericism, magic and poetry, and in recalling all that 'modern' poetry and the revolution of the sensibility operative from the end of the eighteenth century and throughout the nineteenth owed to the magical vision of the universe, in a will to restore an open and dynamic system of correspondences.

> Even if we have reservations about its basic principle, esoterism at least has the vast advantage of maintaining the system of comparison in a dynamic state, boundless in scope and that man may use, freeing him to link objects that appear most distant, so partially revealing the mechanism of universal symbolism. From Hugo (recently revealed to have had ties to the school of Fabre d'Olivet) to Nerval (whose well-known sonnets make reference to Pythagoras and Swedenborg), through Baudelaire who notably borrowed from the occultists their theory of 'correspondences' and Rimbaud, the nature of whose readings, at the apogee of his creative powers, can't be overstressed … up to Apollinaire in whom the influence of the Jewish Cabala alternates with the novels of the Arthurian cycle, the great poets of the last century understood this admirably.
> (Breton 1994: 87, translation modified)

And to underline the importance he placed on the 'magical' nature and ambitions of art, Breton added:

> With due respect to certain minds unable to enjoy anything but calm seas and clarity, in art this contact has continued and will continue for now to be maintained. Consciously or not, the process of artistic discovery, if it remains foreign to the entirety of its metaphysical ambitions, owes no less fealty to the form and even the means of advancement of the highest magic. All the rest is indigence and revolting, unbearable platitude: billboards and doggerel.
> (Breton 1994: 87–8, translation modified)

To Breton's mind this approach to art, as a practice restating or declining the ambitions and aims of magic, offered another advantage: it jettisoned 'anecdotal', aesthetic, formal or plastic conceptions of artistic creation. Indeed, Breton and the surrealists refused to see art as having finality *in itself*, of being a simple diversion for the eye or mind. For them, art and poetry did not aim to disperse or divert the creator's or spectator's forces or attention, but proceeded, on the contrary, from a refocusing. The questions they posed, openly or just below the surface, did not derive from a formal, visual or straightforwardly sensory approach, but brought into play the *very meaning* of existence, in its most everyday and intimate aspects, just as in its most universal and atemporal implications. 'Magic art', which for the surrealists was an art conscious of *all* of its prerogatives and power to change and interpret the world, was therefore opposed to the great swathe of 'art for art's sake', an anecdotal and purely sensory art which they rejected in its entirety. To play on words, one could say that the surrealists required and defended a *re-creative* rather than a recreational art. Moreover this is what Breton had defended in a study devoted to Gustave Moreau and Symbolism, in which he opposed Moreau to the decorative vacuity of Impressionism and the superficial exteriority of realist painting.

> The diametrical opposite of these otiose dissertations on a trumpery world is provided by the kind of painting which aims to provide a re-creation of the world in terms of the inner necessity expressed by the artist. Priority is no longer given to the feelings but rather to the deepest desires of the heart and the mind. … Such painting is obviously uniquely able to fulfil Rimbaud's expressed desire for a language which should be "from the soul for the soul" – whereas one can expect nothing from the other sort of painting than, at best, a skin-deep thrill.
>
> (Breton 1972: 357–9)

It was once again to signify the radical refusal of an art that would only constitute a superficial paraphrase or external vision of the world, and to demand, inversely, an art recovering the excesses and demiurgic ambition of magic that Breton clarified in the last chapter of *Magic Art*, devoted to surrealism, that:

> in the history of thought, surrealism is most likely the first intellectual movement to have deliberately intended to put to work the means of artistic expression in the service of something other than anecdote (whether emotive, intellectual or even 'abstract'). The complete recasting of the human spirit which constitutes the most satisfactory reduction of its ambitions could not be satisfied with a pure and simple iconoclasm like that extolled by Dadaism. But encountering art, surrealism had to bring it back to its origins …:

> the 'royal path' along which deep introspection of the mental field and fervent participation in the storms of the cosmos and of passion are one and the same.
>
> (Breton and Legrand 1991: 241)

Indeed, for the surrealists who refuse dualist vision and the specious and artificial separations between conscious and unconscious and real and imaginary (the imagination being 'what tends to become real'; Breton 1992: 50), there exists a direct, although invisible, correspondence between internal desire and external necessity. Art and poetry, by impelling the creator to express himself in an authentic, spontaneous and least-controlled way possible, bring to the surface the internal necessities that run through it; and the externalization of his deepest desires bring in its wake a modification and transformation of external necessity and contingency. The images created by the surrealist painter or poet, just like charms or magical formulae, in expressing the will and desire of the magician, act on reality and metamorphose it in a *performative* way and thus emerge in the form of associations that appear incoherent or distanced from one another, but in reality are *profoundly right* for they reflect in an unconscious (or semi-conscious) way just as much the external as the internal necessity of the artist. Breton expressed this in *L'Amour fou*, when he wrote that '*chance would be the form by which external necessity is made manifest as it makes its way into human unconscious*' (Breton 1992: 690, Breton's emphasis; 1978: 23, translation modified). Breton developed the same idea in a different form in the text 'Langue des pierres' in *Perspective cavalière*, in which, speaking about his addiction for seeking agates, he says:

> Looking for stones disposed with this odd allusive power, provided one is really passionate about it, determines the rapid passage of those who devote themselves to a second stage, whose essential characteristic is *extra-lucidity*. Beginning with the interpretation of a stone of exceptional interest, this soon embraces and illuminates the circumstances of the finding. It tends, in such a case, to promote a magical causality assuming the necessity for the intervention of natural factors that have no logical relation with what is at stake, thereby disconcerting and confusing the habits of thought but nevertheless having the strength to thrill our mind.
>
> (Breton 2008: 962–3)

Moreover, this was how Michel Carrouges, an attentive observer of surrealism, explained the functioning of objective chance and the disturbing premonitions and unexpected 'oracles' that at times emerge within surrealist poetry and painting before finding their realization, as had been the case with the poem 'Night of the Sunflower' which foretold, some years earlier, the meeting between Breton and Jacqueline Lamba (see the account of the 'sunflower night' in Breton *L'Amour fou*, 714–35 (Breton 1992)), or the self-portrait with an enucleated eye painted by Victor Brauner before his accident.

> According to surrealism, this revenge [over reality] will be obtained because the imagination, working through automatic writing, in an apparently subjective and arbitrary manner, discovers on the contrary how closely bound it is to extreme necessity, and discovers within itself premonitory or telepsychic powers. This idea is based on cases like that of the 'night of the sunflower' but it is probable that this belief is founded on a number of recent experiences at least in the realm of the telepathic. That is, in any case, what Breton is inviting us to believe when he concludes that surrealism gives itself over with an intense hope in certain practices of mental alchemy.
>
> (Carrouges 1974: 57, translation modified)

Magic art is the form this 'mental alchemy' assumes which, being joined to Rimbaud's well-known 'alchemy of the word', means that any poet, any authentic artist, cannot be content to experiment with or innovate forms, but is above all a *clairvoyant* whose art, recovering the very principle of ancient magical practices, whether immemorial or traditional, seeks to penetrate the mysteries of the external as well as the internal world in order to transfigure them and, hence, 'transform the world and change life'.

Notes

1 Among those asked to respond to this enquiry we find ethnologists and anthropologists (like Claude Lévi-Strauss, Éveline Lot-Falck, Robert Jaulin and Jean Guiart), philosophers (Martin Heidegger, Maurice Blanchot, Stéphane Lupasco, Raymond Abellio), psychiatrists and psychoanalysts (Dr Jean Vinchon, Dr Bouvet), sociologists (Roger Caillois), specialists in the history of religions and rituals (Milo Rigaud, Jean Herbert), mythographes or specialists in spiritual traditions (like the poet René Nelli or Jean Markale and Lancelot Lengyel, surrealists and specialists in Celtic and Breton myths and legends), historians of art, aestheticians and art critics (Etienne Souriau, René Huyghe, André Malraux, Alain Jouffroy), archaeologists (Jean-Baptiste Colbert de Beaulieu ...), occultists or specialists in occult sciences, alchemy and traditional sciences (Eugène Canseliet, René Alleau, Valentin Bresle)

but also many poets, writers and artists, whether surrealists or not (such as Jean Paulhan, Georges Bataille, Pierre Klossowski, Michel Butor, Benjamin Péret, Octavio Paz, Joyce Mansour, Julien Gracq, André Pieyre de Mandiargues, Michel Carrouges, Malcom de Chazal, Radovan Ivsic, Leonora Carrington, René Magritte, Wolfgang Paalen and Pierre Molinier).

2 André Breton, manuscript text of the enquiry into magic art sent to several selected addressees. Source, André Breton online archives: http://www.andrebreton.fr/fr/item/?GCOI=56600100096400#, accessed 1 June 2014.

3 Breton considered him 'pitiful' (Breton and Legrand 1991: 187).

4 Described by Breton as 'pallid' (Breton and Legrand 1991: 187).

5 This aspect, which links surrealism with alchemical practice, is developed at length by Michel Carrouges (1974).

6 This accords with the phrase, taken from 'Introduction au discours sur le peu de réalité', that Breton's friends had inscribed on his tomb: 'I seek the Gold of time.'

7 As he had defined the initial nature and aim of surrealism in the *Manifesto of Surrealism* of 1924.

8 In his study, Breton moreover distinguishes several forms and degrees of magic art, pointing to an 'intentional magic art' that is, like magic, 'directly linked to efficacy, whether in the exact historical meaning of the word, or *lato sensu* … the art of children, mediums and the mentally ill', an 'involuntary magic art' which is found 'directly (as unrefined objects) or indirectly "within us"' and a 'neither intentional nor unintentional' magic art in which he placed the art of antiquity (exclusively as a precursor of modern art), a certain aspect of modern art 'which arises neither from "art for art's sake" nor from art used for other ends (propaganda, philosophies and also academic counter-propaganda)' and surrealist art (Breton and Legrand 1991: 93).

20 The marvellous

Joyce Suechun Cheng and Michael Richardson

Humanity is characterised by its inexplicable need for the marvellous.
Pierre Reverdy

'The marvellous is always beautiful, anything marvellous is beautiful, in fact only the marvellous is beautiful': these words from André Breton's *First Manifesto of Surrealism* (1924) make the marvellous a paramount category of surrealist aesthetic and the very essence of the beautiful (Breton 1969: 14). But unlike terms such as 'surrealism' and 'psychic automatism', which Breton deemed necessary to define in quasi-dictionary fashion in the *Manifesto*, 'marvellous' appears in need of no additional *surrealist* qualification. An ordinary word referring to the extraordinary, 'marvellous' in the context of surrealism retains its everyday meaning (synonymous with 'wonderful, astonishing, surprising') while at the same time designating a sensibility that surrealism was in the privileged position to theorize. The sensibility is not limited to surrealist works; according to Breton, the 'marvellous' is found readily in all kinds of fantastic literary forms, from Gothic novels and fairy tales to 'religious literature of every country' whereby 'nothing is impossible for him who dares try' (15). Consequently, Breton and other surrealist poets don't so much claim a specifically surrealist territory of the marvellous as aim to show that '*the marvellous is everywhere*', as Pierre Mabille would later write (1998: 14).

If surrealism did not *create* the marvellous, it was nevertheless adept in making it *appear*. 'The marvellous is the contradiction that appears in the real', writes Louis Aragon in *Paris Peasant*, whereas 'reality is the apparent absence of contradiction' (Aragon 1971: 217, translation modified). In this dialectical formulation by one of surrealism's seminal poets, it is worth underlining what the real and the marvellous have in common: both belong to the world of appearances. It is the perceptible, *phenomenal* nature of the marvellous that Mabille emphasizes when he takes the mirror – an everyday object that produces *real illusions* – as its metaphor par excellence. In *Alice through the Looking Glass* and numerous fairy tales, the mirror represents the threshold beyond which we will find the land of the marvellous, yet it is no accident that one should gain access to the marvellous through the act of looking. After all, according to Mabille, the mirror or the specular is part of the etymological root of the term 'marvel' (*merveille*): 'The dictionary says that "marvel" comes from *mirabilia* which itself comes from *miror*, "Things worth looking at"', and 'around the root "mirror" a very strange family has proliferated: to mirror [*mirer*], to be mirrored [*se mirer*], to admire, admirable, marvellous, and its derivatives miracle, mirage, and finally in mirror' (Mabille 1998: 5–6). For Aragon, the marvellous 'appears in the real'; for Mabille, the marvellous is real *because it appears.* The marvellous is therefore no less available to the senses than reality as commonly conceived. In effect, insofar as the marvellous intensifies rather than dampens perception, it can be considered more real than reality. Phenomenologically, the surrealist marvellous is comparable to what Roland Barthes calls the *punctum*, the Latin term for 'sting, speck, cut, little hole – and also a cast of the dice'. If, for Barthes, the *punctum* in a photograph is an unexpected accident captured by the camera that '"rises from the scene, shoots out of it like an arrow"', the surrealist marvellous likewise is an extraordinary appearance that *stands out* instead of retreating from reality (Barthes 1981: 26–7).

Because the surrealist marvellous is a phenomenon of appearing rather than obscuring, it is related to but not synonymous with terms like the fantastic or the mystery. As Breton writes in his 1962 preface for Mabille's *Miroir du merveilleux*, 'nothing defines [the marvellous] better than setting it in opposition to the "fantastic". The fantastic nearly always falls under the order of inconsequential fiction, while the marvellous illuminates the furthest extreme of vital movement and engages the entire emotional realm' (Mabille 1998: xv). That is, at stake in the marvellous is not the extent of departure from reality but the degree of perceptual and affective intensity it contains.[1] Nor is the marvellous to be conflated with the mysterious. Commemorating the 100th anniversary of Symbolism in 1936, Breton distinguishes the marvellous from the mysterious by seeking to transform Symbolism's aesthetic of obscurity (mystery) into one of appearance (marvel) for the benefit of surrealism, for '*mystery* as an end in itself, intentionally injected – at all costs – into art as into life, looks not only like a cheap trick but also like an admission of weakness, of jadedness. Symbolism has not yet sunk into total oblivion only because, forsaking the mediocrity of such stratagems, it occasionally determined to abandon itself purely and simply to the *marvellous*' (Breton 1995: 6). For surreali ving in Symbolism is therefore not Mallarmé' name an object is to suppress three quarte poem, which is made to be divined little by consequential are the fairy plays of Mauric Symbolists 'who accomplishes the miracle of *Serres chaudes* and *Chansons* on a wo… golden rain' (Breton 1995: 5). Instead of relying on th… poetic word, Maeterlinck conjures up – that is, *makes appear* implausible 'wonderland' familiar to children.

Breton's distinction notwithstanding, it is admittedly difficult to maintain a clear separation between the marvellous and the mysterious. To be sure, 'the interest of Maeterlinck lies with the marvellous', as an admirer of Maeterlinck and sympathizer of surrealism pointed out in 1941. But where, in *Pelléas et Mélisande*, does one locate the marvels of Allemonde, other than in its 'vast forests, deep lakes, grottos, a grand castle full of mystery whose doors suddenly refuse to open' (Anderson 1941: 46). Still, it would be too hasty to conclude with Henri Béhar that the surrealists 'did not clearly demarcate the boundary … between the marvellous, the fantastic, mystery or the mysterious'.[2] If the terms are sometimes exchangeable, it does not follow that they are conceptually indistinct. From the history of the surrealist movement itself, perhaps no anecdote illustrates the tension between the marvellous and the mysterious more pointedly than the famous episode when Breton, Roger Caillois and Jacques Lacan deliberated the proper response to the curiosity of the Mexican jumping bean. In this episode, it was Lacan who adopted Mallarmé's preference for obscurity by insisting on leaving the mystery of the bean intact. Caillois, by contrast, wished to cut the bean open immediately. Breton's proposal might be considered the surrealist response to mystery: the poet suggested prolonging the phenomenon until 'the three of us had exhausted the discussion on the probable cause of the movements we had witnessed (this would have required less than a few additional minutes)' (Breton 1995: 179). In other words, Breton embraced mystery with a limited, even relatively short duration (several minutes). This suggests that the surrealist marvellous, in contrast to Symbolist mystery, is not a permanent substance or figure but a temporal experience: thus surrealism would consistently prefer the adjectival 'marvellous', which potentially modifies any object or event, to the substantive 'marvel'. It is also not surprising that Breton should emphasize the importance of historicizing the marvellous, as he does already in the *First Manifesto*: 'The marvellous is not the same in every period of history: It partakes bscure way of a sort of general revelation only the fragments h come down to us: they are the romantic *ruins*, the modern *equin*, or any other symbol capable of affecting the human sensity for a period of time' (1969: 16, Breton's italics). The surrealist narvellous, put simply, has an expiry date. Occurring or appearing in time and producing an ephemeral effect, the marvellous is always *now*, from which it follows that the marvellous of the past – even of the immediate past – can only appear in the form of ruins.

Following Breton, all surrealist accounts of the marvellous must grapple with the paradox of its being a *temporal experience of timelessness*. In his 'Introduction to the Marvellous', published in 1941 in the Martiniquan review *Tropiques*, René Ménil describes the marvellous as a 'Golden Age', a land where '*everything is possible* … a docile world where everything hastens to respond to wishes' (Ménil 1996b: 91, author's italics). At the same time, agreeing with Breton, Ménil notes that the marvellous 'is always historically situated. The marvellous of the age of knights in armour is not the marvellous of the age of merchants' (94). For Ménil, therein lies the necessity to distinguish between a 'ready-made marvellous' and a 'lived marvellous', between a 'conventional marvellous' and an 'imagined marvellous'. Whereas a ready-made or conventional marvellous is the vestige of history, the 'cultural waste that societies and people expel by the very process of evolution', a lived and imagined marvellous is part and parcel of a temporal *becoming*. The latter, according to Ménil, 'lives in the mind with the full force of its emotion and is consequently inseparable from the human body, which *actualizes* it in time and in space' (94).

Ménil, to be sure, is more invested in the 'lived' or 'actualized' marvellous than a 'ready-made' or 'conventional' one. But surrealism does not oppose one mode of the marvellous to another; it seeks to reconcile them. After all, doesn't Ménil admit in the same text that, 'in the land of marvels, contraries can intimately rub shoulders or, more accurately, are able to communicate, to be mutually compelling … life and death, the communicable and the incommunicable, past and future, possible and impossible are interdependent and cease to be perceived as contradictory' (1996b: 92)? In *Mad Love* (1937), Breton provides an instructive case in which the reconciliation between a historical and a contemporary marvellous is less a utopian aspiration than an enchanted experience of the everyday. Specifically, a wooden spoon Breton had purchased at the flea market morphs into Cinderella's glass slipper by virtue of poetic associations. The sequence of these associations is crucial. According to Breton, the oneiric phrase 'Cinderella ashtray' (*cendrier Cendrillon*) had initially inspired him to conceive of a slipper-shaped ashtray cast in grey glass, which he asked the sculptor Giacometti to make for him (in vain). Subsequently, during a stroll at the flea market in the company of Giacometti, Breton bought a peculiar wooden spoon with a shoe-shaped heel. Back in his apartment, the view of this 'ready-made' object in combination with Breton's mental associations actualizes multiple elements of the fairy tale even more effectively than the *never-made* slipper-ashtray:

> Viewed from the side at a certain height, the little wooden shoe, emerging from the handle and aided by the latter's curvature, assumed the figure of a heel and gave the whole object the outline of a dancer's slipper with an upturned toe. Cinderella was indeed returning from the ball! ... The wood, initially graceless, thus acquired the transparency of glass. Subsequently, the slipper on the shelf, with the shoe-heel multiplying, vaguely looked as if it were moving of its own accord. *This movement was synchronized with that of the pumpkin-carriage in the fairy tale.* The wooden spoon had become illuminated, assuming the ardent value of one of the kitchen utensils Cinderella must have used before her metamorphosis.
>
> (Breton 1992: 702; 1987: 33–4, translation modified)

In the slipper-spoon, what Ménil will call the conventional marvellous collides with the lived marvellous. By means of the poetic imagination, Breton doesn't so much reproduce the story of Cinderella as make an ordinary object *re-appear* as the condensation of key images from the fairy tale (slipper, pumpkin-carriage). In turn, the present becomes the ruins of a past marvellous (the wooden spoon is the lost slipper or the *remains* of Cinderella); but it is also the terrain of a living, active marvellous, where the law of metamorphosis continues to disclose 'the marvellous slipper latent within the humble spoon' (Breton 1992: 702; 1987: 34, translation modified).

What is more, Breton's slipper-spoon represents the possible reconciliation between the collective unconscious (the fairy tale of Cinderella in its French rendition by Charles Perrault) and the poetic imagination of the individual. The possibility of such reconciliation is at issue in both Mabille's and Ménil's accounts. Whereas Mabille and Ménil both consider fairy tales and folklore the expression of 'a common wealth, a spontaneous expression of the collective unconscious', Mabille is pessimistic as regards their institutionalization. He considers that the collective unconscious retains the spontaneity of the marvellous only in the form of folklore; no sooner are the marvellous elements of fairy tales appropriated by religion than they degenerate into dogma: 'Religions take possession of them, building them into a stable construction equipped with a moral purpose. Religious systemization captures the marvellous and strips it of its novelty, its freedom. It exploits it for metaphysical and social ends. Dream images are organized according to an iconography precisely calculated to promote a certain dogma' (Mabille 1998: 29). He does not even regard individual artists and poets as wholly trustworthy because they routinely exploit the collective marvellous for their 'self-glorification'. He concludes that only the 'impersonal' incantations of priests, the anonymous songs and stories of troubadours and other cultural forms where 'no one takes pride in being original' qualify as the authentic marvellous (Mabille 1998: 31). Ménil, by contrast, welcomes the notion of the collective marvellous so long as it remains in dialectical relation with the individual marvellous. For the Martiniquan poet, the collective marvellous and the individual marvellous are not contradictory but culminate in different cultural forms: 'If fairy tales … express the collective marvellous, poems represent the individual marvellous. Fairy tales crystallize in myth; the poem takes shape through metaphor' (Ménil 1996b: 93). The scission between the collective and the individual, far from being inherent, arises only as an indicator of a divided society where the collective/social marvellous becomes for certain individuals as oppressive as physical reality. The aim for Ménil is therefore not the recuperation of a collective marvellous that annihilates individual originality but the creation of a 'reconciled society', where 'the individual marvellous and the social marvellous, although not interchangeable, are reconciled in the effervescence of an exalted social life' (Ménil 1996b: 93).

This desire for reconciliation of the collective and the individual links surrealism with the contemporaneous concerns of the Durkheimian school of sociology that would be influential for those sociologically inclined surrealists who founded the College of Sociology in 1937: Georges Bataille, Roger Caillois, Michel Leiris and Jules Monnerot. Although these four men had by this time all broken with the surrealist group constituted around Breton for a variety of reasons, they had all retained the surrealist concern with the tension between the individual and the collective and with seeking ways to reconcile them. The fact that the operative word now becomes 'the sacred' rather than the 'marvellous' represents a change of emphasis, but the underlying concern is precisely with what Ménil called 'exalted social life'.

The vocabulary here was drawn from Durkheim, who had identified a fundamental distinction between the 'sacred' and the 'profane' in the construction of society. With his foundation set firmly in positivist methodology, Durkheim was a strange bedfellow for surrealism (indeed he was among the authors the surrealists in 1922 advised us not to read) but there was an affinity to the extent that both perceived a crisis of the sensibility wrought in modern society by an excess of individualism. For Durkheim this was *anomie*, linked to the way the profane was increasingly discarding the sacred ties that bound society together; for the surrealists this process was made evident by the way art was fetishized, as well as marginalized, as a product of the inspired individual. Hence the surrealists' demand, following Isidore Ducasse, for art to be 'made by all, not by one'.

If the writers we have thus far discussed responded to this crisis through the identification and elaboration of the realm of the marvellous, those who formed the College of Sociology were more concerned to understand in a systematic way the process by which profane society, an aspect of positivism, had expelled, or more precisely nullified, the sacred. It was for this reason that they spoke of establishing an 'activist' or 'sacred' sociology.

This raises issues too complex to be dealt with satisfactorily within the confines of this essay, but looking back over this period of the 1930s, Jules Monnerot, in his book *La Poésie moderne et le sacré*, published in 1945, essentially conflates the two movements of sacred and marvellous in making a link between modern poetry and the sacred. By 'modern poetry' Monnerot means, exclusively, surrealism (his title would make more sense, especially for an English-speaking audience, if it were called *Surrealism and the Sacred*). For Monnerot, only surrealism deserves the status of poetry because it alone had recognized and revealed 'a critical state of the sensibility, morals, expression, thought and the whole social configuration that has produced it' (1945: 68). Despite this it did not (and perhaps could not) go as far as was necessary in actualizing what it had laid open. It was thus, as he put it, 'prayer in a void'. 'Poetry is magic for magic', he tells us, 'magic without hope, and the poet is a magician who devotes himself to the rituals for themselves, expecting nothing from them' (18).

What is missing here is the collective contagion that gave the sacred its active character in earlier societies, a contagion from which arises the communication that enables a society to establish what Mabille, in another of his books, calls an *égrégore*, that dialectical moment in which an entity is transformed, even if only for a moment, into what is beyond itself (Mabille 1977).

What the marvellous and the sacred share is this transformative quality. In earlier times the sacred was the means by which society renewed itself, placing itself in a harmony with cosmic forces that is broken by the human concerns of everyday, profane existence. It was the period of transgression in which the 'world was turned upside down' within defined limits. In modern society, such periods of transgression have been perverted either into harmless festivals that serve no transformative purpose or into destructive acts of violence and war that lacerate more than they bind society and in which any communicative function is rendered void.

For Bataille, Caillois and Monnerot this loss of the sacred quality of old represented a major incapacity within the modern sensibility that surrealism revealed without having the capability to confront. It was why they sought an activist sociology through the College of Sociology. For those surrealists who evoked the marvellous, however, the issue was less clear-cut. They were less concerned with the dynamic of society itself than with the functioning of the individual within society. The marvellous for them was less a means of renewal than a revelation.

In this respect Michel Leiris might be seen as intermediary figure. Less committed to the social aims of the College of Sociology than his three colleagues, he was more concerned to view the sacred in terms of a personal mythology. Consequently his interest in the sacred seems barely distinguishable from the idea of the marvellous as posited by Breton, Mabille and Ménil. Leiris specifically addressed the sacred in his programmatic text for the College of Sociology, 'The Sacred in Everyday Life', in which he explored how the sacred intervened in his personal life, especially through childhood incident and memory. This text occasioned a response from Colette Peignot entitled 'The Sacred'. In it she develops and extends some of Leiris's insights as she equates the sacred with communication and the constitution of society (which she sees as beginning at the moment two people get together). She defines the sacred in a complex way as the 'infinitely rare moment in which the "eternal share" that each being carries within enters life, finds itself carried off in the universal movement, integrated into this movement, realized' (Laure 1995: 41).

Here we move a long way from the Durkheimian notion of the sacred to approach what the surrealists called the marvellous, and this also distances us from the social concerns of the College of Sociology. The sacred is here conceptualized as closer to an alchemical act of transmutation than as a communal consecration effected through ritual. Communication was conceived by her as an unveiling: one reveals oneself in all of one's nakedness. This indeed links with the surrealist narrative tradition initiated with Breton's *Nadja* and that reaches its most resolute expression in the writings of Leiris, especially in the four volumes of *La Règle du jeu*.

Perhaps this partly answers Monnerot's complaint that poetry can only be 'prayer in a void'. The transformative power of the marvellous lies not within ritual enactment and to this extent does not correspond with the social role the sacred has played in historical societies. It is rather enacted – whether at an individual or collective level – through a plunge into the sensibility that annihilates being into a jewel, as Breton demanded in the *Second Manifesto*. The marvellous is therefore less about finding a means of binding society together than it is a revelation of being, one that brings one's own sensibility into question, so making possible a transformation of the world. This transformation will not occur through a renewal of society, since for the surrealists modern society is irrevocably corrupted, but through a revolution of the sensibility itself as the realization of the *paucity of reality* that Breton identified as the modern condition becomes generalized. The necessity is to confront this paucity with the surfeit of being that comes into focus as soon as one approaches the *point of the mind* at which fundamental oppositions will no longer be perceived as contradictory to one another and being itself is annihilated.

Notes

1 Here Breton is following the insight of the poet Pierre Reverdy, who already in 1917 calls attention to the futility of distinguishing between the real and the imaginary. In the domain of the written word, 'whether it is imaginary or real is of no importance, one will remain in the realm of possible events as long as one does not fall upon the marvellous' (Reverdy 1975: 43).

2 Béhar's readings in various surrealist texts led him to conclude that '1. The concept [of the marvellous] is not an entity; 2. The concept is only found in theoretical texts; 3. the surrealists developed their own exegesis of the marvellous; 4. The concept is vague but recurring; it is all the more pervasive as it does not designate a specific object' (2000: 29, our translation).

21 The supreme point

Michael Richardson and Krzysztof Fijalkowski

The supreme point, or the sublime point, defined by Breton in the second manifesto as the location at which 'life and death, the real and the imagined, past and future, the communicable and the incommunicable, high and low, cease to be perceived as contradictions', is the motive point of surrealism. All surrealist activity is directed towards the determination of this point, which constitutes the very substance of surrealist endeavour, in however oblique a way. This notion should not be treated as a metaphor, or as any sort of aesthetic or poetic gesture. Nor is it an effort to go beyond or bring into question binary oppositions, thus causing a collapse of traditional classifications, in the way that certain elements of postmodernist or post-structuralist thought have sought. Indeed, the supreme point is constituted of those very oppositions; if one were to collapse them, then the whole edifice would come apart, the edifice being, in this case, reality itself. We would be cast into a universe of infinite chaos. But nor do oppositions merge. The surrealist aim is not to overcome, abolish or unite oppositions, but to determine the secret that is hidden within their apparent opposition. This 'point' is where they cease to function as oppositions, where opposition itself loses its strength. It has no material or any other sort of 'reality', since it is reality itself. It is a 'point of the mind' (or the spirit) that dissolves at the moment of its realization, since at that moment there will no longer be a 'mind' at all, for it will have consumed itself in universal radiance.

So it is a 'point' that doesn't actually 'exist', being beyond existence. As reality itself, it is a brilliance that may blind us instead of liberate us at the moment of illumination. It is certainly related to, and may even be indistinguishable from, the 'Tao' of Chinese philosophy or the 'gnosis' of Gnosticism. It is also related to the philosopher's stone of Hermeticism and to the eternal fire in Heraclitus and we find a version of it in numerous cultures, such as the alcheringa of the Australians.

Like all of these notions it stands for what is beyond expression and therefore cannot be represented in discourse. This means that discussion of it is inevitably deficient and lacking in precision. Nevertheless the supreme point as understood within surrealism has its own distinguishing characteristics that need to be explored if we are to understand the contribution surrealism has made to the history of ideas.

Philosophically, we find other intimations of the idea in Paracelsus, Nicholas of Cusa, Giordano Bruno and others. In terms of Breton's own formulation, it is most commonly related to Hegel and Hermetic traditions.[1] In the 1950s, Breton himself would be categorical on this issue:

> I hardly need to stress the 'Hegelian' aspect of the idea of surpassing all antinomies. It was undeniably Hegel – and no one else – who put me in the condition necessary to perceive this point, to strain toward it with all my might, and to make this very tension my life's goal.
>
> (1993: 118)

Georges Sebbag has, however, played down Hegel's importance, preferring to speak not of the 'supreme' but the 'sublime' point. He relates this to the 'point of indifference' of Schelling, linking it with the use Ducasse and Vaché also made of indifference. Quoting Émile Bréhier, to the effect that this point of coincidence is a unity and not a synthesis, Sebbag insists that it should be made 'clear that the point of indifference, in which contraries coexist, corresponds neither to an ideal nor to the end of a process of dissolution but to "a point of departure"' (Sebbag 2012: 604).

Sebbag traces Breton's engagement with the notion of this 'point' over twenty years, from the 'point of the mind [or spirit]' referred to in the 1929 manifesto through his discovery of an actual 'Sublime Point' during visits in 1931 and 1932 to the Verdon Gorges in Provence (a specific spot that is not, as one might have expected, an unattainable mountain peak but a viewing point, a 'panorama' from which to look out onto a remarkable landscape). Breton refers to this 'Sublime Point'[2] in 1937 in *L'Amour fou*, returning to speak of the 'point of the mind' as the place at which antinomies are resolved during his 1942 Yale lecture (Breton 1978: 245). According to Sebbag, Breton has so far mentioned neither Hegel nor the term 'Supreme Point' in connection with this 'point of coincidence', which emerge directly for the first time only in the course of his 1952 conversations with André Parinaud. Sebbag ascribes Breton's assumption of the term 'supreme point' to the influence of Michel Carrouges, a Catholic historian with whom Breton had become friendly and who had published his book *André Breton et les donneés fondamentales du surréalisme* in 1950.[3] There is also, however, an earlier significant mention of the supreme point, made in Breton's 1948 essay, 'The Lamp in the Clock' where he writes:

> Whereas the expansion of *desire* in love is illuminated by a powerful projector, its parallel contraction immediately after the climax of the sex act induces a persistent bad conscience that discourages us from reverting to the supreme point that could have been reached and from where, for a moment after all slightly less brief than a lightning flash, without necessarily being alert to it – which would mean betraying pleasure itself and accepting that it betrays us – we had the chance to grasp some unrevealed aspects of the world from a unique angle.
>
> (Breton 1995: 118)

This quotation marks the supreme point as close to Georges Bataille's notion of the Impossible. For Bataille, this involves a determination to achieve a form of sovereign existence, achieved by pursuing what he termed 'an arduous path to the heart of being' (1993: 50). In making this comment, Bataille was actually criticizing the surrealists for having abandoned this path in favour of the 'establishment of works'.[4] In doing so, however, he was marking out what he saw as the true path of surrealism, which is actually one that no surrealist would be likely to disagree with.

The first question to be considered, then, is the determination of this 'point': should it be treated as 'supreme' or as 'sublime'? Or even whether the point of the mind (spirit) of 1929, the sublime point of 1931 and 1936, and the supreme point of 1948 are actually one and the same thing. Might they in fact be different aspects of a contiguous problem? We can agree with Sebbag that in each case we are not talking about a process of dissolution. We can also agree that in no case does it represent a synthesis. We have more difficulty, however, in accepting that this point constitutes a place where contraries coexist. Breton's definition, indeed, seems to preclude this possibility. The contraries don't coexist; they 'cease to be perceived as contradictions'. Nothing, apparently, happens to the contraries themselves, which continue to subsist – or not – as they were, whether as antagonistic or responsive to one another. Breton emphasizes in the second manifesto that the determination of this point involves 'the annihilation of being into an internal and blind diamond, which has no more the soul of ice than of fire' (Breton 1988: 782). If being is annihilated, then its contradictions no longer have any meaning: a transformation has been effected in which everything that was previously taken for granted has altered and the old rules of reality no longer apply. Breton therefore does seem to be speaking of a *sublation* in the Hegelian sense: a place where antinomies are simultaneously surpassed and preserved.

From this perspective, in raising the question of the 'sublime point in the mountain', Breton would seem to be taking a step back from the determination of the point of the mind or spirit of the second manifesto. The sublime point at the confluence of the Baou and Verdon rivers does not 'annihilate being' since, as Breton acknowledges, he is unable to live there. Or at least if he did, as he tells his eight-month-old daughter in *L'Amour fou*, 'it would have ceased to be sublime and myself to be a man'. Even so, he has 'never moved so far away from it that I have lost sight of it, and become unable to point to it' (1992: 780; English translation, 1987: 114). This tends to suggest that the sublime point is not the point where contradictions cease to be perceived but rather a station – a halting place (or a point of departure, if you prefer) – along the way to its possible realization. Might it not even be, far from the point at which contradictions are resolved, the very place where they are formed, where water separates itself from air and, as it makes its way to the sea, forges out the low of the valley from the high of the mountain, and so on? This, indeed, seems to equate with the notion of the sublime, which implies a sense of awe in the face of what cannot be comprehended. It seems, prima facie, to preclude the sort of immersion that an 'annihilation of being' would of necessity involve. Can the place where life and death are no longer perceived as contradictions ever assume a material form of any sort?

In this respect, Breton's perception of the sublime point seems to be analogous with the profound aim of Chinese landscape painting which unites mountain (as form) with water (as formless) (see Jullien 2016: 57). Without making this precise connection, Sebbag (2012: 600) seems to evoke this sense as he relates the sublime point to the technique of decalcomania invented by Oscar Dominguez in 1935 which conjures up, through the chance encounter of gouache, glass and paper, landscapes redolent of the Verdon Gorges in which high and low are confounded. However, as Sebbag notes, Breton refuses to immerse himself in this landscape, presenting himself in *L'Amour fou* rather as a guide to it. Less an object to look at than a place to see from, the 'sublime point' here seems to correspond not so much to the point of the mind of the second manifesto as to the window that Breton demanded of a picture, concerned as he was with: 'what it *looks out on*' (Breton 1972: 2).

In the passage from *L'Amour fou*, Breton is addressing himself to his little girl, whom he named Aube (Dawn), to be read when she became sixteen. In this letter to the future, Breton explains to Aube how he had long regarded having a child as 'the gravest insanity' (1987: 112) which he hopes she won't one day hold against him. By indulging this 'insanity', Breton's letter explains how this birth, this 'dawn', represented for him a commitment to life. As such it implies a retreat from the will to perceive the point at which the conflict between 'life and death' is resolved. It seems to correspond to that period of Breton's life when political realities, above all the threat posed by fascism, entailed a move back from the metaphysical ambitions of surrealism in the 1920s that culminated in the explication of the ultimate aim as the resolution of antinomies, called for in the second manifesto.

Being content to be a guide to the sublime point does indeed seem to take Breton close to Schelling's point of indifference, but did this 'sublime' point assert itself at a time in his life when he was retreating from the point of mind posited in the second manifesto, to which he only returned and named the 'supreme point' at the end of the forties?[5]

Schelling's 'point of indifference' was precisely what Hegel famously criticized as the night of the Absolute in which 'all cows are black' (Hegel 1977: introd. §16, 9). Hegel faults Schelling for presupposing instead of examining the identity of opposites. The 'indifference' thus collapses subjective and objective so that 'each makes itself into its opposite and only the identity of the two is the truth' (Hegel 2009: 205). From this one would have thought the point of indifference can only represent the break up of difference, not the annihilation of being into a jewel as demanded by surrealism. The point of indifference is undoubtedly one of the elements that surrealism embraced in its process of poetic discovery and does seem to correspond to the sublime point in the mountains located by Breton. But as Breton makes clear, it would be impossible to live there. As noted earlier, it constitutes more of a halting spot, a place where one can rest on the way to the absolute of the supreme point, having become more aware of *what is to be done.* In this respect we might relate it to another theme close to the surrealists' hearts: that of the Grail in Arthurian legend. Julien Gracq (1948: 34) has in fact compared the surrealist group to the Arthurian Round Table in regard to its sense of companionship and it can be said that the surrealists, like the Grail-quester, draw back when the circumstances arise in which they could ask the question to free the waters of non-contradiction precisely in order to remain *on this side* of existence and participate in the world. Might not Breton's encounter with the sublime point in the Verdon Gorges then be comparable to the Grail-questor's encounter with the Grail at the Fisher King's castle? By refusing to live there, was not Breton failing – or deliberately refusing – to ask the question that would enable the realization of the Grail and so transform the wasteland (where life and death are held in suspension) and pass into the *other side* of existence? The choice facing the questor is whether to accept this challenge of the absolute – and thus renounce the world of the senses and the living – or return to that world re-energized by the quest and so be better able to contribute to the struggle for freedom in the here and now.

In this respect, we wonder if in naming the 'point of the mind' as 'supreme' Breton might also have been thinking of René Guénon, who saw the encounter at the Grail castle as the first initiatory stage of the journey towards what he called the 'supreme centre': 'even as the Terrestrial Paradise has become inaccessible, so the supreme centre, which is fundamentally the same thing, can cease to be manifested outwardly during the course of certain periods, and then it can be said that the tradition is lost to the great mass of humanity, for it is preserved only in certain strictly closed centres, so that, in contrast to the original state, the majority of people can no longer participate in it in a conscious or effective manner. This is precisely the state of affairs in our present age' (2001: 30).

For the most part, though, the surrealists (with some exceptions) have been *too much in the world* to embrace fully the initiatory path that a spiritual guide like Guénon might advocate. Notwithstanding a generalized disdain for the fact of life and the paucity of existence it implies, and a few extreme cases like René Crevel or Antonin Artaud, for most surrealists – and certainly this is so for Breton – surrealism is more precisely constituted as a 'philosophy of living', placing examination of the phenomenology of our collective existence here and now above any personal liberation that may be offered by a purely spiritual adventure. In emphasizing the Hegelian aspects of the supreme point, Breton himself insisted that surrealism 'can in no way be situated on the mystic plane' (1993: 119).

While the supreme point provides the motive point of all surrealist activity, one should not make the mistake of thinking that this implies any inclination to represent it, something that would in any event be a vain task. If some artists like the Czech painter Josef Šima, with his crystalline landscapes of a land in which eternity becomes hazily apparent, or a work like Max Ernst's *Men Shall Know Nothing of This* (1923) with its union of love in an alignment of celestial bodies, have visually explored the idea of the supreme point, for the most part it is a question of how a recognition of the possibility of the supreme point energizes the fact of living that motivates the surrealists. Moreover, as

Gérard Legrand (Legrand and Patri 1956: 143) insisted, the surrealists never sought to *realize* the Sublime Point, since they recognized that this would be a 'biological impossibility'. In refusing initiatory ritual, surrealism offers each individual the freedom to challenge in myriad ways dominant ways of thinking. This distinguishes surrealism proper from a group like the Grand Jeu (with which Šima was associated), which embraced the initiatory path and sought to engage in the 'great game' that would only be played once. Nevertheless, the supreme point unites both groups in the opposition it represents to what they see as the false path taken by the Western world since the advent of the monotheistic, Abrahamic, religions, which separate the phenomena of existence and seek salvation in a transcendent god, especially since the mentality underlying such religions became socially concretized during the Renaissance and has dominated our world up to the present day. This is why surrealism has placed such stress on bringing into question oppositions such as those of good and bad, life and death, creation and destruction, and has sought to reveal the point or the moment at which such oppositions lose their meaning and the realization of Rimbaud's demand to 'change life' and Marx's to 'transform the world' can become possible.

Notes

1 Magee (2001) has pointed to significant correlations between Hegel and Hermeticism in ways that intriguingly correlate with the surrealists' perception.

2 Before Breton discovered this point, Roger Vitrac had perceived something similar in the Padirac Gorge in the Lot Valley, referred to in his text 'Consuella, ou Méditations sur le Gouffre de Padirac', published in issue 11 of *La Révolution surréaliste*. This text has been translated in Richardson 1994: 45–9. Nietzsche, too, had a comparable experience in encountering the 'Zarathustra stone' on the shores of Lake Silvaplana when he had the revelation of the idea of eternal return.

3 Despite his Catholicism, Carrouges was uneasily accepted within the surrealist milieu until 1951, when he would become the cause or the subject of a major upheaval that would tear apart the French surrealist group. This is known variously as the 'Carrouges affair' or the 'Pastoureau affair'.

4 Bataille doesn't give any instances in support of his contention and we can only wonder who and what he has in mind, and make our own examination of how justified it was.

5 It would seem strange if the surrealist aim could be realized by visiting a tourist spot in the south of France. A significant distinction is contained in the very words 'sublime' and 'supreme'; the definition of the former being what 'inspires awe', whereas the latter refers to what is incomparable; a point at which life and death are not perceived as contradictory seems prima facie to go far beyond 'inspiring awe'.

Chronology of surrealist engagement with ideas

Given the vastness of the surrealist movement, a comprehensive chronology of surrealism would far exceed the bounds of this volume. This is therefore a highly selective record established principally to give the reader some pointers towards the more significant moments in the history of the movement.

1916	André Breton becomes friends with Jacques Vaché.
1917	Breton meets Louis Aragon and Philippe Soupault.
1918	Soupault discovers the work of Isidore Ducasse. Aragon and Breton begin reading the German Romantics and idealist philosophers.
1919	Death of Jacques Vaché. Breton, Aragon and Soupault establish the journal *Littérature*, in whose pages the idea of surrealism will gradually be shaped. They also become friendly with Paul Éluard, who will be the other key figure in its formation; Breton and Soupault write *Les Champs magnétiques* together, establishing the practical basis of automatic writing.
1920	Tristan Tzara arrives in Paris, momentarily galvanizing the activities of Paris Dada but also helping to concretize reservations in the minds of Breton and his friends about its viability.
1921	The 'Trial of Maurice Barrès', accused of 'crimes against the security of the spirit'; Breton visits Sigmund Freud in Vienna.
1922	Breton publishes the essay 'Lâchez tout', saying goodbye to Dada; a group forms around him that will constitute the basis of the surrealist collective. Period of 'sleep experiments'; the group pays homage to Germaine Berton, a young anarchist who assassinated

Marius Plateau, a leader of the proto-fascist Camelots du roi.

1923 Final activity of Paris Dada. Yvan Goll and Paul Dermée, drawing directly upon Apollinaire, lay claim to the term 'surrealism', which is disputed by those around Breton. Marcel Duchamp leaves unfinished his master work, *La Mariée mise à nu par ses célibataires, même* (*Le Grand verre*).

1924 Goll and Dermée publish their journal *Surréalisme* containing Goll's 'Manifesto' in which he asserts surrealism as 'the transposition of reality onto a higher (artistic) level'. The publication of Breton's *Manifeste du surréalisme* later in the year, supplemented by that of Aragon's *Une Vague de rêves*, will reveal the limitations of Goll and Dermée's vision and definitively establish the superiority of their version of surrealism; a new periodical, *La Révolution surréaliste* is established and a Bureau of Surrealist Research opened. The collective tract 'A Corpse', attacking Anatole France, is published. A surrealist group also begins to take shape in Yugoslavia. Enquiry included in *La Révolution surréaliste*: 'Is Suicide a Solution?'

1925 A *Déclaration* made on 27 January 1925 sets out immediate surrealist aims; issue 3 of *La Révolution surréaliste* pronounces the 'death of the Christian era' and includes open letters to the Pope and the Dalai Lama. The surrealists also take a stand against colonialism and the war in Morocco. The invention of the *cadavre exquis* game provides a fresh impetus for collective engagement. Tract 'La Révolution d'abord et toujours!' Surrealist activity begins in Japan.

1926 A surrealist group is established in Belgium. Close collaborations with the Marxist Clarté and Philosophies groups. Breton meets Nadja. Publications: Aragon, *Paris Peasant*; Naville, *La Révolution et les intellectuels*; Breton, 'Légitime défense'; Éluard, *Capitale de la douleur*.

1927 Rapprochement with the Communist Party. The surrealists issue a tract 'Hands Off Love' defending Charlie Chaplin from a media campaign against him due to his 'dissolute life'. Artaud, having been attacked in the tract 'Au grand jour', responds in kind with 'À la grande nuit'. Publications: Breton, *Introduction au discours sur le peu de réalité*; Desnos, *La Liberté ou l'amour*; Péret, *Dormir, dormir dans les pierres*; Crevel, *L'Esprit contre la raison.*

1928 Aldo Pellegrini establishes a surrealist group in Argentina. First issue of the journal *Le Grand jeu*; Buñuel and Dalí make the film *Un Chien Andalou.* Publications: Breton, *Nadja*, *Le Surréalisme et la peinture*, *Lettre aux voyantes*; Leiris, *Aurora*; Aragon, *Treatise on Style*; Péret, *Le Grand jeu.*

1929 Breton, *Second Manifesto of Surrealism.* A meeting is called to discuss 'the Recent Fate of Leon Trotsky' but descends into a disarray that will be the catalyst for significant splits in the movement. Founding of a surrealist group in Belgrade, formalizing activity first initiated in 1924. Publication of the first issue of *Documents* and *Le Surréalisme en 1929*, special issue of the Belgian journal *Variétés.* Publications: Éluard, *L'Amour la poésie*; Bataille, *L'Histoire de l'œil*; Aragon, *Le Con d'Irène.*

1930 The first issue of *Le Surréalisme au service de la Révolution* is published. Former members of the Parisian surrealist group issue a broadside against Breton, *Un cadavre.* René Daumal writes to Breton marking the difference between surrealism and the Grand Jeu. First surrealist objects are made. First screening of Buñuel and Dalí's *L'Âge d'or*; the League of Patriots and the Anti-Jewish League ransack the cinema. Dalí invents the 'paranoiac-critical' method. Publications: Tzara, *Approximate Man*; Breton and Éluard, *The Immaculate Conception*; Aragon, *La Peinture au défi*; Dalí, *La Femme visible.*

1931 The surrealists take an active stance against colonialism, demonstrating against the major Colonial Exhibition in Paris and staging their own counter-show, 'The Truth about the Colonies'. Publications: Crevel, *Dalí ou l'antiobscurantisme.*

1932 The surrealists break with Aragon and Georges Sadoul over their commitment to the Communist Party. Aragon is prosecuted by the French government for encouraging desertion in the army and 'provocation to murder' in publishing an incendiary poem, 'Red Front'.

Despite the break and misgivings about the poem, the surrealists come to Aragon's defence. Étienne Léro, René Ménil and Jules Monnerot, students at the Sorbonne, publish their anti-colonialist journal *Légitime défense*. Surrealist activity emerges in the Canary Islands, centred around the journal *Gaceta de arte* edited by Eduardo Westerdahl. Publications: Crevel, *Le Clavecin de Diderot*; Breton, *Les Vases communicants.*

1933 Breton is expelled from the Association of Revolutionary Writers and Artists. First issue of the journal *Minotaure*, on which the surrealists collaborate. Exhibition of surrealist artworks and objects held in Paris. The surrealists defend Violette Nozière, a young woman who murdered her father whom she accused of having raped her. First issue of the journal *Phare de Neuilly* edited by Lise Deharme. Hans Bellmer begins *The Doll.*

1934 A surrealist group forms in Czechoslovakia.
A surrealist group emerges in Hainaut, organized by Achille Chavée and Fernand Dumont. In response to violent fascist demonstration in Paris the surrealists issue an *Appel à la lutte* seeking the support of other left-wing intellectuals. Breton gives a talk in Brussels on 'What Is Surrealism?' Publication in Brussels of the journal *Documents 34* devoted to surrealism. Publications: Leiris, *L'Afrique fantôme.*

1935 The surrealists participate in the anti-fascist group Contre-attaque. Breton and Éluard are invited to Prague where Breton gives two important talks, 'Surrealist Situation of the Object' and 'Political Position of Today's Art'. A surrealist exhibition is held in Tenerife. Crevel commits suicide after Breton is not allowed to address the International Congress of Writers for the Defence of Culture. Éluard is then permitted to read Breton's text at the end of the conference, after midnight. The surrealists respond with the tract 'On the Time the Surrealists Were Right' making their split with the French Communist Party definitive. Surrealist activity emerges in Copenhagen, organized by Vilhelm Bjerke-Petersen and Wilhelm Freddie around the journal *Konkretion.* First

International Surrealist Exhibition held, *Den Frie Udstilling*, in Copenhagen. First issue of the *Bulletin international du surréalisme* published in Prague. The first issue of *Mauvais temps*, the journal of the Hainaut surrealists also appears. Publications: Dalí, *La Conquête de l'irrationnel*; Caillois writes *La nécessité d'esprit* (not published until 1981).

1936 The second International Surrealist Exhibition is held in London and a British surrealist group develops. Artaud is invited to Mexico where he gives a series of lectures on surrealism and journeys to the Tarahumaras Indians in Northern Mexico. Exhibition of surrealist objects in Paris at the Galerie Charles Ratton. Breton gives an important lecture exposing 'The Truth about the Moscow Trials'. Publications: Mabille, *La Construction de l'homme.*

1937 Artaud is interned in a mental hospital. The third International Surrealist Exhibition is held in Japan. Opening of the Gradiva Gallery in Paris with a door designed by Marcel Duchamp. Surrealist group Art et Liberté founded in Egypt. Publications: Breton, *L'Amour fou*; Artaud, *Nouvelles révélations de l'être.*

1938 Breton visits Mexico, meeting Leon Trotsky with whom he collaborates on the manifesto *Towards a Free Revolutionary Art*. The fourth International Surrealist Exhibition held in Paris. Breton and Éluard produce the *Dictionnaire abrégé du surréalisme* as its catalogue. Breton founds the Fédération internationale de l'art révolutionnaire indépendant. The surrealists break with Éluard. In London Mesens directs the London Gallery and edits the journal *London Bulletin*. In Prague, Nezval attempts to disband the Czech surrealist group, apparently on orders from the Communist Party; the remainder of the group refuse, protesting with their text 'Surrealism against the Current'. A group forms in Chile and publishes a journal, *Mandragore.* Publications: Artaud, *Le Théâtre et son double*; Gracq, *Au château d'Argol*; Mabille, *Egrégores ou la vie des civilisations*; Nicolas Calas, *Foyers d'incendie.*

1939 Dalí is definitively excluded from surrealism for collaborating with the fascist regime in Spain. In Peru, first issue of the journal *El Uso de la palabra*.

Publications: Éluard, *Donner à voir*; Césaire, *Cahier d'un retour au pays natal*; Leiris, *L'Âge d'homme*; Caillois, *Le Mythe et l'homme.*

1940 Fifth International Surrealist Exhibition held in Mexico. Germany invades France, causing dispersal of the majority of the surrealists in France, many of whom are forced to emigrate. Publication of the first issue of *L'Invention collective*, a journal of the Brussels and Hainaut surrealists. A clandestine surrealist group emerges in Bucharest. Several surrealists, including Breton, make their way to Marseilles in advance of the Nazi occupation. Publications: Breton, *Anthologie de l'humour noir* (banned by occupation authorities); Mabille, *Le Miroir du merveilleux.*

1941 In Martinique Breton discovers the surrealist journal *Tropiques* and a friendship develops with its editors. The semi-clandestine group La Main à plume is established in Paris and issues its first publications; several members are Resistance activists, of whom a number would be executed. In Japan, Shuzo Takiguchi and Ichiro Fukuzaki are arrested by the secret police. The surrealists in Marseilles design a new pack of cards, whose suits are Love, Dream, Knowledge and Revolution with, as emblems, respectively Flame, Lock, Star and Wheel. Breton and Ernst reach New York. Péret, who had been imprisoned the year before for his political activities, reaches Mexico; after a breakdown and incarceration in a Spanish asylum, Carrington also moves there. Publications: Calas, *Confound the Wise*; Bataille, *Madame Edwarda.*

1942 Sixth International Surrealist Exhibition, *First Papers of Surrealism*, held in New York. Breton gives a talk at Yale University: 'Situation of Surrealism between the Two Wars'. The journals *VVV* (in New York) and *Dyn* (in Mexico) are established. With the latter, Paalen announces a (temporary) 'Farewell to Surrealism'. Publications: Breton, *Prolégomène à un troisième manifeste du surréalisme ou non.*

1943 Bataille, *L'Expérience intérieure.*

1944 Publications: Breton, *Arcane 17*; Bataille, *Le Coupable.*

1945 Desnos dies in Terezin concentration camp. Michel Fardoulis-Lagrange and Jean Maquet found the journal

Troisième convoi. Breton is invited to Haiti for a lecture series. The first is attended by President Lescot and other members of the ruling class and is considered incendiary. A special issue of the journal *La Ruche* published in Haiti is dedicated to Breton and suppressed by the government. Riots follow, leading to a revolutionary situation which results in the overthrow of the government. Publications: Péret, *Le Déshonneur des poètes*, a pamphlet attacking the poetry of the Resistance; Luca and Trost, *Dialectique de la dialectique*; Georges Henein, *Prestige de la terreur*, a polemic against the nuclear attack on Japan, arguing that it perpetuates the mentality of Nazism and institutes the modern state as 'terrorist'; Christian Dotremont and Marcel Mariën, *La Terre n'est pas une vallée de larmes*; Monnerot, *La Poésie moderne et le sacré*; Bataille, *Sur Nietzsche*. Maurice Nadeau publishes *Histoire du surréalisme*.

1946 Breton returns to Paris. Artaud released from a mental hospital and a special performance is arranged for him at the Théâtre Sarah-Bernhardt in Paris. Magritte, Mariën and Nougé, the manifesto *Le Surréalisme en plein soleil*; Yves Bonnefoy, Iaroslav Serpan and Claude Tarnaud form the short-lived group La Révolution la nuit.

1947 Seventh International Surrealist Exhibition is held in Paris, *Le Surréalisme en 1947*, which will travel to Prague in reduced form. Publications: Breton, *Ode à Charles Fourier*; Christian Dotremont and Jean Seeger publish the tract 'Pas de quartier dans la révolution! Manifeste des surréalistes révolutionnaires en France'. The Parisian surrealists publish the tract 'Rupture inaugurale' to define their political position. First surrealist group in Portugal formed by Mário Cesariny and Alexandre O'Neill. The Egyptian surrealists publish the journal *La Part du sable*.

1948 Artaud, *To Have Done with the Judgment of God*, shelved by French radio the day before it is scheduled to be broadcast. Publication in Brussels of the *Bulletin international du surréalisme révolutionnaire*. Publication of the journal *Neon*, the first by the Paris group since the war. 'À la niche les glapisseurs de Dieu!', an important tract attacking religion is published. Matta is expelled for what is seen as responsibility for the suicide of Arshile Gorky leading to a rupture within the Paris group. Publications: Leiris, *Biffures*; Gracq, *André Breton, quelques aspects de l'écrivain.*

1949 Publications: Maurice Blanchot, *La Part du feu*; Mabille, *L'Initiation à la connaissance de l'homme*; Bataille, *La part maudite.*

1950 Buñuel films *Los Olvidados* in Mexico. Publications: Marcel Jean and Arpad Mezei, *Genèse de la pensée moderne*; Caillois, *L'Homme et le sacré*; Breton and Péret edit the *Almanach surréaliste du demi-siècle.*

1951 In the fallout from 'the Carrouges affair' when Michel Carrouges, a writer associated with the surrealists and a practising Catholic, is expelled, most of the 'old guard' surrealists leave the group; Gracq publishes *La Littérature à l'estomac* attacking the commercialization of literature, especially the vogue for literary prizes. Notwithstanding this, the following year the judges insist on awarding him the Prix Goncourt for his novel *Le Rivages des Syrtes.* His refusal to accept it causes a minor scandal. Záviš Kalandra, former associate of the pre-war Czechoslovak surrealist group, is tried and executed for allegedly participating in a Trotskyist plot.

1951 The surrealists contribute to *Le Libertaire*, the newspaper of the Anarchist Federation. Breton is interviewed for a series of talks on French radio. René Alleau begins a series of talks on alchemy attended by many of the surrealists. A new journal is founded, *Médium.*

1952 Michel Zimbacca and Jean-Louis Bédouin make the film *L'Invention du monde* with commentary by Péret.

1953 The Czech group begins the *Objekt* cycle, its first collective project since the war. Publications: Ado Kyrou, *Le surréalisme au cinema*; Trost, *Visible et invisible.*

1954 In Belgium, the first issue of the journal *Les Lèvres nues* edited by Marcel Mariën. Publications: Breton, *La Clé des Champs.*

1955 'Hongrie, soleil levant', tract in support of the Hungarian revolution. First issue of the journal *Le Surréalisme, même.* Publications: Breton, *Du surréalisme en ses œuvres vives*; Leiris, *Fourbis*; Bataille, *La littérature et le mal*; Césaire, *Discours sur le colonialisme.*

1956 Publications: Péret, *Anthologie de l'amour sublime*; Caillois, *L'Incertitude qui vient des rêves.*

1957 Bataille, *L'Érotisme*; Breton and Gérard Legrand, *L'Art magique*; Bellmer, *Petite anatomie de l'inconscient physique ou l'Anatomie de l'image.*

1958 First issue of the journal *Bief: Jonction surréaliste*; Mariën, *Théorie de la révolution mondiale immediate.*

1959 Eighth International Surrealist Exhibition held in Paris (*Exposition InteRnatiOnal du Surréalisme*, Eros) devoted to eroticism. It includes a 'cannibal feast' organized by Meret Oppenheim and a ceremony presented by Jean Benoît, 'Execution of the Will of the Marquis de Sade'.

1960 Surrealists initiate and sign the incendiary *Déclaration sur le droit à l'insoumission dans la guerre d'Algérie.* Ninth International Surrealist Exhibition, *Surrealist Intrusion in the Enchanters' Domain*, in New York. Publications: Péret, *L'Anthologie des mythes, légendes et contes populaires de l'Amérique.*

1961 First issue of journal, *La Brèche.* Buñuel, *Viridiana.* Tenth International Surrealist Exhibition at Galerie Schwarz, Milan.

1962 Buñuel, *The Exterminating Angel.*

1963 Founding of surrealist groups in Brazil and Holland.

1964 A liberalization of the political regime in Czechoslovakia allows the group in Prague limited scope to exhibit and publish work for the first time since 1948. Dutch surrealists publish the first issue of their journal, *Brumes Blondes.*

1965 Buñuel, *Simon of the Desert*, in Mexico. Eleventh International Surrealist Exhibition, *L'Écart absolu*, held in Paris. Robert Benayoun, *Érotique du surréalisme.*

1966 Death of André Breton. Twelfth International Surrealist Exhibition, *A phala*, in São Paolo. Founding of the Chicago surrealist group. Publications: Leiris, *Fibrilles*; Caillois, *Pierres.*

1967 Buñuel, *Belle de Jour.* Journal *L'Archibras.* Several surrealists attend the cultural conference in Cuba, causing a minor scandal when the Mexican painter Alfaro

Siqueiros is physically attacked by Joyce Mansour for his part in the assassination of Trotsky. Resumption of surrealist activity in England as John Lyle establishes the journal *TransformaCtion* and organizes the exhibition *The Enchanted Domain* in Exeter.

1968 Thirteenth International Surrealist Exhibition, *The Pleasure Principle/Princip Slasti*, Prague, Brno, Bratislava. French and Czech surrealists compose the important tract/manifesto 'Le Plateforme de Prague'.

1969 Schuster announces the dissolution of the French group. First issue of the Czechoslovak surrealist journal *Analogon*. Buñuel, *La Voie lactée.* Publications: Zavis Havlíček, *Connaissance et création.*

1970 Vincent Bounoure launches the enquiry on the future of surrealism, *Rien ou quoi?* Following the enquiry the decision by some participants is taken to reconstitute the group and publish the journal *Bulletin de liaison surréaliste.* Schuster and those who agree with him form the Coupure collective as an extension of surrealist activity but without laying any claim to the legacy of surrealism, as a *cutting* of historical ties without renouncing the necessity of surrealism. A crackdown by the government condemns the Czechoslovak group to a largely subterranean existence until 1989. First issue of the Chicago group's journal, *Arsenal: Surrealist Subversion.*

1971 Legrand, *Préface au système de l'éternité.*

1972 Buñuel's *The Discreet Charm of the Bourgeoisie.* A split within the Coupure collective in Paris results in another group, Maintenant, being formed. In Brussels Tom Gutt founds the journal *Le Vocative*; Legrand, *Sur Œdipe.*

1973 In Paris Jimmy Gladiator founds *Le Melog* and Abdul Kader el Janabi establishes *Le Désir libertaire*, published in Arabic.

1974 Buñuel, *The Phantom of Liberty.*

1976 Fourteenth International Surrealist Exhibition, *Marvelous Freedom/ Vigilance of Desire*, in Chicago. Publications: Bounoure, *Le Civilisation surréaliste* (edited collection); Leiris, *Frèle bruit*; Guy-René Doumayrou, *Géographie sidérale.*

1977	Buñuel, *That Obscure Object of Desire.* Annie Le Brun publishes *Lâchez tout* attacking the new feminism in France.
1978	The surrealists in Chicago organize an exhibition, *One Hundredth Anniversary of Hysteria*, in Cedarburg, Wisconsin. Publications: Caillois, *Le fleuve Alphée*, *Approches de la poésie.*
1980	Special issue of the journal *Cultural Correspondence* in the United States publishes an important anthology edited by Franklin Rosemont, *Surrealism and Its Popular Accomplices.*
1982	Founding of West Coast surrealist group in Vancouver; it will establish a journal *Scarabeus* the following year.
1984	Fifteenth International Surrealist Exhibition, in collaboration with the Phases Movement, in Lisbon.
1985	Founding of a surrealist group in Stockholm. Le Brun, *Soudain un bloc d'abîme, Sade.*
1987	Surrealist group established in Spain and publishes a journal, *Salamandra*. Le Brun, *Appel d'air.* The first feature film by Jan Švankmajer, *Alice.*
1989	The Velvet Revolution makes public activities possible again for the Czechoslovak surrealists; *Analogon* resumes publication the following year, celebrated with an exhibition in Paris *Analogon: Journey through the Colours of Time* organized by Peter Wood.
1991	Le Brun, *Qui vive.*
1992	Guy Ducornet, *Le Punching-ball et le vache à lait*, attacking academic distortions of surrealism.
1994	Founding of the Leeds surrealist group.
1995	Paris group establishes a new journal, *S.U.RR* (*Surréalisme, Utopie, Rêve, Révolte*). Sarane Alexandrian founds the journal *Supérieur inconnu.*
1996	Derrame group founded in Chile.
1999	Sixteenth International Surrealist Exhibition, devoted to *Sacrilege*, in Prague.
2000	Le Brun, *Du trop de réalité*. A surrealist group is formed in Ioannina, Greece.
2001	Curator of the Picasso Museum, Jean Clair, attacks the surrealists, claiming that their promotion of the Orient and demoralization of Western values, lie at the root of the attack on the World Trade Center on September 11. Régis Debray and other leading intellectuals come to

	the defence of surrealism. Alain Joubert, *Le Mouvement des surréalistes ou le fin mot de l'histoire.*
2005	Founding Declaration of the Athens surrealist group.
2008	Seventeenth International Surrealist Exhibition, *O Reverso Do Olhar/The Reverse of the Look*, in Coimbra, Portugal; first issue of the journal of the Leeds surrealists, *Phosphor.*
2012	Eighteenth International Surrealist Exhibition, *Other Air*, in Prague.
2014	The Dutch surrealists celebrate fifty years of activity by publishing *What Will Be: Almanac of the International Surrealist Movement.*

Bibliography

Ades, Dawn (1992) 'Le Surréalisme en Angleterre', in Christian Descamps (ed.), *Surréalisme et philosophie.* Paris: Centre Georges Pompidou, 125–138.

Ades, Dawn and Michael Richardson (eds) (2015) *The Surrealism Reader: An Anthology of Ideas.* London: Tate Publications.

Adorno, Theodor (1997) *Aesthetic Theory*, edited and translated by Robert Hullot-Kentor. London and New York: Continuum.

Adorno, Theodor and Max Horkheimer (2007) *The Dialectic of Enlightenment*, edited by G. Schmid Noerr, translated by E. Jephcott. Stanford: Stanford University Press.

Alexandrian, Sarane (1981) *Georges Henein.* Paris: Seghers.

Alleau, René (1976) *La Science des symboles.* Paris: Payot.

Alquié, Ferdinand (1965) *The Philosophy of Surrealism*, translated by Bernard Waldrop. Ann Arbor: University of Michigan Press.

Anderson, Georgette (1941) 'Maeterlinck et le merveilleux', *Tropiques* 3.

Aragon, Louis (1924) 'L'Ombre de l'inventeur', *La Révolution surréaliste* 1: 22–24.

Aragon, Louis (1927) 'Philosophie des paratonnerres', *La Révolution surréaliste* 9–10: 45–54.

Aragon, Louis (1971) *Paris Peasant*, translated by Simon Watson Taylor. London: Jonathan Cape.

Aragon, Louis (1988) *The Adventures of Telemachus*, translated by Renée Riese Hubert and Judd D. Hubert. Lincoln and London: University of Nebraska Press.

Aragon, Louis (1990) *Une Vague de rêves.* Paris: Seghers.

Aragon, Louis (1991) *Treatise on Style*, translated by Alyson Waters. Lincoln and London: University of Nebraska Press.

Aragon, Louis (2011) *A Wave of Dreams*, translated by Susan de Muth. London: Thin Man Press.

Artaud, Antonin (1976) *Selected Writings*, edited with an introduction by Susan Sontag, translated by Helen Weaver. New York: Farrar, Straus & Giraux.

Artaud, Antonin (1977) *The Theatre and its Double.* London: John Calder.

Bachelard, Gaston (1984) *The New Scientific Spirit* (1934), translated by Arthur Goldhammer. Boston: Beacon Press.

Bachelard, Gaston (2004) *La Formation de l'esprit scientifique* (1938). Paris: Librairie Philosopique J. Vrin.

Baker, Simon (2007) *Surrealism, History and Revolution.* Bern: Peter Lang.

Barthes, Roland (1981) *Camera Lucida: Reflections on Photography.* New York: Hill & Wang.

Bataille, Georges (1962) *Eroticism*, translated by Mary Dalwood. London: Calder & Boyas; San Francisco: City Lights.

Bataille, Georges (1973) *Literature and Evil*, translated by Alastair Hamilton. London: Calder & Boyars.

Bataille, Georges (1985) *Visions of Excess: Selected Writings 1927–1939*, translated by Allan Stoekl. Manchester: Manchester University Press.

Bataille, Georges (1988) *Inner Experience*, translated by Leslie Anne Boldt. New York: State University of New York Press.

Bataille, Georges (1989) *The Accursed Share*, vols 2 and 3, translated by Robert Hurley. New York: Zone Books.

Bataille, Georges (1992) *On Nietzsche*, translated by Bruce Boone. New York: Paragon House.

Bataille, Georges (1994) *The Absence of Myth*, edited and translated by Michael Richardson. London: Verso.

Bate, Jonathan (2000) *The Song of the Earth.* London: Macmillan.

Bateson, Gregory (1972) *Steps to an Ecology of Mind: Collected Essays in Anthropology, Psychiatry, Evolution, and Epistemology.* Chicago: University of Chicago Press.

Bateson, Gregory and M.C. Bateson (1987) *Angels Fear: Towards an Epistemology of the Sacred.* London: Macmillan.

Baudelaire, Charles (1975) *Œuvres complètes*, vol. 1. Bibliothèque de la Pléiade. Paris: Gallimard.

Baugh, Bruce (2003) *French Hegel: From Surrealism to Postmodernism.* London and New York: Routledge.

Beaujour, Michel (1970) 'André Breton mythographe: Arcane 17', in Marc Eigeldinger (ed.), *André Breton*, Neuchâtel: Baconnière.

Béhar, Henri (2000) 'Le merveilleux dans le discours surréaliste', in *Mélusine, Cahiers du Centre de Recherche sur le Surréalisme* 20. Lausanne: Éditions l'Âge d'Homme.

Benayoun, Robert (1957) *Anthologie du 'nonsense'.* Paris: Pauvert.

Benayoun, Robert (ed.) (1977) *Les dignes du nonsense, de Lewis Carroll à Woody Allen.* Paris: Balland.

Benayoun, Robert (1988) *Le Rire des surréalistes.* Paris: Bougie du Sapeur.

Benjamin, Andrew (1988) 'Time and Interpretation in Heraclitus', in *Post-structuralist Classics*, edited by Andrew Benjamin. London: Routledge.

Benjamin, Walter (1999) 'Surrealism: The Last Snapshot of the European Intelligentsia', in *Selected Writings, 1927–1934*, edited by M.W. Jennings, H. Eiland and G. Smith, translated by E. Jephcott. Cambridge, MA: Harvard University Press, vol. 2: 207–221.

Blanchot, Maurice (1988) *The Unavowable Community*, translated by P. Joris. Barrytown, NY: Station Hill Press.

Blanchot, Maurice (1993) *The Infinite Conversation*, translated by Susan Hanson. Minneapolis: University of Minnesota Press.

Bonnet, Marguerite (1980) 'L'Orient dans le surréalisme: Mythe et réel', *Revue de littérature comparée* 54(4): 411–25.

Bonnet, Marguerite (1988a) *André Breton et la naissance de l'aventure surréaliste*. Paris: José Corti.

Bonnet, Marguerite (ed.) (1988b) *Vers l'action politique, Juillet 1925–avril 1926*. Paris: Gallimard.

Bonnet, Marguerite (1992a) 'La Rencontre d'André Breton avec la folie: Saint Dizier, août–novembre 1916', in *Folie et Psychanalyse dans l'expérience surréaliste*, edited by Fabienne Hulak. Nice: Z'éditions, 115–35.

Bonnet, Marguerite (ed.) (1992b) *Adhérer au Parti communiste, Septembre–décembre 1926*. Paris: Gallimard.

Bounoure, Vincent (ed.) (1976) *La Civilisation surréaliste*. Paris: Payot.

Bounoure, Vincent (2001) *Le Surréalisme et les arts sauvages*. Paris: L'Harmattan.

Breton, André (1960) *Nadja*, translated by Richard Howard. New York: Grove Press.

Breton, André (1969) *Manifestoes of Surrealism*, translated by Richard Seaver and Helen Lane. Ann Arbor: University of Michigan Press.

Breton, André (1972) *Surrealism and Painting*, translated by Simon Watson Taylor. New York: Harper & Row.

Breton, André (1978) *What Is Surrealism? Selected Writings*, edited by Franklin Rosement. New York: Pathfinder Press.

Breton, André (1987) *Mad Love*, translated by Mary Ann Caws. Lincoln and London: University of Nebraska Press.

Breton, André (1988) *Œuvres complètes*, vol. 1, edited by M. Bonnet, P. Bernier, E.-A. Hubert and J. Pierre. Bibliothèque de la Pléiade. Paris: Gallimard.

Breton, André (1990) *Communicating Vessels*, translated by Mary Ann Caws and Geoffrey T. Harris. Lincoln: University of Nebraska Press.

Breton, André (1992) *Œuvres complètes*, vol. 2, edited by M. Bonnet, P. Bernier, E.-A. Hubert and J. Pierre. Paris: Gallimard.

Breton, André (1993) *Conversations: The Autobiography of Surrealism*, translated by Mark Polizzotti. New York: Paragon House.

Breton, André (1994) *Arcanum 17*, translated by Zack Rogow. Los Angeles: Sun & Moon Press.

Breton, André (1995) *Free Rein (La Clé des Champs)*, translated by Michel Parmentier and Jacqueline d'Amboise. Lincoln and London: University of Nebraska Press.

Breton, André (1996) *The Lost Steps*, translated by Mark Polizzotti. Lincoln: University of Nebraska Press.

Breton, André (1997) *Anthology of Black Humour*, translated by Mark Polizzotti. San Francisco: City Lights.

Breton, André (1999a) *Break of Day*, translated by Mark Polizzotti and Mary Ann Caws. Lincoln: University of Nebraska Press.

Breton, André (1999b) *Œuvres complètes*, vol. 3, edited by M. Bonnet. Paris: Gallimard.

Breton, André (2008) *Ecrits sur l'art*, in *Œuvres complètes*, vol. 4. Paris: Gallimard.

Breton, André and Paul Éluard (1990) *The Immaculate Conception*, translated by Jon Graham. London: Atlas Press.

Breton, André and Paul Éluard (1991) 'Prière d'insérer', in *L'Immaculée conception*. Paris: José Corti.

Breton, André and Paul Éluard (1992) *Dictionnaire abrégé du surréalisme* (1938), in *Œuvres complètes*, vol. 2, edited by M. Bonnet, P. Bernier, E.-A. Hubert and J. Pierre. Paris: Gallimard.

Breton, André with Gérard Legrand (1991) *L'Art magique*. Paris: Éditions Phébus.

Breton, André and Jean Schuster (2008) 'Art Poétique', in André Breton, *Œuvres complètes*, vol. 4. Paris: Gallimard

Breton, André, Agnès Angliviel de La Beaumelle, Isabelle Monod-Fontaine and Claude Schweisguth (1991) *André Breton, la beauté convulsive: Musée national d'art moderne, Centre Georges Pompidou*. Paris: Éditions du Centre Georges Pompidou.

Breton, Simone (2005) *Lettres à Denise Lévy*, edited by Georgiana Colville. Paris: Joelle Losfeld.

Bureau, Jacques (2008) 'Le Clou' (1943), in Anne Vernay and Richard Walter (eds), *La Main à plume: Anthologie du surréalisme sous l'occupation*. Paris: Éditions Syllepse.

Bürger, Peter (2009) 'The Lure of Madness: On the Problem of a "Surrealist Aesthetic"', in Thomas Röske and Ingrid von Beyme (eds), *Surrealism and Madness*. Heidelberg: Sammlung Prinzhorn, 28–45.

Cahun, Claude (1998) 'Beware Domestic Objects!', translated by Guy Ducornet, in *Surrealist Women: An Anthology*, edited by Penelope Rosemont. Austin: University of Texas Press, 59–61.

Cahun, Claude (2002a) 'Prenez Garde aux objets domestiques!' (1936), in *Écrits*, edited by François Leperlier. Paris: Jean-Michel Place, 539–541.

Cahun, Claude (2002b) *Les Paris sont ouverts* (1934), in *Écrits*, edited by François Leperlier. Paris: Jean-Michel Place. Originally published, Paris: José Corti.

Caillois, Roger (1950) *L'Homme et le sacré*. Paris: Gallimard.

Caillois, Roger (1978) *Approches de la poésie*. Paris: Gallimard.

Caillois, Roger (1981) *Nécessité d'esprit*. Paris: Gallimard.

Caillois, Roger (1991) *Témoignages, études et analyses précédés de 39 textes rares ou inédits*. Cahiers de Chronos. Paris: Éditions de la Différence.

Caillois, Roger (2003) *The Edge of Surrealism: A Roger Caillois Reader*, edited by Claudine Frank, translated by Claudine Frank and Camille Naish. Durham, NC, and London: Duke University Press.

Caillois, Roger (2008) *Œuvres.* Paris: Gallimard.

Caillois, Roger (2015) 'Specification of Poetry', in Dawn Ades and Michael Richardson (eds), *The Surrealism Reader: An Anthology of Ideas.* London: Tate Publications.

Carrington, Leonora (1972) *Down Below*, translated by Victor Llona. Chicago: Radical America.

Carrouges, Michel (1974) *André Breton and the Basic Concepts of Surrealism*, translated by Maura Prendergast. Alabama: University of Alabama Press.

Caws, Mary Ann (1966) *Surrealism and Literary Imagination: A Study of Breton and Bachelard.* The Hague: Mouton.

Celan, Paul (1988) *Der Meridian und andere Prosa.* Frankfurt am Main: Suhrkamp.

Char, René (1930) 'Hommage à D.A.F. de Sade', *Le Surréalisme au service de la Révolution* 2.

Clifford, James (1981) 'On Ethnographic Surrealism', *Comparative Studies in Society and History* 23(4): 539–564. Reprinted with some modifications in his *The Predicament of Culture*, Cambridge, MA: Harvard University Press, 1988.

Crevel, René (1932) 'The Period of Sleeping-Fits', *This Quarter* 5(1): 181–188.

Crevel, René (1986) *L'Esprit contre la raison.* Paris: Jean Jacques Pauvert.

Crevel, René (2015) 'The Noble Mannequin Seeks and Finds Her Skin', in Dawn Ades and Michael Richardson (eds), *The Surrealism Reader: An Anthology of Ideas.* London: Tate Publications, 41–44.

Croce, Benedetto (1915) *What Is Living and What Is Dead in the Philosophy of Hegel*, translated by Douglas Ainslie. New York: Russell & Russell.

Dalí, Salvador (1935) 'Psychologie non-euclidienne d'une photographie', *Minotaure* 7 (June): 56–57.

Dalí, Salvador (1993) *The Secret Life of Salvador Dalí.* New York: Dover.

Dalí, Salvador (1998a) *The Collected Writings of Salvador Dalí*, edited and translated by H. Finkelstein. Cambridge: University of Cambridge Press.

Dalí, Salvador (1998b) *Oui: The Paranoid-Critical Revolution; Writings 1927–1933*, edited by Robert Descharnes, translated by Yvonne Shafir. New York: Exact Change.

Darwin, Charles (1859) *On the Origin of Species by Means of Natural Selection, or the Preservation of Favoured Races in the Struggle for Life*, 1st edn. London: John Murray.

Deleuze, Gilles (1983) *Nietzsche and Philosophy*, translated by Hugh Tomlinson. London: Athlone Press.

Deleuze, Gilles (1985) 'Nomad Thought', in David B. Allison (ed.), *The New Nietzsche.* Cambridge, MA: MIT Press.

Descartes, René (2000) *Discourse on Method and Related Writings*, translated by D.M. Clarke. London: Penguin Classics.

Desnos, Robert (1978) 'De l'érotisme', in his *Nouvelles Hébrides et autres textes, 1922–1930*, edited by Marie-Claire Dumas. Paris: Gallimard.

Drost, Julia and Scarlett Reliquet (eds) (2014) *Le Splendide XIX siècle des surréalistes.* Paris: Les Presses du réel.

Dryje, František and Bertrand Schmitt (eds) (2012) *Jan Švankmajer: Dimensions of Dialogue – Between Film and Fine Art*. Prague: Arbor Vitae.
Duchamp, Marcel (1978) 'The Creative Act', in *The Essential Writings of Marcel Duchamp*, edited by Michel Sanouillet and Elmer Peterson. London: Thames & Hudson, 138–141.
Eburne, Jonathan P. (2000) 'That Obscure Object of Revolt: Heraclitus, Surrealism's Lightning-Conductor', *Symploke* 8(1–2): 180–204.
Eburne, Jonathan P. (2008) *Surrealism and the Art of Crime*. Ithaca, NY, and London: Cornell University Press.
Ellenberger, Henri F. (1970) *The Discovery of the Unconscious: The History and Evolution of Dynamic Psychiatry*. New York: Basic Books.
Éluard, Paul (1924) 'Les philosophes', *La Révolution surréaliste* 2: 32.
Éluard, Paul (1926) 'D.A.F. de Sade, écrivain fantastique et révolutionnaire', *La Révolution surréaliste* 8: 8–9.
Engels, Friedrich (1946) *Ludwig Feuerbach and the End of Classical German Philosophy*. Moscow: Progress Publishers.
Engels, Friedrich (1987a) *Anti-Dühring*, in Karl Marx and Frederick Engels, *Collected Works*, vol. 25. London: International Publishers.
Engels, Friedrich (1987b) *Dialectics of Nature*, in Karl Marx and Frederick Engels, *Collected Works*, vol. 25. London: International Publishers.
Ey, Henri (1983) *La Conscience*. Paris: Desclée de Brouwer.
Felman, Shoshana (1985/1987) *Writing and Madness*. Ithaca, NY: Cornell University Press.
Fénelon [François de Salignac de la Mothe] (1927) 'Vie d'Héraclite', *La Révolution surréaliste* 9–10.
Foster, Hal (1993) *Compulsive Beauty*. Cambridge, MA: MIT Press.
Fraenkel, Théodore (1990) *Carnets, 1916–1918*. Paris: Éditions des Cendres.
Freud, Sigmund (1961) *The Interpretation of Dreams*, translated by James Strachey. New York: Science Editions.
Gablik, Suzi (1970) *Magritte*. London: Thames & Hudson.
Garrigues, Emmanuel (ed.) (1995) *Les jeux surréalistes: Mars 1921–septembre 1962*. Paris: Gallimard.
Girst, Thomas (2014) *The Duchamp Dictionary*. London: Thames & Hudson.
Gould, Stephen Jay (1977) *Ontogeny and Phylogeny*. Cambridge, MA: Belknap Press.
Gracq, Julien (1948) *André Breton, quelques aspects de l'écrivain*. Paris: José Corti.
Grosskurth, Phyllis (1991) *The Secret Ring: Freud's Inner Circle and the Politics of Psychoanalysis*. London: Jonathan Cape.
Grosz, Elizabeth (2004) *The Nick of Time: Politics, Evolution, and the Untimely*. Durham, NC, and London: Duke University Press.
Gruber, Howard E. (1974) *Darwin on Man: A Psychological Study of Scientific Creativity*. New York: E.P. Dutton & Co.
Guénon, René (2001) *The King of the World*, translated by Henry D. Fohr. Hillsdale, NY: Sophia Perennis.

Hale, Terry et al. (eds and trans.) (1995) *4 Dada Suicides: Arthur Cravan, Jacques Rigaut, Julien Torma, Jacques Vaché*. London: Atlas Press.

Hammond, Paul (1991) *The Shadow and Its Shadow: Surrealist Writings on Film*. Edinburgh: Polygon Press.

Harris, Steven (2004) *Surrealist Art and Thought in the 1930s: Art, Politics, and the Psyche*. Cambridge: Cambridge University Press.

Hegel, G.W.F. (1867) *Philosophie de l'esprit*, vol. 1, translated by Auguste Véra. Paris: Germer Baillière.

Hegel, G.W.F. (1971) *Philosophy of Mind*, translated by William Wallace with the *zusatze* in Boumann's text translated by A.V. Miller. Oxford: Clarendon Press.

Hegel, G.W.F. (1977) *Phenomenology of Spirit*, translated by A.V. Miller with an analysis of the text and foreword by J.N. Findlay. Oxford: Oxford University Press.

Hegel, G.W.F. (1991) *The Encyclopedia Logic: Part I of the Encyclopaedia of the Philosophical Sciences*, translated by T.F. Geraets, W.A. Suchting and H. S. Harris. Oxford: Oxford University Press.

Hegel, G.W.F. (2009) *Lectures on the History of Philosophy*, translated by R.F. Brown and J.M. Stewart with the assistance of H.S. Harris. Oxford: Clarendon Press.

Heine, Maurice (1950) *Le Marquis de Sade*. Paris: Gallimard.

Heraclitus of Ephesus (2000) *Fragments*, edited and translated by Robin Waterfield, in *The First Philosophers: The Pre-Socratics and the Sophists*. Oxford: Oxford University Press.

Hollier, Denis (ed.) (1988) *The College of Sociology (1937–39)*. Minneapolis: University of Minnesota Press.

Hollier, Denis (1996) *Absent without Leave: French Literature under the Threat of War*. Cambridge, MA: Harvard University Press.

Hubert, Étienne-Alain (1992) 'De l'umour à la humour noir', in André Breton, *Œuvres complètes*, vol. 2. Paris: Gallimard.

Hugnet, Georges (2005) 'L'Objet utile' (1935), in Emmanuel Guigon (ed.), *L'Objet surréaliste*. Paris: Jean-Michel Place.

Hugo, Victor (1947) 'Les Contemplations', in *Œuvres poetiques*, vol. 2. Paris: Gallimard.

Hulak, Fabienne (ed.) (1992) Facsimile reproduction of André Breton's notes, in *Folie et psychanalyse dans l'expérience surréaliste*, Nice: Z'éditions.

Hussey, Andréw and Jeremy Stubbs (1997) 'Tempête de flammes: Surrealism, Bataille and the Perennial Philosophy of Heraclitus', *Parallax* 4: 151–166.

Hyppolite, Jean (1957) 'Gaston Bachelard ou le romantisme de l'intelligence', in *Hommage à Gaston Bachelard*. Paris: Presses Universitaires de France, 13–27.

Ingr, Blažej et al. (2012) *Antologie modrého humoru*. Prague: Sdružení Analogonu.

Janacek, Gerald and Toshiharu Omuka (eds) (1998) *The Eastern Dada Orbit: Russia, Georgia, Ukraine, Central Europe and Japan*. New York: G.K. Hall.

Jarry, Alfred (1965) 'Exploits and Opinions of Doctor Faustroll, Pataphysician', in *Selected Works of Alfred Jarry*, edited by Roger Shattuck and Simon Watson Taylor. London: Jonathan Cape.

Jean, Marcel (ed.) (1980) *The Autobiography of Surrealism*. New York: Viking Press.

Jullien, François (2016) *This Strange Idea of the Beautiful*, translated by Krzysztof Fijalkowski and Michael Richardson. Calcutta: Seagull.

Kadri, Raihan (2011) *Reimagining Life: Philosophical Pessimism and the Revolution of Surrealism*. Madison, NJ: Fairleigh Dickinson University Press.

Král, Petr (1983) 'Un romantisme du possible', in his *Le Surréalisme en Tchéchoslovaquie*. Paris: Gallimard.

Král, Petr (1984) *Le burlesque ou Morale de la tarte à la crème*. Paris: Stock.

Lacan, Jacques (1966) 'Propos sur la causalité psychique', *Écrits*. Paris: Seuil.

Lacan, Jacques, with J. Lévy-Valensi and P. Migault (1975) 'Ecrits "Inspirés": Schizographie', in his *De la psychose paranoïaque dans ses rapports avec la personnalité, suivi de Premiers écrits sur la paranoia*. Paris, Seuil.

Laure [Laure (Colette) Peignot] (1995) *The Collected Writings*, translated by Jeanine Herman. San Francisco: City Lights.

Lautréamont, Comte de [Isidore Ducasse] (1978) *Maldoror and Poems*, translated by Paul Knight. Harmondsworth: Penguin.

Laycock, Henry (2010) 'Object', in Edward N. Zalta (ed.), *The Stanford Encyclopedia of Philosophy* (Winter 2014 edn), http://plato.stanford.edu/entries/object/.

Le Brun, Annie (1966) 'Le humour noir', in Ferdinand Alquié (ed.), *Entretiens sur le surréalisme*. Paris: Mouton, 1969.

Le Brun, Annie (1976) Untitled essay, in Adrien Dax et al., *Objets d'identité*. Paris: Éditions Maintenant.

Le Brun, Annie (1989) *Sade, aller et détours*. Paris: Plon.

Le Brun, Annie (1990) *Sade: A Sudden Abyss*, translated by Camille Naish. San Francisco: City Lights.

Le Brun, Annie (2008) *The Reality Overload: The Modern World's Assault on the Imaginal Realm*, translated by Jon E. Graham. Rochester, VT: Inner Traditions.

Legrand, Gérard (1971) *Préface au système de l'éternité*. Paris: Le Terrain Vague.

Legrand, Gérard (1992) 'Breton et l'inauguration philosophique du surréalisme', in Christian Descamps (ed.), *Surréalisme et philosophie*. Paris: Éditions du Centre Georges Pompidou.

Legrand, Gérard and Aimé Patri (1956) 'Le surréalisme est-il une philosophie?', *Le Surréalisme, même* 1: 140–144.

Leiris, Michel (1981) *Miroir de la tauromachie*. Paris: Fata Morgana.

Leiris, Michel (1988) 'The Sacred in Everyday Life', in Denis Hollier (ed.), *The College of Sociology 1937–39*. Minneapolis: University of Minnesota Press.

Leiris, Michel (1989) *Brisées: Broken Branches*, translated by Lydia Davis. San Francisco: North Point Press.

Leperlier, François (1992) *Claude Cahun: L'Écart et la métamorphose*. Paris: Jean-Michel Place.

Levine, George (2006) *Darwin Loves You: Natural Selection and the Re-enchantment of the World*. Princeton: Princeton University Press.

Lewins, T. (2007) *Darwin*. London and New York: Routledge.

Lewis, Helena (1990) *The Politics of Surrealism*. New York: Paragon House.

Löwy, Michael (2009) *Morning Star: Surrealism, Marxism, Anarchism, Situationism, Utopia*. Austin: University of Texas Press.

Luca, Ghérasim (2008) *The Passive Vampire* (1945), translated by Krzysztof Fijalkowski. Prague: Twisted Spoon.

Luca, Gherasim and [Dolfi] Trost (1945) *Présentation de graphies colorées, de cubomanies et d'objets*. Bucharest: Sala Brezoianu.

Luca, Gherasim and [Dolfi] Trost (2001) *Dialectics of the Dialectic*, in Michael Richardson and Krzysztof Fijalkowski (eds and trans.), *Surrealism against the Current: Tracts and Declarations*. London: Pluto.

Mabille, Pierre (1977) *Égrégores ou la vie des civilizations*. Paris: Le Sagittaire.

Mabille, Pierre (1998) *The Mirror of the Marvellous*, translated by Jody Gladding. Rochester, VT: Inner Traditions.

McNab, Robert (2004) *Ghost Ships: A Surrealist Love Triangle*. New Haven, CT, and London: Yale University Press.

Magee, Glenn Alexander (2001) *Hegel and the Hermetic Tradition*. Ithaca, NY, and London: Cornell University Press.

Maldiney, Henri (1991/1997) 'Psychose et présence', *Penser l'homme et la folie*. Grenoble: Million.

Mallarmé, Stéphane (1945) 'Réponse à des enquêtes sur l'évolution littéraire', in *Œuvres complètes*, edited by Henri Mondor and G. Jean-Aubry. Bibliothèque de la Pléiade. Paris: Gallimard.

Mandiargues, André Pieyre de (1971) 'Juliette' in his *Troisième Belvédère*. Paris: Gallimard.

Matthews, J.H. (1976) *Towards a Poetics of Surrealism*. Syracuse, NY: Syracuse University Press.

Ménil, René (1996a) 'Humour: Introduction to 1945', in *Refusal of the Shadow: Surrealism and the Caribbean*, edited by Michael Richardson, translated by Michael Richardson and Krzysztof Fijalkowski. London: Verso.

Ménil, René (1996b) 'Introduction to the Marvellous', in *Refusal of the Shadow: Surrealism and the Caribbean*, edited by Michael Richardson, translated by Michael Richardson and Krzysztof Fijalkowski. London: Verso.

Moles, Abraham (1972) *Théorie des objets*. Paris: Éditions Universitaires.

Monnerot, Jules (1945) *La Poésie moderne et le sacré*. Paris: Gallimard.

Motherwell, Robert (ed.) (1989) *The Dada Painters and Poets: An Anthology*. Cambridge, MA: Harvard University Press.

Mundy, Jennifer (2011) 'The Naming of Biomorphism', in O. Botar and I. Wünsche (eds), *Biocentrism and Modernism*. Farnham: Ashgate, 61–76.

Nadeau, Maurice (1968) *The History of Surrealism*, translated by Richard Howard. London: Jonathan Cape.

Nancy, Jean-Luc (1991) *The Inoperative Community*, translated by P. Connor. Minneapolis: University of Minnesota Press.

Naville, Pierre (1977) *Le temps du surréel: L'Espérance mathématique*. Paris: Galilée.

Nietzsche, Friedrich (1974) *The Gay Science*, translated by Walter Kaufmann. New York: Vintage Books.

Nietzsche, Friedrich (1998) *Twilight of the Idols, or How to Philosophise with a Hammer*, translated by Duncan Large. Oxford: Oxford University Press.

Norris, Margot (1985) *Beasts of the Modern Imagination: Darwin, Nietzsche, Kafka, Ernst and Lawrence*. Baltimore: Johns Hopkins University Press.

Nougé, Paul (1980) 'Les Images défendues', in *Histoire de ne pas rire*. Lausanne: Éditions l'Âge de l'Homme.

Nougé, Paul (2015) 'Notes on Poetry', in Dawn Ades and Michael Richardson (eds), *The Surrealism Reader: An Anthology of Ideas*. London: Tate Publications.

Okazaki, Akira (1986) 'Man's Shadow and Man of Shadow: Gamk Experience of the Self and the Dead', in M. Tomikawa (ed.), *Sudan Sahel Studies*, vol. 2. Tokyo: Institute for the Study of Languages and Cultures of Asia and Africa.

Okazaki, Akira (1999) *Open Shadow: Dreams, Histories and Selves in a Borderland Village in Sudan*. PhD thesis, School of Oriental and African Studies, University of London. London: British Library, e-theses Online Service.

Parkinson, Gavin (2008a) *Surrealism, Art and Modern Science*. New Haven, CT: Yale University Press.

Parkinson, Gavin (2008b) *The Duchamp Book*. London: Tate Publications.

Parkinson, Gavin (2009) 'Emotional Fusion with the Animal Kingdom: Notes towards a Natural History of Surrealism', in F. Brauer and B. Larson (eds), *The Art of Evolution: Darwin, Darwinisms, and Visual Culture*. Hanover, NH: Dartmouth College Press, University Press of New England.

Pascal, Blaise (1958) *Pensées*, translated by W.F. Trotter. London: J.M. Dent & Sons.

Paulhan, Jean (2006) *The Flowers of Tarbes, or, Terror in Literature*, translated by Michael Syrotinski. Urbana: University of Illinois Press.

Paz, Octavio (1996) *The Double Flame: Essays on Love and Eroticism*, translated by Helen Lane. London: Harvill Press.

Peckham, M. (1959) 'Darwin and Darwinisticism', *Victorian Studies* 3(1): 19–40.

Péret, Benjamin (1955) *Livre de Chilám Balám de Chumayel*, translated with an introduction by Benjamin Péret. Paris: Denoël.

Péret, Benjamin (1956) *Anthologie de l'amour sublime*. Paris: Albin Michel.

Picabia, Francis (1960) *Dits*. Paris: Losfeld.

Pierre, José (ed.) (1980) *Tracts Surréalistes et Déclarations Collectives*, 2 vols. Le Terrain Vague. Paris: Losfeld.

Pierre, José (1987) *André Breton et la peinture*. Lausanne: Éditions l'Âge d'Homme.

Pierre, José (ed.) (1992) *Investigating Sex: Surrealist Discussions 1928–1932*, translated by Malcolm Imrie. London: Verso.

Queneau, Raymond (1965) *Bâtons, chiffres et lettres*. Paris: Gallimard.

Reverdy, Pierre (1975) 'Essai d'esthétique littéraire', in *Œuvres complètes*. Paris: Flammarion.

Richards, R.J. (2008) *The Tragic Sense of Life: Ernst Haeckel and the Struggle over Evolutionary Thought*. Chicago: University of Chicago Press.

Richardson, Michael (ed.) (1994) *The Myth of the World: Surrealism 2*. Sawtry: Dedalus.

Richardson, Michael and Krzysztof Fijalkowski (eds and trans.) (2001) *Surrealism against the Current: Tracts and Declarations*. London: Pluto.

Richter, Hans (1965) *Dada: Art and Anti-Art*, translated by David Britt. London: Thames & Hudson.

Rimbaud, Arthur (1986) *Collected Poems*, translated by O. Bernard. London: Penguin.

Ristić, Marko (2015) 'Humour as a Moral Attitude', in Dawn Ades and Michael Richardson (eds), *The Surrealism Reader: An Anthology of Ideas*. London: Tate Publications.

Robinson, T.M. (1987) *Heraclitus: Fragments*. Toronto: University of Toronto Press.

Roudinesco, Elisabeth (1990) *Jacques Lacan & Co. A History of Psychoanalysis in France, 1925–1985*, translated by Jeffrey Mehlman. Chicago: University of Chicago Press.

Roudinesco, Elisabeth (1997) *Jacques Lacan*, translated by Barbara Bray. New York: Columbia University Press.

Ruskin, John (2010) *Love's Meinie: Lectures on Greek and English Birds*. Charleston, SC: Nabu Press.

Sanouillet, Michel (1965) *Dada à Paris*. Paris: Pauvert.

Schlegel, Friedrich (1984) 'Rede über die Mythologie', in *Romantik*. Stuttgart: Reclam.

Sebbag, Georges (1988) *L'Imprononçable jour de ma naissance 17ndré 13reton*. Paris: Jean-Michel Place.

Sebbag, Georges (2012) *Potence avec paratonnerre: Surréalisme et philosophie*. Paris: Hermann.

Sedgwick, Eve Kosofsky (1985) *Between Men: English Literature and Male Homosocial Desire*. New York: Columbia University Press.

Spiteri, Raymond (2015) 'Convulsive Beauty: Surrealism as Aesthetic Revolution', in André Erjavec (ed.), *Aesthetic Revolutions and Twentieth-Century Avant-Garde Movements*. Durham, NC, and London: Duke University Press.

Stewart, Jon (ed.) (1996) *The Hegel Myths and Legends*. Evanston: Northwestern University Press.

Sulloway, Frank J. (1979) *Freud, Biologist of the Mind: Beyond the Psychoanalytic Legend*. Cambridge, MA: Harvard University Press.

Surya, Michel (2002) *Georges Bataille: An Intellectual Biography*, translated by Krzysztof Fijalkowski and Michael Richardson. London: Verso.

Thévenin, Paule (ed.) (1988) *Bureau de recherches surréalistes, octobre 1924–avril 1925*. Archives du surréalisme 1. Paris: Gallimard.

Thirion, André (1975) *Revolutionaries without Revolution*, translated by J. Neugroschel. New York: Macmillan.

Trost [Dolfi] (1947) *Le Même du même*. Bucharest: Collection Surréaliste Infra-Noir.

Tzara, Tristan (1977) 'Dada Manifesto 1918', in *Seven Dada Manifestoes and Lampisteries*, translated by Barbara Wright. London: John Calder.

Tzara, Tristan (1981) *Grains et issues*. Paris: Flammarion.

Valéry, Paul (1985) *Littérature*, in Paul Valéry, André Breton and Paul Éluard, *Pleine Marge* 1 (May), edited with notes by Marie-Paule Berranger. Paris: Le Temps Qu'il Fait.

van den Berg, Hubert F. (2006) 'Towards a "Reconciliation of Man and Nature": Nature and Ecology in the Aesthetic Avant-Garde of the Twentieth Century', in D. Hopkins (ed.), *Neo-Avant-Garde*. Amsterdam: Editions Rodopi.

Viot, Jacques (1932) *Déposition de blanc*. Paris: Gallimard.

Viot, Jacques (1933) *Malaventure*. Paris: Gallimard.

Wahl, Jean (1932) *Vers le concret: Études d'histoire de la philosophie contemporaine*. Paris: Vrin.

Whiteside, Kerry H. (2002) *Divided Natures: French Contributions to Political Ecology*. Cambridge, MA: MIT Press.

Wilson, Edward O. (1998) *Consilience: The Unity of Knowledge*. London: Little Brown & Co.

Zürn, Unica (1994) *The Man of Jasmine and Other Texts*, translated by Malcolm Green. London: Atlas Press.

Index